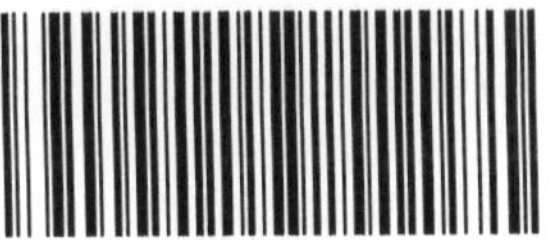
MW01248412

Seasons of Love

3 Romance Novellas That Take Place
in the Upper Peninsula of Michigan

Joan Deppa

ISBN 978-1-959182-84-9 (paperback)
ISBN 978-1-959182-85-6 (hardcover)
ISBN 978-1-959182-89-4 (digital)

Scripture quotations are from the Holy Bible, NIV and NLT.

Rushmore Press LLC
1 800 460 9188
www.rushmorepress.com

Printed in the United States of America

What Others are Saying about Joan Deppa's Books

Whiter Than Snow

"*Whiter Than Snow* was written with enough detail to enable me to feel like I was right there with the characters in their emotions and their surroundings in the UP. Brad and Bonnie had to deal with real-life struggles that could make or break their relationships. It is a gentle, pleasant read that shows you can overcome your past hurts and build a healthy relationship."

Kate

"...Written in a calming manner with a focus on faith and the charm of the region, this novella packed a lot of miles into a shortened story. Sweet, graceful, and engaging. I found *Whiter Than Snow*, by author Joan Deppa, to be an inspirational read with a gorgeous book cover."

Savurbks

"Seeing the struggles that Bonnie and Brad faced in their relationship are real in any relationship. Context may be different, but no relationship is perfect and there are struggles to overcome. Throughout the book, I found myself rooting for them. I can't wait for the next book to come out."

Kayla

"Perfect for any snowy day with a cup of warm cocoa! Highly recommend!!"

Faith

"Wonderful descriptions of all the UP has to offer in the winter. Took me back to my skiing and snowshoeing days. Enjoyed the story as Brad and Bonnie bring out every day life in spiritual and loving ways."

Pat

Summer Dreams

"Once I started reading it, I could not put it down. I finished it by the time I went to bed last night… I feel that there was things that the characters in this book go through that all of us battle on a daily basis. Order this book, you won't be disappointed."

Kayla

"Highly recommend this read!!! Perfect for your summer reading list."

Noah

"*Summer Dreams*" looks utterly great and it's absolutely brilliant."

Frank Parker, *PaperClips Magazine*

Summer Dreams, the second book in Joan Deppa's, *Season of Love* series, is a fun, well-paced story. You will journey alongside young adults looking to build meaningful relationships and seek God's will for their lives. April's professional goals and relationship struggles and triumphs are familiar ones, as are all the characters personalities and flaws. You'll finish the book feeling you have spent time with a group of good friends."

Goodreads Reader

"Aaron and April make their dreams come true with understanding and prayers. I liked the author's descriptions of Lake Superior, the 'Porkies.' and even remodeling a house."

Pat

Autumn Discoveries

"Missy's fears of becoming a Pastor 's wife was overcome by spiritual guidance, self-assurance, and Mike's love. A story giving greater meaning to old-fashioned family ties and faith in God."

Pat

To the memory of my father, who longed to be loved and accepted.

To the memory of my mother, who loved to read and passed on that love of reading to me. I passed it on to my daughter and hope it will go on for many generations to come.

To my loving husband, Jerry, who has always been by my side to support and encourage me to write down my stories to share with others. For loving and accepting me for who I am, for encouraging me to use my abilities for Christ, and for allowing me to be his wife.

To our children, who were PKs, and had to put up with "living in a glass bowl"—we love you, just for being you, and always will.

To those who have been divorced or have family members who have gone through a divorce—there is hope and healing.

To those who have dreams of what they would like to do—take courage.

Most of all, to Jesus Christ, who removes our fears and pain and fills our hearts with His perfect love!

Acknowledgments

I would like to thank my husband, Jerry, for his help and wisdom with the remodeling aspect of this book, as well as my friend, Ken, and brother, Russ. I appreciate all your time, recommendations, and wisdom.

Introduction

The western Upper Peninsula (UP) of Michigan is rich in culture, beautiful scenery, and known as the "big snow country." For winter recreation, there are many groomed snowmobile and cross-country ski trails, as well as ski resorts for downhill skiing and snowboarding. It is bordered to the north by the magnificent Lake Superior, which allows for summer boating, fishing, kayaking, and picnics. There is also an abundance of waterfalls, inland lakes, hiking trails, biking, camping, and the natural beauty of the rolling hills, especially Porcupine Mountain - the state's largest park and highest elevation, which can be enjoyed in any season. The colors of the leaves in autumn, and sunsets over the lake are breathtaking and not to be missed. This is the setting for *Seasons of Love,* where you'll meet friends in three different stories who learn to appreciate and enjoy God's creation. But they also learn about God's love and forgiveness, how to release their fears and follow their dreams, and understand that God has a special plan for each one of our lives.

In *Whiter Than Snow, B*onnie Turner has recently moved to the UP of Michigan and is enamored by its beauty in the wintertime. While enjoying the beauty, Brad Jorgenson bumps into her and takes it upon himself to show her the sights and how to enjoy winter in the UP. But will Bonnie be able to show Brad how to release the anger and bitterness he's carried since childhood and introduce him to the Creator of the beauty he enjoys? Can God's love and forgiveness really make his heart "whiter than snow?"

In *Summer Dreams,* April Phillips is a sixth grade teacher who loves children but feels she should never marry due to the history of divorce in her family. Instead, she pursues her dream to learn to kayak and buys an older house that she can make into the home of her dreams. However, Aaron Matthews has his own dreams, to marry April and have a family of their own. But first, he needs to help her realize that God is able to break her chains of fear and give her a love that paddles through the storms and difficulties of life and thrives. Whose dreams will be realized? Can they both win?

In *Autumn Discoveries,* Missy enjoys helping people but has a low self-esteem and often feels she doesn't measure up to other people's expectations. So when Mike starts showing an interest in her, she feels he's definitely not the man for her because of his position and what would be expected of her. But as she faces some of her insecurities; begins to understand her strengths, weaknesses, and loneliness; and realizes what's important to her—she discovers that God may have a special plan for her life after all. Will it be much better than what she had planned? Does God have a special plan for each one of us?

Book I

Whiter Than Snow

"Cleanse me with hyssop, and I will be clean;
wash me, and I will be whiter than snow."

—Psalm 51:7

Chapter 1

The snow was gently falling from the sky, kissing Bonnie's face as she looked up. It had already covered the branches on the trees like a soft blanket and made a thick, white carpet on the ground. It was a beautiful winter wonderland. Bonnie loved being out in the woods on a day like this—just her, God, and nature.

"Hey, look out!" screamed a voice from behind Bonnie, but too late to stop her from landing on her backside as she tried to get out of the way.

She looked around to find the person responsible for the outcry and saw that he too was on the ground—skis pointing to the sky, poles on either side of him, and his back toward her. But not for long. As he turned around, she could see the angry expression on his face, and she braced herself to hear about the trouble she had caused.

"What do you think you're doing, standing in the middle of the ski trail like that?" The man stood up on his skis and came toward Bonnie.

"I'm sorry," Bonnie said, as she awkwardly tried to get up.

But the snow on that side of the trail was softer, and she was having a hard time getting her feet under her.

A hand reached down to help her. As she looked up into his face, it looked less angry and more concerned for her welfare.

"Here, let me help you up. Are you hurt anywhere?"

"No. Thankfully, I had the snow to cushion my fall. How about you? Are you all right?"

"Yes, although I'm sure we'll both have some bruises we didn't have before. Don't you know you're not supposed to walk on the groomed trails? It ruins it for cross-country skiers, and coming down this hill it's hard to stop. I didn't see you until I came around that turn. What are you doing here?"

"I was enjoying the beautiful day, just like you. I like walking in the woods, but my boots kept sinking into the deep snow and it was hard to walk, so I stayed on the edge of the trail where it was packed down so I wouldn't keep sinking. You mainly go down the middle, so I didn't wreck your stupid trail!" She planted her fists on her hips. "Besides, where's a person supposed to walk anyway? You're not the only one who likes to be out in the woods."

She hoped her stern expression would convey her seriousness, as her five-foot-three stature wouldn't intimidate him as he looked down on her.

"Okay, okay, I get the point. But you're endangering yourself and others on this trail when you stand there gawking that way. Why don't you get yourself some cross-country skis, then you can enjoy the trails more safely?"

"It does look like fun, but I don't know if I could do it."

"I could teach you. I have a ski shop in town. You could rent some skis at first to see how you like it and go from there. By the way, my name is Brad Jorgenson, owner of the Lake and Snow in Bessemer, and you are?"

"Bonnie. Bonnie Turner. I recently moved to Ironwood, Michigan, and have found it to be a beautiful area."

"That it is. In any season. But for now, let's get you out of the woods safely. You stay on the edge of the trail, and I'll take the middle. I'll help you get back to your car, as it should only be about a mile or so."

"Oh please, don't stop skiing on my account. I can make it back on my own."

"I don't want to worry about you getting run over by another skier. I can come back another time." Brad smiled. "Besides, like you said, it's a beautiful day to enjoy the woods."

So they continued on through the trees and across the white carpet of packed snow. Bonnie, however, got a good view of not only the woods but also Brad's back, as he was able to go faster on the downhill parts of the trail on his skis than she could on foot. He looked to be about five feet ten and muscular, which told her he was an outdoorsman. His dark hair, partly covered by his stocking cap, had soft waves in it. Whenever he stopped and turned to make sure she was all right, his blue eyes sparkled in the sun that was beginning to peek out of the clouds and through the trees.

As they got closer to the parking lot and Bonnie's car, the trail widened and was flatter, so Brad pointed out the different kinds of trees and small animals frolicking in the snow. It seemed like all of God's creation was enjoying this beautiful day as well.

When they got to the parking lot, Brad put his skis and poles into his red SUV, and Bonnie started walking to her car.

"I want to thank you, Brad, for walking with me and making sure I got back safely. And I promise not to walk on your groomed ski trails again. I'll have to find another place to walk. Or maybe I'll try cross-country skiing. We'll see."

As she got into her car, Brad came over and put his hand on the door before she could shut it.

"Would you like to get a cup of hot chocolate before you go home? I know a little café down the road that has the best homemade pies and the creamiest hot chocolate you've ever tasted. My treat—for running into you."

"Oh, that's not necessary."

"Please. Maybe we can even talk about those ski lessons for you," he said with another smile.

"All right. Hot chocolate does sound good. I'll follow you."

As Brad said, the café was not far down the road. It wasn't very busy, so they chose a booth by the window. A waitress came right away, and Brad ordered apple pie à la mode with a cup of hot chocolate; and Bonnie ordered just a hot chocolate. It didn't take long to get their order, and Brad was right—the hot chocolate was rich and creamy. It really hit the spot.

"So what brought you to Ironwood?" Brad asked as he cut into his pie.

"Actually, a friend of mine lives here. April and I went to college together at the University of Minnesota in Duluth. After we graduated, April got a job teaching in the elementary school in Ironwood. I got a teaching job in the Minneapolis area but didn't really like living in the big city, as I'm more of a small-town girl. So when April heard about an opening in her school district, she told me about it. I applied, got the job, and here I am."

"So what grade do you teach?" Brad asked as he continued eating his pie.

"The third grade. It's a nice age. The kids still like their teacher, are excited with all the new things they're learning, but are able to do a lot of things on their own. My class has twenty-one students, so it's a nice size to work with. How about you? Have you lived in the area all your life?"

"Yes, pretty much. I graduated from Bessemer High School and then Gogebic Community College in Ironwood, where I got a degree in business. Now I have my own business doing what I enjoy—skiing, snowmobiling, fishing, boating, and just being in the great outdoors. Which reminds me, when should we set up your first cross-country ski lesson?"

"Well, I don't know. Are you sure you can fit me into your busy schedule?"

"I'll make the time," Brad said with a smile. "I'm sure you're pretty busy during the week with school and all, so how about next Saturday afternoon about one-thirty? You can meet me at my shop, we'll fit you with some skis, and I'll take you to some trails that would be good for you to start out on. I have someone helping me on the weekends, so I can take some time off when I need to. Here's my business card. It has the shop address and phone number."

"All right. I guess if I'm going to live here, I better learn how to ski and enjoy the beauty of the Upper Peninsula. Thank you for the hot chocolate," Bonnie said as she grabbed Brad's business card and her coat. "I guess I'll see you next Saturday then."

They left the café, and Brad walked her to her car.

"Until next Saturday," he said as Bonnie got into her car and shut the door.

Chapter 2

The week went by fast, and Bonnie was anxious for her first skiing lesson on Saturday afternoon, not to mention seeing Brad again. On Saturday morning, Bonnie and April cleaned the apartment they shared, went on some errands, and ate a quick lunch. Then Bonnie was off to Brad's ski shop.

Arriving a little early, Bonnie was able to look around the shop while Brad was taking care of a customer. She was amazed at all the different types of snow gear that were in his shop: goggles, skis, snowboards, snowshoes, and many other items.

It can get expensive to enjoy the snow, Bonnie thought.

She wasn't sure how far her teaching salary would allow her to enjoy the recreation this area offered. But soon, Brad came over, took her by the hand, and led her to the back of the shop.

"I keep my used skis and boots back here and use them for my rentals. We'll start you out on one of these to see how you like it. I put aside some skis that I thought would work well for you. Let's try them out and see how they fit. I guessed at your height and weight, as I know it's not polite to ask a woman those things. But it's important to know when fitting you for a pair of skis. Is five-feet-three and about a hundred and twenty pounds pretty close?"

"Yes, that's close," Bonnie answered with a shy grin.

"Okay. What size shoe do you wear?"

"Size seven."

"All right. Have a seat right here, and I'll get you a pair of boots."

As he went to get the ski boots, Bonnie took off her snow boots and was wondering if she should have put on an extra pair of socks to keep her feet warm. But Brad soon came back with ski boots and a pair of socks as well.

"Here, put these on first. They're smart wool socks, not bulky but really warm. Your feet will be warm as toast."

Bonnie put them on, and Brad helped her with the ski boots.

"Okay, now stand up and see how they feel. We don't want them too loose and floppy, but we don't want them too tight either."

Brad took Bonnie's hand and helped her stand up. It felt different at first, but they seemed to be a perfect fit.

"All right, now let me lay the skis down, and I'll show you how we hook the boots into them. Lift up your right foot and slip the toe of the boot into the bindings. Then rest your boot down, and you'll hear it click into place."

Bonnie did as he directed, heard the click, and was pleased that it was going so well.

"Good. Now we'll do the left one. Why don't you hang on to my shoulder? Lift up your left boot and slip it into the left ski."

Bonnie did as he said and was grateful that she was hanging on to Brad's shoulder or she would have lost her balance. Maybe this wasn't as easy as it looked.

"You're doing fine," Brad assured her. "Now just stand for a while and get your balance."

Soon Bonnie felt steady on her own, so he moved away and got her ski poles.

"Here, hang onto these poles, and they'll help you balance."

Bonnie did so and felt more secure.

"Okay, I think everything fits you well. Sit back down again, and we'll take the skis off and load them into my SUV. You might as well leave the boots on as we'll be going directly to the trail from here."

After Brad loaded the skis and poles into his SUV, they headed out for Bonnie's first ski lesson. Bonnie was excited and scared at the same time. Many questions went through her mind.

What if I make a fool of myself? Will I be able to get the hang of it? Will I be wasting Brad's time?

Brad seemed to sense her uncertainty as he placed his hand on hers and said, "Don't worry. You're going to be fine! This is supposed to be fun, you know, not a test."

Bonnie smiled and tried to relax. When they got to their destination, they got out and unloaded the skis. Brad helped Bonnie with hers and then put his own on.

"All right, we're ready. This trail is pretty level and doesn't have any sharp turns. It's also wide so we can ski side by side. It's like walking—only you don't pick up your feet as much, so it's more of a gliding motion. Use your poles to push off, and let's go."

It was actually easier than Bonnie had expected. After she got the hang of it, Bonnie was able to look around and enjoy some of the scenery around them—the bare branches reaching toward the heavens, the birds and squirrels frolicking in the snow, and the sun peeking through the clouds.

Brad talked more about the area and mentioned other trails he thought she would enjoy. Skiing was definitely good exercise, for she could tell she was using muscles she didn't normally use every day.

"We don't want to overdo it for your first time, but you seem to be catching on very quickly. We'll turn you into a Yooper yet," Brad exclaimed.

"What's a 'Yooper'?" Bonnie asked.

"A Yooper is a person who lives in the Upper Peninsula of Michigan, or the UP. Someone who is used to the snow and cold, says *yah* a lot instead of *yes* and calls this place home."

"Well, I don't know if I qualify yet, but I hope to become a Yooper one day," Bonnie affirmed.

"Let's go up to that next curve and then head back. That will be about one mile. That's long enough for your first time."

Bonnie was thankful for his understanding and glad when they got back to his SUV, for she was getting short of breath and the muscles in her legs were sore. She gratefully accepted the bottle of water Brad offered.

"Wow! I'm tired, but it's a nice tired. I feel exhilarated by the exercise and the fresh air, and I really enjoyed the view. I think I'd like to do this again," Bonnie realized as she said it. "How much do you charge for a lesson?"

"I'll tell you what," Brad replied with a smile on his face, "you cook me supper, and we'll call it even. As far as future lessons go, well, we'll figure that out later."

"You've got yourself a deal. I share an apartment with my friend, April. You'll be able to meet her, as I'm pretty sure she wasn't going anywhere."

They were soon loaded up and headed back to Brad's shop.

"I have some work to do at the shop. We close at five, so I can be at your apartment about five-thirty. Does that work for you?" Brad asked as he parked.

"Sure," Bonnie said as she got out of the SUV and walked toward her car. "Let me make sure it's okay with April first."

Bonnie called April on her cell phone and got her approval, gave Brad their address, got in her car, and headed for home.

Bonnie was grateful they'd cleaned the apartment that morning so they didn't have a lot to do when she got home. Of course, April had a lot of questions for her while they prepared supper. Bonnie started preparing some baked potatoes and chicken breasts, while April got out makings for a salad. Bonnie had picked up some buns and a pie at the store, so they had that to add to their menu. With both of them working together, supper was ready when Brad arrived.

They enjoyed getting acquainted while they ate and cleaned up the dishes. After the dishes were done, April excused herself to her bedroom to work on a project for her sixth grade class. Bonnie and Brad headed to the living room and sat on the sofa.

"So what did you do for fun in the wintertime when you were growing up?" Brad asked.

"Well, I grew up in Minnesota and came from a large family, so we did things pretty simply. We made forts in the snow piles that were there after my dad plowed, went sledding down nearby hills, skated on the neighbor's pond, made snowmen and snow angels, and, of course, had snowball fights. When you come from a large family like I did, you can't afford to do things that cost a lot of money. But we never felt left out. We had each other, and we did with what we had. What about your family?"

"Oh, my parents split up when I was little, and I grew up in a foster home. They had a logging business, so I worked outside quite a bit. We wore snowshoes out in the woods when the snow was deep. With all the ski hills around here, I would go skiing whenever I could save up enough money. I guess I just liked being outdoors. It was peaceful, nobody bothered me, and I could do my own thing."

"Did your foster family have any other kids?"

"Yah, they had one son, but we didn't get along very well."

Bonnie could tell that Brad didn't feel comfortable talking about his foster family, so she tried to change the subject.

"How did you come to own your own business?"

"After high school, I went to work for Joe, the previous owner of the Lake and Snow. He let me stay in the back of his shop and encouraged me to get a business degree at Gogebic Community College. I continued to work for Joe, and when he retired, he sold the business to me. Of course, it's not all paid for yet, but I'm my own boss, and I'm doing what I like to do. It can't get any better than that."

Brad had a smile back on his face again, and after a short pause asked, "So do you have any plans for tomorrow? You'll probably be a little sore after the exercise you got today, but we could take a drive, and I could show you around some more of the area."

"Well, I'll be going to church in the morning, and I have some work I need to do on the Christmas program for my third grade class. I could probably spare a couple of hours in the afternoon though. What time were you thinking of?"

"How about I pick you up at about one? I promise I'll have you home by three-thirty at the latest so you'll have plenty of time to work on your program."

"All right. I've been so busy since I arrived here—getting settled in and ready for my class and finding where things are in town—that I haven't taken the time to really see the area. Now that I've had a taste of the beauty around here, I'm anxious to see more."

Brad got up and Bonnie went to grab his coat out of the closet.

"Thank you so much for my first ski lesson. You were very patient, and I'll definitely want to try it again. It was a lot of fun, though I'm sure I'll be sore in the morning. I didn't realize how out of shape I was."

"Cross-country skiing is definitely a good workout, but you did great for your first time. And thank you for the delicious supper. It more than covered your first ski lesson, so I owe you. Whenever you're ready for lesson two, just let me know. Tell April goodbye for me and that it was a pleasure meeting her."

As Brad looked into Bonnie's eyes he smiled and said, "I look forward to seeing you tomorrow."

With that, he opened the door and was gone.

Bonnie leaned against the door and felt her heart beating against her chest. She had never felt like this before.

Take a deep breath, Bonnie, she told herself.

As she did, her heart slowed down a bit, but she smiled as she shut out the lights and went to her bedroom. It looked like tomorrow would be another wonderful day.

Chapter 3

Brad was looking forward to his afternoon with Bonnie. She was delightful to be around, she could cook, and she was real, not phony like some women. He could tell she wasn't trying to make a good impression or put on an act, but was kind and fun to be with, not to mention good looking. Her just below shoulder-length, brown hair shone when the sun hit it, and he had been tempted to feel how soft it was. Her eyes were hazel with green flecks in them, and her beautiful smile made her whole face light up.

Brad knocked on her apartment door, but didn't have long to wait before Bonnie opened it. She looked beautiful in a pair of jeans and a green knit sweater, which made her eyes look the same shade of green as her sweater, and they sparkled as she smiled.

"Let me get my coat, and I'll be ready to go."

Brad helped Bonnie with her coat, and then they went to his SUV parked out front.

"I thought I'd take you to Black River Road. It's one of the popular sites in the UP and a beautiful drive this time of year. There are lots of things that I think would interest you. It ends at Black River Harbor, which isn't plowed this time of year, except for the boat ramp, but you can get a look at Lake Superior anyway."

Brad opened the door for Bonnie, waited until she was settled, shut the door, and went around to the other side.

"Are you ready?"

"I sure am. It's nice to have a tour guide who knows the area and can show me the best sights. I've heard about Black River Road but haven't had a chance to check it out. I'm excited!"

"Good, then let's get going. It's not far and will only take us about twenty minutes to get there. I'll take you down Lake Street, but we'll come back a different way so you can see other things on the way back."

They rode in silence for a while as Bonnie took in the route so she could remember the way, in case she wanted to go again on her own.

"At this four-way stop we'll take a right onto Airport Road. I'm sure you'll want to come again, and it's a pretty easy route."

They hadn't driven far when they drove by the Gogebic County Airport.

"Mostly small company planes use this airport, but some small passenger planes come in also, so it gets used quite a bit," Brad explained.

A few miles further, they came to a T in the road.

"This is Black River Road. We'll take a left and go down to Lake Superior, but there are several interesting things I want to point out to you along the way. The first will be Copper Peak. It's the highest ski slide in the world, which is 469 feet long. Ski jumpers used to come from all over the world to train for the Winter Olympics there. They would strap on a pair of 8-foot skis, accelerate to 65 miles per hour down the run, and soar more than 600 feet to the bottom of the hill. To get up to the top, there's an 800-foot chairlift and then an 18-story elevator ride to the main observation deck. Then there's another 8 stories to climb to the very top of the slide. They don't use it so much now, as they need to do some work on it."

"You've got to be kidding! Here in the UP?" Bonnie was surprised to find something so amazing in this small-town area.

"They don't call this area the 'big snow country' for nothing. We get well over two hundred inches of snow here in the wintertime."

"Wow! I guess I better learn to like snow. We had snow in Minnesota but not that much. No wonder there are so many snowmobilers and skiers in the area."

"Here we are at the turnoff that goes to Copper Peak," Brad said as he took a road that veered off to the right. It wasn't long before they came to the amazing ski jump. They couldn't see the top from inside the vehicle, so they got out to see it better.

"This is amazing! People actually ski off of that? You wouldn't get me up there. I'm not too crazy about heights."

"People are able to go up on the observation deck in the summer and fall and can see some eighty-five miles across Lake Superior to northern Minnesota on a clear day. You can see the Apostle Islands, which is forty miles away; Isle Royale, eighty miles away; and Porcupine Mountain is twenty-five miles away. The view is spectacular, especially in the fall."

"Have you ever gone up there?" Bonnie asked.

"Yes, Joe took me up there once in the fall. It was really awesome."

"Well, I think that will be one thing I'll pass on," Bonnie decided with a shiver. "I'd rather stay closer to the ground, thank you very much."

"You're getting cold. Let's get back into the vehicle. I kept the motor running and the heater on."

They got back into the vehicle, and the warmth felt good. However, Bonnie wasn't sure if her shiver was from the cold or her fear of heights.

"Actually, you can get an even better view of how high the slide is from a distance. We'll see it later coming back.

Brad retraced their way to the Copper Peak turnoff and continued their drive down Black River Road.

"This road is called the Black River Scenic Byway because it follows the Black River and has many beautiful sights along the way. Black River got its name from all the hemlocks that grow along it. The seeds from the hemlocks give it the dark color. There are five waterfalls that you can walk to within a short distance. The first one is here on the right called the Great Conglomerate Falls. The trail is a little less than a mile through the woods. You'd love it! It's a beautiful walk, and the waterfall is breathtaking. We'll have to come back in the spring after the snow melts. It's more difficult to get to with all the snow."

In the spring? That must mean he wants to spend more time with me. Is that what I want also? What do I want? Bonnie wondered.

Brad was definitely good looking, fun to be with, and very polite; and she enjoyed having him share his love of nature with her. But did he know the One who created all this beauty that he enjoys?

"Here are the second and third waterfalls called the Potawatomi and Gorge Falls. It's only a short walk in and has a boardwalk that goes along the river and even a small picnic area."

They didn't go far before they came to the fourth waterfalls sign.

"The parking lot to Sandstone Falls is just off this road, but there are a lot of stairs that go down to get to the waterfall. However, the view is definitely worth it. We'll have to be sure and come back to see this one in the spring too. That's when the water is really high and rushing. It will definitely take your breath away. You'll get your exercise walking back up also. The last one is Rainbow Falls. You can get to it from here or across the river by the harbor. Either way, it's beautiful, especially in the fall when the colors are changing. And to the left is a national campground. Do you like to go camping?"

"Yes, we went as a family several times. We just had a small trailer and a tent, but it was always something we looked forward to in the summer."

"Well, this is a nice campground. The sites are good sized, surrounded by trees for privacy, and several have a good view of Lake Superior. They don't have electricity, so it's more for people who like to rough it and don't need all the fancy stuff. But there's nothing like sitting around and cooking over an open campfire."

Bonnie could tell by the faraway look and smile on Brad's face that he really enjoyed camping.

"And this is the harbor. We can only drive down to the boat ramp because of all the snow, but this is Lake Superior from the Michigan side," Brad said after he stopped his vehicle at the boat ramp.

They surveyed the view in front of them, and Bonnie was glad there were no other vehicles so they could just stay and take in the beauty.

"If you look down the shore, you can see Porcupine Mountain in the distance."

There was ice on the edge of the lake, but it had open water further out. The shimmering blue water sparkled as the sun hit it. To the right and in the distance was Porcupine Mountain. Bonnie had never seen mountains before; though these weren't big like the Rocky

Mountains out west, they were mountains just the same, and she was totally thrilled to see them. It took a few minutes for her to speak, but Brad gave her the time to take it all in.

"It's so magnificent! I've never seen anything so beautiful! Thank you for bringing me here, Brad. When I went to school in Duluth, we saw Lake Superior, but it was so commercial with all the boats, trains, buildings, bridges, and grain elevators. Here it's just the lake, trees, sky and the mountains. It's awesome!"

"I knew you'd like it. That's why I wanted to bring you here." Brad reached over and took Bonnie's hand, and they just sat silently, enjoying the view.

After a few minutes, Brad let go of her hand and started turning around.

"Well, I promised to have you home by 3:30 p.m., so we'd better head back. I still have a few more things to show you."

As they drove back down the road, Bonnie had a chance to look through the trees and see the terrain of the area. There were rolling hills, rocks, hardwoods, and pines, all covered in the beautiful white snow. Everything looked so clean and white. It reminded her of the words to the chorus of that old hymn "Whiter Than Snow":

Whiter than snow, yes, whiter than snow;
Now wash me and I shall be whiter than snow.

She felt reflective and started humming the tune, but Brad's hand on her arm interrupted her. "Look! Now you can get a good view of the ski jump and really see how high it is."

Brad pulled off to the side of the road and pointed to the ski jump that stood high above the trees. It looked even taller than it had when they were up close, as the ski hill had made it hard to get a perspective on its true size.

"Boy, you can really see it from here. It's even taller than I imagined. I can't understand how anyone could build something like that so high up, much less climb it. It has to be a beautiful view from up there though."

Brad soon pulled back onto the road and started talking about Joe, the man who took him in after high school and taught him to run the ski shop.

"Joe's father grew up in Finland. A lot of people in this area have family that came from there. During World War II, he was on the ski patrol, as he practically grew up on skis. He loved the snow, loved to ski, and taught Joe to ski. He told Joe lots of stories about when he was growing up, about the war, and coming to America. He worked in the mines when he first came here but didn't like it. He couldn't see the sky, so he started the business in Bessemer. It was tough going at first, but over the years, he and Joe built it up to what it is today. There are five downhill ski hills within ten miles of Ironwood. There are miles of groomed cross-country trails, and with snowshoes, you really don't need trails, so it's a good business.

"Coming up is one of the ski hills in the area called Big Powderhorn Mountain. That's where I've done most of my downhill skiing. People snowboard there too, but I like skiing better. As you look straight ahead, you can see the ski hill with some of the ski slopes."

As Bonnie looked, she saw a snow-covered mountain with trees on top and patterns of ski slopes, chairlifts, and skiers at different spots along the side of the mountain. What a spectacular sight. In her mind, she could picture Brad skiing down that mountain, and it made her want to join in the fun.

They lost the view for a short while as the road went around a bend, but then Brad took a turn to the right; and she noticed the road was called Powderhorn Lane. She soon found out why, for straight ahead was the resort. She could see the skiers—some coming down the hills, others going up on the chairlifts, still others coming out of the lodge, carrying their skis and poles to their vehicles after an afternoon of fun.

Brad pulled to a stop where they could sit and watch as the skiers wove down the mountain. They looked so graceful and made it look so easy.

"Do you think you would like to try it?" Brad asked.

"You know, I did go skiing once with our youth group from church when I was in high school. But I never made it off the bunny hill. It looks like fun and much safer than the ski jump, but maybe I should get cross-country skiing down first before I try something else."

"Okay. Well, it's time I got you home."

Brad backed out of the parking lot, and they headed back to Ironwood.

Bonnie had seen so much in a short time that she was in awe and a bit overwhelmed with the beauty of the area she now called home. She sent up a prayer of thanks to God for bringing her here and for letting her enjoy the beauty of His creation.

She turned to Brad and said, "I can't thank you enough for this afternoon and everything you've shown me. Everything was just beautiful, and you were a wonderful tour guide."

"It was my pleasure. You let me know when you're ready for your next ski lesson. There's a lot more places I'd like to show you."

Brad soon pulled into the parking lot of her apartment building.

"You have my business card, but let me also give you my cell phone number in case you can't reach me at the shop."

Brad pulled out a piece of paper and pen and wrote down his cell number and handed it to her.

He got out of his SUV and came around to open her door and walked Bonnie to her apartment.

"Well, I got you home safe and sound and on time. I suppose I need to let you go so you can get your work done for your class tomorrow. Thank you for allowing me to show you some of my favorite places. You have my number, so feel free to call me anytime."

"Thank you again. I had a wonderful time. And I'll call and let you know when I can do that next ski lesson. You have a good evening."

Brad turned and went back to his vehicle, and Bonnie went into her apartment. It was going to be difficult to concentrate on preparing for her third-graders after spending the afternoon with Brad and seeing all he had shown her.

Chapter 4

Only two weeks of school remained before Christmas break, so besides their regular schoolwork, Bonnie's students were also practicing for the Christmas program and making Christmas gifts for their parents. The children were excited about Christmas, and it was contagious, but Bonnie wasn't ready for it yet. She and April still had to get a Christmas tree and decorate their apartment, and she had Christmas shopping left to do.

Bonnie was hoping to get most of it done this weekend, but Brad had called on Thursday evening, asking if she wanted to have her second ski lesson this Saturday afternoon. Her arms, shoulders, and legs had been pretty sore for a few days after the first lesson; but she had really enjoyed being outdoors. She found she enjoyed cross-country skiing, and the company was definitely enjoyable as well.

If she was going to learn to ski, it was best not to put it off and to keep at it. And since she wanted to get into shape, skiing would be a good way to do it and enjoy the area at the same time. So she told Brad she'd meet him on Saturday at his shop at one-thirty. However, she'd have to get some Christmas shopping done in the morning.

She woke up early Saturday morning, determined to get some of her Christmas shopping done, as well as some decorations for their Christmas tree, which they hoped to purchase and decorate that evening. She had written a list the night before, so hopefully it would help make her shopping more efficient. April was going to pick up some groceries they needed, and she had already given her money for her portion of the grocery budget. So she quickly took a shower, got dressed, read her Bible, ate breakfast, straightened up a few things in the apartment, and was out the door with her list by eight-thirty.

Getting the lights and Christmas tree decorations, the supplies for her school project, and some candles she wanted were the easy part of her shopping. She even found a gift for April right away, but gifts for her family were more difficult. She wanted them to be something they could use but not too practical; special but not too decorative. She soon found something for her younger brothers, but her older brothers and parents were more difficult. Whenever she asked her parents what they'd like, they would say, "Oh, I don't need anything. I have everything I need." Though she knew that wasn't true, some things they needed she couldn't afford, like a new car, or a new roof for their house.

But they had the most important things—love for one another being something money couldn't buy. She hoped she would someday find someone to love her the way her parents loved each other. Someone who would be there in good times and bad, someone with whom she could talk to and share her dreams, but, most of all, someone who shared her faith and wanted to serve the Lord in whatever capacity He would lead them.

Could Brad be that person? Was he a Christian? Did he share her faith? Even though they seemed to get along well, liked some of the same things, and he was very kind and polite—they hadn't talked about God. Did he even go to church? She would have to ask him that afternoon, which would be upon her soon. She needed to finish up her shopping, run things back to her apartment, and grab a quick lunch. She found a sweater for her sister and a book on airplanes for one of her brothers and headed for home.

Brad had everything loaded and was waiting for her when she got to the ski shop.

"I'm sorry I'm late," Bonnie said as she got out of her car. "I was trying to get some Christmas shopping done this morning."

"You're not that late, it's only 1:35 p.m. We weren't that busy, so I thought I'd get everything loaded before you got here, since I knew which skis worked for you. Are you ready to go?"

"Yes. It's colder today than it was last week, but I put on those smart wool socks you gave me, and I'm dressed pretty warm, so I should be fine."

Bonnie got into Brad's SUV, which was already warmed up, and they headed out.

"Actually, you don't want to dress too warm because as we get going, you warm up pretty fast. It's best to layer so you can remove clothes as you go. Also, the thinner insulated clothes like I'm wearing are good because they're warm but not bulky so you can move easier. We can look at some for you at the shop if you want."

"Well, I think it'll have to wait until after Christmas. By the time I get my Christmas shopping done, there won't be much money left for that. I looked at some last week while I was waiting for you, and they're kind of expensive."

"Yes, they're an investment. You can use what you have for now and pick up a piece now and then. They last a long time, though, and if you keep skiing and enjoy it, it's worth it."

"Spoken like a true businessman," Bonnie commented with a smile.

"I'll take that as a compliment," Brad said as he smiled back. "Well, here we are. I thought we'd start off with the same trail but go a little farther so you can try some smaller hills. It's fun when you can glide down a hill, and then it gives you the momentum to get up the next."

They had arrived at the ski trail, so Brad got out of the SUV and said, "Wait here, and I'll get your boots and help you put them on."

Brad helped Bonnie with her boots and laid out her skis. She clipped her boots into the skis, grabbed the poles and her gloves, and was ready to go. She had bought a pair of Thinsulate gloves, which helped her feel like she was on the way to looking more like a skier. Brad put on his skis, and they went off down the trail.

It was cloudy and snowing lightly, and the wind made it colder than the last time they'd skied, but like Brad said, she warmed up quickly once she got going. She remembered what he'd taught her the week before, so was able to move along pretty well. When they got to the rolling hills area, it was a challenge to get up the first hill but then she glided down and didn't have to work quite as hard getting up the next one. She was enjoying it more and more.

"You're really getting the hang of this," Brad said.

"I'm really having fun, and you're a good teacher. I think you've got me hooked, but I definitely understand what you were saying about the thinner, less bulky clothes and layering. It would be easier to move without this bulky coat and clothes."

"Let's take a right here, and it'll take us back to my SUV. I don't want you to get too overheated."

When they got back, they loaded up and headed back to town.

"April and I were planning to get a real Christmas tree and decorate it this evening. Do you know a good place where we could get one that won't lose its needles right away and isn't too big or expensive?"

"I sure do. You can pick out the size you want, and I can cut it down for you, free of charge."

"Really. And where can we find such a deal?"

"At my place. I have forty acres south of Bessemer with all kinds of trees on it—hardwoods and pines of all shapes and sizes. Some of the smaller trees need to get thinned out now and then, as there isn't enough room for all of them to grow. I can show you some that would make a nice Christmas tree. You pick the one you want, and it's yours. We have a couple of hours of daylight left. I don't need to go back to the shop, so if you want, we can pick up April and go pick one out now."

"Could I use your cell phone and give her a call to see if she can go right away?"

"Sure, here." Brad gave Bonnie his cell phone.

April was thrilled with the idea of picking out and cutting down a live tree, so they picked her up and headed back to Bessemer.

When they got to Brad's place, Bonnie was amazed to see a beautiful log cabin that Brad said he had built with Joe's help and had gotten the logs off his own property.

"Since my foster family had a logging business, I'd learned quite a bit about logging and trees over the years, so I decided to put it to good use."

"You certainly did that," Bonnie acknowledged.

The house was one level and had a porch with railings that went across the front of the house. It had a stone chimney at the back of the house where a fireplace must be, and the house looked big enough to have two or three bedrooms.

"That had to have been a lot of hard work," Bonnie stated bluntly.

"That it was but definitely worth it. Now let's go find you that Christmas tree. We'll take my tractor back into the woods. I still have the trailer hooked up to it, so you can ride in the back of it. Let me just get my saw."

He soon came back, Bonnie and April climbed into the trailer, and they went down a path that led to the woods. It looked like Brad had made logging trails through the woods when he built his house, as they were wide enough for his tractor to go through easily.

They hadn't gone far when they came upon a grove of pine trees. Some were very large, and some were seedlings, with many sizes in between.

"We'll stop here first and you can walk around and see if you see anything you like," Brad offered.

As they walked, they found many nice trees. However, Bonnie and April didn't want anything too big since they didn't have a lot of room in their apartment. They thought something about five feet would be about right.

"What about this one, Bonnie?" April asked.

It was about the right height, but it had some empty spaces between the branches, and Bonnie was hoping to find one a little fuller.

"It's a possibility, but let's look around a little more and see if we can find one we like better."

They'd walked only a little farther when Brad called out from their left, "Here's a nice one that's about the size you're looking for."

When they saw the tree he was pointing to, Bonnie and April both knew that this was the one they wanted.

"You sure know your trees, Brad. This one is perfect," Bonnie announced.

"Well then, let me get my saw, and I'll cut it down for you lovely ladies."

Soon, he had the tree cut, took it back to his SUV, and tied it onto the top. Then they were on their way back to Ironwood.

"So do you have your tree up already, Brad?" April asked.

"No, I don't bother with a tree since it's just me."

April and Bonnie looked at each other, nodded, and soon had a plan in place.

"Why don't we pick up some burgers and fries on the way home and you can help us decorate our tree?" Bonnie asked. "It would be nice to have a man to help us put the tree in the stand and string the lights. Are you game?"

"Well, how can I say no to two lovely ladies in need of help?" Brad smiled. "And when there's food to go along with it, you can count me in."

Brad pulled into the McDonald's drive-through. After ordering, they picked up their food and headed for the apartment. It didn't take long to devour the food, as they were all hungry after being out in the fresh air and trekking through the woods. Then it was on to setting up the tree. Bonnie and April were glad Brad agreed to help with putting the tree in the stand. It took all three of them to get it upright, straight, and tightened down so it wouldn't fall over.

Then they went on to the lights. Bonnie bought a new strand of lights so they wouldn't have to worry about untangling the string or having lights not working, but they all had a different view of how they should be put on the tree and how close. Brad and Bonnie decided to let April do that job, and they started getting out the decorations to put on the tree. They had some new and some they'd each used in previous years, so it was quite an assortment. When the tree was decorated, it looked very festive. They also set out some table decorations and candles. When everything was all done—the tree lights turned on and the candles lit—they turned off the living room lights and sat on the couch to admire their handiwork.

"Well done," Bonnie said with satisfaction. "We make a pretty good team."

They sat quietly for a few minutes, taking in the beauty of the tree, the candlelight, and the festive mood of the decorations.

"Well, I suppose I'd better get going," Brad said, breaking the spell.

"Would you like to come to church with us tomorrow morning, if you don't go anywhere else?" Bonnie asked. "It starts at ten-thirty."

"No, I don't think so," Brad said, while putting on his coat. "I used to go with my foster family when I was young, but I haven't gone since I've been on my own. Thanks for letting me join you this evening. I'll call you later, Bonnie."

And with that, he left.

"Whoa! What was that about?" April asked. "Everything was going good, and all of a sudden, Brad turned cold and left in a big hurry."

"I don't think Brad got along very well with his foster family. Maybe the tree brought back some bad memories. We'll have to keep him in our prayers. I think he's really hurting," Bonnie said. "Well, let's get these boxes put away and get things cleaned up. It's been a long day and I'm really tired."

Chapter 5

Monday was another busy day at school. In the afternoon, they worked on their songs and lines for the Christmas program, which was scheduled for Thursday afternoon. The kids were excited to perform for their parents. The first through third grades were doing a "Winter Wonderland" theme, and the fourth through sixth grades were doing the nativity story with traditional carols.

For their art project, Bonnie had asked her students to bring plastic grocery bags to school so they could make a large snowman for their winter scene. She had brought three white kitchen garbage bags, and the children stuffed them with the grocery bags to make three different-sized makeshift snowballs. They covered them with the blanket snow she had bought when she was shopping on Saturday. Then they glued on buttons for eyes, made a carrot nose of orange construction paper, and used red licorice for the mouth. More buttons went down his front, and a hat and scarf she'd found in the prop room finished off their five-foot snowman. They were all pretty proud of their creation.

The only thing she hadn't thought of was something for the arms. She'd call Brad after school and ask him if he could cut her some branches they could use for the arms. Hopefully, he'd be in a better mood today. Maybe he even had some old skis and snowshoes they could use for props on the stage. They already had a plastic toboggan, a snow tube, large snowflakes to hang, a couple of artificial Christmas trees, and, of course, their large snowman; but a few more items would fill in the gaps.

When Bonnie called Brad at the shop after school and explained what she needed, he seemed more than happy to help out and apologized for leaving so suddenly on Saturday night. He even asked if he could take her out for supper that evening when he brought over the items she needed for the program. She hesitated for a moment but decided to accept.

Maybe she could find out the reason for Brad's quick change of mood on Saturday.

Brad arrived at 6:30 p.m. and they had a pleasant conversation during supper. He talked about some experiences he had at the shop, and she shared how excited the children were and how much fun they had making their snowman.

"I can tell you really love working with children. They're lucky to have you as their teacher," Brad said.

"Thank you. I do enjoy teaching, and the children in my class are wonderful. They can be challenging at times, but it stretches me to be an even better teacher, understand my students, and do all I can to help them learn and have a healthy self-esteem. Some of my children come from difficult homes and need a lot of love—at times, appropriate discipline, individual help with their lessons, and just someone to listen to them."

"If you're done eating, do you mind if we go for a little drive? I promise I won't keep you out too late, but I think I need to explain why I left like I did on Saturday."

"That would be fine," Bonnie said simply.

Brad drove up to a spot where they could overlook the city of Ironwood. The streetlights were on, and some of the houses were lit up with their Christmas lights. It was a peaceful sight, but Bonnie could tell Brad didn't share that peace. She waited for him to speak.

"As I mentioned, my parents split up. My dad took off, and my mom kept my sisters, but my brother and I were placed into different foster homes. I was only six at the time, and I didn't understand what was happening or why. While I lived with my foster family, I never really felt accepted. The social worker would come from time to time and recommended that the family adopt me, as I had been with them for some time. But whenever she left, I was told that they had no plans of adopting me and that I would never be considered their son. I felt rejected and didn't know what I'd done to make me so unworthy of their love or why my parents didn't want me. Even at

Christmastime and birthdays, while they lavished gifts on their son, I received only one small gift.

"I was given chores to do, usually the jobs their son didn't want. I was even told that I would never amount to anything. As I got older, I realized I was taken in for free labor and the money they received from the county, not because they cared about me. Oh, they took me to church and on family outings, but it was all for show. They wanted to give people at church and in the community the impression that they were good Christian people. I guess that's why I quit going to church when I left them. If that was what Christians were like, I didn't want any part of them."

"That's very understandable. I'm sorry you had to go through all that." Bonnie laid her hand on his. But she sensed there was more, so she waited for him to continue.

"As I told you, I went to work for Joe at the Lake and Snow after high school, and he let me stay in the back of his shop. We got along well, and he taught me a lot about the business, skiing, fishing, and all the things he enjoyed. His wife had died several years before I met him, so he was just as lonely as I was, and we became close friends. In fact, he became the father figure that I never had.

"He recommended that I go to the community college and get a business degree, and I became his apprentice. The forty acres I have used to belong to Joe. He helped me build the cabin and said when I was able, I could make payments to him for the land. Shortly after we got the cabin done, Joe decided to retire and sold me the business. I found out soon after that Joe had been diagnosed with cancer and had only a few months to live. I was angry at God for taking away the only person who ever cared about me. Hadn't I been through enough?"

By this time, tears were running down Brad's face, and he couldn't go on. Bonnie reached over and put her hand on his shoulder, letting him grieve for his friend and mentor. She tried to soothe him with soft words of comfort. When he was finally able to speak again, he wiped his face with his handkerchief, blew his nose, and continued.

"Before Joe died, he asked for a minister to come to the hospital and show him how he could know for sure that he would go to heaven when he died. Joe knew his beloved wife, Anna, was in heaven, and he wanted to see her again. The minister came and talked to him for quite a while. The next time I saw Joe, he was smiling and said, 'My sins are washed away and now my heart is washed whiter than snow. I'll be seeing my Anna soon.' There was no longer the struggle of pain and anxiety on his face. Instead, there was a look of acceptance and peace, like he was just waiting for his time to go. He died a few days later.

"I never understood what he said, but I've sensed that same peace in your life. You go to church and have shown me such kindness and acceptance. When I was at the apartment with you and April for supper that first night, and again when we set up and decorated your Christmas tree, I felt included, welcomed, and a part of a family, so to speak. I never had that growing up, and Joe never really celebrated Christmas. So that was the first Christmas tree I've ever decorated where I felt included, where my opinions, suggestions, and help were wanted. It meant a lot to me. Then when we looked at the finished product, I guess it made me realize what I've missed all these years, and I felt so sad I just had to leave. I don't know if that makes any sense to you, but—"

"It does make sense, perfect sense," Bonnie said as she put her hand on Brad's arm. "You've been through a lot of pain in your life, and I'm sorry you had to go through all that. I can't say I understand why God allows us to go through such difficult times, but I sense that some of the children in my class are going through similar situations, and it saddens me. Maybe after hearing your story, it will help me understand them better, and I'll know how to reach out to them, make them feel important, accepted, and loved.

"But, Brad, you need to realize that all this time, even when your parents and your foster family didn't love you, God loved you! He placed you on this earth for a reason, and I'm glad He did. I've come to appreciate your friendship, your willingness to share with me your love of nature, this beautiful area, and the skiing lessons. I've learned a lot since we bumped into each other a few weeks ago."

"Yes, a lot has happened since then, hasn't it?" Brad managed a crooked smile. "Maybe God even had a hand in us meeting." He turned to look at her. "Do you mind if I come to church with you on

Sunday? If there are more Christians like you in your church, maybe I can give it another try."

"I would be delighted to have you come with me to church on Sunday," Bonnie said with a smile. "Church starts at ten-thirty, so why don't you come to the apartment at ten and we can ride together. And if you can get away this Thursday, our Christmas program at the school is at one-thirty. You could come see the program, pick up your props, and meet some of my students. We'll be serving coffee, punch, and Christmas cookies to the students and parents after the program."

"That sounds good. I can't promise for Thursday afternoon, as I'll have to see if I can get Kevin, my employee, to cover the shop, but I'll do what I can. If I'm not there Thursday afternoon, just bring my things to your apartment and I'll pick them up on Sunday. But now, I need to get you home. Thank you for listening to me and being so understanding. I've never met anyone like you, Bonnie, and am looking forward to spending more time with you and getting to know you better."

"So am I," Bonnie stated with a smile.

Brad returned her smile and took her home.

All the students were very excited, though nervous, on Thursday to perform for their parents. But there was also much confusion while everyone got their props, reviewed their lines, and kept peeking around the curtain, trying to see where their parents were sitting. Bonnie even sneaked a peak now and then to see if Brad had been able to come.

A few minutes before the program was to start, she saw Brad come in with a bouquet of roses and find a seat toward the back. Her heart skipped a beat, but then it was time to get the children in place and start the program.

Bonnie was proud of her students as they recited their lines and sang their songs. A good number of parents and grandparents had come, and she could tell they were proud also.

After the program, Brad came up to Bonnie and handed her the roses he'd brought and expressed how happy he was to have been able to come and watch the children perform. She felt him watching her as she helped serve the refreshments and interacted with the students and their parents. He watched as she made family members feel welcome and saw her students express their affection for her. They proudly introduced their parents to her with a smile, and she told them how much she enjoyed having their child in her class.

After everyone left, Bonnie was able to introduce Brad to her fellow teachers, get Brad's props from the stage, and he put them in his vehicle. Then she retrieved her roses from the refreshment table and smelled them again. How thoughtful of Brad to bring them for her. Bonnie took Brad to see her classroom and retrieve her coat, and then they headed for the school parking lot.

"Thank you so much for coming and for the flowers," Bonnie said with a smile. "I love roses."

Brad grinned. "I'll have to remember that. I enjoyed the program very much. I could tell that you're a great teacher, and the children really respond well to you."

When they got to Bonnie's car, Brad asked, "By the way, do you have any plans for after church on Sunday?"

"No, I don't have any plans. I know April will be going to her mom's for dinner after church, and I was just planning on having a quiet afternoon. Why, what did you have in mind?"

"Well, I thought we could pick up a sandwich after church and then go for a snowmobile ride. There are some groomed trails that go through the woods by my place, and it's supposed to be a nice day. I have an extra helmet you can wear, and I promise I won't go too fast. Have you ever been on a snowmobile?"

"You're going to think I've never done anything fun in the wintertime, but no, I haven't," Bonnie replied. "So if you promise to take it easy, then yes, I'd love to go. I guess I'm more of an adventurer than I realized. I've never done so many new things before."

"Good. I'll see you Sunday then."

Brad opened Bonnie's car door; and she got in, set her roses carefully on the seat next to her, and started the car. Brad shut the car door, and Bonnie waved goodbye as he turned to walk toward his vehicle. As she let her car warm up for a few minutes, Bonnie smiled and reflected on how happy she felt. Brad came to the Christmas program and brought her flowers; he was planning on going to church with her on Sunday for the first time; and he wanted to spend time with her in the afternoon as well.

Lord, you brought Brad into my life. Help me show him that You love him and desire to have a relationship with him. I know that You're willing to forgive his sins and make his heart whiter than snow. May he hear Your message on Sunday and be willing to respond to Your word.

And, Lord, I think I'm beginning to care for Brad maybe more than I should. He's been very thoughtful, fun to be with, and so kind. I've never been with anyone like him. But I know he's not a Christian, and I need to share with him my convictions about not dating a nonbeliever. Help me to just be his friend. Amen.

Chapter 6

Brad seemed nervous and uncomfortable as they entered the church on Sunday. Bonnie introduced him to some of the people their age, and a few recognized him from his business. When they went into the sanctuary and sat down, the worship team started the singing. Bonnie noticed that he wasn't familiar with many of the songs, but he did sing along with one, and she found he had a great tenor voice. He seemed to listen intently to the message, and Bonnie shared her Bible with him. She was anxious to ask him later what he thought of the service.

They stopped at her apartment so she could change clothes and then went to Subway to grab a couple of sandwiches to go. Brad wanted to eat at his home and then head out to the snowmobile trails.

While they ate, Bonnie decided to broach the subject of the church service.

"So, Brad, what did you think of the service this morning?"

"Oh, it wasn't so bad. The music has changed since I went to church. All we ever sang were the old hymns. I liked the livelier music, even though I didn't know the songs. And your minister seems to know the Bible and was much more interesting to listen to than what we had when I was a kid. I didn't even embarrass you and fall asleep," he said with a smile. "The people seemed friendly enough. I guess I could go again if you don't mind me tagging along."

"I wouldn't mind at all," Bonnie stated honestly.

"Well, if you're done eating, I'll put the dishes in the sink, go change clothes, and then grab some snowsuits. It can get pretty cold out there when we're moving along on the trail. I'll grab the helmets too. They'll keep us from getting wind burnt and our eyes from watering too much. It's clouded up a little, but that's almost better.

We won't have the sun glaring in our eyes. You wait here," Brad said after he put their dishes in the sink.

While he was gone, Bonnie looked around his lovely home. The kitchen, dining space, and living area were all one big room, with the logs on the outside walls exposed. The large windows had no curtains and looked out over his beautiful, spacious yard.

The kitchen cupboards and island were made of natural wood and a simple design, with a durable polyurethane sheen on them. The countertops were made of green marbled granite. His dining room table and chairs were made of the same wood as the cupboards and island and set with four woven green placemats.

His living room couch and chairs had a natural, log-style frame with comfortable cushions in a green, plaid pattern. The hardwood floors were a darker color with several green scatter rugs to make the room feel warm and cozy. The focal point of the large open area was the beautiful stone fireplace on the back living room wall. Though there was no Christmas tree in the room, the wooden mantel was decorated with fresh pine boughs, holly berries, and candles.

She was standing by the fireplace and admiring it when Brad returned with the snowsuits and helmets in his hands.

"Did you build this too?" Bonnie turned and asked him.

"Yes, with Joe's help, of course. I couldn't have done it without him. I smashed a few fingers laying those rocks, but it was worth it. I'll make a fire when we get back from snowmobiling. Are you ready to suit up?"

Bonnie put on the snowmobile suit Brad gave her. It was a little big, but at least she wouldn't be cold. Brad got into his suit, and they both pulled on their boots. Brad gave her a helmet, and they went outside to where he had the snowmobile parked. Bonnie put on her helmet and sat behind him.

"Grab onto my waist and hold on," Brad said, putting on his helmet. "It may get a little bumpy at times. Are you ready to go?"

Bonnie put her arms around his waist, motioned she was ready, and they were off.

They took the path along the road for a short distance until they reached a snowmobile trail that led into a wooded area. Bonnie couldn't see the speedometer, but Brad did take it easy as promised, and she enjoyed the view as they went through the woods and along some streams and rivers. As he'd said, it did get bumpy as they went over the rolling hills and ridges, but she didn't really mind. It was quite a comfortable and safe feeling to have her arms around Brad's waist. She felt protected and warm, as his body also blocked much of the wind.

They couldn't talk much over the roar of the motor, but she could tell he was enjoying the ride as much as she was. He definitely enjoyed being outdoors, with the beauty of nature all around him.

After riding for about an hour, they headed back to Brad's home. As promised, he made a fire while Bonnie heated some water in the microwave for making hot chocolate. Then with two steaming cups in hand, she made her way to the couch in front of the fireplace. Brad joined her after the fire was blazing and he'd lit the candles on the mantel. They sat in silence for a few minutes as they enjoyed the warmth, watched the fire, listened to the crackle of the wood, and sipped their hot chocolate.

Then Brad broke the silence with a question. "So what did you think of your snowmobile adventure?"

"I enjoyed it very much! I'm glad you didn't go too fast. That way, I could take in the view along the way. I don't know why people go so fast that they can't see what's around them."

"I guess it's a guy thing," Brad said with a laugh. "Guys like speed—the faster, the better. But I'd have to agree with you. Sometimes people go so fast that it becomes dangerous, and they definitely miss the view, although I think the view here is pretty good too. You look good, even with your hair all rumpled up and your cheeks and nose rosy from the cold," Brad said with a smile, touching her nose and cheeks with his finger.

Bonnie's hands went right away to her hair, and she tried to run her fingers through it to make it look more presentable, but he stopped her.

"Leave it," he said with a kiss on her forehead. "I like it just the way it is."

He put his arm around her shoulders. She relaxed and leaned her head on his shoulder; and they enjoyed the fire, the quiet, and just being together.

"So which do you like better, snowmobiling or cross-country skiing?" Brad asked after about ten minutes.

As she lifted her head and looked into his face, she answered, "I'd have to say I like cross-country skiing better, mainly because I'm enjoying the exercise. I'm really not into the speed and noise of a snowmobile. I like being able to look around and enjoy the view and peace and quiet around me."

"Yes, I guess I found that out three weeks ago when you were enjoying the view the day we met," Brad acknowledged with a smile. "It doesn't seem possible that we've only known each other for three weeks."

He became serious as he said, "I've shared more things with you than anyone else, except Joe. I feel very comfortable with you and want to spend as much time with you as possible."

Bonnie sensed he wanted to kiss her, but that little inner voice reminded her that he wasn't a Christian and she needed to let him know that they should remain friends and not let their relationship get too serious.

She pulled back, as hard as it was, and with a prayer in her heart began to speak.

"Brad, there is something I have to say to you. I want you to understand that I like you very much. You've been so kind and patient with me, and I enjoy being with you. You're easy to talk to, you've introduced me to so many fun things to do, and we both love nature. But I'm a Christian, which means that I've accepted Jesus Christ into my life. And according to the Bible, I can't have a serious relationship with someone who's not a Christian. So our relationship can't go any further than friendship unless you also accept Jesus Christ as your Savior and Lord."

"But I've started going to church with you. Doesn't that mean anything?"

"Going to church is good, but it doesn't make you a Christian. You have to acknowledge that you're a sinner and in need of a Savior and then ask Him to forgive you of your sins and become the ruler of your life."

"So I'm not good enough for you? Is that what you're saying?" Brad stood up angrily and walked toward the fireplace.

"No, that's not what I'm saying." Bonnie stood, walked up to him, and put her hand on his arm.

But Brad shrugged it off and walked away.

"I think it's time I take you home," Brad said as he grabbed their coats.

Bonnie nodded, realizing that he wasn't about to listen to any more explanations right now, so she put her arms into her coat as he held it out for her.

It was a quiet ride back to her apartment, and she prayed that God would somehow help him understand.

"Wednesday is the last day of school before Christmas break. I'll be here for a few days, and then I'll be going back to Minnesota to spend time with my family between Christmas and New Year's. Will I see you before Christmas or should I get your Christmas present now?" Bonnie asked when they arrived at her apartment and before getting out of the vehicle.

"You got me a Christmas present?" Brad asked.

"Yes. It's not much, but I wanted to let you know how much I appreciated all that you've done for me, your kindness and friendship."

"I'll tell you what," Brad stated with a calmer tone than when they had left his home. "Why don't you hang on to it, and I'll see you at the Christmas Eve service at church on Friday evening. If all we can have is friendship for now, I guess it's better than nothing. I don't want our relationship to end like this. If God means that much to you, I guess I need to find out why. So if you don't mind, I'd like to continue attending your church."

"I don't mind at all," Bonnie said with a smile. "I'll see you on Friday evening then."

With that, she opened the vehicle door and went into her apartment, praying that God would work in Brad's heart and help him accept Jesus Christ into his life.

Chapter 7

Bonnie and her students were glad when the last day before Christmas vacation was over. Everyone was ready for a break and excited to spend Christmas with family and friends. April left the next day to spend the holiday with her sister downstate, so Bonnie would have the apartment to herself for a few days before she left for Minnesota.

She had a few more presents to buy and some wrapping to do. She also baked some special Christmas goodies to wrap and give to their neighbors, as well as take some for the fellowship time after the Christmas Eve Service. She stayed busy until Friday evening, but her mind kept drifting to thoughts of Brad and his reaction to her profession of faith. She prayed for him often.

When she got to church on Friday evening, she waited in the foyer for Brad to arrive. A few minutes before the service started, Brad came in dressed in black pants, a red shirt, and a black tie. He looked very handsome and festive. They sat toward the back of the church, and the service soon began. It was a candlelight service with Christmas carols, interspersed with readings and acting out the Christmas story. Brad sang along with the Christmas carols he knew and seemed to listen carefully to the Christmas story as it unfolded.

Following the service, people gave Christmas wishes to one another and enjoyed the punch, coffee, and Christmas goodies that the ladies had brought. Everyone was friendly toward Brad, but he seemed uncomfortable, so Bonnie suggested they go to her apartment where she could share her Christmas baking with him and make some hot chocolate. She wanted to give him the gifts she'd gotten him and hoped he'd accept them with the care and understanding that she meant them to have.

Bonnie hung up their coats, and Brad went into the living room to put a box he'd carried in under the Christmas tree. Bonnie went into the kitchen to make their hot chocolate. When she came into the living room, Brad had turned on the Christmas tree lights, lit the candles, and cleared a spot on the coffee table in front of the couch for their mugs and plate of Christmas goodies.

"I thought since I don't have a tree at my house, I'd enjoy yours," he said. "I forgot how nice it looked all lit up. We did a pretty good job of decorating it, didn't we?"

"Yes, we did," Bonnie agreed with a smile. They enjoyed the tree lights, the candlelight, hot chocolate, and her Christmas baking.

"Mmm, these are really good. You made all these?" Brad asked.

"Yes. I wanted to make a variety to put in the Christmas baskets I took to some of our neighbors and also for church tonight. You can take what's left home with you. I sampled plenty while I was baking and making up the baskets."

"I'll need to ski ten miles to work off what I've eaten tonight. I'm not used to all these home-baked goodies. Why don't you just freeze it or take it to your family when you go to Minnesota?" Brad suggested.

"Because Mom will be baking up a storm before I arrive, and then we'll be doing more while I'm there. I'm afraid I'll gain back the pounds I've lost. It sure goes on much easier than it comes off. I'll have to do a lot of skiing this winter to make up for this Christmas break. In my family, we do a lot of cooking, eating, and visiting but not much exercising, though we do usually get in a snowball fight and maybe some sledding."

"Speaking of sledding, I have something I wanted to give you." Brad got up and grabbed the box he'd put under the tree and handed it to her. "Merry Christmas!"

"Thank you, but you didn't have to get me anything." Bonnie looked over the package. "It sure is pretty paper. I almost hate to rip it off. Did you wrap this yourself?"

"No, you'd know if I wrapped it. I had my employee's mom, Molly, do it for me. She did a really nice job, but it's only paper, so go ahead and rip it off."

She tore off the paper and opened the box to find some of the Thinsulate skiwear that she'd seen in Brad's shop. As she pulled out each item, she found two black pants, a pink long-sleeved top, a mint-green top, and two pairs of smart wool socks.

"Oh, Brad, I wanted to get some of this Thinsulate skiwear, but this is too much! I saw the prices of these items, and I sure didn't expect all this."

"I want you to have them. Let's just say you now have a start in your ski wardrobe. I enjoy skiing with you, and this will keep you warmer without the need for so many layers. Besides, I get them wholesale. You can take them with you to Minnesota for sledding, and I won't have to worry about you getting cold."

"Thank you. You're so sweet," Bonnie said and planted a kiss on his cheek.

"Wow! If this is the response I get, I'll have to bring you presents more often."

"Now it's time for you to open your presents," Bonnie said as she got up and retrieved two presents from under the tree, handing them to Brad.

"Two? You got me two presents?" Brad asked.

"I just wrapped them separately. You put all my presents in one box," Bonnie said.

"Okay, which one should I open up first?"

"The bigger one."

Brad looked like a little kid ripping off the paper with a smile on his face, anxiously opening the box. He reached in and pulled out an emerald-green sweater. He pulled it over his head.

"How do I look?" Brad asked, with a big boyish grin and his arms spread out wide.

"Like a Christmas ornament," Bonnie said, smiling.

With the red collar of Brad's shirt above the sweater, he looked very festive.

"I couldn't decide what color to get, but after being in your home, I figured you liked the color green. If you don't like it, you can exchange it for something else. I put the gift receipt in the box."

"I love it! It's very soft and warm, and I do like the color green, especially in your eyes when you're wearing green, like you are tonight." Brad was looking into her eyes with a look that said he was in no hurry to look away.

Bonnie knew she had to do something to break the spell, so she quickly looked down and noticed the second package that Brad hadn't opened yet.

"Look, you still have one more present to open. But this one doesn't come with a gift receipt, as I hope you'll keep it and use it. I also hope you won't be angry with me for giving it to you."

"You've made me curious," Brad said as he started to open the second present with as much gusto as the first one.

When he removed the paper, he saw that it was a Bible. As he removed it from the box, Bonnie was praying that he wouldn't reject her gift and understand that she wasn't trying to be pushy but hoped it might answer some of his questions and help him find the hope and love he was searching for.

"I know you feel God doesn't care about you because of the way your parents and foster family treated you, but God does care. If you would read His love letter to you and realize to what extent He's gone to have a relationship with you and make you His child, maybe you could see things differently. This was once my Bible, but I have another just like it.

"The notes on the bottom of the pages really helped me understand what the verses are saying, and I underlined verses that were meaningful to me too. I recommend you start reading in the Gospel of John. I marked it with the silk ribbon in the Bible. If you want, we could even read it together. I may not be able to answer all your questions, but I'm sure the pastor at our church would be happy to answer anything you'd ask. I hope you don't think I'm being too pushy or preachy, but—"

"Whoa," Brad cut her off. "I don't think you're being pushy. It means a lot to you, so that makes it special to me. I promise you I'll read it, but let me take it at my own pace—at least, to start out with."

"Okay," Bonnie agreed.

"So how soon do you head for Minnesota?" asked Brad.

"I'll be leaving on Monday morning. That will give me a few days to rest up before I travel. My parents are spending Christmas with one of my brothers and his wife as they'll be spending New

Year's with her family and won't be with us the following weekend. I'll be driving back here on Sunday after church, since school starts up again on Monday, January 3. Do you have plans for Christmas dinner tomorrow?"

"Yes, Molly, the one who wrapped your gift, invited me over for Christmas dinner. How about you?"

"A family from church invited me to join them, but they said I could bring a friend, if you didn't have any place to go," stated Bonnie.

"I'm set. So I guess I'll see you at church Sunday morning?" Brad asked as he grabbed his gifts and got up to leave.

"Yes, I'll see you then," Bonnie said as she followed him to the door.

"Since it's Christmas, how about one more tradition before I leave?" Brad asked as he pulled mistletoe from his coat pocket. "Do you mind if I give you a Christmas kiss, just as a thank-you for making this Christmas so special for me?"

"Why not? It is Christmas, after all."

Bonnie lifted her face to his, and as their eyes met, she knew this was going to be more than a friendly kiss. As Brad's lips met hers, they were soft and gentle and then gradually became more passionate as their arms wrapped around each other.

"Merry Christmas, Bonnie," Brad said as he finally stepped back, gave her a smile, and then left.

This Christmas was definitely not like any Christmas she'd ever had before—neither was that kiss one she'd soon forget.

Chapter 8

Bonnie helped with the dishes after Christmas dinner at the Thompsons' home the next day but excused herself shortly after. She wanted to be alone to think about her response to Brad's kiss on Christmas Eve. Was she falling in love with him? Was he falling in love with her? What was she going to do about their relationship? It was obvious that it would be difficult to just remain friends. How should she respond to him on Sunday when she saw him at church?

She opened her Bible and began reading some passages. First Corinthians 7 stressed that marriage was definitely a lifetime commitment. Ephesians 5 compared a husband-and-wife relationship to that of Christ and the church and stressed the importance of mutual love and respect for each other. If a husband would love his wife as much as Christ loved the church, that would be quite a love, since Christ was willing to die for His bride, the church. And if a wife would respect her husband as the head of the home, as we need to respect and obey God, that's quite a commitment of respect and obedience as well. First Peter 3 stressed that we need to live our lives as an example to our spouses, as well as to others, in a way that is loving, respectful, and honoring to God. Wow, that was a tall order!

Yes, she'd always dreamed of marrying and having a family one day, but was she ready for that kind of commitment? Had God brought Brad into her life as a possible future husband or just to introduce him to what a real relationship with Jesus Christ would be like? Could she wait for him to become a Christian? What if he never did turn his life over to God? So many questions ran through her mind!

As she continued reading her Bible, she came across 2 Corinthians 6:14–16, which reads,

> Do not be yoked together with unbelievers. For what do righteousness and wickedness have in common? Or what fellowship can light have with darkness? What harmony is there between Christ and Belial? What does a believer have in common with an unbeliever? What agreement is there between the temple of God and idols? For we are the temple of the living God. As God has said: "I will live with them and walk among them, and I will be their God, and they will be my people."

"Okay, God, I get the picture," Bonnie prayed as she looked up toward heaven. "I'll leave my future and who I'll marry someday in Your hands. I'll be obedient to You and take one day at a time. I'll be faithful in sharing Christ with Brad and pray that he'll come to know You as his personal Savior and will leave the outcome to You. Thank You for showing me in Your Word what I needed to see and help me be what You want me to be. Amen."

After Bonnie prayed, she felt a peace she hadn't felt in the last few days. She knew her future was in God's hands and that she could trust Him to guide her in the days ahead. She spent the next several hours listening to Christmas music and enjoying her Christmas tree and decorations, which Brad had helped with. Then she watched her favorite Christmas movie, *It's a Wonderful Life*.

The Sunday morning worship service the next day was a real time of celebration, with Christmas music and a message from God's Word. Everyone seemed to be in the Christmas spirit, smiling and greeting one another with Christmas joy. Even Brad was smiling and talking with some of the people in the church after the service. Bonnie noticed that a couple of young adults were gathered around Brad and talking to him about something that he seemed very interested in.

He soon caught her eye and motioned for her to join the group.

"Aaron, Mark, and Sally are seeing who can get together this afternoon at Indianhead for some downhill skiing and snowboarding. Are you game?" Brad offered. "You said you don't leave until Monday. How about going skiing so you can try out your new ski clothes? I'll help you on the smaller hill until you feel comfortable with the longer ones."

"Oh, no, you'd have a lot more fun without me," Bonnie said. "I'm sure you'd rather go down the longer slopes than babysit me all afternoon. Besides, I need to pack and get ready for my trip to Minnesota."

"I don't mind helping you on the smaller hills," Brad countered. "As fast as you picked up cross-country skiing, I don't think it will take you long to catch on to downhill either."

"Yah, come with us!" Aaron, Mark, and Sally all echoed.

"Oh, all right," Bonnie gave in. "I do want to try out the new ski clothes you gave me for Christmas, but don't laugh too much if I spend more time falling than skiing. And I sure hope the snow is deep enough to cushion my falls, as I certainly don't need any broken bones."

"You'll do fine," Sally declared.

As they left the church, Brad informed Bonnie that he'd follow her home so she could change. Then they'd take his SUV, grab a sandwich at Subway, stop and pick up some downhill skis and boots for both of them from his shop, and drive over to Indianhead, which was just a few miles past Bessemer.

When they got to her apartment, Brad whispered in her ear, "Wear the green top. I love what that color does to your eyes."

By the time they got to the ski hill, they found out that about twelve others from church had agreed to go skiing and snowboarding. This didn't help Bonnie's nerves, but Brad insisted he'd stay by her side, and he did. He was very patient and an excellent teacher. He helped her with the towrope, taught her how to snowplow, turn, and stop. Once she got the hang of it, Bonnie thought it really was quite fun.

"So are you ready for a longer hill?" Brad asked. "They have the chairlifts rather than the towrope, but it's a similar principle."

"I think so," Bonnie said hesitantly, watching a group of people going down the hill. "It does look like they're having a lot of fun. Let's go before I chicken out."

The hills were covered with snow; the sky was a brilliant blue; the pine trees were a deep green, edged with white from the previous night's snowfall; and the hardwoods stood proudly with their strong, bare branches, basking in the bright sunshine. What a day it was to be out enjoying God's creation. She was glad she had agreed to come.

However, as Bonnie looked down, she wasn't so sure she was ready. But Brad reassured her and reminded her that if she was going faster than she was comfortable with, she should snowplow the way he'd shown her and it would slow her down. Eventually, Brad and Bonnie started down the hill. They gradually sped up, and Bonnie was actually enjoying the faster pace and a longer run. She even felt kind of a rush as they sped down the hill. Then halfway down, she felt she might be going faster than she could control, so she started to snowplow and slowed down a little. She noticed that Brad stayed with her and copied her speed, which helped her stay relaxed and not fall. When they reached the bottom, she was smiling and felt excited that she'd actually done it!

"Wow, that was really fun!" she said. "I even liked going a little faster and feeling the wind in my hair. It was very exhilarating."

"You ready to try it again?" Brad asked.

"Sure, let's go."

When they got to the top, Brad suggested she try weaving down the hill like they had seen some people doing and see if that slowed her down enough to make her feel more comfortable. Brad went in front of her, but to one side to show her how yet give her enough space so she wouldn't feel like she might bump into him. She found it was not too difficult, and the speed was more comfortable. It was also very graceful, almost like ice skating. She was really enjoying herself.

They went down a few more times and then decided to take a break and go in for some hot chocolate. They met some of the others as they went into the building and sat down together, enjoying their hot chocolate and warming their hands on the hot cups.

"Boy, Bonnie," Aaron said, "for your first time, you're really catching on quick. You look like you're really enjoying it."

"Yah, you're really doing great," agreed Sally.

"Well, I have a good teacher. And yes, I am enjoying it, though my legs are getting a little shaky. But I think I'm getting the hang of this UP snow. And it sure beats sitting inside just looking at it. Though it's beautiful to look at, it's much more fun to experience it."

"I think we've got her hooked," Mark stated. "Maybe you'll want to try snowboarding next?"

"No, let me get used to two skis first," Bonnie said, shaking her head.

They visited some more while they drank their hot chocolate and then went back to enjoy the slopes. The group skied for another hour, some of them trying different slopes, but Bonnie stuck with what she was comfortable with—although she did have to admit she was enjoying this new experience, as well as the fellowship with the other young adults. When Brad and Bonnie were ready to leave, Aaron stopped them and mentioned that they were hoping to start a young adult Bible study in January after the holidays and invited them to come.

"It will be at the church on Thursday evenings at 7:00 p.m.," Aaron said. "It'll be informal, with a time of sharing and studying the Book of John. We hope you both will come. And we'll plan some more fun activities like this as well."

"Thank you for inviting us today. We had a great time," Brad said, looking at Bonnie, who nodded with him. "And we just might be at your meeting too."

"Yes, thank you, Aaron," Bonnie agreed. "I had a wonderful time today. And the Bible study sounds interesting too. It would be an opportunity to get to know more of the young adults better also."

As Brad drove Bonnie home, they talked about the skiing and her trip to Minnesota. She was anxious to see her family and tell them about her new experiences and the friends she'd made while in Ironwood. Although she'd miss Brad and all the fun times they had while she was gone.

But, she wondered, would Brad read the Bible she'd given him? Was he serious about going to the young adult Bible study in January? Was it just a coincidence that they would be studying the Book of John, the same book she'd asked Brad to read? Only time would tell.

Chapter 9

Bonnie arrived at her parents' home on Monday around noon, after a five-hour drive. Hugs and Christmas greetings were given by her parents, her brothers who were home, and her sister, Carrie. Then their mom announced that after everything was carried in, lunch would be ready. When they were all seated and had asked the blessing on the food, everyone started asking questions of Bonnie about her class at school, how she liked the UP, and what she'd been doing with her spare time. Her parents wanted to know if she was attending any new Bible studies. Her sister was more interested in knowing if this guy Brad that she often talked about was her boyfriend.

She answered their questions the best she could but avoided the boyfriend question, though she knew it would come up later. She'd called home and talked about some of her activities and let them know how she was doing, so they already knew the basics. But she did tell them about her most recent downhill skiing experience and that she planned to attend a new young adult Bible study, which would start after the holidays.

After the table was cleared and the dishes done, Bonnie went to her old room to unpack her suitcase. Of course, it wasn't her room anymore, since she'd been away from home for six years now and was only there for short visits. It was now fourteen-year-old Carrie's room, but she was willing to share it with her. She'd even emptied a drawer for her to put some of her things in and made room in her closet for some hanging clothes.

Carrie obviously wanted the scoop and wouldn't be happy until Bonnie gave it to her, as she'd followed her into the bedroom and plopped on the bed.

"So tell me about this Brad guy," Carrie began. "How old is he? How did you meet? Is he cute? Are you going to marry him?"

"Whoa, slow down," Bonnie cautioned with a smile.

Carrie, her only sister, was ten years younger than her and at the age where she was interested in boys.

"Brad is just a friend, and he has been giving me cross-country ski lessons and also helped me this last weekend when I went downhill skiing. He's twenty-six, owns his own ski and fishing business, and yes, I guess you could say he's cute."

"So are you going to marry him?" Carrie asked the second time.

"Carrie, I said we're just friends. Let's not jump to conclusions," Bonnie cautioned.

Still, to be honest, I'd like to know the answer to that question myself, Bonnie told herself inwardly.

Bonnie kept busy helping her mom with baking, cooking, and other preparations for the family's New Year's get-together. She was even able to use her new ski clothes when she went sledding with her brothers and sister down a sledding hill they'd made in the woods. The area where her family lived in Minnesota was mostly farmland and pretty flat, no ski hills there. She had started to miss the rolling hills of the UP, and there definitely wasn't as much snow in Minnesota. That did mean less shoveling though. They also went ice skating one evening on the neighbor's pond. There was a bright yard light that shone on the ice, so they were able to see after dark.

She enjoyed doing things with her family again, but she missed Brad too. She often wondered what he was doing.

Does he miss me as much as I miss him? Bonnie wondered. *Has he started reading the passages I suggested in the Bible I gave him for Christmas?*

Brad missed Bonnie while she was in Minnesota visiting her family. Since he had help in the shop during the Christmas holiday break, he did some cross-county skiing during the day in preparation for the SISU Ski Race, which would be in the middle of January. But his mind kept going to thoughts of Bonnie and how she'd enjoy one trail or the view from the top of another slope. Even when he tried to go snowmobiling in the evening to pass the time, it just wasn't the same without Bonnie, especially after feeling her arms around his waist.

So he got out the Bible she'd given him and started reading through the Book of John, as she'd suggested. Some of the things he read were familiar from when he went to church as a child, but they still didn't make much sense to him. The notes that Bonnie had pointed out on the bottom of the pages helped, but he still didn't understand why Jesus would be willing to let the Romans hang Him on a cross. He healed people, fed thousands with just a small lunch, and even raised a man named Lazarus from the dead. So if He could do all that, why didn't He let someone else die on that cross? Why Him? He hadn't done anything wrong.

Brad was thinking about going to the Bible study Aaron told them about. Aaron said they would be studying the Book of John. He definitely needed some help in understanding what he was reading.

It probably wouldn't hurt to read it a second time through, Brad thought. *Maybe that would help.*

He certainly had the time, now that Bonnie was gone.

Bonnie went to church with her family on Sunday, then drove back to Ironwood. As she drove, her thoughts went back to the wonderful times she had with them—the laughter around the table and the fun they had playing games, sledding, and skating together. The talks with her mom as they worked together in the kitchen were special too. Everyone loved the things she'd brought them, and she loved the gifts she'd received as well. They weren't large or expensive gifts but thoughtful gifts that she knew came from the heart.

They didn't see each another as often as they used to. Some had moved away from home and were living their own lives. As the second oldest of eleven children and having gone away to college, she'd missed some of the younger children's growing-up years. But now she had some more memories to treasure and pictures to share with April.

But what about Brad? He doesn't have any happy family memories, Bonnie worried. *Would he enjoy hearing about my family and looking at my family pictures or would it make him feel lonelier for what he'd missed? April comes from a divorced home and doesn't have a lot of happy family memories either, but she enjoys hearing about my family and looking at our pictures. Maybe Brad would too.*

Chapter 10

Brad called Bonnie Sunday evening to make sure she arrived home safely. He sensed that she was tired after the long drive and unpacking, so they didn't talk long. But he did tell her he'd missed her. She invited him over for dinner after church the next Sunday to tell him more about her trip and show him her pictures. April would be there as well, so they could both have their pictures uploaded onto their computers to share.

Monday morning it was back to school for both Bonnie and April with their normal routines. But the week passed quickly, and they went grocery shopping together on Saturday. With both of them gone during the holidays, they hadn't stocked the cupboards before they left, so they were looking pretty bare. Bonnie also wanted to get the things she needed for their Sunday dinner. She planned on making lasagna, corn, a salad, garlic bread, and a chocolate cake for dessert, which she knew was Brad's favorite.

At church on Sunday, they announced that the young adult Bible study would begin on Thursday evening at seven. Aaron made it a point to personally invite Bonnie, April, and Brad to attend. So they talked about it while they were getting the food on the table for dinner. Brad said he wanted to go and was willing to pick up both Bonnie and April at six-thirty on Thursday evening.

"I've read over the Book of John twice now, and I still don't understand it," Brad admitted. "Maybe this study will help explain things for me."

Bonnie and April caught each other's eye at what Brad said. April knew that Bonnie had given him a Bible for Christmas, but neither of them knew if he would read it.

"I think it's always helpful when you can discuss the Bible with others," April said. "Different people pick up different insights that you may not see and can learn from."

"And having fellowship with other people our own age is a plus too," Bonnie said. "I really enjoyed our time at the ski hill last week and getting to know some of those who were there. Going to church on Sunday just isn't enough time to get acquainted with people on a personal level. I really haven't gotten to know many in the church since I've been here."

Over dinner, they told each other some of the things they'd done during the holidays.

"I'm glad I was able to spend some time with my sister and her children in Lansing," April said. "Since her recent divorce, she's having a real hard time of it. She's got a good job, but she's away from the kids so much and has them in daycare. She puts in long hours, plus with keeping up the house, laundry, and the kids, she's always tired. I took care of the kids while she was at work and did some cleaning around the house. They're really sweet kids, but they don't understand why their daddy isn't there anymore. The youngest cried every night, and it just about broke my heart. I've got pictures of them to show you after dinner. You'll fall in love with them when you see them."

"It's definitely not easy for kids to understand why families don't stay together," Brad agreed sadly. "I know that from experience."

"Oh, Brad, I'm sorry. I didn't mean to bring up bad memories," April said.

"No, it's okay, April. It happens more and more all the time. I don't understand why families can't stay together and love each other the way the home was designed. I feel for your sister's kids. It won't be easy for any of them, but at least they have their mom who loves and wants them. They can be grateful for that."

Bonnie tried to change the subject to a lighter topic.

"I was able to use the ski clothes you gave me for Christmas, Brad. There aren't any ski hills near my parents' home, but I did some sledding and ice skating with some of my brothers and sister. They really were warm and comfortable. My sister, Carrie, says she'd like some too and to tell you her favorite color is purple."

"I'll have to remember that. But I don't think I'll be able to remember all your brothers' names. Nine brothers can get pretty confusing. How did your mother remember them all?"

"Well, there were times when she went down the whole list before she got the name right, but we always knew who she meant when we were in trouble. Then she used our first, middle, and last names," Bonnie said with a laugh.

They continued sharing while they cleared the table, put things away, and washed up the dishes. It was amazing how well the three of them worked together and enjoyed each other's company. But soon they were done and went back to the table with Bonnie's and April's computers to look at the pictures they'd taken of their families.

Brad enjoyed seeing Bonnie's family and the things they did together but said he'd never be able to keep track of who was who. When April showed the pictures of her niece and nephew, Bonnie had to agree that they were sweet-looking kids. They all wondered how a man could up and leave his family like that.

"Well, I didn't have as exciting a time as you two," Brad said. "I basically worked at the shop but took a few days off to go cross-country skiing in preparation for the SISU Ski Race next Saturday. I went again yesterday and will need to get out again a few more times this week. I hope you ladies can be there to cheer me on."

"I've heard of it, but I don't know much about it," said April.

"I don't know anything about it," said Bonnie. "You'll have to fill us in."

"Well, the SISU Ski Fest has been in existence for a few years now and offers both a full and half marathon for classic and freestyle racers, as well as a 'taste 'n' tour' with food stops along the way. I'm just doing the half marathon this year, which is 15K, since I've been busy at the shop and haven't had the time to ski as much this year. All races start at the ABR ski trails and finishes downtown in Ironwood. We'll be skiing past scenic bluffs, river views, and through historic mining areas. There's also evening entertainment at the historic Ironwood Theater. So it's a pretty big deal for the area. I'll have to take you on some of the trails, Bonnie. There are really some amazing sights and great views along the way. ABR has over fifty-eight kilometers of scenic trails of varied terrain along the Montreal River."

"It sounds like great fun! You can count on me being there," Bonnie replied excitedly.

"Yah, me too," April agreed.

"Great! I'll look forward to seeing both of your lovely faces. But I suppose I should be going while I still have a couple of hours of daylight to ski." Brad stood and went to get his coat. "I want to thank you, Bonnie, for another delicious dinner. You certainly are a good cook and made all my favorites. But then, I guess most foods are my favorites since I like to eat. I just don't take much time to cook."

"You're most welcome! I enjoyed doing it, and you both helped, so that made it pretty easy. We'll see you on Thursday then?"

"Yes, I'll be here at six-thirty," Brad said, giving Bonnie a look that told her he wanted to say more. "Can you walk me out?"

"Sure, let me get my coat."

Brad helped Bonnie with her coat, and as they walked to his SUV, he took her hand in his and gave it a slight squeeze. She looked into his face and saw a tenderness there that she hadn't seen before. When they reached his vehicle, he turned to face her and put his hands on her shoulders.

"I sure missed you when you were gone," Brad began. "I felt so empty and lonely. You've come to mean a lot to me, and I know you want to just remain friends, but I miss our times together. I'm looking forward to the Bible study on Thursdays and you being there on Saturday to cheer me on at the SISU race. But can we continue your ski lessons again when my schedule lightens up a bit after the race? I've got some other places I'd like to take you to."

"Yes, I'd like that," Bonnie said, looking into his eyes.

She knew he could see the pleasure that she felt when she was with him.

"Good!" Brad said and kissed her on her forehead. "I'll see you on Thursday then."

He got into his SUV with a smile and was gone.

Chapter 11

There were about twenty young adults at the Bible study on Thursday evening. The chairs were placed in a circle so everyone could see each other—some of them Bonnie had seen at church and at the ski hill, others she hadn't met before.

Aaron led the evening and started by asking each one to say who they were and something about themselves. He then opened in prayer and began by sharing a good way to study the Bible.

"The goal of studying the Bible is to understand it and be able to apply it to our lives. Otherwise, why take the time to read it, right?"

Everyone nodded in agreement as Aaron went on.

"I've got a handout that I want you each to take, and it will explain some things that I've found helpful as we get into the book of John."

As Aaron talked, the papers were passed around the circle.

"In order to understand the Book of John, you'll need to read it thoughtfully and repeatedly, not just once and think you got it. Look for things while you're reading; such as the purpose, repeated phrases, and who the people are to whom John is talking. Notice what the events are and where they are happening. What is the time sequence? What is he trying to get across?

"After that, take each chapter and write a title that will help you remember what the content of that chapter is about. The title should be brief. Describe each paragraph. Be specific but creative so you can remember it. Then ask questions. The obvious ones are *who, what, where, when, how*, and *why*. Are there things that are similar, different, repetitive or that are contrasts? Is there a cause and effect? Is there a movement from general to specific? Is there a progression?

Are there questions and answers? Are there problems and solutions? Are there any commands or promises? Now you won't find all these questions in one chapter. These are just things to look for and jot down. I highly recommend you start a journal or notebook so you can jot down your thoughts and findings.

"You also need to take into consideration the context of the book or what was happening at the time this book was written. Check out the cross-references in your Bible and even read different translations or commentaries on the Book of John," Aaron continued. "Then you can begin to ask questions that will help you apply what you've read to your own life: How should I change my life in light of this truth? How will I carry out these changes? After that, write out a personal prayer expressing the change desired."

As Aaron was talking, Brad realized why he didn't understand the Book of John, even after reading it twice. There was more to studying and understanding the Bible than he realized. He was glad that he decided to come to this Bible study. He had a feeling he was going to learn a lot more about the Book of John than he would on his own. And he would definitely have to get a notebook in which to write things down.

"We'll work through all these steps together as we go through the study. But to conclude for tonight, let's end by turning to John 20:30–31." Aaron waited until everyone found it. "These verses tell us the reason why John wrote the book. April, will you read it for us?"

"Jesus did many other miraculous signs in the presence of his disciples, which are not recorded in this book. But these are written that you may believe that Jesus is the Christ, the Son of God, and that believing you may have life in his name," April read.

"Thank you, April. So the purpose of the book of John is so that, first, you'll believe that Jesus is the Christ, the Son of God and, second, that you may have life in His name. So that will be the goal for each one of us throughout this study. All right then. For our meeting next week, I want you all to read John 1 several times, go through the handout I gave you, and answer the questions that relate to it. Then come up with a title for the chapter and discover what God wants you to learn and apply to your life. Let's close in prayer."

As the study ended, many stood around visiting and helping themselves to the drinks and snacks that were provided, but Brad went to talk to Aaron.

"Thank you, Aaron, for inviting me and sharing how to study the Bible. I'm sure it will be very helpful," Brad said. "Bonnie gave me a Bible for Christmas and asked me to start by reading the Book of John. I've read it twice, but I didn't understand much of it. This study is going to be a big help and so will this handout."

"I'm glad you came, Brad. God has a lot to say to us in His Word, and I'll be praying that He'll give you understanding. Being in a group like this helps a lot too, especially hearing people share about what they're learning."

As Brad took Bonnie and April home that evening, they each said how much they were looking forward to the study and getting to know more of the young adults in the group. Brad walked Bonnie and April to their door but didn't go inside. He had a busy day on Friday working in the shop in the morning and preparing for the SISU race in the afternoon.

"So I'll see you on Saturday at the race then?" Brad asked Bonnie after April went inside.

"Yes, I wouldn't miss it. It sounds exciting!"

"Well, be sure to dress warm. Bringing blankets to wrap up in wouldn't be a bad idea either. It's supposed to be in the twenties, but the wind will be cold. Of course, you'll be able to warm up in your car between stops, and they'll have coffee, hot chocolate, soup, and other food that can be purchased at the three different locations. But it'll definitely be cold out there. So you know where to go, right? Meet me at the ABR where we'll begin, and then I'll see you again at Norrie Park and then at the finish line in downtown Ironwood."

"Yes, don't worry! April knows where to go, and I promise I'll dress warm."

Saturday morning started out cloudy, but by race time, the sun was out. However, as Brad said, the wind was cold. Bonnie was grateful for her warm clothes and the hot tea that April had brought in her thermos.

They were both surprised at the number of racers that participated in the SISU race. There were skiers of all ages, and they were all anxious to get started. They even had a race for children the day before. This was definitely a skiing community.

As the racers took off, Bonnie and April cheered them on with the rest of the crowd. They watched until all the racers were out of sight and then went on to the next stopping point at Norrie Park. There they were able to purchase muffins, soup, and coffee or hot chocolate while they waited for the skiers to arrive. They could tell when the first skier became visible as the crowd began to yell and cheer as they looked for their family member or friends.

When Bonnie was able to spot Brad, she joined in the cheering and waved to him as he went by. His cheeks were red from the wind and cold. She couldn't see his eyes as he was wearing goggles to keep his eyes from watering from the cold wind, but she did see that he had a big smile on his face and seemed to be enjoying himself as he kept his smooth, steady pace.

At the finish line in downtown Ironwood, Brad came in fifth in the half marathon race. He said he felt good about his finish as he hadn't skied as much as he would have liked to in preparation for the race. Bonnie was proud of him, and she and April both congratulated him for his good finish. They watched more of the skiers cross the finish line while Brad loaded his skis into Kevin's pickup to take back to the shop. Kevin worked for Brad at the shop, and they had become good friends as well.

All four of them then went for a delicious bowl of hot chili and enjoyed the warmth of the restaurant. They were in no hurry to go back out into the cold; but the warmth made Brad sleepy after the fresh air and exertion from the race. He reluctantly got up to go home for a shower and nap before the evening festivities. Kevin would give him a ride back to the ABR for his SUV.

As they left the restaurant, Brad took Bonnie aside and asked, "How about we go on another new adventure and I take you snowshoeing tomorrow after church? There's a place called Peterson Falls that I'd like to show you. I know how much you like walking in the snow through the woods, and with snowshoes you'll be able to do it without sinking to your knees, I might add. I'll even bring lunch and we can have a picnic. There's a spot off the trail that would be perfect!"

"A picnic in the wintertime?" Bonnie asked.

"Sure, just dress warm. I'll bring a blanket for us to sit on during our picnic," Brad answered with a smile as he got into Kevin's pickup.

Chapter 12

After church the next day, Bonnie went home to dress for her new adventure. The prospect of being with Brad, snowshoeing for the first time, and having a picnic in the winter was exhilarating. She had done a lot of different things since coming to the UP, and she wouldn't trade it for anything. It's amazing that when you allow God to direct your life, He gives you the abundant life He promises. Would Brad find that abundant life as well? She would continue praying that he would.

Brad picked her up at twelve-thirty, drove across the Wisconsin state line and soon turned onto a road that had a sign that read, "PETERSON FALLS." After driving a short distance, he pulled over and parked where the plowed portion of the road stopped. They got out and Brad took out snowshoes for Bonnie and buckled them on over her regular boots, as she didn't need special boots for them. She was glad the snowshoes were made of aluminum and lightweight. They also had clawlike teeth on the bottom to grip the snow. He gave her a pair of ski poles to help her balance and told her to try walking around in them while he put his snowshoes on.

She felt like a duck waddling through the snow, for as she picked up her feet, she barely broke the surface of the snow. But she also learned quickly that she had to be careful not to trip over the long tail on the back of the snowshoes. She laughed at herself as she figured out how to use the snowshoes, but soon realized that this was a much better way to walk in the snow. For she didn't sink down to her knees as she had the first time she went walking in the snow—the day she'd met Brad.

After Bonnie had time to practice for a little while and Brad put on the backpack with a blanket and their lunch inside, they headed down the trail. Soon they turned and entered a wooded area that was narrower, so they had to go single file. Brad led the way. Bonnie felt like they were in their own realm—just her, Brad, and God, enjoying the beauty of God's creation all around them—the snow-covered ground, the branches of the trees blanketed with fresh snow and moving with the breeze, and the sun shining down on them. She even noticed that the wind blowing around her was much gentler now that they were in the woods. She always felt a sense of reverence when she was in the woods. She didn't even want to speak loudly but only whispered for fear of disrupting the presence of God.

"Do you feel it?" Bonnie asked.

"Feel what?" Brad whispered back.

"The presence of God," Bonnie answered with a smile and an angelic look on her face.

After they'd gone farther, they began to hear the rippling sounds of the Montreal River. With the river on their left and cliffs on the right, Bonnie was so busy looking at the scenery that she stumbled over a branch that had fallen onto the trail and was frozen in the snow. However, she kept herself from falling by digging her poles into the snow for support.

"These poles come in handy, don't they?" Bonnie called out to Brad.

"Yes, they do," Brad answered back. "You don't always need them while snowshoeing, but they give you extra support when going through deep snow, climbing, or need to catch yourself. Are you okay?"

"Yes. I just need to watch where I'm going," Bonnie answered.

As they went farther down the trail, the river got louder, and she could glimpse it through the trees. Though there was ice along the edges, the water was running swiftly down the middle. It was exciting to see the white snow along the banks, large rocks here and there in the middle of the river covered in snow, and the water splashing as it sped around the rocks. As they went farther and the river became wider, she could see even more large rocks with huge mounds of snow on top of them. She started to giggle, as they looked like a Smurf village from the cartoon she'd seen as a child.

Just past the Smurf village was the waterfall. It wasn't large but still breathtaking as she saw the sunlight filtering through the trees and the water sparkling as it tumbled over the rocks, fallen logs, and into the river below. She just stood there gazing at the waterfall, in awe of the wonder of God's creation.

"I thought you might like this spot," Brad said with a confident grin. "If you'd like, we can go up this hill a short distance and sit on a log and eat our lunch. Then you can have a good view of the waterfall and river while we eat."

"Oh, that would be wonderful!"

Once Brad found the perfect spot, he took the blanket out of his backpack and laid it across a large fallen tree for them to sit on. He set out their lunch, and Bonnie said the blessing, thanking God for the beauty all around them and for the food. The atmosphere was beautiful, the company was great, and the food was simple, but tasted really good after their trek through the woods.

"Well, what do you think of our winter picnic now?" Brad asked after the food was eaten and they spent some time just relaxing, looking at the river.

"It's better than I ever imagined!" Bonnie confessed as she looked into Brad's eyes. "You keep amazing me with new adventures, and each one just keeps getting better," she said with a smile and a little shiver.

"You're getting cold!" Brad put his arm around Bonnie's shoulders and pulled her close. "We should head back soon. I don't want you catching a cold and getting sick."

But at the moment, with Brad's arm around her and nestled against him, she felt very warm and comfortable, not at all in a hurry to head back.

They spent a few more minutes watching the water flow over the falls, birds flying from tree to tree, and the snow dropping off the branches; and then they decided to head back. Bonnie felt cold again after Brad removed his arm, but she didn't stay cold for long as the snowshoeing through the woods warmed her quickly. This was a new adventure she wouldn't soon forget, but even more memorable was Brad's strong arm around her and how it made her feel so warm and protected.

Chapter 13

Brad envied Bonnie's relationship with God and wondered if he would ever understand what it was like to feel the presence of God. That was why he enjoyed spending time with Bonnie; she was not only beautiful and fun to be with, but she had a godly character that he knew wasn't an act to impress him, but was real. It was refreshing!

Brad was learning a lot from the young adult Bible study on Thursday evenings as well. The insights that Aaron shared and the discussions with others in the group were very helpful. Bonnie and April even shared things that they'd learned from their study. He admired their knowledge of the Bible and wished that he could understand it more. But Bonnie assured him that it would come in time, with diligent study and prayer for understanding. That was the other thing he didn't understand—the concept of praying to God.

When some of the people in the study group prayed, it sounded like God was right in the room with them and they were talking to Him like He was their best friend.

Is it possible to have a relationship with God like that? Brad thought. *How I wish I could. But if God was real, where was He when I was growing up? When my parents abandoned me and when my foster family were so unloving?*

They were now on the third chapter of John when Nicodemus came at night to talk to Jesus. The concept of being born again was as confusing to Brad as it had been to Nicodemus thousands of years ago. What did it really mean? When they came to verse 16, the one you hear everyone quoting and he'd even learned as a child, he was hoping to glean some understanding: "For God so loved the world that he gave his one and only Son, that whoever believes in him shall not perish but have eternal life."

Okay, so it says God loves me so much that He sent His Son to earth as a baby. That's why we have Christmas. That much I know, Brad mulled. *He did miracles while He was here on earth…I already read about that, and they were pretty amazing! No ordinary person could do the things that Jesus did.*

Then the Romans put Him on the cross and killed Him. No way did He deserve that. But then it says later in the Book of John that He rose again the third day, was seen by many witnesses to prove He was alive, and that's why we have Easter. But what I don't understand is why Jesus had to die. What is its significance and how does that help people have a relationship with God and go to heaven?

Brad knew he would have to continue with the study in order to find the answers.

"The ABR's candlelight ski event is next Saturday. It's always a lot of fun, especially if you have a special someone that you want to bring along," Aaron announced at the end of the class. "I think it'd be great if we could have a number of us go to that event. If you'd like to participate, please let me know by next Thursday evening. If you don't have your own cross-country skis, you can rent them from ABR, Whitecap, or"—he winked at Brad— "from Brad at the Lake and Snow in Bessemer. I don't want to be accused of not representing all of our local businesses in the area. The event starts at eight in the evening, but please be there by seven-thirty, so you'll be ready to go by eight. They'll be serving hot chocolate and coffee at intervals along the trail to help ward off the cold.

"Then I have one more announcement. The church is planning a couple's banquet on the Saturday night after Valentine's Day for the married and engaged couples. They've asked us to help with the decorating and serving for that event, so if you're available to help that evening, please let me know. Okay, let's close in prayer."

After Aaron prayed, Brad didn't hesitate to walk toward Bonnie. He really wanted to take her to the candlelight ski event. She said they couldn't date, but since the whole young adult group was invited, maybe he could just suggest that he pick her up and bring the cross-country skis.

Bonnie and April had ridden to the Bible study together, so he wouldn't be taking her home. He approached Bonnie expectantly.

"Good Bible study tonight, wasn't it?" he began.

"Yes, it was," Bonnie said. "Is it starting to make more sense to you?"

"To some degree, but that born-again stuff is still kind of confusing," confessed Brad. "I'm sure I'll get it eventually."

Bonnie prayed he would.

"I was wondering," Brad continued, "if I could pick you up for the candlelight ski event next Saturday. You're doing very well at cross-country skiing, and I could bring the skis you've been using from my shop. April, you could come too if you'd like."

"Count me out!" replied April. "I'm not into being out in the cold and cross-country skiing, especially at night. I think I'll just spend the evening cuddled up under a blanket with a good book."

"I think it sounds like fun, if you think I'm skiing well enough," Bonnie said with a smile. "Being out in the woods with just the stars and candlelight sounds great! The hot chocolate sounds inviting too."

"Oh, you'll do fine. I'll be right there with you if you have any trouble, and the trails are pretty wide and lit up. I'll pick you up at seven next Saturday evening then," he promised. "You ladies have a good evening, and I'll see you again for church on Sunday?"

"Yes, we'll be here," Bonnie said with a smile.

The evening of the candlelight ski event was cold, only about ten degrees above zero, but the sky was clear and filled with bright, twinkling stars. Bonnie dressed warm and wore the ski clothes Brad had given her for Christmas. She was looking forward to another new adventure—which, again, included Brad. It seemed she always looked forward to seeing Brad, no matter how hard she tried not to. But this night's event included others from the young adults' group, as well as those from the community, so it wasn't like a real date. At least that's what she kept telling herself.

After Brad helped her with her skis and handed her the poles, they joined the others at the trail, awaiting their instructions. She could see the candles flickering along the trail ahead. It looked so romantic!

"So how was it? Did you fall much? Was it pretty cold out there? Who else was there? Did Brad try to kiss you?" April bombarded her with questions the next morning when she entered the kitchen.

"Please, one question at a time," Bonnie insisted, putting up her hand to stop April from asking any more questions.

"Well then, start with the info, and I'll get your breakfast. What do you want, cereal or toast, apple or orange juice?" April started in again.

When Bonnie gave her "the look," April responded, "Hey, there's not a lot of time before we have to leave for church, so you'd better talk fast if I'm going to get all the details by then."

"Okay, I'll just have a piece of toast with peanut butter and a glass of apple juice," Bonnie began as she sat at the kitchen table. "There were about fifty people there, we had a wonderful time, and I only fell once. It was kind of cold, but the hot chocolate helped. And the stars—they were magnificent! That's when I fell. I was looking up at the stars, not paying attention to where I was going, and I tripped over a root that was across the trail and fell. But Brad helped me up. Then we stayed more toward the back so I could look at the stars and take in the effect of the candles along the sides of the trail without holding other people up."

"You were looking at the stars in the sky or in Brad's eyes when you fell?" April asked with a smile as she put Bonnie's toast and apple juice on the table.

"The stars in the sky," Bonnie stated matter-of-factly, but she could feel her face flush to a brilliant pink.

She took several bites of her toast and drank some of her juice before she was able to look up again.

"So did Brad try to kiss you while you were in the back all by yourselves?" April asked with a smirk on her face. "Come on, I need details. I'm your friend, you can tell me."

"No, he didn't. And that's all I'm going to say. I still have to take a shower and get ready for church." Bonnie quickly finished her toast and juice.

But as she showered and got dressed, she remembered the moment when they'd stopped to look at the stars in the sky and then found themselves looking into each other's eyes. She didn't know which were brighter—the stars in the sky or Brad's eyes. She knew he wanted to kiss her, but just in time, they both looked away and continued down the trail. They didn't speak for a while, but then Brad finally said, "Sorry, I guess I got carried away by the moment."

Just like I get carried away every time I think about Brad. Lord, You need to help me here! Bonnie told herself. *I can't stop thinking about him or wanting to be with him. I know he's not a Christian, so we can't become serious about each other. Please, Lord, help him understand that You love him and want to have a relationship with him. Help him understand what it means to be born again, to become a child of God, and one who is forgiven. Help me live my life as an example and wait on You for Your direction.*

At the end of the worship service, Aaron approached Bonnie, April, and Brad about helping at the couples' banquet, which would be held in just two weeks.

"I could sure use your help if you're available. I need people to set up tables and decorate them—in the kitchen; cooking and doing dishes; serving; and then taking down tables and cleaning up afterward. Can I count on your help?"

"What day is it again?" April asked.

"It's the Saturday evening after Valentine's Day. We'll need to do the setup at 4:00 p.m. Then the cook will need help in the kitchen, and we start serving at 6:00 p.m. We'll start cleanup after 8:00 p.m. You'll get a free meal, and I hear it will be really good. So what do you think?" Aaron asked again.

"I'm willing to help," volunteered April.

"Sure, me too!" Bonnie chimed in. "I'm not doing anything that day anyway. We might as well make it special for the married couples. They deserve a nice evening out."

"Yah, count me in too," Brad agreed.

He was willing to do anything to spend time with Bonnie. He really liked her, and though he felt she liked him too, she still kept him at arm's length. He knew it had something to do with her relationship with God. But he was going to church, reading and studying the Bible, and trying to stay within the boundaries she had set. What more did Bonnie want?

Chapter 14

Valentine's Day was a fun day for Bonnie's third graders. Her students brought in their decorated Valentine boxes, which were all unique and special. Bonnie had also made one to set on her desk for the cards she received from her students. It was a shoebox wrapped in a pink cloth with red roses all over it and then red and white silk roses on top. Several moms had volunteered to help with the party that afternoon and brought cupcakes and juice boxes. It was a fun, sugar-filled afternoon.

When Bonnie arrived home after school, she was tired yet excited. Brad had asked her out to dinner that evening—"Just as friends," he'd added. She knew he wanted to be more than friends, and in her heart, she was feeling more than friendship for him as well. But as a Christian, she knew she couldn't commit to any more than that.

He seemed to enjoy going to church with her and April and was attending the young adult Bible study on Thursday evenings. He continued to read the Bible she gave him for Christmas but was often confused by what he was reading, compared to what he'd grown up with. She needed to continue praying that God would give him the understanding he sought.

April went to a friend's house after school to spend the evening watching some chick flicks and eating junk food. Bonnie decided to wear a simple red A-line dress with a wide empire waistband she'd bought a few years ago for Christmas but added a new silver necklace, earrings, and shoes she'd purchased, as well as a lacy silver shawl. It looked dressier than it had before. She was ready when Brad arrived, and he seemed pleased with her attire when she opened the door.

"Wow! I made reservations to eat out, but maybe we should stay in so I don't have to share you with the rest of the restaurant crowd," Brad exclaimed.

He came in with a beautiful bouquet of red and white roses, just staring at her, unable to say another word or take his eyes off her.

"You look pretty handsome yourself," Bonnie complimented.

Brad looked really sharp in his black dress pants, white shirt, and red tie.

"Are those for me?"

"Oh, yes. I know you like roses, and I thought these red and white roses looked nice together. I hope you like them," Brad said, handing her the flowers.

"They're lovely! I'll get a vase to put them in," Bonnie said as she walked into the kitchen

Soon the roses sat in a vase on the counter next to the Valentine box she had brought home from school.

"Did you make this box?" Brad asked.

"Yes, I did. We had our Valentine party at school today, and the kids passed out cards to one another. They like to give the teacher one too, so I made this box to put on my desk. What do you think?"

"I think it definitely shows your love for roses and looks like I picked the right colors for your bouquet. You have the same colors on top of your box. Look, they match." He smiled and looked very pleased with himself, gazing into her eyes.

"I also think I never had a teacher as pretty as you when I was in school. I might have been a better student if you were my teacher." He caressed her cheek with his fingers. "Then again, I might have paid more attention to the teacher than my studies."

Bonnie blushed. It was hard to look away, but finally, she glanced down at the floor, breaking the spell.

"Why don't I get my coat and we can go? I'm sure you're getting hungry."

Brad helped her with her coat, and they left for the restaurant.

After a delicious dinner, and their dishes had been cleared from their table, Brad pulled a small, black, rectangular box with a red ribbon around it from his jacket pocket and presented it to Bonnie.

"Goodness, you didn't need to get me anything. The flowers and dinner were more than enough," Bonnie said as she hesitantly took the gift.

"I wanted you to have something to remind you of all the fun times we've had the last few months."

This made her curious, and when she opened it, she found a silver charm bracelet with a white snowflake hanging from it, a green Christmas tree, a snow skier, a red snowmobile, a pair of snowshoes, and a silver star.

"The charms represent some of the things we've done together this winter, and there's room for more. I'm hoping I can add more as we continue our friendship."

As Bonnie looked up, her eyes were filled with tears, and she had a hard time expressing her gratitude.

"Oh, Brad, this is very thoughtful and special, but it's too much! You shouldn't have gone to all this expense. First the flowers, and now this!"

Brad put his fingers under her chin, keeping her eyes focused on his, and said with a smile, "Bonnie, you mean a lot to me. You listened to me when I shared my past and didn't reject me. You've encouraged me and even respected me and my ideas. You're very patient as I try to study the Bible and understand what it says. I feel accepted and free to be who I am around you. I haven't had that since Joe died. I like spending time with you, doing things together that we both enjoy and watching the excitement in your face when you do something new for the first time. I even enjoy seeing the love and concern you have for your students. Oh, and you're a good cook too."

"Well, my mother always said that the way to a man's heart is through his stomach," Bonnie said without thinking, then felt her cheeks blush to a bright pink.

"You have my heart, that's for sure, Bonnie Turner. But it's not just because of your cooking. You're a very special person, and I'm glad I bumped into you on that ski hill. My life hasn't been the same since."

Bonnie looked down with embarrassment, and Brad removed his hand.

"I got something for you too, but I left it at the apartment. But I don't know if I should give it to you after you've been so generous," Bonnie said, looking at the charm bracelet again.

"All I ask is that you'll keep the bracelet and allow me to put it on you. That's the only gift I need," he said, giving her an expectant look.

She gave him a smile, nodded, and he fastened the bracelet on her wrist.

"There, that looks really nice with your dress and other silver jewelry. If you're ready to go, I'll take care of the check and help you with your coat."

"Yes, I'm ready to go."

Brad paid for their dinners and helped Bonnie out of her chair and into her coat. It made her feel very special. It wasn't something she was used to, but she sure liked it.

She often glanced at the charm bracelet on their way back to her apartment. She hoped he would accept her gift with the same gratitude that she had his. When they got to her apartment, she made them some hot chocolate and brought it into the living room.

Brad was sitting on the couch looking relaxed after having loosened his tie and top button.

"I hope you don't mind," he said, pointing to his shirt and tie. "I'm not used to wearing these things."

"That's fine. I think you've suffered long enough. But I did appreciate you dressing up for the occasion. I felt like a princess this evening, and you were my handsome prince."

She sat down next to Brad, handing him his hot chocolate.

"We'll have to do it again sometime then. I'd be willing to suffer through this shirt-and-tie thing just to see you all dressed up and looking so pretty. But you're a princess to me, no matter what you wear."

Brad put his arm around her shoulders and gave her a squeeze.

"Flattery will get you burned if you're not careful," Bonnie said as she leaned forward and set her cup down, thankful it wasn't full or it would have spilled on Brad's lap, as well as her own.

"Sorry!" he said as he scooted over to give her a little more space.

"April will be home soon. Why don't I get your gift so you can open it before she gets here?" Bonnie got up, went to her bedroom, and returned, carrying a large, rectangular package wrapped in red paper with a big, white bow.

"Wow, is it Christmas again already?"

"No, silly! When I was at your house, I noticed you didn't have any pictures on your walls, so I thought you could hang this up. Actually, we were both thinking on the same line. You got me this charm bracelet to remember our times together, and I got a picture blown up and framed of us at the ski hill when we went with the young adults' group."

Brad tore it open and stared at the picture, amazed and pleased.

"Where did you get this photo? I don't remember anyone taking our picture."

"Aaron had taken some that day and showed them to April. When she showed them to me, I asked if I could have a copy of this one. I had it blown up to an eight by ten and bought a matted fourteen-by-sixteen frame for it." Bonnie smiled as they both looked at the picture, pleased with how it had turned out.

Brad kissed her on the cheek, and his eyes were shimmering with tears as he smiled at her.

"Thank you! You don't know how much this means to me. And I already know where I'm going to put it—on the center of the fireplace mantel."

"I'm glad you like it."

Bonnie couldn't look away but felt mesmerized by Brad's face so filled with gratitude and awe. Only when the door opened and April came in did they both look away and greet her.

"Sorry for intruding. Oh, you opened your gift! What do you think of the picture?" April asked with excitement. "Didn't it turn out great?"

She hung up her coat and threw her purse and bag on a chair.

"When I saw that picture, I just had to show it to Bonnie."

"It's absolutely the greatest! I didn't even know Aaron was taking pictures that day."

"Well, you had your mind on other things," April smiled as she looked at the picture again, then at Brad and Bonnie. "Anyway, I'll leave you two alone. Sorry again for interrupting your evening. I'm tired and am going to bed."

She yawned on the way to her bedroom.

"Good night, Bonnie. Good night, Brad."

"Good night, April," they both replied.

"I should go too as you have school in the morning," Brad said as he turned and looked at Bonnie. "Thank you for a wonderful evening. I enjoyed our dinner together, and I *love* the picture. I'll pick you up on Saturday afternoon then when we go to work at the Valentine banquet."

"Okay. Thank you so much, Brad, for everything! This has been a very special evening, and I'll never forget it," she said as they walked to the door together and Brad put on his coat.

"Neither will I." He looked at her face and, as if asking permission, slowly leaned down and placed a soft kiss on her lips. "Happy Valentine's Day, Bonnie."

And with that, he opened the door and was gone.

"Happy Valentine's Day, Brad," Bonnie said in a whisper as she closed the door.

Chapter 15

On Saturday, Brad and the rest of the guys from the young adult group set up the tables for the Valentine banquet in the gym of the church, and then the ladies decorated them. What a transformation! The gym now looked like a banquet hall, with round tables covered in white linen tablecloths and set with red napkins, silverware, stemmed glassware, and candles. Brad helped put buns in baskets for each of the tables, while others got salad dishes ready to take out on trays later. Still others made punch, filled water and coffee servers, and made everything ready for the couples to arrive. The meal smelled temptingly delicious, and Brad was glad when he was asked to leave the kitchen and help take the coats of the couples as they arrived and hung them on the coat racks. They even had a photo room set up so couples could get their picture taken before they went into the gym. It was going to be a special evening.

They had all been instructed on how to serve the couples, with two servers per table of six, one holding the trays and the other serving from each person's right side. They brought the drinks, the salad, and then the main course, which was a choice of either marinated chicken or stuffed pork chop, baked potato, and California blend. It worked out well, and everything went without a hitch. No trays were dropped, no coffee was dumped on anyone's lap, and the couples enjoyed being waited on and made to feel special.

After they finished the main course and the dishes were removed from the tables, a program began for the couples, and the young adults were able to take a break and eat. The food was as good as it smelled. They all felt pleased that they had a part in something that came off so well.

When they finished eating, Aaron spoke up and said, "You all did a really fine job setting up, getting things ready, and serving tonight. I'm really proud of the way you were willing to do whatever was asked of you. And there were no spills or catastrophes, just a job well done."

"It was actually kind of fun to see the transformation of the room, the smiles on the couples' faces, and how well the serving went when we worked together," April spoke up. "It went much better than I expected."

"Serving others without expecting anything in return is an interesting concept and one that is rewarding in itself," Bonnie commented.

"I think Valentine's Day and the idea behind it is very nice, but I think we need to make people feel special every day, not just once a year," stated another volunteer. "We need to think of ways to let people know that we care and tell them we appreciate them."

"I agree," Aaron acknowledged. "At our next Thursday night meeting, as we continue in the Book of John, plan on sharing ways that Jesus showed his disciples that He cared about them, as well as other people He came in contact with. But now, we still have a kitchen to clean and dessert to serve, so pick up your dishes and let's get back to it."

Brad thought about what had been said, how the group had worked together without complaining, and the reaction of the couples they served the rest of the evening. Even the concept of Jesus showing people that He cared for them made him pretty quiet and reflective as he dropped Bonnie and April off at their apartment. He would have to read over the Book of John again and see what was so different about this Jesus and how He made people feel special.

Does Jesus really care about me? he thought. *My biological parents didn't. My foster parents sure didn't. Joe was the first person who showed that he cared about me. Bonnie seems to care about me too. I know I care for her. Aaron has become a good friend, and I enjoy his teaching. But why would God care for me? Why would Jesus, God's Son, want to die for me?*

Burdened with many thoughts, Brad definitely had a lot to consider.

The next few weeks, Brad continued to ponder about Jesus and again read through the Book of John and some of the other books in the New Testament. He read that God had sent Jesus, His Son, to earth to be born as a baby to a woman named Mary. Joseph became His earthly father and cared for Him as if He were his own flesh and blood. When Jesus became a man, He chose twelve men to be His disciples. He performed many miracles—healed the sick, raised the dead, changed water into wine, and fed five thousand people with only five loaves and two fish.

Jesus was no ordinary man, so He had to be God's Son. But if He was, why would He care for someone like himself? He would never be good enough for God to accept him, no matter how hard he tried.

As Brad sat in church the last Sunday in February listening to the pastor talk about Jesus and God's love, some of the things he was saying started to make sense. None of us will ever be good enough for God to accept us, for as the pastor quoted, "For all have sinned and fall short of the glory of God" (Rom. 3:23).

Then the pastor read the verses in John that Brad had read so many times already:

> For God so loved the world that he gave his one and only Son, that whoever believes in him shall not perish but have eternal life. For God did not send his Son into the world to condemn the world, but to save the world through him. Whoever believes in him is not condemned, but whoever does not believe is condemned already because he has not believed in the name of God's one and only Son … But whoever lives by the truth comes into the light, so that it may be seen plainly that what he has done has been done through God. (John 3:16–18, 21)

When Brad heard those verses again, it was like a light came on in his head.

It's not what I can do that makes the difference but what God already did! Brad reasoned. *I just need to believe it and accept it.*

He was determined to speak to the pastor after the service. Brad didn't care who or what was going on around him, but went straight to the pastor and said, "Pastor, can I talk to you in your office?"

The pastor took Brad to his office and explained to him the wonderful plan of salvation and gave him the promise in Acts 16:31: "Believe in the Lord Jesus, and you will be saved."

"There's nothing you can do to earn salvation, and you can never be good enough for God to accept you. He takes you just as you are, loves you, and wants to forgive your sins—if you but ask Him," explained the pastor. "It's a gift that you only need to receive. Jesus paid the price for your sins when He died on the cross and then was victorious over sin and death when He rose again the third day."

"I want to accept God's gift," Brad affirmed. "I want my sins forgiven."

"Then all you need to do is pray and ask God to forgive you. Talk to Him, just like you're talking to me right now," instructed the pastor.

"Dear God, thank You that You love me just as I am. And, God, I know I'm a sinner and have done wrong. I've been angry at my parents for not wanting me and my foster parents for not loving me. I'm sure glad You love me and sent Your Son, Jesus, to die for my sins. Please forgive me of my sins and anger. I don't want to carry them anymore. Help me live the way You want me to live. Thank You, God. Amen."

Brad opened his eyes and lifted his head with a smile on his face.

"Wow! I feel so clean and like a heavy burden has been lifted from me. I have a peace that I've never felt before!"

"That's because you're forgiven, you've been made clean—'whiter than snow,' as the Bible says—and are now a beloved child of God. You can claim Him as your Father now, and He will always love you and will never leave you or forsake you. That's His promise! Satan will try to trick you into believing that you're not forgiven, that you're not a child of God. But you know different because God's Word is true, and He never goes back on His promises. You'll need to keep reading God's Word, and His Spirit will guide you in the way He wants you to live."

"Thank you, Pastor. I'm forgiven, cleansed from my sin, and my heart definitely feels whiter than snow. Bonnie said that once, but I didn't understand what it meant. Now I do. I need to go tell her."

Brad got up from his chair, shook hands with the pastor, and left the room to find Bonnie.

As he went out into the foyer of the church, he saw Bonnie, Aaron, and April standing in a circle, praying for him while he was in with the pastor. Brad reached out for Bonnie, and she went into his arms with tears running down her face.

"I did it, Bonnie. I believed in the Lord Jesus Christ, and God forgave my sins. My heart feels whiter than snow, just like you said, and I know now what that means. Thank you for praying for me. Thank you for being patient with me and caring for me."

"Oh, I'm so happy for you!" Bonnie exclaimed through her tears.

"Welcome to the family of God, friend," Aaron said as he placed a hand on Brad's shoulder.

Bonnie broke away from Brad's arms, and Aaron gave Brad a brotherly hug.

"Hey, I need a hug too." April joined in and gave Brad a hug.

Drying her tears, she said, "This calls for a celebration! Why don't we all go for lunch together? I'm buying."

"That sounds like a winner to me," Aaron said. "Never let it be said that I turned down a free meal. Besides, I'm starving!"

They all left the church with smiles on their faces, Brad with his arm around Bonnie's shoulder and April and Aaron chatting about what they were going to order.

Chapter 16

Brad enjoyed reading his Bible that week, but there were still things he didn't understand. When they'd gone to lunch together on Sunday, Aaron said that he would meet with Brad each week on Tuesday evenings to talk about things he didn't understand and they could pray together. This was a great help and encouragement for Brad. He knew he could also talk to Bonnie about the Bible, and he did share with her what he was learning. But it was good to share his questions with another man. The pastor was also helpful in answering many of his questions.

He'd never had so many people come up to him and tell him what a wonderful thing he'd done as there were in that church. It was like they had accepted him into their family—their church family. It was a great feeling for Brad. He'd never felt a part of a family before. Now he had a very large family.

Bonnie and Brad planned to go snowshoeing on Saturday afternoon. It was the first weekend in March, and it had warmed up quite a bit, so there wasn't a lot of snow on the ski slopes. Even the cross-country ski trails had grassy spots here and there, so it wasn't good for cross-country skiing either. With snowshoes, they could go into the woods where the sun hadn't melted the snow as much.

"Remember when I took you for a ride that first Sunday after we met to see some of the area?" Brad asked as they were driving to their destination.

"Yes. I remember I was fascinated with all the snow, the ski jump, and the beauty all around. Is that where we're going?"

"Yep. I told you I'd bring you back in the spring, which it will be soon, but it's also a good place to snowshoe. We'll get a good workout and see some waterfalls, and maybe even Lake Superior will have started to open up."

"That sounds great. I just hope I can keep up with you. I haven't been getting as much exercise the last few weeks as we did earlier."

"Oh, we're not going to be in any hurry. We're just going to enjoy the beautiful day and scenery and having the afternoon together," Brad said as he parked the SUV. "Here we are at our first stop. Normally we can drive in closer to Potawatomi Falls, but they don't plow this side road in the wintertime. Come on, I'll help you with your snowshoes."

Bonnie hung onto his shoulder as she stepped into the snowshoes that Brad placed on the snowy ground. He tightened them and then handed her the ski poles.

"Okay, you're all set. It looks like we're not the only ones snowshoeing here, for I see other snowshoe and cross-country ski tracks. We'll see which is easier, to follow their tracks or make our own. It will just take me a minute to put mine on, and then we'll be ready to head down to the waterfalls."

"I'm amazed at all the different ways there are to enjoy the snow here," Bonnie commented as she looked down the path ahead of her. "Downhill skiing, snowboarding, snowmobiling, cross-country skiing, and snowshoeing—when I was growing up, it was just making snow angels and snowmen or having snowball fights and making snow forts."

As she started to move forward, snow hit her from behind. When she turned around, Brad was getting ready to throw a second handful of snow.

"Hey, what's the big idea? I thought we were snowshoeing, not having a snowball fight!"

"I just wanted you to feel at home, but the snow isn't sticky enough right now for a really good snowball," Brad said with a grin and tossed it to the ground.

She stooped down to grab a handful of snow and threw it at him.

"Yah, too bad. I used to be pretty good at throwing snowballs," she said, smiling. "Lead the way, O mighty warrior. I'm anxious to see this waterfall. How far down the road is it?"

"Well, if we could have driven down this road to the parking lot, it would only have been a short distance. But since we have to walk in from the road, it's more like half a mile."

As they continued on, they decided to use the cross-country ski tracks already there. They were more compacted, and it was easier going than in the untraveled snow. Bonnie was amazed at how much of a workout snowshoeing was. They stopped now and then to rest and look at the scenery all around them—the snow falling from the tree limbs, the sun peeking through the trees, and the birds pecking at the snow, looking for something to eat and then flying back into the trees.

But when they got to the waterfalls, Bonnie could only stop and stare in awe at the sight before her. There was still some ice in the river, but water was rushing around the rocks and ice, and the sun was gleaming off the water as it rushed down the waterfalls, causing sudsy-looking foam as it continued down the river. They'd gotten a lot of snow this last winter, so with the snow melting, the water in the river was high and the current powerful.

The trees on the rocky hills along both sides of the rushing river were standing as if in reverence to the Creator who made all this possible.

"How could anyone look at this and not believe that there is a God who created the world—that it didn't just happen? The power that we see here is just a glimpse of the power God has, for He controls the whole universe, and He made all this for us to enjoy. Isn't God good?"

"He sure is. He made all this," Brad agreed as he stretched his arm out to encompass everything around them.

He then turned Bonnie to face him and looked into her eyes.

"Most of all, I'm thankful that God brought you here, that I met you, and that you shared your faith with me, and then lived it so I couldn't deny it. I'm thankful that God loved me enough to die for my sins, forgive me, and make me His child. I feel so alive now, so free to love others, and even to forgive my parents and foster parents. I guess if God can forgive me, He wants me to forgive them also.

"I can't personally ask for their forgiveness, since I don't know where my parents are, and my foster parents have passed away. But

God has removed that anger and bitterness from my heart, and I feel like a new person. Bonnie, maybe this is too soon—and I have no right to say it—but I love you. I hope someday I'll be someone you can come to love too because I can't imagine life without you."

Bonnie couldn't take her eyes away from Brad's. She could see that he was sincere and that the love in his eyes for her was real. She knew in her heart that God was finally giving her the chance to confess her love as well.

"Oh, Brad, I already love you! I have for some time, but I couldn't express it since you weren't a believer. But now that you are, I know that God brought us together for a reason, and I can't wait to see what He has for us in the future."

"Me neither, but right now, I want to kiss you in the worst way," Brad said as he bent his head down.

But he didn't have far to go as Bonnie met him halfway with a kiss that started out gentle and increased with passion. But it didn't last long—as, when they tried to embrace each other, they almost tripped over their snowshoes.

"We'll have to try this again without the snowshoes," Brad said with a smile. "I think it'll work better."

"I agree," Bonnie said, laughing. "Let's head back."

When they got back to the SUV, Brad took off Bonnie's snowshoes and then his own and put them in the back.

"Well, have you had enough exercise for today? We could snowshoe the campground down the road, which would be about another mile. They have a great lookout spot where you can get a good view of Lake Superior. Or we could drive down to the harbor as far as the boat launch and see the lake from there and then go and get some pie and hot chocolate. Which would you prefer?"

"I know I could use the exercise, but I don't know if I could do another mile. So I vote for the second option. If that's okay with you."

"It sounds good to me. Let's go," Brad said as he opened her car door.

When they got to Lake Superior and stepped out of the vehicle, Bonnie was surprised at the huge buildup of ice chunks piled against the rock barriers and along the shoreline. Farther out, however, there was open water as far as the eye could see.

"Because Lake Superior is so deep, it doesn't always freeze over," Brad explained. "So when the wind blows and the weather warms up, it breaks up the ice and the waves push it closer to shore. It can be very dangerous to fish Lake Superior in the winter or in any season, as the winds can shift and come up very quickly."

"I've always enjoyed looking at Lake Superior," she said with awe. "It's so big and beautiful, but it can be very dangerous too. Have you ever fished on it?"

"Oh yes, many times. I'll take you this summer if you like."

"Oh my, more new adventures for this Minnesota country girl? Are you sure you're up to the challenge?"

"I would enjoy it immensely," he said with a reassuring smile that left no doubt in her mind. "But for now, let's go get that pie and hot chocolate. I can see the wind is picking up out here in the open, and you're getting cold."

He wrapped his arms around her shoulders and pulled her close as they walked back to his SUV.

The next morning during the worship service, one of the songs they sang was called "White as Snow." Brad just stood and listened to the words, for he realized that was what had happened to him—his sins were as scarlet, but Jesus washed them away, and now he was clean and forgiven. All because Jesus loved him enough to die for him and shed His blood on the cross.

After listening to the song and with tears in his eyes, Brad whispered to Bonnie, "That's what happened to me. That's what Jesus did to my heart. He washed it white as snow."

"I know," Bonnie stated simply with a smile and tears in her eyes. "Isn't it wonderful?"

Chapter 17

Bonnie and Brad enjoyed reading the Bible together and going to the young adult study group. They would finish their study in the Book of John by Eastertime, which was in April this year. It was a good study, and with Bonnie and Aaron's help, Brad understood more and more of it each week.

It was even more meaningful with Easter approaching. To realize that God loved him so much that He was willing to let His Son pay the penalty for his sin by dying an awful death on the cross was still amazing to him. Thankfully, Jesus was victorious over death and rose again on the third day and was now in heaven, preparing a place for him. To be loved by God and now by a wonderful woman like Bonnie—Brad's life was good!

Bonnie had asked Brad to go to Minnesota with her during spring break in the middle of March to meet her family. Since the snow was melting and not many people were buying or renting skis or snowboard equipment, he figured Kevin could handle things on his own, so he decided to take some time off. He was nervous at the thought of meeting her family, however. Would they like him? Would her parents approve of him dating their daughter? Would they give their approval for him to marry her one day?

Bonnie came from a large family. How would he ever remember all their names? She had talked of them often and mentioned their names, but putting the right name with the right person—that would be a challenge. At least she only had one sister, Carrie. He should be able to get that name right. He had sent Carrie a purple ski top and gray ski pants to go with it, which she had requested when Bonnie had gone home at Christmastime. He'd received a very nice thank-you note from her.

Their drive to Minnesota went very quickly, as they talked and enjoyed the passing scenery. However, when they got close to her family's home, Bonnie tried to fill him in with as much about her family as possible. This made Brad even more nervous, and he felt like he was cramming for an exam.

"Please stop!" he insisted. "My brain can't hold any more information. I'll do my best not to embarrass you and remember what I can. But let's try to relax and have a good time. They'll just have to take me for who I am."

"I'm sorry, you're right. But I'm sure they'll fall in love with you, just as I have." She leaned over and kissed him on the cheek. "Turn left at the next road, and it's the first driveway on the right."

Brad did as she said and tried to calm his nerves at the same time.

He found Bonnie's family to be very welcoming and friendly, and since her brothers weren't all currently living at home, he didn't have as many names to remember. However, Bonnie's sister, Carrie, was not easy to forget, as she seemed to always be around and was either asking him questions or beating him at Skip-Bo, which seemed to be the favorite family game.

Bonnie helped her mom in the kitchen but still had time to go for walks around the property with him and into the nearby woods. She showed him where the gardens would be planted, and shared how she had spent many hours planting, weeding, harvesting, and then canning and freezing the many crops that they grew. It helped feed their large family, and she was grateful for all she'd learned.

Bonnie said she even hoped to have a garden of her own someday.

"Watching things grow," she went on, "always reminds me of how awesome God is. Nature reflects God's glory, His creativity, His love of color, beauty, and diversity, as well as His love for mankind. God put us on this earth to take care of it and enjoy all the beauty He created. It gives us just a glimpse of who He is and what heaven will be like. For if the earth—in all its imperfections—is this beautiful, heaven will be awesome and unimaginable! I guess that's why I've appreciated that you enjoy nature and have shown me all the places you have. It's something that we can share together, and now that we also share the same Savior—well, that's the best of all!"

Bonnie's father shared her love of nature and also took Brad for a walk. He, however, had a different purpose in mind.

"So how long have you known my daughter?" he started by asking.

"Since December," Brad responded nervously.

"I've been watching you, and you seem to care for my daughter a great deal for having known her for such a short time," her father said.

"Yes, sir, I do. She's a very wonderful and caring person. We both enjoy the outdoors, and I've enjoyed showing her the beauty we have in the UP in the wintertime. Now that it's warming up, there are many other things I'd like to show her. She says she enjoys Lake Superior, and we're not far from it, as well as many waterfalls."

"Yes, she's always enjoyed seeing the water, though she hasn't learned to swim yet. That's something I'd like her to learn if she's going to be around Lake Superior a great deal."

"I didn't realize she can't swim, but I would be more than happy to teach her, sir."

"Well, don't let on that I told you she can't swim. She may not have wanted me to disclose that information."

"I'll be very tactful, sir," Brad responded seriously.

"And I would appreciate it if you stopped calling me *sir.* Since we'll probably be seeing more of each other, why don't you call me Bill? It's a lot less formal and won't make me feel so much like a drill sergeant."

"Very well, sir—I mean, Bill. Thank you," Brad said, trying to relax.

"Bonnie informed us that you recently accepted Christ as your Savior. Have you been reading your Bible and growing in your faith?" Bill asked.

"Yes, I have. In fact, Bonnie gave me a Bible for Christmas, and I've been reading it ever since. I've also been attending the young adult Bible study at our church where we've been studying the Book of John. At first, I didn't understand a lot of it, but now it makes much more sense to me. Bonnie's been very helpful in explaining things to me. Aaron, the leader of our group, has helped me a lot too. He's becoming a great friend and mentor, and we meet together weekly for Bible study and prayer."

"Well, it sounds like you've come a long way in a short time. I'm pleased. Tell me about your family."

"I was put in a foster home when I was six years old after my parents separated. It was not a good situation, and I never felt loved or accepted into their family. They had one son and owned a logging business. I guess I felt more like a hired hand than a son—only without the pay, though I did get room and board. Whenever we were around other people at church, in town, or around friends or relatives, they put on a front to make it look like I was part of their family, but I never felt like I was."

"I'm sorry to hear that, son," Bill replied.

His genuine concern made Brad feel good that someone who didn't even know him would sympathize with him and even call him *son*.

"Thank you, Bill. That means a lot to me."

"Brad, we have a big family, and it seems to keep growing as the kids get older, bringing special friends home for us to meet and, eventually, marry. If you would someday become a part of our family—and it looks like that's a possibility—I'd be glad to call you son," Bill said as they stopped and he put his hand on Brad's shoulder.

As Brad's eyes misted over, he looked into Bill's eyes and said, "I would be very proud to be a part of this family."

They walked the rest of the way back to the house in silence as they both contemplated what had just transpired—Bonnie's father realizing that he might soon be giving away his daughter and Brad feeling accepted into an earthly family. Much had happened to him since Bonnie came into his life: Bonnie accepting him, becoming a child of God and being accepted into God's family, and now being accepted into Bonnie's family. He was overwhelmed with joy.

Chapter 18

As Bonnie prepared for the Easter egg hunt she'd planned for her third graders, she was glad Easter was in April when it was warmer. For now the snow was gone, except for the piles, and the ground was drying up so she could hide the eggs outside for her students. They had decorated Cool Whip bowls for their Easter baskets, which the students had brought from home, and used pipe cleaners for handles.

She was always pleased to see the creativity her students displayed. Each one was unique and showed their individual personalities. The girls' baskets were mostly done in pink or purple, with stickers of cute little bunnies, baby chicks, or Easter eggs. The boys' decorations, however, varied in color and design—from trucks and cars, to Spider-Man, Mario, and other video game characters. Bonnie had designed hers by using a soft yellow fabric held on by a rubber band and decorated with Easter symbols of the cross and the empty tomb.

She was grateful that a few other children chose a more religious theme as well. When the children would ask questions about the symbols, she was happy to answer and tell them of the true meaning of Easter. She could tell some had never heard of Jesus dying on the cross and couldn't understand why someone would die for someone else.

She often prayed, "Lord, may they someday understand and accept Your gift of salvation. Please help me to be an example and show them how much You love each one of them."

The Easter egg hunt went as planned, and the children enjoyed running around the designated area of the schoolyard to find the hidden eggs. Some of the children found more eggs than others, and she was glad that she'd explained that there would be a prize for the one who found the most eggs and that the eggs would all be put into a large basket and distributed equally after the party. The eggs contained jelly-beans, small prizes, and, of course, some chocolates. But the food for the party would offer more healthier foods and less sugar. She had asked the mothers who volunteered to bring small sandwiches of meat, tuna, or egg salad and fruit. Bonnie brought juice boxes for drinks.

Once school was done for the day and Bonnie and the mothers had cleaned up after the party, she was exhausted. But she was looking forward to going to the Good Friday service at church that evening. Brad said he and Aaron would pick up supper and bring it to their apartment so neither she nor April would have to cook. Then they'd go to the service together

Since they didn't have to worry about cooking supper, April suggested Bonnie shower and change first while she straightened up the apartment and set the table. After showering and changing into her black dress pants and lavender sweater, Bonnie felt refreshed and ready when she opened the door for Brad and Aaron, who arrived with their supper. April was still changing.

"Mmm, supper sure smells good! What did you all get?" Bonnie asked as they unloaded the bags of food onto the kitchen counter.

The aroma made her realize how hungry she was.

"We got fried chicken, mashed potatoes, coleslaw, buns, and cheesecake for dessert," Aaron said as they finished emptying the bags of food.

Bonnie took their jackets and laid them on a chair in the living room.

"My, don't you look handsome this evening," she said to Brad as she returned to the kitchen.

Brad was wearing black dress slacks, a gray shirt with a black-and-white printed tie, which she knew he wasn't fond of wearing, and a black leather vest. His hair was still damp from his shower, and he looked nervous, as if it was their first date.

Even April gave a whistle when she came into the kitchen.

"Wow, Brad, you're wearing a tie and everything! You look good too, Aaron."

"Thanks, I think," Aaron replied with a quizzical look. "Let's go into the dining room. It looks like the table is all set and looks very nice, by the way."

"Yes, April used our best dishes, goblets, fancy napkins, and even candles. You really set a lovely table, April."

"I was just following orders. Brad said to do it up nice and that he wanted candles too, so that's what I did," April replied.

"So why don't you ladies have a seat?" Brad asked as he pulled out a chair for Bonnie, and Aaron followed suit for April. "I'll light the candles, and then Aaron and I will serve you this evening."

After the candles were lit, the men went into the kitchen to get the food.

"I could get used to this kind of service," April said with a smile as she placed her napkin on her lap.

They heard banging in the kitchen as cupboard doors were opened and shut, but soon, the men returned with the food in serving bowls and platters. Brad asked Aaron to say grace, and then they all started eating.

"I always say that food tastes better when you don't have to cook it yourself. This tastes even better than it smelled," Bonnie said after taking a few bites. "And you brought all my favorites. You're going to spoil me."

Brad smiled at her and looked back down at his plate.

Bonnie shared how well her Easter egg hunt went, and they all listened attentively. However, she sensed Brad was nervous about something and tried to find a topic that would help him relax.

"Brad, now that the weather is warming up, do you have any plans for working on your property before fishing season starts up?"

This subject didn't seem to help, as Brad actually blushed a little, cleared his throat, and said slowly, "Y-yes…as a matter of fact, I want to get some more clearing done around the house, but it's still a little too wet."

He looked down, took a deep breath, and started in again, looking at her with anticipation in his eyes.

"I was hoping maybe you and April could come over sometime and give me some advice. I want to clear a spot for a vegetable garden and maybe plant some flowers or bushes around the house. Make it look a little homier. When we were at your parents' home, you mentioned how much you liked to garden, plant flowers, and watch things grow. I know you can't do that here at your apartment, so I thought maybe you and April could plant some things at my place."

"Oh, that would be wonderful!" Bonnie said with excitement. "I was wondering how I would fill my time this summer when school was done. April, would you like to help?"

"I don't have your green thumb, but I could help some. I'm sure some flowers around your house, Brad, would look very nice, though I couldn't see much with all the snow that was there in December.

"What kinds of vegetables do you think you'd like to plant?" asked Bonnie.

"Well, I suppose the usual—corn, beans, potatoes, tomatoes, and I liked that broccoli you made. But no asparagus or brussels sprouts. You can't get me to eat that stuff!"

"Okay, that's a good start." Bonnie said with a laugh. "What kind of flowers would you like?"

"I'll leave that up to you ladies. I don't know much about flowers, although we'll definitely have to plant roses, as those are your favorite. What other kinds of flowers do you like?"

"Oh, just about all kinds. Dahlias and begonias are beautiful, and geraniums do nicely in a flower box or pot. Some hanging baskets would look nice on your porch too." Bonnie's eyes lit up with excitement as she went on. "I've always thought red salvias are majestic and rich looking when planted in a group setting. And snapdragons are really pretty and fun. Did you know that if you pinch the blossom from its side that it looks like a dragon's mouth opening? That must be where they got its name. My brothers and I used to do that when we were kids."

Brad just smiled and seemed to relax as Bonnie went on about the flowers she'd like to plant.

Soon they were finished with their food, and Brad said, "I hope you all saved room for dessert, because I bought Bonnie's favorite—strawberry cheesecake. You ladies relax, and Aaron and I will clear the table and bring your dessert."

"You guys are going to spoil us," Bonnie commented as the men cleared the table. "If you keep feeding us like this though, we'll get so fat, we won't be able to bend over and plant your garden."

"I'm not worried," Brad said with a look of such love and devotion that it almost took her breath away. "Besides, the pieces are small. You'll work it off in no time if you plant all those flowers you're talking about.

Brad and Aaron soon came back, each carrying two plates of strawberry cheesecake. Aaron placed one in front of April and the other at his place and sat down. Then Brad placed one in front of Bonnie and one at his place and sat down as well.

As Bonnie picked up her fork and looked at her plate, she gasped, for in the middle of her cheesecake was a beautiful, shiny diamond ring.

Brad got up from his chair, knelt down beside her, took her hand in his, and said, "Bonnie, I thank God every day that I ran into you in the woods. You've accepted me, loved me, supported me, and made me laugh. But most of all, you showed me that God loves me, and now I'm forgiven and a part of His family. Bonnie, I can't imagine my life without you, and I want to spend the rest of my life loving you, caring for you and maybe someday having a family of our own. I asked your parents for their blessing, and they granted it, so, Bonnie, in front of our friends as witnesses, I want to ask you if you will marry me and be my wife?"

With tears in her eyes threatening to overflow, Bonnie smiled.

"Yes! Oh yes! I love you, Brad, and it would be an honor to be your wife."

With that, Brad stood and lifted Bonnie into his arms and was kissing the tears away as they spilled down her cheeks, while April and Aaron looked on, clapping and cheering! Brad took the ring, wiped off the cheesecake, and placed it on Bonnie's finger. Then he gave her a kiss that made her feel loved and cherished.

April and Aaron congratulated them.

Aaron patted Brad on the back and said, "Well done!"

"You were in on this weren't you?" April smiled and enquired of Aaron.

April then turned to Brad and said, "No wonder you wanted everything so perfect. You did good!"

Then she gave Bonnie a hug and said, "I'm so happy for you!"

Brad took Bonnie in his arms again and kissed her with joy. With all the excitement, however, they forgot about the cheesecake waiting for them on the table.

Finally, Brad looked at his watch and said, "It looks like we'll have to eat our cheesecake later or we'll be late for the Good Friday service."

Bonnie and April put the cheesecake in the refrigerator while Brad and Aaron got their coats. They didn't have far to go, and they made it to church just as the singing started, so they slipped into one of the back rows.

But Brad had a hard time concentrating on the service and smiled at Bonnie every time he caught her looking at her engagement ring. She seemed radiant that evening, and it made his heart glad to know she was as delighted with their engagement as he was. Though he tried to concentrate on what the pastor had to say, he had to admit that he couldn't remember much of what was said. However, the words to the last song, "Oh, How He Loves You and Me," at the end of the service really grabbed his attention and touched his heart.

Wow! Brad thought. *Jesus loved me so much that He was willing to die for me. That's a lot of love. Do I love Bonnie like that?* He thought so, but during the closing prayer, he thanked God for loving him and being willing to send His Son to die a gruesome death on the cross in order to pay the penalty for his sins. He also committed to loving Bonnie the way God wanted him to love her, care for her, cherish her, and, if necessary, be willing to die for her—as Jesus had died for him.

Chapter 19

Bonnie, Brad, April, and Aaron went back to the apartment after the service and ate their strawberry cheesecake.

As they enjoyed their dessert, April exclaimed, "Boy, love must really be in the air. You two weren't the only ones from our young adult group to get engaged this week—three other couples got engaged! I've never seen so many smiling faces and rings sparkling after a service."

"Well, I have to say, I like my ring the best." Bonnie smiled as she looked down, admiring her ring again.

It was white gold and had a brushed look to it with a small stone placed on each side of the diamond in the middle.

"Besides, it's not important how many carats your diamond has but the love you share—and that you put Christ first in your marriage."

"Yes, and I want you all to know, especially Bonnie," Brad said as he took her hand and looked into her eyes, "that I am committed to loving you with all my heart and asked God this evening to help me to love, care for, and cherish you for the rest of my life."

He then looked at April and Aaron as he continued, "I know I haven't had many good examples of this in the past, but God is my example now. I have His word to guide me, and I'd like to ask the two of you to keep me accountable."

"You can count on me," April assured. "I know you love Bonnie, and I've never seen her happier."

"I'm in too," Aaron agreed. "We can continue studying the Scriptures together and learn from each other. That's what friends are for."

"Thanks, both of you! We appreciate your support," Brad said as he and Bonnie held hands, smiled, and nodded in agreement. "But it's getting late, and Aaron and I better let you ladies get to bed. I have to be at the shop in the morning, but would you have time in the afternoon, Bonnie, to help me pick a garden spot for the vegetables and let me know what flowers you want to plant? April can come too. I want to get to work as soon as the ground is dry enough to start clearing and tilling the soil."

"So you were serious about this garden thing and it wasn't just a line?" April asked, smiling at Brad. "I'm sorry, but I already have plans to take my mom down to my sister's downstate over the Easter holiday. Though I don't think I'd be much help anyway, and I'd probably just get in the way. I've never done much gardening, but I'll help once you get the plants, as long as you tell me what to do. I don't mind digging in the dirt."

"I can help with whatever you need too," Aaron added. "Just give me a call."

"Thanks, both of you," Brad said as he and Aaron got up to get their coats. "I'll pick you up about one-thirty, Bonnie, so Kevin can get his lunch break in before I leave. Does that work for you?"

"Sure, that will be fine," Bonnie agreed. "It will give me time to get a few things done around here in the morning. There's no school on Monday, due to the Easter holiday, so I don't have anything pressing for tomorrow."

"Good! I'll look forward to seeing you tomorrow then. You better bring your boots as it's still pretty muddy out there." He took Bonnie in his arms and kissed her good night but had a hard time letting her go.

As Brad looked longingly into her eyes, he said, "I hope you don't want a long engagement because it gets harder and harder to leave you. Start thinking of a date when you'd like to get married and maybe we can talk about it this weekend."

"Okay, though I'm still getting used to the idea of being engaged, much less getting married. But don't worry, I don't want to wait too long either. This summer will probably be best as I wouldn't have school to worry about. Would that be okay with you? Though it does take some time to put a wedding together, you know."

"This summer sounds good to me, but I think it's more important to put a marriage together than a wedding. Let's keep it simple. I really don't want anything too fancy."

"No, I don't picture you as the fancy type, though I have to admit, you do clean up pretty well. You looked very nice tonight in your dress shirt, tie, and vest."

"Only for you, my love," Brad said as he kissed her again. "Well, Aaron is waiting for me so I better go. I'll see you tomorrow afternoon."

"Good night, I'll see you tomorrow." Bonnie closed the door, went into the kitchen, and found April washing off the counter. "Well, this was quite a night. Did you know about this, April?"

"I wasn't sure, but I had my suspicions when Brad wanted everything to be so perfect, with candles and everything. I'm so happy for you, Bonnie!" April came over and gave her another hug. "It looks like you have a wedding to plan."

"Yes, and I would like you to be my maid of honor. You have been my dearest and best friend."

"I would love to," April assured her. "Anything else you want me to help with, just let me know. But now, I'm going to bed. It's been a long and exciting day, and I have a long drive tomorrow. Good night, Bonnie, and sweet dreams."

"Good night, April. I'll be praying that you have a safe trip and a wonderful visit with your mom, sister, and those adorable kids of hers. I'll see you when you get back, and thanks again for everything. You helped make this an evening I will never forget."

And with that, they hugged each other again and went to their separate bedrooms. Bonnie didn't know how soon she would fall asleep after all the excitement of the day, but she knew her dreams would be sweet.

Chapter 20

Brad arrived at 1:30 p.m. and they were both anxious to get to his place to check out the garden spaces. Bonnie had been thinking of some ideas as she worked around the apartment that morning and was excited to share them with Brad when they arrived at his home.

"Now that the snow has melted," she said, "it's easier to see the grounds around the house and yard. We should probably start with the area in front of the house. Hanging baskets on the porch would look lovely and add a lot of color and curb appeal. How does that sound to you?"

"Sounds good. I've seen that on other houses, and it looks very nice and homey," Brad agreed. "How many were you thinking of?"

"Well, it's quite a long porch, so I'd say probably three on each side would be enough. We don't want to block too much of the view when we look out the windows from the inside or when sitting on the porch. Petunias or impatiens always look nice in hanging baskets. We can even use different colors if you'd like."

"Okay, that takes care of the hanging baskets, but I'm sure you have more ideas, so go on."

"Well, I've always loved red geraniums, so I think a large pot of them on each side of the front door would look lovely, and they'd make a nice welcoming statement. Then in front of the porch, on each side of the steps, we could plant some perennials, as they come up every year and you don't have to replant them."

"I really like that idea!" Brad exclaimed. "It would be a lot less work and money."

"Well, they do cost more up front, but yes, in the long run, they're more cost effective. They spread out over time, so we'd have to give them some space when we plant them. Bushes on each side of the steps and at the ends would help ground the space, with taller flowers in the back and shorter flowers in the front between the bushes. But when you dig up the space, you'll want to round the edges and clean out all the grass and weeds so it doesn't look too boxy.

"I'll buy a gardening book that has a variety of perennials in it," she went on. "We can look at it and draw out a plan with the choices of bushes and flowers we'd like to plant. It'd be a fun project to do together. Do you have a tape measure we can use to measure the space? And we need to decide if you want to go all the way across the front or just partway or if you want to just do one side of the porch and leave the other side grass, as it could get quite expensive."

"Well, if they're going to be perennials, which will come up every year, I'd rather do both sides at once so they'll grow up the same. And like you said, if we round the edges, starting with the end of the steps and angle it in, it wouldn't have to be that deep, so that will cut down on some of the plants."

"Very good! It will also make it easier for me to keep it weeded if it's not so deep that I can't get to the plants without stepping on something. And I agree that it would look much better to have plants on both sides of the porch. So I guess we're in agreement?"

"Yes, we are. This is going better than I thought. Of course, it helps to have someone who knows what they're doing," Brad observed.

"Well, I can't say I know that much about perennials. That's why I suggested buying a book that will tell us how much space they need, what grows best in this area, whether they need shade or sun, what the different varieties are...maybe we should talk to someone at a nursery too and get their recommendations."

"Boy, there sure is a lot more to planting flowers than I realized," said Brad. "There's more to it than digging a hole and putting them in the ground."

"That's for sure! But if we're going to invest money into the plants, we want to make sure they'll grow and thrive for years to come."

"Okay, I'll get the measurements of each side of the steps, you get a book on perennials, and we'll get together and plan that space for the front of the house. What about the vegetable garden you wanted? Where would be a good spot for that?" asked Brad, leading them around to the back.

"Well, it needs to get plenty of sunlight and be level so rain doesn't puddle in spots and kill the plants and not too close to the buildings," Bonnie suggested.

"Okay, how about to the right of the driveway or back here?" Brad pointed to some open, level spots. "It's far enough away from the house and sheds, level and gets plenty of sunshine, and it's not too close to the woods."

"Yes, either one looks like a good spot," she said. "My only concern is all the wildlife you have out here. I think we'll have to put a fence around it or the animals will get more food than we will."

"You have a good point. It'll cost a lot of money to fence in a large garden. It may not be that much cheaper to plant our own food after all." Brad looked very discouraged.

"I tell you what," Bonnie said as she turned to face him. "We have a wedding to plan and get ready for and you have a job that keeps you busy, so why don't we just concentrate on the flowers for this year and I can pick up a few things at the farmer's market that some of the teachers have told me about? That will give us some fresh fruit and vegetables without all the time, money, and work. I think doing the flowers in the front will keep us more than busy this summer."

"You would be okay with that, even after I promised you a vegetable garden?" he asked doubtfully.

"Of course. I was getting a bit overwhelmed anyway with all the things we're talking about and the amount of work it would take. I know I have the summer off, but I was hoping to have time for some fun and not all work. I'm sure we'll have to make many adjustments and changes as we plan our wedding and throughout our marriage. That's part of life."

"Wow, you are quite a woman! I thought you'd be upset. No wonder I love you."

"Why would I be upset? Really, I'm relieved. Now we'll have more time to talk about the wedding, what you had in mind, and which dates would work out best for you and your business."

"I'm so thankful that you agreed to marry me. I'm truly blessed. Have I told you lately how much I love you?" Brad asked with a smile as he leaned down toward her lips.

"Not since last night. But a girl can never hear it too much," Bonnie said before she accepted his kiss.

His kiss lingered, and Bonnie finally stepped back, feeling flushed, and said, "Let's go sit on the porch steps, look at a calendar, and see if we can come up with some dates."

"Good idea! I'll get us something to drink, bring out a calendar, paper and a pen," he said as they walked back to the house.

Bonnie made herself comfortable while he went inside. Soon he came back out with a calendar under his arm and a tray with two glasses of tea, some paper, and a pen.

"Here you go," Brad said as he handed Bonnie the tray, pulled the calendar out from under his arm, and sat down. They each took a sip of their drink and gave a sigh.

"Okay, you did say you don't want to wait too long, didn't you?" asked Brad hopefully.

"Yes," she answered. "This is April, and school is done the first week in June. I've always thought June was a nice month for a wedding, but it wouldn't give us much time to get everything ready since May is pretty busy for me with all the things to do at the end of the school year."

"May starts the summer fishing season, so I'm stocking up now with all the fishing supplies. June and July are pretty busy, with fishing in full swing and all the fishing tournaments in the area. Things start to slow down in August. So how would that work for you? Though I was hoping it would be sooner," Brad admitted with a grin.

"Well, with all I have to do to get ready for the wedding—planting flowers, packing, and getting the house ready—I think that's our best choice. Do you have any idea who you want to stand up with you?" she asked.

"Well, Aaron for sure," Brad replied, smiling. "He's become a very good friend and mentor. And probably Kevin. He's been working with me for a little over a year now and we've become pretty close. And I've been invited to his home several times. His mom's a great cook. I'll have to introduce you to her sometime when you're both at the shop. She helps out once in a while, does my bookkeeping, and, of course, other odds and ends like wrapping presents for me. She does a much better job than I would. How many did you have in mind?"

"Well, I already asked April to be my maid of honor, and I'll be asking my sister, Carrie, to be a bridesmaid too. We said we wanted to keep it simple, so I think two would be enough. What do you think?"

"I think that sounds perfect," Brad agreed. "But that's enough thinking for a while. Would you like to go for a walk with me? I'd like to show you around the property. I'm glad you wore your boots as there's still some snow in the woods, and some spots are pretty muddy. But it's a nice day for a walk."

"That sounds wonderful!" Bonnie said, smiling, as her husband-to-be helped her stand. "It's such a beautiful spring day, and as you know, I love walking in the woods."

Bonnie enjoyed their walk as he showed her where his property lines were and told her some of the names of the trees on his property. He also showed her where he got many of the trees that he'd cut down to build the house. She could tell that he truly loved the outdoors and knew that they'd be taking many walks together in the future. She always felt close to God when she walked in the woods and was surrounded by nature, and now God had brought someone into her life who shared her love of nature and God.

The Easter service at church the next morning was a real time of celebration and worship of their risen Lord. The songs proclaimed that Christ was no longer dead or in the tomb but was risen, just as He'd said and the prophets had proclaimed would happen. The scripture that was read and the message given had new meaning for Brad, for now he understood that Jesus had done it all for him and anyone else who would believe in Him. He still could not fathom all the love that God had for him or why He chose to forgive him, but he was sure glad He did.

The closing song was "Because He Lives," written by William Gaither, and Brad sang it as his testimony and with tears in his eyes:

> Because He lives, I can face tomorrow,
> Because He lives, all fear is gone.
> Because I know, He holds the future,
> And life is worth the living,
> Just because He lives!

Chapter 21

After their Easter dinner, Bonnie and Brad called her parents to tell them of their engagement. They were happy for them, congratulated them, and asked questions about when they thought the wedding would be. Carrie screamed with excitement when she found out she'd be a bridesmaid and would be able to come to Ironwood for a week in June to help pick out dresses for the wedding.

The reality that Bonnie was engaged and would be getting married in August was finally starting to sink in. The teachers she worked with and her students all wanted to see her ring, congratulated her, and peppered her with questions that she didn't have answers for yet. There was more involved in getting ready for a wedding than she realized.

But time went fast, and before she knew it, it was May. Her class made May baskets on the first of the month, and she told them the story of what to do with them. Some of the children hung their baskets on people's doors and came back excited to share the excitement of those who'd found them. Spring was such a happy time, with new life springing up all over—green grass, daffodils, tulips, and, soon, peonies. Bonnie was also busy browsing the garden books she had purchased, and she and Brad drew up plans together for the perennial garden they wanted to plant in front of their home. They decided it would be best, though, to show their plans to someone at a garden nursery before they purchased the plants, just to make sure they had chosen the right ones for their garden spot.

Then fishing season opened, and Brad was excited to share his love of fishing with Bonnie. She had fished offshore with a cane pole as a child and caught a turtle, a bullhead, and some branches of a tree with her hook; but never had she been on a boat or learned to cast. She was about to embark on another new adventure.

Brad had her practice in his backyard first with no hook so she could get used to casting, but now they would be in his boat. Brad decided to take her to Gile Flowage in Wisconsin, which was a small lake, instead of Lake Superior and made sure she had on a life jacket since he'd learned that she was afraid of the water and didn't know how to swim.

"Okay now, do just as I showed you when we practiced in the yard. To begin casting, hold the rod about waist level, grasping it so that the reel is above the rod and your thumb falls naturally on the button at the base of the reel. The bait is about eight to ten inches below the tip of the rod. Now go ahead and let some of the line out by pulling it gently with your hand then pushing and holding the button with your thumb. Pull the rod tip back above your head so the tip sweeps over your right shoulder, and then bring it forward swiftly, pointing the rod tip at your target on the water. As the rod comes forward to your shoulder, release the button so that the weight of the bait pulls the line from the reel. When the lure hits the water, reel once to engage the bait, and then you can slowly reel the line in again to entice the fish to snatch at the bait."

"It looks so much easier when you do it," she remarked after she watched Brad cast his line into the water.

"It gets easier with practice," he assured her.

It did get a little easier, but soon Bonnie had enough and set her rod down. She decided she liked riding in the boat, looking around at the scenery, and watching Brad and the other fishermen rather than fishing herself. She congratulated Brad whenever he caught a fish and handed him the bucket after he took it off the hook. She felt sorry for the poor fish but knew God had created fish for man to eat, so she looked forward to their fish fry later that evening.

The rest of the month of May was busy for Bonnie and her students, with field trips, end-of-the-year activities, and finalizing their studies. Bonnie was proud of what all her students had accomplished that past year. She had fallen in love with each one of them. Yes, some had been a challenge at first, but once she understood why and came alongside them to care and help them, they had flourished as well.

She would miss having them in her class next year but was sure she would fall in love with her new students the following year as well.

⁂

Bonnie, Brad, April, and Aaron spent the last Saturday in May planting the flowers Bonnie and Brad had purchased from the Country Store in Hurley, Wisconsin. The salespeople had been very helpful in their selections and seemed to stock the nicest plants in the area. They decided to get impatiens of different colors that were already in the hanging baskets so all they'd have to do was hang them from the porch.

"Please hang them low enough on the chain so I can reach them without having to get a stool when I need to water them," Bonnie asked Brad and Aaron.

While they hung the chains and the hanging baskets, Bonnie and April planted red geraniums and some baby's breath in two large pots with a stand, one for each side of the front door. The flowers really added a lot of color and hominess to the front of Brad's house.

Brad had already dug up the ground in front of the porch and got rid of the grasses and weeds, so it was ready to plant. The owner of the Country Store had recommended several bushes and perennial plants that were more deer resistant. And since it would take a while for the bushes and plants to grow and fill out, he also suggested they plant some annuals among the perennials to add some color, so they purchased marigolds of various colors, which would also keep the deer and rabbits away. When they were finished, they put brown mulch around the plants to keep the ground moist and the weeds down.

It was a big job, but with the four of them working together, it went much quicker than they expected. Part of the incentive to get the job done were the grilled steaks, potatoes, and vegetables, as well as chocolate pie with whipped cream for dessert, which Bonnie and Brad had promised April and Aaron. But the best part for Bonnie was to step back and see the finished product.

"Wow!" she exclaimed with a smile. "It makes such a big difference to have more color around the house. The red in the geraniums by the front door and the pink, salmon, and white of the impatiens in the hanging baskets make the porch come alive. Then with the plants in front, all the different greens and reds of the bushes and perennials, the yellows and oranges in the marigolds, and the dark brown mulch make everything look inviting and pop with color. I couldn't be more pleased."

Brad put his arm around her shoulders and kissed her on the cheek.

"I'm glad you like it. It makes it worth all the aches and pains of digging and bending over those plants to see the glow and smile on your face."

They both admired the view for a few minutes.

Brad then got Bonnie a cold drink and said, "Here's a glass of cold iced tea."

After she took a drink, Brad turned her to face him and said, "You are much more beautiful and precious to me than these flowers. I thank God every day that He brought you into my life, and I look forward to the day when you'll become my wife."

When he pulled her close and kissed her, she forgot how tired, sore, and hungry she was. She felt totally satisfied just to be held in his arms and feel his love.

But soon, Brad let her go and said, "I'll go wash up and get the grill going. Then I'll bring out a table and some chairs on to the porch so we can eat out here."

The food was a great reward indeed, as was the company and the view of their labor.

It rained on Sunday, but Memorial Day promised to be nice, so Bonnie and Brad decided to spend the afternoon at Black River Harbor and hike in the woods, walk along the beach, have a picnic, and just relax. They hadn't been there since March when there was ice and snow on the lake. Now it was seventy degrees, the grass was green, there was a soft breeze, and Lake Superior was a beautiful blue with soft ripples from the wind. The sky almost matched the blue of the water, but a few puffy clouds set it apart.

They went for a hike first on the trail that went to Rainbow Falls from across the bridge of the river. It was quite a climb up the wooden stairs, and then they walked along the ridge that followed Black River through the woods. Soon they could hear the water thundering down the rocks, but when they saw it and felt the mist as the water hit the river at the bottom, it made them stop in awe at the beauty and majesty of it all.

Brad couldn't help but reverently exclaim, "God created all this beauty for us to enjoy. What a great God we have!"

When they got back to the harbor, they enjoyed the picnic that Bonnie had prepared and then took a leisurely walk along the beach of Lake Superior, hand in hand. When they returned to the park area, they sat on some rocks overlooking Lake Superior and watched the gorgeous sunset with the reds, oranges, and yellows.

When Brad took her home that evening, she said with a sigh, "Thank you for such a perfect afternoon and evening! That sunset was a gorgeous way to end a beautiful day, a productive weekend, and an eventful month. It was like a promise from God that He has even more wonderful things in store for us in the future."

"He does—a lifetime with each other, and I'm looking forward to it!" Brad exclaimed as he released her from his arms, kissed her good night, and left.

Bonnie sensed that he struggled with letting her go, but knowing that God wanted him to flee from temptation, he left quickly. Brad had grown much in his faith, and she thanked God that he was willing to listen to the Spirit's prompting. She was also thankful that she had saved herself for her husband and looked forward to how God would bless them and their love for each other after they were married.

Chapter 22

After school was out, bulletin boards taken down, her room cleaned up, and report cards turned in, Bonnie was finally able to concentrate on wedding plans. She and Brad had decided on August 6 for their wedding, which would give them time to get everything ready and have a weeklong honeymoon before Bonnie had to be back and get ready for another school year. Brad said he would take care of the honeymoon plans and let Bonnie, April, her mom, and Carrie work out the details for the wedding plans but was willing to be there to help when needed.

They talked to the pastor and informed him of the date they decided on, reserved the church for the fifth and sixth of August, and scheduled marriage counseling sessions. A friend from their young adult group offered to design their wedding invitations and came up with three options for them to choose from. They chose one they both liked, and Brad took it to be printed.

Bonnie's mom and sister would come and stay with her the last week in June to help shop for her wedding dress and bridesmaid dresses and order flowers for the wedding. Her father and brothers who still lived at home would join them on the Fourth of July weekend for some sightseeing and the Fourth of July festivities. So she had much to look forward to.

The summer looked to be a busy one. April had set a goal of learning to kayak over the summer, and Aaron was more than happy to help her with that. They seemed to be spending a lot of time together, but April kept saying, "It's nothing serious, we're just friends." Only time would tell.

Brad had also set a goal for Bonnie to learn to swim. Lake Superior was too cold, so he took her to a pool in the area.

"It will definitely make being around water safer and more enjoyable for you," he said with love and concern.

They went on Tuesdays and Thursdays when Brad finished with work, and then they would have supper together. She also went to his shop when he got large shipments in and helped with pricing and shelving the new stock, hanging clothes, and arranging items on the wall hooks. It helped her learn about the fishing equipment and other inventory, and she could see all that Brad did. It even gave her a chance to meet Kevin's mom, Molly, and they became fast friends.

She was very kind, caring, and always willing to help, and she definitely did more than bookkeeping when she was there. She was a widow, and her children were all grown; and though Kevin still lived at home, he worked at the shop, attended classes at the college, was very active, and was seldom at home. Like Brad, he was an outdoorsman and loved skiing, snowmobiling, and fishing.

One of Molly's daughters had recently gotten married, and Molly told Bonnie, "If you need any help with the wedding plans, I would be more than willing to help. It can get pretty overwhelming at times, trying to remember everything that needs to be done."

As they visited over lunch, Molly mentioned some items that Bonnie hadn't even thought of.

"I tell you what, my daughter made a checklist of things that she wanted to get done before her wedding. Why don't I get a copy of that from her and bring it to you? You may not need everything on her list or need to make some changes, but it may be helpful for you. I can even give you the names of a caterer and a woman who makes great wedding cakes whom we contracted for her wedding. They were very good and not too expensive."

"Oh, that would be very helpful! Thank you, Molly. I have a couple of brothers who are married, but I wasn't that involved in their weddings. My only sister will soon be fifteen and isn't at that stage yet. I've attended weddings but have no experience in planning them. My mom and sister are coming at the end of the month to go dress shopping, but any help in the meantime would be very helpful."

The list Molly gave Bonnie was definitely helpful, though she did make some changes to it. Now she felt like she had some direction, knew what she needed to take care of, and would feel a sense of accomplishment when she could check things off when completed. There was definitely more to planning a wedding than she realized. Her mom hadn't planned any weddings since her own, which was very simple and a long time ago, so Bonnie was grateful for the help Molly had given her.

Bonnie's mom called also, saying, "After talking with your dad and the family, your older brothers said they would be willing to be ushers, so you can check that off your list. Also, we'll take care of preparing the rehearsal dinner and cleaning up the church after the wedding."

"Thanks, Mom! That's wonderful and a very big help. We also have someone to take pictures. She's in our young adult group and has done several weddings already. Brad and I have seen some of her pictures, and she does a really good job. We have talked to a caterer and ordered the cake, so we're making progress. Oh, and since I don't have any nieces or nephews able to be a flower girl or ring bearer and Brad doesn't have any family, I've asked two of my third graders from this last year, who also attend our church, to be our flower girl and ring bearer. I think that will really make it special. And while you and Carrie are here, April wants to have my bridal shower so you'll both be able to attend."

"Oh, that will be so nice! Since the wedding won't be here and many from the church won't be able to attend your wedding, the ladies said they'd like to make you a quilt for a wedding gift and want to know what colors you'd like."

"That is really awesome! Please tell the ladies that I really appreciate that. Can I get back to you on the colors in a week or so? I want to check with Brad and also look at his house again. I've been in the kitchen, living room, and bathroom but only glanced at the bedrooms as I walked by."

"Yes, I'm sure that will be fine. In fact, as a mother, I'm grateful to know that you haven't been in his bedrooms."

"Mom! You know that as a Christian, I would never do that."

"That's every mother's hope and prayer, but I also know that there are temptations that are common to all of us. After all, we're still human. But God is able to help us through any temptations we may have." Bonnie's mom paused for a while. "Well, that's enough preaching. Carrie and I will be there in a week, and we'll help with whatever we can. Carrie is excited about trying on dresses for the wedding. Hopefully, it won't take too long to pick them out. Do you have some idea of what you're looking for?"

"I've been looking online and at some bridal magazines, so I will print or copy the styles that I like. Hopefully, that will narrow it down some so it won't take too long."

Bonnie and April had decided that while Bonnie's mom and Carrie were staying with them; Bonnie would share April's room, Bonnie's mom would have Bonnie's room, and Carrie would sleep on the couch. Later when Bonnie's dad and brothers joined them for the Fourth of July weekend, that would allow Bonnie's mom and dad to have her bedroom, and Brad said the boys could bunk up at his place. He would take care of the arrangements. So they moved some things around, and when Bonnie's mom and Carrie arrived, they were all set.

They went to Duluth to shop for dresses for the wedding, and Bonnie was able to find a wedding dress that they all fell in love with and thought was just right for her. It was an elegant lace A-line dress with a jeweled waist, had cap sleeves, and a V neckline. The skirt flared out at the waist to make it move easily as she walked. She felt like a beautiful bride yet comfortable. She knew Brad would love seeing her in it as she walked down the aisle.

They tried on both long and short dresses for April and Carrie but finally decided to go with short dresses, since the wedding was in August and would likely be very warm. Her mom also mentioned that the short dresses could be worn again rather than just once. They chose a short dress in a silky green material that had cap sleeves and a fitted bodice with a modest scooped neckline.

The slightly flared skirt had a filmy lace overlay that was a lighter green with pink flowers on it. It made the pink flowers pop and looked very summery, cool, and elegant. Both April and Carrie loved the dresses and looked beautiful in them. They were also happy with the idea that they could wear them again for other occasions.

They would wear tan sandals with an open toe and block heel to finish off the look.

Even Bonnie's mom found a dress for the wedding, as they were having a great sale. She chose a pink short-sleeved dress in a classic A-line style made of chiffon and lace. It looked very elegant and stylish. The women went for lunch together and then left Duluth satisfied that they had accomplished their task, had a great time, and got to know each other better.

The next day, they went to the floral shop. There was a new one in Ironwood that was recommended, and they found the owner to be very helpful. Bonnie said she wanted red roses and white baby's breath for her bouquet, and after hearing about the colors of the bridesmaid's dresses, the florist recommended pink roses and white daisies for their bouquets, with a few greens for contrast. The flower girl would carry a bouquet of white daisies tied with a green ribbon, which would go nicely with her pink dress. They also ordered the boutonnieres for the men and corsages for Bonnie's mom and other women helping in the wedding. The floral shop would also rent them the silk rollout for the aisle and a white archway. So now more items were accomplished that Bonnie could cross off her list. They were making great progress.

With this feeling of accomplishment, Bonnie and April were able to spend some time showing Bonnie's mom and Carrie around their community. They showed them the school where they both taught, the church where they attended, and also the pool where Bonnie was taking her swimming lessons, for which her mom was grateful.

"I'm so glad Brad is willing to teach you. Your brothers all taught themselves and Carrie has taken swimming lessons, but I've always been worried about you, especially since you're around so many lakes here."

Then they drove by the grocery store and the downtown area. One of the highlights was taking them to the Ben Franklin store, which had many items unique to their area. It had a good variety of jewelry, silk flowers, material, home décor, and craft items, as well as pictures and framing supplies, clothing, and many other items unique to the Upper Peninsula. Bonnie's mom was able to purchase a few items that she hadn't been able to get in their own area, and Carrie was fascinated by all the bear figurines and "up north" décor.

"Are there really bears in this area, Bonnie?" Carrie asked with concern.

"I've heard there are, but I haven't seen any," Bonnie assured her.

"Boy, you really do live in the sticks up here, don't you?"

"I guess you could say that," she said with a laugh. "But it's home and a pretty safe place to live."

After they left the Ben Franklin store, Bonnie had one more place she wanted to take them.

"Next I would like to take you to Brad's shop in Bessemer," Bonnie explained. "It's about six miles east of here, and you'll be able to see where he works and what type of items he has in his shop. I also want you to meet Kevin, who works for him, and will be one of his groomsmen. Kevin's mom, Molly, will be there also, and I want to introduce you to her too. She's Brad's accountant, among other things, and has become a great friend and help to me with the wedding."

As they traveled to Bessemer, Bonnie shared with them that once her dad and brothers arrived, she and Brad would take them to other sites in the area that they would enjoy seeing.

Carrie was captivated with the many items that Brad had in his shop. She also was excited to meet Kevin, since he was the one who would walk her down the aisle at the wedding. But she had to wait for him to finish with a customer. In the meantime, Brad introduced them to Molly. She was delighted to meet them, and as she and Bonnie's mom visited, Bonnie could tell that they hit it off right away. So while they visited, Bonnie, April, and Carrie browsed around the shop until Kevin was finished with his customer, and then Bonnie introduced them.

They were pleased to meet him, especially Carrie, but he didn't have much time to talk, as another customer needed his attention. He seemed very knowledgeable about the products, and one could tell he really enjoyed the sports he talked about. However, Carrie was only concerned that he was good looking and she would be with him at the wedding and he'd be walking her down the aisle. Such was the mind of a teenager!

During the evenings, Bonnie, her mom, April, and Carrie addressed the wedding invitations that Brad had picked up for them and got them stamped and ready to mail out. Bonnie was grateful for the family and friends' names and addresses that her mom had brought with her. Though some wouldn't be able to come to the wedding because of the distance, they still would like an invitation so they could send a card. They were expecting between 100 and 150 to attend the wedding.

Chapter 23

The Fourth of July weekend promised to bring much excitement and activity. Bonnie's father and some of her brothers were able to join them on July 1, around one in the afternoon, for a four-day weekend. Bonnie and Brad looked forward to spending time with them and showing them around to some of their favorite spots. Brad knew that the boys would want to do something active after sitting in the car for five hours, so they started out with a stop at Copper Peak. Then they hiked to some of the waterfalls on Black River Road and ended up at Lake Superior for a swim. The water was cold; but Brad, Bonnie's brothers, and Carrie said that once you got used to it, it wasn't so bad.

Bonnie and her parents decided to go for a walk along the shore. On the way back, Bonnie took off her shoes and walked along the edge of the water where the sun had warmed it. Then they sat on the beach under a nearby tree and watched everyone enjoy the water. They were definitely having a good time, and it cooled them off. Then they went to Brad's home for a cookout of hamburgers, bratwursts, potato salad, beans, and ice cream for dessert. It was a fun evening of getting to know one another better and relaxing after a busy day. Bonnie, Carrie, and their mom and dad went back to her apartment as dusk fell, eager for a good night's sleep.

The next morning, after they had a simple breakfast of cereal, toast, and juice, Bonnie and her mom started putting together a lunch for the day's activities. They tried to do it quietly, as Carrie was asleep on the couch, but didn't succeed.

Carrie finally got up and said, "I'm going to take a shower. I can't sleep anyway with all this noise."

With Carrie up, they didn't have to be as quiet and felt free to make some noise while making brownies, cooking noodles and chicken for their salad, and other preparations. April had gone to be with some friends, and Bonnie's father was kept occupied with some magazines Bonnie had about the Upper Peninsula of Michigan.

"You know," he concluded, "I didn't realize all that you have to see here. It really has some unique and beautiful areas. And the activities that are available in all seasons are amazing! It would take a lifetime to see and enjoy it all. You know, honey, I think we'll be coming up here quite often, now that Bonnie has decided to call this place home."

They met the boys and Brad at his home at eleven and then went on to Presque Isle, a beautiful spot in the UP which Bonnie had not yet seen. Brad had told them to bring their cameras as they would be able to get some amazing pictures. There was a covered picnic area available so they could get out of the sun for a while. They enjoyed their lunch of chicken salad, carrot sticks, dinner rolls, brownies for dessert, and bottled water.

When everything was put away, they followed a walking trail into the woods; and Bonnie, Carrie, and some of her brothers had their cameras ready to take pictures. And they weren't disappointed, for the trail led them to a boardwalk that went along Presque Isle River where there were several waterfalls, with steps to go down to give them a closer view. They also saw awesome sights of what the power of water could do to the rocks along the shore as it wound its way down the river. After more steps, they came to a bridge that crossed the river and took them to a different part of Lake Superior than they'd been to the day before.

Since Brad had told them to wear their swimsuits under their clothes and bring sunscreen, they would again have a chance to swim and enjoy Lake Superior. This time, Bonnie decided to go in the water and join the fun, so she could have a chance to cool off. There were a lot of driftwood and logs on the shoreline, so her mom and dad found a place to sit in the shade and watch the activity.

"You know, dear," Bonnie's dad commented while they watched the activity in the water, "I think Brad is going to fit in very well with this family."

"I think you're right," Bonnie's mom agreed with a smile.

Sunday was the day of Bonnie's bridal shower, so after church, Brad took her dad and brothers out to lunch. The ladies stayed at the church; and after lunch, the guys went to Brad's home to have an afternoon just to relax, throw some balls around, take a walk in the woods, or take a nap—which was what Bonnie's dad said he wanted to do.

The bridal shower was very nice. Kathy, one of the teachers with whom Bonnie and April worked at school, and Missy from their young adult group had helped April plan, decorate, and prepare the food. Because it was on a holiday weekend, some women were not able to attend, but a good number were there.

Bonnie was very grateful that her mom and Carrie were able to attend as well. Bonnie had her mom and Carrie help her when it was time to open the gifts, and it made them feel very special. When it was over, Bonnie's dad and Brad came to help load up the gifts and take them back to Brad's home. There were a lot of lovely and useful items that they would not have to purchase. Bonnie looked forward to putting them to good use.

However, Brad had a surprise for her when they arrived at his home. He had made a porch swing, which was hanging from the right side of the porch roof when they arrived. He had painted it the same green as the roof and shutters of the house. The swing looked wonderful and would be great for sitting in the shade of the porch, enjoying the scenery. They all took turns sitting on it once the vehicles were unloaded and found it to be very relaxing. Bonnie was looking forward to many evenings of sitting on the porch swing with Brad in the future.

"Thank you, Brad, for such a wonderful surprise," she said when she finally had a chance to sit in it with him.

"You're welcome! I started working on it after we planted the flowers in front. They looked so nice, I figured we needed someplace on the porch to sit and enjoy them. The flowers are really filling out and starting to bloom, I might add. Your brothers helped me hang the swing. It was a good project for us to do together. They're really quite handy, and I appreciated the extra muscle."

"I'm sure you did, and we definitely will spend a lot of time enjoying this. It's so beautiful out here. I enjoy the soft breezes and the shade that the porch offers. In fact, we can even use it on rainy days—watch it rain and still stay dry. This is going to be wonderful!" she said with a smile.

She gave him a kiss, put her head on his shoulder, closed her eyes, and relaxed with a sigh of contentment.

Bonnie and Brad decided that they would put away the gifts later when they had more time to look them over and read the cards together. But since her mom was there, Bonnie wanted to show her the house and decide on the colors for the quilt that the ladies in her home church were making for her. There was a lot of green in the main area of the house, which was an open floor plan, including the kitchen, dining area, and living room. Her mom thought it was very roomy, casual, but comfortable; and the large stone fireplace really made it homey and unique. They walked into the master bedroom to see a large bed, wooden dresser and chair, and a walk-in closet but no curtains; and the only color was in the faded green blanket Brad had on the bed.

"You know, I was thinking about what colors to choose for this room since you called and asked about colors for the quilt," Bonnie said. "I really would like to go with something different than green, but not too feminine. What do you think of blues and reds? The blues would keep it masculine looking, but I could also add some femininity and elegance with red roses on the dresser and other accents."

"That is totally up to you and Brad," her mom said. "It's going to be your home, and it's very lovely, I might add. Brad put a lot of love and hard work into this home when he built it, but it definitely needs a woman's touch. It will be interesting to come back and see how you decorate it and make it both of yours. I think blues and reds might be a good option, but you need to talk it over with Brad."

After talking with Brad later, he liked her choice of colors and said, "Go for it!"

So Bonnie informed her mom of their color choices and would look forward to seeing the finished quilt on their bed.

That evening, they all went to Wakefield to see the fireworks as they were shot over Sunday Lake. There were a lot of people with lawn chairs or blankets scattered on the grass enjoying the colors and sounds of the fireworks display. It was a spectacular ending to a great day.

Their last day together started early, as Brad wanted to take them to Porcupine Mountain, another place Bonnie hadn't yet visited. April and Aaron were going to join them, and they all looked forward to the trip. After eating a quick breakfast, Bonnie and April packed a lunch of sandwiches, chips, and leftover fruit and desserts from the bridal shower the day before, along with bottles of water and Gatorade to drink.

While they made their lunch, Carrie and her mom and dad packed up their things, as they would have to leave later that afternoon for Minnesota. Aaron was to pick them up at eight-thirty, and they would meet up with Brad and her brothers at Sunday Lake in Wakefield where they had watched the fireworks the night before. Then they would follow Brad to Porcupine Mountain.

It would take about an hour to get there, so an early start was necessary. Brad said they wouldn't be able to see everything but would get a good taste of what was there and then could come back another time to see more.

"Porcupine Mountain is Michigan's largest state park—sixty thousand acres—and is one of the few remaining large wilderness areas in the Midwest," Brad told his guests. "It has tall virgin timber, secluded lakes, and miles of wild rivers and streams. A visit to the 'Porkies' is a trip to remember, and people come back to it again and again."

Their first stop was to the visitors' center. They watched an informative film about the park, its history, and some of the main sights. They learned that the park was named Porcupine Mountain because from a distance, the mountains looked like the hump of a porcupine. The visitors center had maps of all the hiking trails, a large topographic map of the park, and a room that explained some of the past mining and logging that took place, as well as some of the fish and animals that could be seen in the area. They all agreed that they wouldn't be able to see it all in one day. A gift shop offered a variety of things they could purchase to remind them of the park, but they would come back to that later.

Then they drove through the campground, just to see what it was like. It had great sites, some along the lake and others up on a little hill closer to the shower and bathroom facilities. Bonnie knew her brothers would like to come back and camp there sometime. After they left the campground, they drove up Porcupine Mountain until they reached the top where they came to the famous Lake of the Clouds.

They got out of their vehicles and followed the boardwalk until they came to the lake. What a breathtaking view they saw! The lake was nestled in a valley between the mountains and trees with a river flowing to it. From there, you could see for miles. They even saw a pair of eagles gliding over the treetops.

"This is so amazing!" Bonnie said to Brad, and everyone else agreed.

They spent about ten minutes taking it all in and then decided they had to move on if they were to see other things as well.

They drove back down the mountain and stopped at a picnic area overlooking Lake Superior to have their lunch. They shared with each other their favorite activities and sights from the weekend as they ate, enjoyed the view of the shimmering lake, and watched boats skim across the water. But they knew they must move on, so they stopped again at the visitor center to pick up some mementos to remember their time at Porcupine Mountain. Bonnie and Brad purchased matching T-shirts to remember their visit and promised each other they would return soon.

Their last stop before returning to Ironwood was the famous Summit Peak. It was a long walk up to a wooden lookout tower, with several stops along the way to enjoy the majestic view of the mountains and trees. When they got to the tower at the top of the peak, they still had many steps to climb to reach the platform. Bonnie's mom opted not to climb all those steps but would enjoy the view from the ground. Her dad stayed with her as well. The rest of them climbed the steps to the observation platform, and all exclaimed that it was definitely worth the effort. You could see for miles, and the views were absolutely breathtaking.

"Can you just imagine what it would look like in the fall with all the colored leaves?" one of Bonnie's brothers asked with an air of reverence. "I definitely want to come back here again in the fall, camp out, and see more of the park."

Her other brothers agreed.

As they walked back to their vehicles, her brothers tried to fill their parents in on the views they had seen and tell them of their plans to return in the fall for a camping trip.

Her dad answered with the usual, "We'll talk about it later."

When they returned to Ironwood, her family got their vehicle packed up and were ready to head out shortly after three, which was their desired time of departure. They all shared how much they enjoyed their visit, the sites they'd seen, and getting to know one another better. It was hard for Bonnie to see her family leave, but she knew they would be back again in another month for the wedding. She so appreciated the time she had with her mom and Carrie, their help with the wedding preparations, and their chance to get to know Brad. But even more so, she appreciated the time she'd spent with Carrie.

Because of their difference in ages and her being away at college and work, she hadn't been able to spend much time with Carrie and really feel like sisters. The past week helped them discover each other for who they were and appreciate one another. It had really been a good week that she would cherish for a long time.

"I've never had a family to enjoy and feel a part of," Brad also shared with Bonnie. "Thank you for sharing your family with me."

"They're going to be your family too. Besides, I could tell that they really liked you, enjoyed spending time with you, and appreciated all that you did to make this time fun for them. So now you'll have a large family with more siblings than you bargained for. Do you think you can handle that?"

"I sure can," he assured her, "especially when I get you as my wife in the process. You are my greatest gift and treasure, and I can't wait until our wedding day when you will become Mrs. Brad Jorgenson. We'll make a wonderful life together, raise our family, and teach them all that we've learned from God's Word. It will be a dream come true for me."

"Me too!" She raised her head to give Brad a kiss, but he met her halfway and enfolded her in his arms.

Their kiss was a promise of what the future held for many years to come.

Chapter 24

The remainder of July was very busy. Bonnie and Brad spent several evenings looking at the gifts she had received at the bridal shower, reading the cards, laundering the sheets and towels, putting things away, and writing thank-you notes. Bonnie also had started packing her things in the apartment and taking them over to Brad's home. The reality that their wedding was actually going to happen—and soon—was starting to sink in. Most of Bonnie's list was checked off, and all they had left to do was purchase gifts for those who would participate in their wedding, which they planned to do the following week.

Brad had a fishing tournament the third weekend in July; so he, Aaron, and Kevin decided to spend an evening, several days before the tournament, to fish Lake Superior to see where the fish were biting and get a take on the kinds, sizes, and numbers of fish they could expect. Brad had suggested that April and Bonnie go to his home during the afternoon while he was at the shop to measure the windows for the curtains that Bonnie wanted to put up and then go shopping after. They asked Molly to help them as well, so they were able to get quite a bit accomplished.

They got all the window measurements and talked about colors that would look good in each of the rooms. Because the house was situated back off the road and in the woods, there weren't a lot of privacy issues. Bonnie and Brad both liked to look outside at the views all around the house, and with the porch on the front of the house, there wasn't a big issue of having to block the hot sun of summer in the living room area. So they didn't need any long, heavy drapes.

"I was thinking of white valances in the kitchen area to brighten up the space and green valances with white blinds for the living room windows, which we could leave open during the day and close for privacy when needed," Bonnie shared with them.

As they moved on to the bedrooms, she continued, "In our bedroom, I want to go with blues and reds, so Brad already painted the two sheetrock walls this blue-gray color called drizzle. It reminds me of Lake Superior on a rainy day and kind of brings the outside in. So I was thinking that longer red curtains with tiebacks would look nice, accent the beautiful woods in the room, and still let in plenty of light.

"My home church is making us a quilt for the bed in white, blues and reds, and I can add more blues and reds for accents as we get them. In the bathroom, I'm thinking of a café curtain and valance in blue and white to offer privacy and color but still lets the light in. And we'll have to find a shower curtain that will go with it also. We'll have to see what they have when we get to the store. In the laundry room, probably just a white valance on the back door, similar to the kitchen. The second bedroom faces west, so I'm thinking of going with a yellow print, which would make the bedroom feel warm and cheery."

Bonnie was looking forward to their shopping trip. It would be interesting to see if three different women could agree on curtains for her home.

However, there was no need to worry, for the shopping trip was not only a great success but a lot of fun. They laughed at some of the choices one would jokingly suggest, but soon realized that they all liked similar styles. It was even helpful to hear their different perspectives and suggestions after Bonnie shared her ideas. They found curtains that would not only look good but enhanced the style of their home and personalities. The men had a very successful fishing trip and brought home enough fish so they could all get together for a fish fry the next evening.

When the day of the fishing tournament came, Bonnie said she would help Brad.

"As long as I don't have to touch the fish," Bonnie added.

Brad agreed and gave her the clipboard to keep record of the names of the fishermen, types, weights, and lengths of the fish as they were brought in.

There was a lot of excitement when the fish were brought in and recorded, but Bonnie told Brad at the end of the day, "I'm going to go home and take a shower, and I don't want to see, smell, or eat another fish for at least a month."

Brad just laughed, gave her a hug, and congratulated her for being such a good sport and helping him with the tournament.

The following weekend, April and Aaron wanted Bonnie and Brad to go kayaking with them. Aaron had been teaching April to kayak, and for the last two months, they had gone different places and seen many different things. April found that she really enjoyed it and wanted Bonnie to see her progress, hoping that maybe she would come to enjoy it too.

Bonnie was hesitant.

"I'm getting married in a week. I want to live to be able to attend my own wedding."

"But you're not afraid of the water like you used to be," Brad assured her. "You have learned to swim a little, and you'll be wearing a life jacket. Besides, I'll be with you and won't let anything happen to you. We can even use a two-seated kayak so you won't be alone."

"Yes, please come with us," April and Aaron chimed in together.

"Boy, you guys won't let me get out of this, will you?" Bonnie said with a sigh.

"Not a chance," all three agreed.

"Okay," Bonnie said reluctantly.

They decided that for Bonnie's first time in a kayak, they would go to Gile Flowage where they wouldn't have to worry about waves rocking the kayak. It was a calm, cloudy day, and the sun wouldn't be in their eyes; so that was okay.

Brad and Aaron gave her some general instructions, and Brad assured her that they would stay close to the edges of the lake so she would feel more secure for her first time. April and Aaron each had their own kayaks and led the way, with Brad and Bonnie following.

After a while and with more instructions, Bonnie started to get the hang of it. She began to feel more comfortable and paddled *with* Brad instead of *against* him, and they went straight instead of in circles. She even started to relax and enjoy the ride and the scenery. She noticed the ducks along the shoreline, other boaters in the water, and people at the park enjoying the summer day.

They kayaked for about an hour, went back to the boat launch area, and Brad helped Bonnie get out of their kayak.

"Well, what did you think?" April asked while the men loaded up.

"You know, once I got the hang of it and relaxed a little, I kind of liked it," Bonnie admitted. "I can see now why you like it so much. You really looked comfortable out there, as if you knew what you were doing."

"Aaron is a good and patient teacher, and I really do enjoy it. It helps me relax, and they say that a kayak is even safer than a canoe. It's lightweight and much easier to handle than a canoe."

"Well, I enjoyed it too, once I relaxed. I just may try it again."

"Good!" April said and gave her a hug. "You know, I'm really going to miss you. We have shared an apartment together for only a year, but it's been the best year of my life. We get along so well together, have similar likes and dislikes, go to the same church, and even share the same values. It's going to be hard to find someone to replace you."

"Hey, I'm not going away. I'm just getting married."

"I know, but it won't be the same. Your life will be with Brad, and we won't be spending as much time together," April insisted.

"Well, we'll still see each other at school and church, and we'll have each other over for dinner a lot. You're still my best friend, and that will never change."

"That's good! I'll hold you to that."

They gave each other a hug, with a promise to always be there for each other.

Chapter 25

Most of Bonnie's family arrived the Thursday before the wedding to help decorate, get the meal ready for the rehearsal dinner on Friday evening, and pitch in on other preparations. Brad decided to let Bonnie's family use their home while they were in town, and he would stay with Aaron for the few days before the wedding. He brought in some cots and borrowed an air mattress and extra bedding from Molly for the boys. Brad had also made arrangements with Molly to change the bedsheets, pick up the extra bedding, cots, and air mattress and make sure everything was ready for their return after the honeymoon. Bonnie's two married brothers would rent rooms at a hotel in town when they arrived on Friday.

The day of the wedding was predicted to be in the nineties but with no rain. Bonnie was grateful that the wedding was going to be at seven in the evening, so hopefully, it would cool off by then. And with no rain predicted, they could have the reception line outside. Everything was going as planned, and she was excited and nervous at the same time. The rehearsal dinner was delicious, with many of the family's favorites—lasagna, lettuce and fruit salads, garlic bread, and several different kinds of bars for dessert. The rehearsal was a little chaotic at first, but once they understood when to come in and where they were supposed to stand, it went smoother. The pastor even promised that when it was time to say their vows, he would keep the phrases short so they could repeat them without a problem.

The church was decorated simply but beautifully. When Bonnie walked down the aisle on her father's arm, all she saw was Brad in his tux. He looked very handsome, with the biggest smile on his face and his eyes fixed only on her, as if they were the only two people in the room. The service was very special; the music, the pastor's words, the candle-lighting ceremony, their vows, and the exchanging of rings were all very meaningful to them both.

Brad said his favorite part was when the pastor said, "You may now kiss the bride."

That was very special, but Bonnie thought that the most memorable thing for her was when the pastor introduced them for the first time as "Mr. and Mrs. Brad Jorgenson."

Wow! I am really married! Bonnie marveled. *Brad is my husband, and we will spend the rest of our lives together. I thought this day would never come, but here we are, and I couldn't be happier.*

As the people went through the reception line, she felt grateful that so many people had come to celebrate this wonderful day with them. She also felt honored and blessed to introduce her new husband to those who had not met him before. Afterward, the photographer took pictures of the wedding party and family outside, while the volunteers from their young adult group set up the tables and chairs in the sanctuary for the reception.

Everything was happening quickly, but Bonnie wanted to talk to Carrie before they went in for the reception.

"Carrie, I want to say how proud I am of you," Bonnie began. "You have become such a lovely young lady, and I'm glad you were able to have a special part in my wedding."

"Thank you, Bonnie," Carrie said with tears in her eyes and a big smile. "I know we haven't spent much time together in the past, with you being older and moving away, but our time together this summer has meant a lot. I'm happy to finally get to know my big sister, and I want you to know that I'm proud of you too. You picked a good man, and I hope I'll do as well as you."

They hugged each other, just as Brad and Kevin came to collect them. They joined April and Aaron and together walked into the reception area.

Since it was an evening wedding, they had chosen a light, summery meal of chicken and pasta salad with sliced apples, celery, and grapes in it, along with small party buns, nuts, and mints. The wedding cake had three tiers of chocolate cake on one side and three tiers of white cake on the other, with a bridge in between where the bride and groom stood. It had solved their issue of what kind of cake to order, chocolate or white.

Molly had agreed to serve the cake for them, saying, "I would be honored." And she did it with a smile.

After the reception, Bonnie threw the bouquet in April's direction, hoping she would catch it—and she did. Then the couple said their goodbyes and headed off to Duluth, where they would spend their first night as husband and wife.

Brad had still not told her where they were going on their honeymoon, saying only that they would fly out of Duluth the next morning. She was glad it was only a two-hour drive. With all the preparations and commotion over the last few days, she was looking forward to spending some quiet time alone with her husband.

The next morning, Brad told her that their destination was to be a quiet lodge in the Smoky Mountains of North Carolina.

"Remember when we talked months back about places where we would like to go someday?" Brad said. "We both mentioned a place in the mountains with a lake and woods where we could watch the sunsets, enjoy the water, walk in the woods, and just enjoy the quiet and each other. Well, I found a place just like that and booked it for us for five nights. I hope you like it."

"I'm sure I will! I can't believe you remembered that."

"Of course I remembered that! I've been thinking about it and planning it ever since. I wanted this to be special for you."

"Being with you makes it special! The mountains, lake and woods are just a bonus," Bonnie said and rewarded him with a kiss.

"Amen to that!" Brad kissed her again.

The view of the mountains from their room at the lodge was spectacular. They spent time taking long walks, enjoying the gardens and the lake, and they even did a little fishing. The lodge also recommended a tour of nearby historical sites. Being a teacher and interested in American history, Bonnie enjoyed the tour immensely. Brad enjoyed it as well, but mostly because he enjoyed watching Bonnie taking it all in and her excitement over everything she saw.

The Southern hospitality made them feel like royalty, and the cuisine was delicious!

"I don't know, Brad. I'm getting so spoiled I may never want to leave this place."

"Well then, I guess I'll have to spoil you when we get home too. How about I promise to kiss you awake every morning, make you breakfast while you shower, and give you a back rub in the evening after a long day at school? We definitely have woods and lakes at home, and I promise to treat you as my queen as long as I live."

"Well, how can a woman say no to that?" Bonnie asked with a smile. "Take me home, Mr. Jorgenson."

"I'd be happy to, Mrs. Jorgenson."

Epilogue

January 1 of the following year

Bonnie awoke on New Year's Day, glad that neither of them had to go to work that day. She just wanted some time to reflect on the past year and dream of ~~what~~ the new year would bring. She had many new adventures in the past year, but they were about to embark on an even bigger adventure.

As she looked out the window, she saw that it had snowed during the night. The trees were heavy with snow, and it sparkled as the rising sun's rays hit it. It reminded her of another day when she was enjoying the beauty of the white snow—the day she'd met Brad.

Bonnie turned to look at his sleeping face. He looked so peaceful and content, she didn't want to wake him. So she crept out of bed quietly, went to the window, and sat on the bench Brad had built her. She always enjoyed looking out the window in the mornings, checking out the weather and enjoying the scenery before she started her day, so Brad made her a window bench. Molly made the cushion for the seat, covering it with beautiful fabric in blues and reds, which went well with the colors in their bedroom. Bonnie added some pillows that leaned against the wall and windowsill to give it a finishing touch.

Lord, she prayed silently as she bowed her head, *it's me again. You have made us another beautiful day, and I'm so grateful. Thank you for the beautiful white snow on the trees and ground. It makes everything look so clean and white, just like our hearts when you forgave us of our sins—making them whiter than snow! Thank you for my husband, who loves me, and I so dearly love him. But best of all, we both love You, and You have walked with us through many adventures. But, Lord, we are about to embark on another adventure that excites me and scares me at the same time. Be with us! Give us Your wisdom and strength! In Your Precious Name. Amen.*

When she looked up, Brad was standing next to her.

"Are you okay?" he asked as he sat down next to her and put his arm around her.

"Yes, I'm fine. I have something I need to tell you."

She paused for just a minute, realizing that she was calmer since she'd prayed, and then continued.

"When I went to the doctor the other day, he did a pregnancy test, and it came back positive. Brad, we're going to have a baby."

"A baby? Wow, that's wonderful!" Brad held her close and kissed her. "So then what's the matter? Aren't you happy?"

"Yes, I'm very happy…but scared at the same time. Brad, this is a new adventure for us. That's why I was sitting here praying. Being pregnant, raising a child, teaching him or her how to live—that's a big responsibility!"

"Yes it is! That's why I think you did the right thing and prayed about it. And that's what we will continue to do—ask God to give us wisdom, strength, and the ability to raise our child to love Him and desire to serve Him. That's what you did with me, isn't it? When we first met, I didn't know the Lord, and you prayed for me, lived a godly life, and showed me that God was a loving and caring Father. That's what we'll do for our child too."

"You're right! Thank you for helping me put things in the right perspective. I guess I just felt so overwhelmed by all the uncertainties that I forgot to put my trust in God. We'll just take one day at a time and ask Him to get us through each situation as it comes."

"That's my girl. And we'll do it together. Besides, I think you'll be a wonderful mother. Look at all the siblings you have, and as a teacher, you've had a lot of experience with children. It's me who should be scared. I didn't come from a loving home, and I haven't had much experience with kids."

"But you are a very, loving person. Just look at how much you've loved me, and I know you have much more love to give."

"That's because God loved me first and because of your love for me as well. Let's pray together and thank God for this wonderful blessing."

They both bowed their heads, and Brad prayed aloud.

"Lord, we thank you for blessing us with this baby to love and cherish, just as You loved us. Thank You for bringing Bonnie into my life. I pray that You will keep Bonnie and the baby healthy throughout her pregnancy. Give us patience and understanding during this time of uncertainty, and help us to rely on Your wisdom and strength to be the parents that You desire us to be. Take away our fears and give us Your peace, love, and joy. In Jesus's name, Amen."

"Thank you, Brad. It's so good to know that I have you by my side and that we'll go through this together, with God's help. Now, look at the beautiful day God has given us. And more snow! How would you like to celebrate our good news?"

"First with this," Brad said as he kissed his wife. "Then with this." He held her tight. "Then like this." Brad then stood and lifted her off the bench and twirled her around.

"Stop! You're making me dizzy," Bonnie exclaimed, laughing.

Brad put her down but gave her another kiss.

"You know, I have always liked snow because I can ski and snowmobile," Brad began. "But now, I like snow even more because it reminds me of when we met. It's when we found out we're going to have a baby, and it also reminds me that God washed my sins away and made my heart whiter than snow. I like snow, but I love God. I love you, Bonnie. And I love you too, little one."

Brad knelt down and patted Bonnie's stomach. He felt so blessed!

Book II

Summer Dreams

"And so, we know and rely on the love God has for us.
God is love! … There is no fear in love.
But perfect love casts out fear."

—1 John 4:16, 18 (NIV)

Chapter 1

"Yah, school's out! Bye, Miss Phillips!" the children shouted as they left their sixth grade classroom on the last day of school.

Some lagged behind and gave Miss Phillips a hug before they left her room. She hugged them in return and knew she would miss them. Her eyes even got watery as she watched them leave, excited for their summer vacation. It had been a good year, and she loved her students. Some of her most difficult students at the beginning of the year were now her favorites. They had come a long way in nine months. But now, she needed a break from the challenges of preparing and correcting lessons, answering their many questions, and the rigorous schedule throughout the year.

April had a week's worth of work to clean and pack up her room and prepare report cards, and then she had the summer to look forward to. She had big plans for the summer, and she was anxious to get started.

One of her plans was to be the maid of honor at her best friend, Bonnie Turner's, wedding. She taught third grade at the same school, and April was on her way to Bonnie's classroom now as the halls were emptying of all their students.

"Well, Bonnie, we did it! Another year of teaching behind us, and our students have acquired more knowledge than when they came to us and are now ready to move on to new adventures," April said as she entered Bonnie's classroom.

"Yes, but I hope they acquired not just knowledge but also important life and relationship skills as well," Bonnie returned. "Some of my students come from very difficult homes, and I hope I was able to give them some skills in coping and building good relationships with their family and friends."

"You are so right. But if anyone can do it, you can. Look at the change in Brad's life since you two met, and now you're engaged and getting married soon. By the way, have you set a date yet?"

"No, not yet. We know it will probably be in August but no specific date yet. Once I get my classroom cleaned up and report cards turned in, then I can concentrate on wedding plans."

April and Bonnie had graduated together from the University of Minnesota in Duluth, with teaching degrees in elementary education. After graduation, April had gotten a teaching job in her hometown of Ironwood, Michigan, which was in the Upper Peninsula; while Bonnie had taken a teaching job in Minneapolis, Minnesota. However, when a third grade teaching position opened up in Ironwood a year ago, April informed Bonnie about it, and she was hired for the position. They now shared an apartment and enjoyed being back together again.

"Well, I'm in no hurry for you to move out, so don't hurry on my account. But I couldn't be happier for you, Bonnie. You and Brad make a perfect couple."

"Well, it was definitely the Lord who brought us together and made the changes in Brad's life, not me," Bonnie clarified. "Let me grab my purse and we can head home. I'm starving and can't wait to put my feet up and relax this evening. Just think—we have no papers to grade and no lessons to prepare tonight."

"So let's celebrate and pick up two chicken dinners from Mike's for supper," April suggested as they walked down the hall, arm in arm.

As April and Bonnie ate their fried chicken, fries, and coleslaw when they got home, it reminded them of another supper when they shared a similar menu.

"Remember another time we had fried chicken here?" April asked. Brad had brought supper over on Good Friday, and he proposed to you. It was so special when he gave you that piece of cheesecake with a ring on the top of it, kneeled down, and proposed. I was surprised and excited at the same time. I should have guessed when he asked me to set the table and have everything so perfect, but only Aaron was aware of what was going on. We were almost late for church that night and had to eat our cheesecake after we got home."

"How could I forget?" Bonnie answered with a smile. "It's a night I will always remember! Brad was so nervous and acted so strange and mysterious all through supper, but was so sweet, loving, and caring. They both waited on us and treated us like queens that night, remember? So what about you and Aaron? You two have been spending a lot of time together lately. Is it getting serious between you two?"

"We're just friends," April stated and got up to take their empty plates to the kitchen. "How about some ice cream for dessert? We have chocolate or Moose Tracks."

"Quit trying to change the subject. I think Aaron is really interested in you," Bonnie countered.

"Well, I don't think of him that way, so subject closed!" April insisted.

"Okay, whatever you say," Bonnie said. She dropped the subject but wondered about her friend's tone of voice and insistence. "I'll take chocolate if you're dishing up."

Aaron Matthews was a friend of Brad's but was also the young adults' Bible study leader at their church, which they had been attending since January. The four of them had become fast friends and spent a lot of time together.

"Here's your ice cream," April said as she handed Bonnie her bowl. "I'm sorry for snapping at you. I just don't want to talk about it right now."

April sat back down and began to eat her ice cream.

"Okay," Bonnie replied, eating a few bites before beginning again. "So I have a wedding to plan and get ready for, and I'm hoping you'll help me with it. But tell me, what do you want to accomplish this summer?"

"You know I'll help you with your wedding, you're my best friend. It's going to be such fun. Are your mom and sister going to be able to come and help with some of the plans as well?"

"Yes, it looks like they'll be here by the end of June, and then my dad and some of my brothers will join us for the Fourth of July holiday. It will be fun to have them here and show them around to some of the things that we have here in the UP."

"Well, I better get going on planning your bridal shower then too. We can have it when your family is here and it will make it even more special," April said as she finished off her ice cream.

"That would be great, but you're avoiding my question. What do you want to do with your summer? Anything special?" Bonnie asked again.

"This may sound strange to you, but I would really like to learn to kayak," April finally said after hesitating for a while. "So many people around here kayak and talk about it all the time, but I've never even tried it. So that is my goal for this summer—learn to kayak."

"I think that's wonderful, April!" Bonnie exclaimed, hugging her best friend. "When I came here last year and was awed by all the snow that's here in the winter, Brad taught me how to cross-country ski, took me snowmobiling, snowshoeing, and even downhill skiing. I did a lot of things I'd never done before. I think it's wonderful that you want to try something new. You go for it, girl!"

"Thanks, Bonnie. I appreciate your support, but it's kind of scary too. I don't own a kayak and I don't even know where to begin."

"Well, there must be someone who can give you lessons. That's how I got started with cross-country skiing."

"Yah, Brad gave you lessons, and the rest is history," April said with a laugh.

"We can ask around. Maybe Brad knows someone who can teach you or a class where they teach kayaking. With so many people kayaking, they all had to start somewhere. We can even ask at our next young adult group. A lot of them go kayaking."

"Okay, but let me do the asking. I don't want a lot of people knowing about it until I find out more and see if I can do it."

"All right," Bonnie promised.

They then took their ice cream bowls to the kitchen, rinsed them, and put them in the dishwasher.

"You want to watch a movie since we're celebrating that school is out?"

"Sure, why not? You pick one while I finish cleaning up the kitchen."

When they both settled onto the couch, they enjoyed a relaxing evening watching a family classic DVD entitled, *Dreamer.*

Chapter 2

April turned in her report cards, her classroom was in order, and she left it with a sense of completion, but also anticipation for what the summer would bring. She had asked Kathy, one of their teacher friends, to help with the planning of Bonnie's bridal shower while her family was in town, and she graciously accepted. She had also talked to Aaron, after their young adult Bible study on Thursday evening, about who she could contact about taking kayak lessons.

"I would be happy to teach you," Aaron offered. "I've been kayaking since I was fourteen. I'm also an instructor and guide some of the trips for Whitecap Kayak in the summer when I can get time off work."

April tried to hide her amazement and embarrassment but didn't think she succeeded very well.

"I knew you did some kayaking, but I didn't know you were an instructor."

"Yes. I like to go to the Apostle Islands to see the sea caves, as well as kayak down the rivers in the spring when the water is high. It's a lot of fun, and I'm sure you'll come to enjoy it too. Once you get the hang of it, I can show you some of the sea caves. They're pretty amazing."

"Whoa, slow down! Let's see if I can get the hang of it first," April said with a laugh. "So when would you have time to teach me and what do I have to do to get started? I don't have a kayak, know what to look for, or even what kind to get. You'd be dealing with a novice here."

"Don't worry about it," Aaron replied. "I have one and can borrow a friend's until you try it, see how you like it, and what kind would work best for you. Why don't I pick you up Saturday morning at nine and we'll go to Gile Flowage and start with some basics? I even have an extra life jacket I'll bring for you. Just be sure to have some water shoes with you."

After thinking for a minute, Aaron added, "Do you know how to swim?"

"Yes, why? We won't be doing anything crazy or go where there are high waves right away, will we? Do they tip over easily?" April asked with some reservations.

"We'll stay close to shore until you feel comfortable and get the hang of paddling. Actually, kayaks are safer than canoes, and I'll teach you how to balance while you're in the kayak." Aaron put his hand on April's arm reassuringly. "Believe me, April, I wouldn't let anything bad happen to you."

As April looked into Aaron's eyes, she knew he meant it and wondered if Bonnie was right, that Aaron did care for her as more than a friend.

Maybe having Aaron teach me to kayak isn't such a good idea after all, April reasoned. *But I do feel safe with Aaron and don't know who else to ask.*

"Okay! I'll be ready by nine on Saturday. And thank you, Aaron, for being willing to do this. How much do you charge for your instruction?"

"Let's not worry about that now."

On Saturday morning, April woke up with anticipation, excitement, and a small case of nerves when she realized that she was actually stepping out and trying something new. But she felt confident with Aaron teaching her, so she got up, straightened up her bedroom, had breakfast with Bonnie, and was ready when Aaron arrived.

"Are you all set to go?" Aaron asked when April opened the door. "Looks like you have your water shoes, but you might want to bring a light sweatshirt too. It's always cooler on the water than on land."

April went to get a light zippered sweatshirt, said goodbye to Bonnie, and followed Aaron to his Jeep, where he had two kayaks fastened on the top.

"Wow! This is really happening, isn't it?" April said as she got in the Jeep.

"Yes, and you're going to do great!" Aaron said with confidence.

When they arrived at Gile Flowage, which was a small lake in Wisconsin, just a few miles from Ironwood, they unloaded the kayaks, paddles, and lifejackets. Aaron then started teaching April the basics. Aaron showed her how to get in and out of the kayak from the shore and the dock. She learned how to hold the paddle, how to paddle through the water, and how to balance the kayak so it wouldn't flip over.

"That's my greatest fear!" April informed Aaron.

"That's why I want to teach you these things before you even get out on the water," Aaron affirmed. "It dispels some of the fears. So do you think you're ready to try it? We won't go far from shore, and we'll practice the strokes I've shown you, as well as getting in and out of the kayak until you feel comfortable."

"Okay then, I guess I'm ready. If I'm going to learn, I need to get out and do it, right?"

"That's right! And I'll be with you all the way. Here's a life jacket for you to put on. Make sure it's tight and won't slip off your head," Aaron said and then tested it to make sure it was tightened properly. "I want you to get in the kayak from the shore, and when we come back, I'll have you get out at the dock so you can practice both ways."

Aaron talked April through each step of getting into the kayak and was pleased with how much she remembered. Then he pushed her out into the water and watched as she began paddling. He then got into his kayak, and they paddled side by side for a while.

"You're doing really well! You're sitting straight against the backrest, your knees are flexed out, feet against the footrests, and you're holding your paddle with your arms at a ninety-degree angle and paddling not past your hips so you're well balanced. Now you just need to try and relax and enjoy it."

They went a little further, and April seemed to relax a bit.

"Okay now, if you want to turn to the right, you stroke the paddle back further on the right side until you've turned as far as desired, then paddle normally from both sides," Aaron said as he demonstrated it, then watched as April tried it. "Good! Now if you want to turn to the left, you stroke the paddle further back on the left side until you've turned as far as desired, and then paddle normally from both sides."

Again, Aaron demonstrated and then watched April do the turn successfully.

"Excellent! You're really getting the hang of this! To go backward, you just stroke normally backward instead of forward."

They continued paddling along the outside of the lake until April felt comfortable with the strokes and turning.

"I think I'm getting the hang of it," April commented after a time of silence and concentrating on her strokes. She was even starting to enjoy the scenery around her, noticing other boats and even ducks swimming in the water.

"Yes, you're doing very well for the first time. But I want you to relax your grip on the paddle a little more and relax your legs too. Otherwise, they could cramp up." Aaron watched as April relaxed her grip on the paddle and her legs, and she seemed more comfortable. "That's better!"

"Yes, it feels better too. I didn't realize I was so tense," April acknowledged.

They kayaked for another thirty minutes, and then Aaron advised that they head back to the dock. Aaron got out of his kayak first so April could watch how he did it, and then he motioned for April to come alongside the dock. He held her kayak while he instructed her how to get out of the kayak when alongside the dock. She did it without falling in the water and actually fairly well.

"Getting in and out of a kayak alongside a dock is actually harder than from shore, but it's good to know how to do it safely both ways."

"Boy, I have to get used to being on land again after being on the water. My shoulders are a little sore too from paddling," April realized.

"That will improve as you get used to it and relax more while you paddle. You'll get better with practice. So do you think you'll like it and want to continue with the lessons?" Aaron asked April.

"Oh yes! I like being on the water. It just seems so peaceful, and the scenery is gorgeous! You are a good and patient teacher, and I'm sure I'll get better with practice."

"There's no doubt in my mind, April. You did very well for your first time. Let's load up the kayaks, and how about if we get some lunch before I take you home?"

"That sounds good. The fresh air and exercise really made me hungry. What would you like me to carry?"

"Why don't you hold on to the paddles. I'll take one of the kayaks to the Jeep, and you just stay here with the other one. I'll be right back for it, and we can load everything up and get something to eat. What are you hungry for?" Aaron asked.

"Burgers and fries sound really good right now," April suggested.

"That sounds good to me too! I'll be right back," Aaron said as he hoisted the first kayak above his head and headed toward his Jeep.

Soon he was back for the second, and April carried the two paddles and lifejackets.

"Either you are really strong," April said as she admired the flexed muscles on his arms, "or those kayaks aren't as heavy as they look."

"Actually, they aren't very heavy. These are sea kayaks and are fairly light and easy to move around. That's the other reason I like kayaks better than canoes. They're made of much lighter but durable material."

April helped Aaron tie down the kayaks and put the paddles and lifejackets in the back of the Jeep, and then they headed for the Iron Nugget in Hurley, Wisconsin, for lunch.

Chapter 3

April had much to do to get ready for Bonnie's bridal shower and her family coming in two weeks. Missy, a friend from church who also attended their young adult Bible study, asked if she could help with the bridal shower, and April gratefully accepted. They got together with Kathy to plan the menu and decided who was going to bring or make what, who would give a devotional, and which games they would play.

April was glad when Kathy volunteered to take care of the games, and Missy said she preferred to be in charge of the food. April would bring a short devotional and thoughts about Bonnie and Brad.

Things were progressing quickly with the preparations for the shower, as well as her kayak lessons. She had completed another lesson with Aaron, and he seemed very pleased with her progress. She was relaxing more and was really enjoying it. She was learning to twist from her torso when paddling, which she found made her shoulders less sore. They again went to Gile Flowage, but Aaron said they would try other places when she felt ready to move on. She was so glad that she had decided to learn to kayak and that Aaron was willing to teach her. Aaron worked for a construction company, so he worked long hours in the summertime. But he said giving her lessons was a good excuse for him to get out and do some kayaking also.

One Thursday evening, after their Bible study, Aaron approached April and asked, "How about if we change up your kayak lesson this Saturday and go to Black River Harbor and try kayaking there? The harbor is usually pretty calm, would give you some different scenery, we could go swimming, if the water isn't too cold, and even have a picnic afterward. I have to work the morning, but I can pick you up about 1:30 p.m., and we can have an enjoyable afternoon."

"That sounds really good. I have some things I need to take care of in the morning anyway. I have to do some shopping for Bonnie's shower coming up," April explained.

"That's right, her family is coming soon. When do they arrive?"

"Her mom and sister will be arriving a week from Monday. While they're here, we'll be shopping for dresses for the wedding, picking out flowers, and showing them around the area. Then on that Friday, her dad and some of her brothers will arrive to spend time with Bonnie and Brad for the Fourth of July holiday."

"Wow, that is going to be a busy week!" Aaron exclaimed.

"Yes it will. We also want to squeeze in Bonnie's bridal shower on that Sunday afternoon while her mom and sister are here, so you better not plan on a kayak lesson for next week."

"That is totally understandable!" Aaron affirmed. "Will this Saturday be okay though to go to the harbor?

"Yes, that will be fine. It will be nice to have a relaxing afternoon before all the chaos starts. And I'll have all next week to get everything ready for Bonnie's family and the shower. Bonnie's mom and sister will be staying with us at our apartment, and when the rest arrive, her brothers will be staying at Brad's home, and her dad will join her mom in Bonnie's bedroom. Bonnie's sister will sleep on the couch, and Bonnie will share my room."

"Well, it sounds like you two have it all worked out. So I'll pick you up at 1:30 p.m. on Saturday then."

"Great! You'll be bringing the kayaks and life jackets, so I'll bring the food for the picnic."

"Sounds good. I'll look forward to seeing you on Saturday."

April was excited for her lesson at Black River Harbor on Saturday and had gotten up early to make some brownies for their picnic. She wanted to get her shopping done in the morning and then have time to finish her food preparation when she returned home. She had made a list, so her shopping went quickly, and she was able to have their lunch ready and packed up when Aaron arrived. It was a nice day, with some puffy clouds but no threat of rain, and temperatures were expected to be in the upper seventies—perfect weather to enjoy the water.

When they arrived at the boat ramp of the harbor, April helped Aaron unload the kayaks. They placed them near the edge of the water and then got their paddles and life jackets. While Aaron parked the Jeep, April put on her life jacket.

"Okay, we'll kayak up the river until just before we get close to Rainbow Falls," Aaron said as he made his way to April. "We don't want to get too close, as the water will get rough the closer we get to it. But it is an awesome sight to see from the river rather than above the falls on land. Have you ever been on the trails to the five waterfalls on Black River?"

"Not all of them," answered April. "Only the Potawatomi Falls, and it was gorgeous! You know, it's really a shame that I live so close to all this beauty and haven't taken advantage of it. Bonnie has seen more sights in our area than I have since she met Brad."

"We'll definitely have to remedy that, starting today," Aaron replied with a smile. "Now we'll be paddling upriver, so it will definitely be more difficult, but we aren't in any hurry and the view along the river is breathtaking, so let's just enjoy it."

"Sounds good to me, let's go!" April said with enthusiasm.

She got into her kayak first and pushed off onto the river, but Aaron wasn't far behind. Right away she could tell it was different from the lake and that they were paddling against the current. But she tried to remember everything Aaron had taught her and began to relax and enjoy all the beauty around her.

The trees along the river towered above them and seemed very majestic as she looked up at them. The river made a soft ripple effect as they glided through the water, and the birds soared above them, also enjoying this beautiful day.

"How are you doing, April?" asked Aaron as he watched her paddling and enjoying the view. "You seem to be getting more comfortable in the kayak and with your strokes."

"Yes, I am! I'm so glad I decided to learn to kayak and that you were willing to teach me. It just seems like I'm closer to nature and enjoy it so much more here on the water," replied April with a smile. "Does that make sense?"

"It sure does! I feel the same way," assured Aaron.

They paddled on silently for a while, and as they got closer to the waterfall, they could hear its roar and feel the water became choppier.

"We should be able to see the waterfall just around the next bend, but we won't go much further as it will get too rough. Paddle closer to the shore on the right, and the water will be calmer."

Just as Aaron said, when they rounded the next bend of the river, they saw the waterfall and felt the spray it created as the water crashed down the rocks.

"Wow, look at that!" April exclaimed.

She stopped paddling and just stared, amazed at the power of the water and the roaring sound it created. But she soon found herself going backward with the current, so she put her paddle into the water to slow her downstream progression.

"Earlier in the spring, when the river is really high from all the melting snow, my friends and I come to Black River and kayak down some of the waterfalls. The current just takes you down, and you feel like you're almost flying through the water. It's pretty amazing!" Aaron said with excitement.

"Well, I don't plan on doing any of that!" April exclaimed. "I just want to paddle through the water nice and easy and enjoy the scenery as I go."

"Okay, well, let's turn around then, and the current will take us downriver nice and easy and you can enjoy the view to your heart's content," Aaron said with a smile.

After they turned around, the river did take them downstream, and they didn't have to paddle much at all at first. She even felt like she was bobbing along like the ducks she had seen earlier on the river. As they got closer to the harbor, she had to paddle more but definitely not like she did when they went upstream.

As they rounded the last curve to the harbor, Aaron pointed to the sky and said, "Look, April! There's an eagle soaring up over the trees."

They both stopped paddling and just watched as the eagle glided effortlessly in the sky.

"That is so awesome! You know, I kind of feel like that eagle riding the wind. Like it's just me and God enjoying His creation, the peacefulness, and I don't have a worry in the world," April said with a sigh.

"I know what you mean," Aaron confirmed. "It's like the great outdoors is God's cathedral and you just can't help but praise Him for all the beauty He created and for loving us, even though we're so unworthy of His love and goodness."

"Amen!" April agreed reverently.

They watched the eagle a while longer until he flew out of sight. Then they paddled to shore, loaded the kayaks on to the Jeep, and stowed away the life jackets and paddles.

"So do you want to go swimming or just go for a walk along the beach?" Aaron asked.

"I'm sure Lake Superior is still pretty cold for swimming. Why don't we just walk along the beach? I feel kind of lazy today, and just a relaxing stroll sounds good."

"All right, a nice relaxing stroll it is then," Aaron said as he shut the door to the Jeep and took April's hand.

Aaron taking her hand seemed to fit her mood of not having a care in the world and being willing to trust her day into the hands of the handsome man at her side. She seemed to have taken on the peaceful mood of the eagle and was just gliding along wherever God led her. She hadn't felt like that in a long time, and she liked it.

Chapter 4

After April and Aaron's stroll along the shore of Lake Superior, they decided they were hungry and retrieved the lunch April had brought from the Jeep. They found a picnic table where they could watch the boat activity going in and out of the harbor and ate their lunch in comfortable companionship.

"Are you up for another walk? There's a trail that goes up that hill by the harbor and follows along Lake Superior to the campground. There's a lookout bench by one of the campsites where we can sit. It has an awesome view of the lake, the sky, and the boats going in and out of the harbor."

"Sounds good. I'm game if you are," April acknowledged. "Let's pack up our food containers and put them back in the Jeep."

After they had stored away the cooler and grabbed two bottles of water, they headed toward the trail Aaron had mentioned.

"I'm definitely getting more exercise and fresh air this summer than I have in previous years," April confessed.

"That's good! Fresh air and exercise are a good thing. I'm glad I'm a good influence on you," Aaron said with a smile as he pointed to the beginning of the trail.

It began with wooden steps and a railing that wound up the side of the hill. Halfway up was a bench, for which April was grateful. After sitting down, she took a drink from her water bottle.

"Boy, it isn't as easy as it looks, is it?" April commented after catching her breath. "I guess I'm more out of shape than I thought."

"Just take your time. It's so beautiful from up here. Look down there at that big fishing boat going out of the harbor and onto the lake. They catch fresh fish and sell them to some of the local restaurants in the area. And look there," Aaron said as he pointed to a smaller boat further out in the lake. "It looks like they are done fishing and coming back into the harbor."

They watched the smaller vessel as it entered the harbor with two men and a teenage boy who were talking together and seemed excited about their catch. Once they docked, one of the men got out to get the pickup and trailer to load the boat on to. The teenage boy grabbed their poles while the other man lifted a cooler onto the dock. They both admired their catch, smiling and excited about the fish they'd caught. Even others on the dock came to admire their catch. Once the truck and trailer arrived, they loaded their things into the back of the pickup and helped load the boat onto the trailer. After that, they drove off, all with smiles on their faces.

"It looks like they had a successful day," Aaron observed. "Are you rested up and ready to climb the rest of the way?"

"Yes, I am. And you were right, it is a great view from here," April said as she stood up.

"Wait 'til we get to the top. It only gets better," Aaron said as he followed her up the hill.

Part of the trail was a dirt path, and part of it was a wooden path with a railing to keep anyone from falling and getting hurt. When they reached the top and came to an opening in the trees, they could see the water again. It was breathtaking!

"Wow, look how far you can see from up here!" April said with amazement. "Those sailboats look so small over there, and the sky and water seem to go on forever!"

"Yes, it's something, isn't it? I never tire of looking at it." Aaron said in awe.

"The shades of blues in the sky and the water, the white puffy clouds, the wind that ripples the water and makes the waves—those are just a sample of God's artistry. Even the sun that warms us on this beautiful summer day and all the different kinds of trees and vegetation remind us that God is the great Creator!" April said in reverence.

As they moved on toward the campground, they noticed the different styles and sizes of campers and tents. There were no showers in this campground, as it was more rustic and didn't have as many sights, but they were very spacious and had trees around each site for privacy and shade. The people camping there seemed to be enjoying themselves. Some had just finished eating and were putting away food supplies. Others were sitting around the campfire relaxing while their children rode their bikes or played with their toys.

"I remember when I was younger and went camping with my family," Aaron said with a smile as he remembered times past. "We had some fun times riding our bikes, swimming, and sitting around the campfire. There is nothing like food cooked over an open fire, sleeping in a tent, and listening to the crickets, frogs, and other nights sounds. I ate and slept really good when we went camping. How about you?"

Aaron glanced at April as they walked along the camp road. "Did you go camping when you were young?"

"No," April answered with her head down, not wanting to look at the families who were enjoying themselves. "My father left us when my sister and I were young, and my mom had a hard time just making ends meet. There was no extra money for camping or anything else, for that matter."

"Oh, I'm sorry, April. I didn't realize. It must have been hard for you, your sister, and your mom."

"Yes, it was. My mom did the best she could and worked quite a bit. My sister and I got jobs to help out when we became teenagers. I wouldn't have been able to go to college if it hadn't been for the grants and scholarships I received. My mom remained strong though and kept saying we needed to trust in God for our needs and that God would provide. I guess you could say He did but not always the way I would have liked," April concluded.

"Are you bitter against your dad and God, April?" Aaron asked.

"I was for a while, but then I realized that my bitterness against my dad hurt me more than it did him. So I released my bitterness to God, and a huge weight was lifted off my heart. I also realized that I needed to pray for my dad," April confessed. "I knew God loved me, and I could see ways that He did provide for us. But the thing that hurts now is that my sister, Jenny, is recently divorced and has two young children to take care of. Why would God let this happen to her all over again? She went through so much pain when we were kids."

"I don't know the answer to that, April. Nobody does. That bench I was telling you about is just down this path. Let's sit down and ask God about it," Aaron said as he guided April to sit on the bench looking over Lake Superior.

Aaron took April's hand and turned her to face him. "April, do you mind if we pray together?"

April shook her head, closed her eyes, and bowed her head. Aaron paused a moment and began praying.

"Lord, we don't always understand why things happen to us. But You are all knowing and in control of everything in this universe. You made that evident to us today as we viewed Your creation and all that is in it. Lord, You created the sky, the sun and the moon, and all the stars. You created the waters and the fish that live in them. You created the trees, the flowers, and all the food that we eat. And, Lord, You created us and have promised to take care of us. But we are a sinful people, our mistakes have consequences, and other people are hurt by those mistakes.

"Lord, April is Your child and You love her, but she has been hurt by her earthly father. Please wrap Your loving arms around her and show her that You will be her Father and will always love her and never leave her or forsake her. Thank you for giving her a mother who loves You and has taught her to trust in You. But it's not always easy, and sometimes, we doubt that You have a purpose when things go wrong.

"And Lord, April's sister is going through a hard time right now, and we don't understand it, but You do. Please help April to trust that You will be with her sister now, just as You were when they were growing up. Help her know that You will wrap Your arms around Jenny and her children through this difficult time and will never leave them or forsake them either. Thank You that Jenny has April and her mom to love, care, and pray for her through this time. May You undertake for their needs and give April Your peace and knowledge that You will provide for them. Help April to trust in You and believe that You will do as You say. In Jesus's name. Amen."

"Lord, I believe. Please help my unbelief. Watch over my sister Jenny and her children, Nick and Arietta. They are so sweet and don't deserve this. I love them so, and I know that You love them even more than I do. So I entrust them to Your loving hands. Amen."

As April finished her prayer in tears, Aaron put his arms around her and held and comforted her.

When April's tears finally subsided, Aaron handed her a handkerchief. She wiped her eyes, blew her nose, and when she looked up, she saw the beginning of a beautiful sunset. The sky was lit with the sun glowing in a radiant yellow halo, surrounded by the sky and clouds colored with beautiful oranges, pinks, and purples as the sun began to sink from the sky. The colors were also mirrored on the water to give a double-exposure effect.

"Wow! Look at those colors!" April exclaimed. "It's almost like God is giving me His promise that He has everything under control and I just need to trust Him!"

"I couldn't have put it better myself!" Aaron said in awe as he looked at the colorful sky. "But we better head for the Jeep if we want to get back before it gets too dark to see where we're going. Come on, let's get going," Aaron said as he took April's hand again and led her back to the Jeep.

They arrived at the Jeep, just as the sun set. As they drove down Black River Road and headed back to Ironwood, they were able to enjoy bits of color in the clouds before darkness engulfed them. Then they began to watch for the stars to sparkle in the sky. What a wondrous show of majesty God was displaying for them tonight.

Chapter 5

In preparation for Bonnie's mom and sister's arrival, they moved some of Bonnie's things into April's room and made sure everything was clean and comfortable, had extra towels and bedding available, and stocked up on extra food that would be needed. In the evenings, they looked at bridal dresses in magazines and online, printing the styles of wedding and bridesmaid dresses they liked to show Bonnie's mom and sister when they arrived. They planned on going to Duluth to shop, as that was the closest place where bridal stores were available. Bonnie and Brad had chosen August 6 for their wedding date, with the ceremony at 7:00 p.m. August was usually pretty warm, but hopefully it would be somewhat cooler in the evening.

April had met some of Bonnie's family when they came to visit her at the University in Duluth and also when they helped Bonnie move into her apartment in Ironwood. However, she hadn't really had the chance to get to know them personally, so April was looking forward to this time. Once they arrived, she found Bonnie's mom and sister to be very nice, easy to get to know, and talk to. Her sister, Carrie, who was almost fifteen, was full of energy and excited to be involved in Bonnie's wedding plans. They looked at the pictures Bonnie had printed, gave their opinions, and were able to narrow down some of their choices.

During the trip to Duluth, which was a two-hour drive, they were able to get even better acquainted by the time they arrived. As Bonnie tried on dresses, April was surprised at how similar their tastes were, and it didn't take long to find one they all agreed was the perfect dress.

"This is the one," April said, grinning. "When you have it on, your face glows, and it fits your figure perfectly. You have never looked more beautiful!"

They all agreed, and it was even at a price that Bonnie's mom thought was reasonable, though Bonnie insisted she was paying for her own wedding.

Then it was time to pick out bridesmaid dresses. Bonnie had chosen pink and green for her wedding colors, and April and Carrie started out by trying on long dresses. But they couldn't find anything they all liked.

"You know, a lot of weddings are going with shorter dresses, especially in the summertime. I think we should look at some of those instead," Carrie suggested.

Bonnie's mom also pointed out that a short dress would be able to be worn again and would be more practical. So they grabbed several options and went back to the dressing room. It was easy to tell what Carrie thought of the dresses, for her facial expressions said it all. So it was back and forth to the dressing room until they found one that brought a smile to her face, as well as everyone else's.

It was a short dress with cap sleeves, fitted bodice, a modest neckline, and slightly flared skirt in solid green, made of silky material, but had a filmy lace overlay that was a lighter green with pink flowers on it. The pink flowers popped off the dress and looked very summery, cool, and elegant. Carrie twirled in her dress and made them all laugh with satisfaction and joy that they had finally found the right dress.

"I think tan sandals with an open toe and block heel would finish off the look. April and Carrie, what do you think?" Bonnie asked.

They both agreed and were surprised that they were able to complete their task so quickly and all in one store.

"We're doing so well, Mom, maybe you should look for a dress while we're here, especially since the store is having such a great sale," Bonnie suggested.

Her mom wanted something very simple and was able to find a pink dress that had short sleeves in a classic A-line style, but the material made it look very elegant and stylish. Even Carrie liked it on her, so it got a *yes* vote all the way around. It was a successful day! They went for lunch together and were able to be home by three. April thought that if it kept going like that the rest of the week, it wouldn't take Bonnie long to get things crossed off her to-do list for the wedding.

The next day, they went to the floral shop, and they found the owner to be very helpful. Bonnie said she wanted red roses with white baby's breath for her bouquet, and after hearing about the colors of the bridesmaid's dresses, the florist recommended pink roses with white daisies and a few greens, which would make the flowers pop in their bouquets. The flower girl would carry a bouquet of white daisies tied with a green ribbon and would go nicely with her pink dress. Bonnie also ordered the boutonnieres for the men and corsages for the women. The flower shop also had available the silk rollout for down the aisle and the white archway that could be rented. So now more items were accomplished and crossed off Bonnie's list. They were making great progress.

With this feeling of accomplishment, April and Bonnie spent the rest of the day showing Bonnie's mom and Carrie around their community. They showed them the school where they both taught, the church where they attended, and the grocery store, as well as other shopping areas that were available. One of the highlights was the Ben Franklin store, which had many items unique to their area. It had a good variety of jewelry, silk flowers, material, home décor and craft items, as well as pictures and framing options. They even had some clothing and other items unique to the Upper Peninsula. Carrie was fascinated by the bear figurines of all types and sizes and the "up north" decor.

"Are there really bears in this area, Bonnie?" Carrie asked with concern.

"I've heard there are, but I haven't seen any," Bonnie assured her.

"Boy, you really do live in the sticks up here, don't you?"

"I guess you could say that," Bonnie said with a laugh. "But it's home and a pretty safe place to live."

After the Ben Franklin store, Bonnie had one more place she wanted to take them.

"Next, I would like to take you to Brad's shop in Bessemer," Bonnie explained. "It's about six miles east of here, and you'll be able to see where he works and what type of items he has in his shop. I also want you to meet Kevin, who works for him, and will be one of his groomsmen. Kevin's mom, Molly, will be there also, and I want to introduce you to her too. She's Brad's accountant, among other things, and has become a great friend and help to me with the wedding."

As they traveled to Bessemer, Bonnie shared with them that once her dad and brothers arrived, she and Brad would take them to other sites in the area that they would enjoy seeing.

Carrie was captivated with the many items that Brad had in his shop. She also was excited to meet Kevin, since he was the one who would walk her down the aisle at the wedding. But she had to wait for him to finish with a customer. In the meantime, Bonnie, April, and Carrie browsed around the shop until Kevin was available. Bonnie then introduced them.

They were pleased to meet him, especially Carrie, but he didn't have much time to talk, as another customer soon needed his attention. He seemed very knowledgeable about the products, and one could tell that he really enjoyed the sports he talked about. However, Carrie was more concerned that he was good looking and she would be with him at the wedding and he'd be walking her down the aisle. Such was the mind of a teenager!

During the evenings, April, Bonnie, her mom, and Carrie were able to address the wedding invitations that Brad had picked up and got them stamped and ready to mail out. Brad also helped them when he was able. They were all having a great time working together.

Chapter 6

The rest of Bonnie's family arrived around one on Friday; and after they ate the lunch that April, Bonnie, and her mom had prepared, they were off for some more sightseeing. April stayed behind and worked on Bonnie's bridal shower for Sunday afternoon. She made bars, vegetable and fruit dips, and also made a list of everything she needed to bring to the church or purchase before Sunday. She was getting together with Kathy and Missy the next day to finish any shopping they had left to do and making the centerpieces for the tables. She was grateful for all their help and suggestions.

At church on Sunday morning, Bonnie and Brad sat with her family, which took up a couple of rows of chairs, so April sat with Missy, and Aaron soon joined them.

"Bonnie has quite the family with her today," Aaron said with a smile as he watched them converse with one another. "I know Brad was raised in a foster home and never felt like he belonged or was loved. Looks like he's going to get a family after all when he marries Bonnie. I think Brad is going to fit in quite well with all those boys."

"Yes, I do too. I'm happy for Bonnie and Brad both," April replied.

The praise band began the song service, and they all worshipped together, praising God for His love and care for each of them. It was an encouraging service and seemed to match April's spirit of being thankful for her friends and family, as well as the love Bonnie and Brad had for each other. For April, it had been interesting to watch their relationship grow over the last eight months and to see how much Brad had changed since He gave his life to the Lord.

When the service ended, Aaron offered to help April, Kathy, and Missy set up the tables and chairs for the shower in the fellowship room. Then he left and April's mom also helped to get things set up. So it was true that "many hands make light work," and they had everything ready when people arrived so they could greet their guests as they came in.

They served a variety of salads, buns, vegetable and fruit trays, and bars for dessert, as well as punch, water, and coffee for drinks. There was plenty to go around, and they received many compliments on the food. Then Kathy did a great job with the games, and everyone seemed to enjoy themselves. April followed with a thoughtful devotional.

Bonnie then opened her gifts. Her mom sat with her to write on the back of the cards, and Carrie brought her the gifts. Bonnie got a good variety of items she could use for the house, as well as some personal items. She was very appreciative of everything and couldn't stop smiling as she opened each gift.

After the shower, Brad and Bonnie's dad came to load everything into the van and took the gifts to Brad's home while April, Kathy, and Missy cleaned up. Although the day was exhausting, they all felt very satisfied and enjoyed doing this for Bonnie.

April would definitely miss Bonnie after she got married and moved out. Should she look for another roommate? She didn't know if she wanted to live in that apartment alone again. But would she find someone that she could get along with so well? April had some decisions to make.

They were shooting fireworks that night at Sunday Lake, and Aaron had asked April to go with him and some of their friends. But after a busy day, she decided not to go and spent a quiet evening at home. She put on some music, read from a devotional book she had purchased, and just spent time thinking and pondering about what the future may hold for her. She went to bed early and was asleep before Bonnie and her family came back to the apartment.

The next day, April and Aaron had been invited to go with Bonnie, Brad, and her family to Porcupine Mountain. April had never been there, so she was as excited as Bonnie and her family for this new adventure. After eating a quick breakfast, April and Bonnie packed a lunch of sandwiches; chips; and leftover fruit, vegetables, and bars from the bridal shower, along with bottles of water and Gatorade to drink.

While they made the lunch, Carrie and her mom and dad packed up their things as they would have to leave later that afternoon for Minnesota. Aaron was to pick them up at eight-thirty, they would meet up with Brad and Bonnie's brothers at Sunday Lake in Wakefield, and then follow them to Porcupine Mountain. It would take about an hour to get there, so an early start was necessary.

Brad said they wouldn't be able to see everything but would get a good taste of what was there and have to come back another time to see more. Porcupine Mountain was Michigan's largest state park and consisted of sixty thousand acres and was one of the few remaining large wilderness areas in the Midwest.

Their first stop was to the visitors' center, where they watched a film about the park, its history, and some of the park's highlights. They then drove through the campground just to see what it was like. After they left the campground, they drove until they reached the top of Porcupine Mountain where they came to the famous Lake of the Clouds. They got out of their vehicles and walked along the boardwalk until they came to the lake.

What a breathtaking view all around them! The lake was nestled in a valley between the mountains and trees with a river flowing to it. They could see across the region for miles and even saw a pair of eagles gliding over the treetops.

"This is so amazing!" Bonnie said to Brad, and they all agreed. "You can't help but look at all this beauty and realize that there is a God who created all this. That it didn't just happen."

They spent about ten minutes taking it all in and then decided they had to move on if they were to see other things as well.

They drove back down the mountain and stopped at a picnic area overlooking Lake Superior for their lunch. As they ate, Bonnie's family shared some of their favorite things they had seen and done over the weekend, and they all enjoyed the view of the shimmering lake and watched the boats skimming across the water. But then they had to move on, so they stopped again at the visitors' center to pick up some mementos to remember their time at Porcupine Mountain. April was amazed that she had lived so close to this amazing place and had never been here before. Aaron promised to bring her back again when they had more time.

Their last stop was to the famous Summit Peak. It was a long walk up to a wooden lookout tower, with several stops along the way to enjoy the majestic view of the mountains and trees. The tower went even higher, with many steps to climb. Bonnie's parents opted not to climb all those steps but would enjoy the view from the top of the hill. The rest of them climbed the steps to the observation platform, and all exclaimed that it was definitely worth the effort.

"What a tremendous view! You can see for miles," April said with awe. "The different greens in the trees and the blues of the water are so amazing. I took a picture with my camera, but a picture just won't do it justice. You really have to see it to believe it!"

"If you think this is amazing, I'll have to bring you back here in the fall when the colors are at their peak," Aaron offered. "That would *really* be a sight to behold!"

"I can't wait," April said, staring at the valley below.

Aaron enjoyed watching her as she took in the view and promised himself that he would do whatever it took to show this beautiful and talented woman how much he enjoyed being with her and seeing her try and see new things. Her excitement was contagious, and he could see why she was such a great teacher and why her students loved her so. Because, he realized, he did too.

Chapter 7

Aaron asked April to go with him for some ice cream after Thursday evening's young adult Bible study.

After they ordered and sat at a table, Aaron asked April, "You've been kayaking for about a month now. Do you think it's something you would like to continue doing and possibly purchase your own kayak or do you want to keep using my friend's kayak for now?"

"Oh, I would definitely like to continue!" April said with excitement. "I'm enjoying it even more than I thought I would. About how much do you think one would cost?"

"Well, like I said before, it would depend on what kind you get, and the lighter the weight, the more it will cost. Since we're so close to Lake Superior, I would recommend you get a sea kayak, or it's also called a touring kayak. Then I could take you out to see some of the islands and sea caves."

"Do you think I'm ready for that?"

"Maybe not now, but you will be by the end of the summer," Aaron affirmed. "We can look at some on Saturday if you'd like and then still have some time to do some kayaking afterward."

"Okay! Can you give me an idea about the cost? I don't want to be too shocked by the prices when I get to the store."

"I think you should plan on between $900 and $1,500 for one that is comfortable, lightweight, and will move easily in the water, especially once we start going on Lake Superior to some of the islands. There are views that will take your breath away, and I can't wait to show them to you."

"That was more than I'd expected!" April said surprisingly. "But I suppose if you think of it as an investment that I would be using for years to come, it makes sense to get one that has some quality to it."

"You don't have to buy one now if you're not ready. My friend is out of town for the summer, so he's not using it."

"Well, we can look on Saturday, but I'll have to think about it for a while before I purchase one."

"That's fine," Aaron affirmed. "I'll pick you up at nine, we'll look at some kayaks to give you an idea of what's available, and then I have a new spot to take you that will let you see more of the beauty in the area. So bring your camera and wear your bathing suit under your clothes in case you want to take a swim. We'll see some magnificent cliffs and waterfalls along the way and then find a place to stop for our lunch and enjoy the view."

"I can't wait!" April said as they got up from the table and left the café.

On Saturday morning, April and Aaron looked at some kayaks that Aaron recommended. She was finding out that it would definitely be an investment to purchase a good, quality kayak, plus all the accessories that went with it, which counted up quickly. However, she did have her eye on a yellow one that she really liked. But for now, she was grateful that Aaron's friend was letting her use his while she took some time to think about her purchase.

They picked up their lunch at Subway to eat later, and then Aaron took her to Saxon Harbor where they would kayak along Lake Superior.

"This is a great day trip that I think you'll enjoy. We'll paddle between Saxon Harbor and Little Girl's Point. Less than a mile from there, we'll then come to the mouth of the Montreal River and kayak a short distance through the last portion of the river canyon that goes to a forty-foot final cascade of Superior Falls," Aaron informed as they headed out on the water. "We'll have lunch on a gravel bar just below the falls, swim, take pictures, and enjoy the beauty."

The trip was everything Aaron said it would be and more. Seeing the cliffs from the water was so different from looking down from above. The cliffs were so tall, majestic, and had such unique formations. On top of that, Superior Falls was amazing! The power of the water as it cascaded down the rocks was breathtaking. They had several hard rains recently, so there was a lot of water coming down the waterfalls. They stopped by one of the smaller waterfalls to eat their lunch, swim, and talk of all the wonders they had seen. April took a lot of pictures and was anxious to share them with Bonnie, her mom, and even her students when school resumed in the fall.

April's mom invited her and Aaron over for dinner after church the next day, so April had downloaded her pictures onto her computer to show what they had seen during their kayak trip. April's mom, Barb, enjoyed seeing her daughter trying new things and the company of a good Christian man. April's mom was a good cook, and Aaron helped himself to seconds. They decided to wait on dessert until after looking at the pictures, so they all helped clear the table to make room for the computer.

April and Aaron both talked about the different pictures as they came up on the screen, and April's mom marveled at the beauty that was displayed.

When the slides were done, April's mom sat back and said, "My goodness, I have lived in Ironwood all my life and haven't seen half the sights you have seen in the last month or so. I didn't know there was so much beauty in this area!"

"Aaron is a good teacher, Mom. Maybe he can give you lessons too. It's amazing what you can see on the water and how different everything looks."

"No, I'm too old to start something like that. You just keep taking pictures and showing them to me. I'll enjoy them that way," April's mom insisted. "Now, how about some dessert? I made chocolate cake. I believe that's your favorite, right, Aaron?"

"I would never turn down chocolate cake, count me in!"

So they all enjoyed their dessert and visited for the rest of the afternoon.

Bonnie and Brad's wedding was only a few weeks away now, so Bonnie was checking off all the things that needed to be done, including packing up some of her things in the apartment to take to her new home. April was going to really miss her friend. While Brad was at work the next week, April and Bonnie went to Brad's home—soon to be Bonnie's as well—to put away some of her things. As they pulled up to the log home, which Brad and his friend and mentor had built a few years ago, April noticed how much the flowers and bushes in front of the porch had grown since she and Aaron had helped plant them on Memorial weekend.

The two large pots with red geraniums and white baby's breath on each side of the front door, which she and Bonnie had planted, were now taller, more filled out, and very elegant looking. They were like sentinels, greeting them and inviting them in. Bonnie also showed her the swing that Brad had built and her brothers helped hang from the porch ceiling while they were at Bonnie's bridal shower.

April set the boxes down on the porch that she had carried from the car and sat on the new swing.

"You two will definitely get a lot of use out of this swing. What a nice surprise!" April said excitedly.

Bonnie joined her, and they sat enjoying the new swing and taking in the view of the beautiful summer day. The leaves were blowing in the soft breeze; the birds were singing; they could even smell the soft fragrance of the flowers blooming. Because the house was located in the country and off the main road, they enjoyed the peace and quiet for a few minutes.

"Well, this isn't getting the car empty, these boxes carried in, and things put away. Come on, you said you came to help, so let's get going," Bonnie said with a smile.

"I'm coming, you slave driver!" April said laughing as she got up off the swing.

It didn't take long to get the car unloaded, and Bonnie directed her to where the boxes needed to go. They emptied the ones for the kitchen first, then the bedroom, and last, the decorations and knickknacks Bonnie had brought for the living room.

"Boy, with the things you got at the shower and now some of your personal things, it's really starting to look homey. Brad's a good carpenter, but he's definitely not a good decorator. Now it's getting the woman's touch it needed."

"Yes, it's coming along. But it still needs some curtains to give the rooms more color and hominess. Next week, when the guys go on their fishing trip, I'm hoping you and Molly will help me measure the windows and we can do some shopping."

"Count me in!" April confirmed.

April looked forward to their shopping trip but wondered if three different women could agree on a style and color of curtains for Bonnie's new home. But there was no need to worry, for the shopping trip was not only a great success but a lot of fun! They laughed at some of the choices one would jokingly suggest, but soon realized that it was helpful to hear their different perspectives and suggestions after Bonnie shared her ideas. They found curtains that not only looked good but enhanced the style of their home and Bonnie's and Brad's personalities. Brad, Aaron, and Kevin also had a successful adventure and brought home enough fish so they could get together for a fish fry the next evening.

April and Molly helped Bonnie put up the curtain rods and then iron and hang the curtains the next afternoon. They were all pleased with the completed look. After their fish supper, Bonnie, April, and Molly cleaned up the dishes while the guys visited in the living room. The guys talked fish stories, while the ladies talked wedding plans and gave Bonnie compliments on how nice her home was looking. However, working with Bonnie on her new home made April again realize that soon she would no longer have a roommate.

Should I look for a new roommate? April wondered. *Who would be as compatible as Bonnie and I have been? Is this even a good time to move on to another dream I've had for some time now—to buy a home and fix it up, just the way I want?*

Seeing Bonnie's home, helping her purchase new things to make it her own, and watching it go from a bachelor's pad to a home that Bonnie could be proud of had really given April something to think and pray about.

Chapter 8

On the Saturday before the wedding, April and Aaron had invited Bonnie and Brad to go kayaking with them, for April was excited to show Bonnie all that she had learned. They decided that for Bonnie's first time in a kayak, they'd go to Gile Flowage. It was a calm, cloudy day, but that was okay, as the sun wouldn't be in their eyes.

Brad and Aaron gave Bonnie some general instructions, and Brad assured her that, for her first time, they would stay close to the edges of the lake until she felt more secure. April and Aaron led the way, with Brad and Bonnie following in a two-man kayak that Brad had brought along. It wasn't long before Bonnie started to get the hang of it, was feeling more comfortable paddling *with* Brad and not *against* him, and they were going straight instead of in circles. She even started to relax and enjoy the ride and the scenery. They kayaked for about an hour and then went back to the launch area. Aaron and Brad loaded up the kayaks.

"Well, what did you think?" April asked while the men loaded up.

"You know, once I got the hang of it and relaxed a little, I kind of liked it," Bonnie admitted. "I can see now why you like it so much. You really looked comfortable out there, as if you knew what you were doing."

"Aaron is a good and patient teacher, and I really do enjoy it. It helps me relax, and they say that a kayak is even safer than a canoe. It's lightweight and much easier to handle than a canoe."

"I just may try it again."

"Good!" April said and gave Bonnie a hug. "You know, I'm really going to miss you. We've shared an apartment together for only a year, but it's been the best year of my life. We get along so well together, have similar likes and dislikes, go to the same church, and even share the same values. It's going to be hard to find someone to replace you."

"Hey, I'm not going away. I'm just getting married."

"I know, but it won't be the same. Your life will be with Brad and we won't be spending as much time together," April insisted.

"Well, we'll still see each other at school and church, and we'll have each other over for dinner a lot. You're still my best friend, and that will never change."

"That's good! I'll hold you to that," April said as they gave each other a hug, with a promise to always be there for each other.

The next week was crazy, with final preparations for the wedding and Bonnie's family arriving on Thursday. Brad decided to let Bonnie's family use their home while they were there, and he stayed with Aaron for the few days before the wedding. Missy, who had helped her with Bonnie's bridal shower, approached April about sharing her apartment after Bonnie's wedding, as she was looking for an apartment.

This was a true answer to her prayer, and April thought the arrangement would work out well—at least, until she decided whether or not to buy a house. In the meantime, it would help her save more money for a down payment. Aaron, Brad, and Kevin helped move Bonnie's furniture out of their apartment, so Bonnie shared April's room the last few days before the wedding.

The day of the wedding was in the nineties and with no rain in the forecast. As maid of honor, it was April's job to keep Bonnie cool and calm, but it wasn't going to be easy as she was just as nervous as Bonnie. Aaron was Brad's best man and would be walking her down the aisle. At the rehearsal, as Bonnie and Brad rehearsed their vows, Aaron gazed at her with such a look of love, it almost mirrored Brad's face.

April had been concerned that Aaron was starting to care for her more than she wanted him to. She had wanted to just remain friends, but it didn't seem like that was what Aaron wanted. She would have to be careful and not spend so much time with him, even though she enjoyed his company.

During the wedding, April tried to avoid looking at Aaron, concentrating on her best friend Bonnie who was a beautiful bride and glowed with happiness. During the reception line, she even tried to stay busy, introducing people to Bonnie's sister, Carrie. While the pictures were being taken, she stood wherever the photographer directed and smiled, but it didn't come from her heart. This was a happy time for her best friend, and she tried to be happy for her, but she knew that things would be different and their relationship would change. She realized that her relationship with Aaron had changed too—Aaron wanted more from April than what she was willing to give.

After the reception and just before the bride and groom left, Bonnie threw her bouquet and, as she suspected, right to April. April caught the bouquet and stared at it, not knowing what to do next.

Aaron came up to her and said, with a big grin on his face, "Well, does that mean our wedding is going to be next?"

"No! I will never marry! It just will never be!"

She dropped the bouquet and fled through the church, down the hall, and out the back door, crying as she went.

Aaron picked up the bouquet and followed her, not understanding what had just happened.

When he reached her, he turned her around to face him and asked, "April, what's wrong? What do you mean you'll never marry?"

"I just can't!" April said through her tears. "I watched my mom go through a divorce after my dad left and all the pain and heartache she went through. Now my sister's going through the same thing! My family has gone through so much divorce and pain that I just can't take the chance—my grandparents, parents, some of my aunts and uncles, cousins, and now my sister. You don't want to marry me. My family is doomed with bad marriages!"

"But that doesn't mean it would happen with us. We have God on our side. He can break that cycle. I love you, April!"

Aaron tried to lift April's chin so she would look at him, but she held firm and would not look up. He turned dejectedly and saw that

April's mom had followed them also. She motioned for him to go and whispered, "I'll try and talk to her."

Aaron handed her the flowers and left.

April's mom went to her daughter and held her while she sobbed. Thankfully, she had grabbed some Kleenex when she saw April run out of the church crying. She gave them to April so she could wipe her face and blow her nose. April's mom directed her to a place where they could sit down.

"Now what do you mean you never want to get married?" Barb asked.

"Oh, Mom, I remember how awful it was with you and Dad—the fighting, the crying when he didn't come home at night, and then when he left for good. It was all so horrible! And you had to work so hard raising us girls on your own. I know it wasn't easy for you. And now Jenny is going through the same thing. I just don't want that to happen to me. It would be better just to stay single and avoid all that pain."

"Oh, sweetheart, I didn't know you felt that way." April's mom put her arm around April and held her until her crying calmed. "No, it wasn't easy going through the hurt, but I still had you two girls, and that was what was important. I know it wasn't easy with me working so much and we didn't have a lot of things, but we still had each other. And I loved you girls more than life itself.

"Honey, your dad and I made mistakes, and it caused you to go through a lot of pain and hurt. But that doesn't mean it will happen to you. Aaron is a good Christian man and loves you very much. I think you care for him too."

"But it wouldn't work! Jenny thought she would be happy when she got married but look what happened! Now she's raising her two children by herself."

With that, April got up, went to her car, and drove home, thankful that Bonnie wasn't there to see the state she was in and that Missy hadn't moved in yet.

After April left, April's mom prayed, "Lord, please help her! She's hurting because of my mistakes. You forgave me years ago and healed my heart, now please heal my daughter's heart too."

April threw herself onto her bed and, without getting undressed, cried herself to sleep. When she awoke the next morning, her eyes were red and swollen, and she had no intention of going to church looking like that. So she took a shower, put on her robe, and placed a cold cloth on her eyes.

Later she had some toast and juice for breakfast and got dressed, sat on her bed, and noticed her Bible on the nightstand. She picked it up and opened it to where she had left off in her devotions. She had been reading through the Book of Psalms and was on chapter six. As she began reading, she found out that David had felt the same as she did:

> Have compassion on me, Lord, for I am weak. Heal me, Lord, for my bones are in agony. I am sick at heart. How long, O Lord, until you restore me? Return, O Lord, and rescue me. Save me because of your unfailing love… I am worn out from sobbing. All night I flood my bed with weeping, drenching it with my tears. My vision is blurred by grief; my eyes are worn out because of all my enemies. Go away, all you who do evil, for the Lord has heard my weeping. The Lord has heard my plea; the Lord will answer my prayer. (Ps. 6:2–9, NLT)

David had been in agony just as she was. She didn't know what his problem was, but if God heard his prayer, she knew He would hear hers as well. And so she started praying.

"Lord, I know You will hear my prayer and I know You heard all my crying last night too. Lord, I'm asking You to restore my heart, as You did David's. My family has gone through so much pain from broken marriages that I don't want to take the chance of it happening to me as well. I know Aaron is a good Christian man and loves You, and that he has come to care for me. To be honest, I care for him too, but why can't we just be friends? Why can't we just leave things as they are?

"So much is changing right now in my life, with Bonnie getting married and not living here anymore. I know Missy will be moving in, but I don't know her as well as Bonnie. Lord, this is really sounding like I'm having a pity party here, I'm sorry! I know that You are always with me and will never leave me or forsake me, and I thank You for that. Also, thank You for Your unfailing love. Help me accept Your will for my life and to trust that You know what is best for me! Help me to release my will for Your will, and I will give you all the glory and praise that You deserve. Amen!"

April felt better after she prayed and realized that she had gotten a better perspective of the situation after talking out loud to God. No wonder David did it so often. In many of the Psalms, he would start out complaining to God about his problems; but at the end, he was praising God for His goodness and mercy. She realized that she was feeling lonely, sorry for herself, and wasn't willing to let go of the pain of her past. Did God want her to release it and be open to His plan for her life? She had stepped out and learned to kayak this summer and found she enjoyed it. What else did God have planned for her life?

Chapter 9

Aaron called several times that day, but she just let the voicemail take his calls. She didn't want to talk to him until she had time to think things through. Her mom stopped by after church to see how she was doing.

"Mom, I'm better now, but I just need some time."

Her mom made them some sandwiches, they had lunch together, but she didn't push April to talk. She did, however, encourage her to text Aaron if she wouldn't talk to him and let him know that she was okay and would call him after she had time to think and pray about their relationship.

Missy moved into April's apartment on Tuesday evening. April helped her carry some of her things up the stairs, and the new youth pastor, Mike, and Jeremy, from their young adult study group were there to help with the bedroom furniture and heavier boxes, for which they were grateful. Before they were done, they all wished there was an elevator in the building. But Missy didn't have any living room furniture or kitchen stuff, as she had moved from her parents' home, so it was mostly her personal belongings and bedroom furniture.

April decided to visit her sister before school started up again, so left early on Friday morning for Lansing, Michigan. Her mom was able to get time off work, so she went along to help drive, as long as April did the driving through the large cities and across Mackinac Bridge. Barb didn't feel comfortable driving in the high-traffic areas. April was happy to have her along, and they would have a good time visiting with Jenny and the kids.

It was a quiet ride as they started out. The sun had barely come up, so they both enjoyed the tranquility of the early morning, but April could tell that her mom's mind was working, and she eventually started asking her questions.

"April, what do you want out of life?"

"What do you mean?"

"You went to college, you achieved your dream of becoming a teacher, and you are a good one, I might add. I couldn't be prouder of you! Then this summer, you decided to learn to kayak and have found that you enjoy it. So what's next?"

"Well," April started out slowly, "I have actually been thinking about buying an older house and fixing it up. Now that Bonnie has moved out, I realize that it won't be the same without her. My lease is up in a few months, and I've been thinking that this may be a good time to turn it over to Missy, now that she's moved in. Maybe she has a friend who would want to share it with her. That would give me time to look for a house, and Missy would have time to find another roommate."

"I had no idea that you wanted to buy a house," April's mom stated. "Do you have something in mind?"

"Well, there are a lot of older homes in Ironwood that are selling really cheap right now, and I could fix it up the way I want. I really like the older homes with the enclosed front porches, wide wood trim, arched openings, and wood staircases. I think they have so much charm and character," April admitted to her mom.

"It sounds like you've been thinking about this for a while and are really excited about it."

"Actually, I only recently have been noticing some of the older houses as I've been driving around town, and I've also been looking online at some of the realty websites. I started thinking about it after I helped Bonnie with her home. Aaron and I helped them plant flowers and bushes around their home in May, and then I saw how nice they looked after they'd grown and filled out in July.

"It was amazing what a difference it made and how inviting and cheery the house looked. Then I helped her move her things in, and Brad's friend Molly and I went shopping with Bonnie for curtains for the windows. It was really fun to pick out colors and watch the house become transformed into a real home."

"Well, my friend Lori is a realtor who could look for houses for you, and I'd be happy to come with you to look at houses if you'd like. I think it would be really exciting for you!" Barb turned toward her daughter and was getting as excited about it as she was. "But you would really have to talk to Missy first and see if she's willing to take over your lease and look for another roommate. This is a big step for her to move out of her parents' home and be on her own. She seems very mature and responsible, but you would definitely need to discuss it with her first."

"Oh yah, I'd planned on that. But she really seems to like the apartment and the idea of living on her own and setting up house. She would have to get more furniture and kitchen items, but maybe whomever she'd have move in with her would have some of those things already. Or maybe she'd like to find stuff she likes and make it her own style."

"Well, just make sure you're not running from the fact that you'll miss Bonnie and have a fear of change," warned her mother.

"What do you mean?"

"Please don't take this the wrong way, but you have a tendency to run away from things that frighten you, like new relationships, fear of change, or fear of being hurt. Those are all normal, and you need to learn to work through them. You knew Bonnie from college, so it was a comfortable transition to have her move into your apartment when she came here. Now that she's married and moving on, you feel alone and left out. You know Missy from church, so that should be comfortable for you. But I want you to look for a house for the right reason, not because you're afraid of something new."

April thought for a while before she responded.

"Thanks, Mom, for your words of caution. But I really think I'm ready to move on. Not just because Bonnie moved out, but because I've found that I like being open to trying new things and pursuing my dreams. I've been doing the same things for a long time and playing it safe. Now it's time to make my dreams become a reality. Teaching was one of my dreams, and I thoroughly enjoy it and love my students. This summer, I decided to learn to kayak and found out I enjoy that too. Now I want to go for other dreams I'd like to pursue—like buying a house and making it my own."

April's mom prayed silently before broaching the next topic.

"And what about the dream of falling in love and getting married? Is that one you will pursue as well?"

"Oh, Mom!" April said with a sigh. "I just don't know if I can go down that road. I would rather stay single than go through what you went through, and what Jenny's going through now."

Barb thought for a moment and then said, "April, I think it's time I told you my story.

"Your father and I came from very dysfunctional homes, and we were both anxious to get away from our situations and have someone to love and care for us. We had good times when we dated and enjoyed each other's company, so we thought getting married would solve both our problems. But we had no idea how to relate to each other on a daily basis or how to put each other's needs above our own. We were both very self-centered, didn't even know the meaning of true love, or how to communicate without yelling or demanding our own way. So we left our dysfunctional homes and started another.

"When you girls came along, I found real purpose in my life—someone to love and who loved me back. But your dad felt left out, so he found someone else who would give him the attention he was looking for. So, honey, we both made mistakes! It wasn't just your dad's fault.

"After your dad left, I knew I needed help and some direction in my life, so we started going to church. I learned about God's sacrificial love, became a Christian, and had the support and love of my new church family. It still wasn't easy, but I didn't feel like I was going through it alone. I made some special friends at church who encouraged me and prayed for us, and I knew God was watching over us and would always be there for us. You girls kept me going, and I was able to find a job as a receptionist at the clinic to pay the bills. We didn't have much extra, but we managed. Because my job was during the week, I was able to have weekends off so we could spend time together and go to church on Sundays."

"Mom, I'm thankful for all you did for us. I know it wasn't easy, and I'm sorry if I sound like I'm complaining. But don't you ever wish things could have been different?"

"Of course! But we can't change the past. We can only learn from it and move on by God's grace. Sometimes God even brings someone across our path who's going through a similar situation so we can come alongside them, encourage them, and pray for them. Like we're doing for your sister."

Some time passed before April responded.

"Mom, do you think you would ever marry again? Dad did, a couple of times. But he still doesn't seem happy. Jenny thought she was in love and got married, now she's divorced. So what makes a marriage last and a couple live happily together?"

"That's a good question, and God answers that in His Word. In the fifth chapter of the book of Ephesians, it says that 'wives are to submit to their husbands, just as they would to God.' So just as we are told to obey God, wives ought to obey their husbands. Husbands, too, are told to love their wives, just as Christ loved the church and gave His life for them. Even to love her as he loves himself. So if a husband loves his wife with a sacrificial love as Christ did, puts his wife first, and cares for her as much as he does himself, then it would be easy to obey him and not a drudgery. So there needs to be a mutual love and respect between both the husband and wife in order for it to work."

"Wow, that's a tall order! No wonder most marriages end in divorce. That's impossible to do all the time. So why even get married then?"

"Because God designed it from the beginning," Barb explained. "When God made Adam, he said, 'It is not good for man to be alone. I will make him a helper suitable for him' [Gen. 2:18, NIV]. It isn't possible for us to do on our own, that's why we need to ask for God's help. And when we make mistakes or hurt our spouse, we need to ask for forgiveness and be willing to forgive in return. I wish I had known all this before I got married. Perhaps things would have been different. Also, that is why our church requires counseling before they marry a couple—to give them some biblical instruction on which they can build their marriage."

"Yes, I'm sure that would be helpful. But even with counseling, I'm sure there are problems that come along."

"Yes, there are. As with any relationship, you need to work at it in order for it to succeed. You need to put the other person's needs first, you need to forgive, and be considerate of one another. You need to spend time with them, listen to them, encourage them, and just enjoy being with them. It's a lifetime commitment, not something you bail out of when things get tough or don't go your way."

"Wow, Mom, maybe you should become a marriage counselor. You really know a lot about it."

"No, April. I've just learned from my mistakes and what *not* to do and, from God's Word, what is the *right* thing to do. But the biggest thing to remember is to marry someone who loves the Lord as you do. When you have that going for you and both of you value what God says in His Word and are committed to the relationship for life, then that's a good foundation to build on."

"Well, Mom, you've definitely given me a lot to think about."

"So you've been driving for about five hours now, and we're almost to the Mackinac Bridge. After we cross it, why don't you let me drive for a while and you can have some time to think on it?"

"Sounds good to me! Maybe I'll take a short nap too. I didn't sleep well last night."

April hadn't returned any of Aaron's calls, but he did get a text message saying she needed to take some time to think about their relationship and would be gone for a week to visit her sister in Lansing.

Okay, so where does that leave me? Aaron asked himself. *April says she never wants to get married. I know I love April and I know God brought her into my life to be my wife and lifetime partner. Did I misunderstand? What should I do now?*

Aaron was glad they were busy at work and he had plenty to keep him busy. He was able to take out some of his frustration while pounding nails, sawing boards, or cleaning up at the construction sites.

However, the evenings and weekends were lonely and gave him time to think. It was hard to go to church on Sunday and the young adult Bible study on Thursday night and not see April there. On Thursday nights, they were now studying the Book of Hebrews and would be finishing with chapter 11, known as the "faith chapter" or "faith hall of fame."

As Aaron was preparing for the lesson, he was drawn to the first verse, which gave the definition of faith: "Now faith is being sure of what we hope for and certain of what we do not see" (Heb. 11:1, NIV). They had studied and looked into the background of each "by faith" situations and were going to conclude with vv. 32–40 that week. He was realizing that it wasn't easy to follow God 'by faith'; for many were persecuted, ridiculed, put in prison, stoned, and even killed. Then the chapter concluded with the verses, "These were all commended for their faith, yet none of them received what had been promised. God had planned something better for us so that only together with us would they be made perfect." (Heb. 11:39–40, NIV).

The Old Testament people were not able to see the fulfillment of the promised Messiah, the coming of Jesus Christ on earth, whose death and resurrection brought salvation and forgiveness of sins. Yet they believed in the promise. So how did these verses pertain to him and his relationship with April?

Should I wait for God's promise of a helpmate to be fulfilled? Aaron thought. *Is April not the one God had planned for me? Is God's plan for April to remain single? If that's the case, why do I have such strong feelings for her? And how does faith fit into it?*

Aaron read the definition of *faith* over and over again, reading silently from his Bible, "Faith is being sure of what we hope for and certain of what we do not see.

"So no matter what the cost to myself, I have to trust that God knows what He is doing and then be certain that if God wants me to marry April, it will happen," Aaron thought out loud. "But I have to do what God has called me to do. And if I truly love April, what am I called to do?"

He then turned to 1 Corinthians 13—the "love chapter"—and began memorizing some of the verses.

> Love is patient, love is kind. It does not envy, it does not boast, it is not proud. It does not dishonor others, it is not self-seeking, it is not easily angered, it keeps no record of wrongs. Love does not delight in evil but rejoices with the truth. It always protects, always trusts, always hopes, always perseveres. (1 Cor. 13:4–7, NIV)

Yes, that's what I need to do! Aaron realized. *I will love April the way God wants me to and leave the rest to Him. Then, by faith, I will trust my future into God's hands!*

"Thank you, Lord, for teaching me from Your Word!" Aaron prayed out loud. "I know that it won't be easy to put what I want aside and love April selflessly, but that is what You did for me, and with Your help, I will do it for April too!

"Please be with April as she spends time with her sister. Help April to encourage her and give Jenny and her children the love and care that they need right now. Also, help April to realize that You are the One who ordained marriage and can break the cycle of divorce in her family, remove her fears, and help her put her past behind her. Lord, I do love April! Give me the faith to hope that we can have a future together, if it is Your will. In Your Precious and Holy Name, amen!"

Chapter 16

April and her mom were having a good time visiting with Jenny and her two children. While Jenny was at work, they got to spend time with Nick and Arietta playing; taking them to the park; swimming; and even going out for burgers, fries, and ice cream.

"You're spoiling my kids, and they'll expect this all the time now," Jenny said, trying to sound like she was complaining but actually was very grateful.

"That's what grandmas are supposed to do," her mom said with a smile and a wink.

"And don't forget, Friday night is girls' night, so Mom said she'll put the kids to bed, go to her room with a book, and we can put in a movie, eat popcorn, brownies, and any other snacks we come up with and then talk 'til midnight," April reminded Jenny.

"I won't forget. In fact, I'm looking forward to it, but I don't know if I'll make it 'til midnight. After working all week, I may not be able to stay awake that late. Also, we need to save some energy because we need to go shopping for the kid's school clothes and supplies on Saturday. School starts in a couple of weeks."

"Yes, I know!" April said with a sigh. "I've got my work cut out for me when I get back. I need to finish getting things ready for my class before school starts."

On Friday night, they chose a comedy, which was just what they both needed to get their minds off their troubles. They laughed, ate snacks, and felt like they did when they were teenagers.

"Oh, this was fun! We haven't done this in a long time! I wish you lived closer so we could do this more often, Jenny," April said.

"But I like living in the city," Jenny replied. "I have a good job, and I certainly wouldn't make the money in Ironwood that I do here. With Brent's child support, I'm able to keep the kids in a good Christian school, and they have much more opportunities here than they would in Ironwood. Besides, the kids need to spend time with their dad, and since Brent lives here, we need to stay here."

"I suppose you're right." April pondered a moment before asking her next question. "So how are you doing Jenny, really?"

"Oh, April," Jenny said with a sigh. "It hasn't been easy, and it still hurts. But I'm starting to realize that I can't blame it all on Brent. When we met in college and started dating, I couldn't think of being with anyone else but him. I fell head over heels in love with him, and I know he loved me too. But God and church weren't a priority in our lives, and after we graduated from college, we both let our careers take priority over our relationship as well. Then when the kids came along, I realized we needed to make some changes and started nagging Brent about going to church and spending more time at home. In reality, my nagging, anger, and pressure pushed him away from us."

Jenny grabbed a Bible that was on the end table by the couch.

"The kids and I have been going to church regularly now, and I've started reading my Bible again. God brought me to 1 Peter 3 where it says:

> In the same way, you wives must accept the authority of your husbands. Then, even if some refuse to obey the Good News, your godly lives will speak to them without any words. They will be won over by observing your pure and reverent lives. Don't be concerned about the outward beauty of fancy hairstyles, expensive jewelry, or beautiful clothes. You should clothe yourselves instead with the beauty that comes from within, the unfading beauty of a gentle and quiet spirit, which is precious to God. This is how the holy women of old made themselves beautiful. They trusted God and accepted the authority of their husband. (1 Pet. 3:1–5, NLT)

"April, I definitely wasn't living a pure and reverent life. And though I can't change the past, I now know that I need to pray for

Brent and show him more respect when he comes to get the kids and not be so hurtful and angry. In fact, I've asked him to forgive me for my hurtful words and pressuring him, and we've been praying for Brent together as a family.

"I don't know what the future holds for us, but I know that I don't have to go through this alone, because God is with us. I have a peace that God is in control, and it has even helped with the tension in our home. When I'm more at peace, the kids sense it and are less agitated as well."

"You are definitely different than you were at Eastertime when I was here. Like you said, 'more at peace.' I'm glad for you and the kids. And I will pray for Brent as well. It can't hurt."

"Prayer is powerful, and so is forgiveness! I didn't realize what a weight I was carrying with my anger and bitterness against Brent. He hasn't forgiven me yet, but at least I feel free and forgiven by God," Jenny said, giving a big yawn. "But I'm very tired, and we have a big day of shopping tomorrow. Brent gave me his credit card for the kids' clothes and school supplies, so I just have to pay for our lunch."

They both got up, stretched, and April smiled and said, "Lunch is on me tomorrow. It's the least I can do."

She gave her sister a hug, they picked up their snack bowls, carried them to the kitchen, and told each other good night. Looking at the clock, April realized that they had stayed up 'til midnight and hoped their few hours of sleep would prepare them for their busy day of shopping.

The kids were full of energy the next morning. Nick was seven and going into the second grade, and Arietta was five and going into kindergarten. Nick wasn't too keen on trying on clothes, but Arietta couldn't wait and went into great detail of what clothes she wanted to get over breakfast.

They finished their clothes shopping by lunchtime, and the adults plopped down at their table at the restaurant with exhaustion. Nick was frustrated and wanted to go play with his friends, but

Arietta couldn't stop talking about all her pink and purple outfits that looked so beautiful on her.

"Jenny, why don't I take the kids to the park after lunch and you and April can get the school supplies they need?" her mom suggested. "It would be less stressful, take less time, and the kids would have a chance to play and let off some steam."

"Oh, Mom, that would be wonderful!" Jenny said with a sigh. "But are you sure you can handle it? You look pretty tired yourself."

"I'll be fine," she assured. "I'll just sit and rest on one of the benches while I watch the kids play. We'll be fine, won't we, kids?"

"Yeah!" Nick and Arietta agreed with nods and smiles on their faces.

The next morning, they went to the early church service with Jenny and the kids and then left for Ironwood. It would be another full day of driving. April started out while her mom took a nap. Once they got past the city traffic, April would have time to think about all that went on this past week—the discussion she had with her mom on the way to Lansing, the time they spent with Jenny and the kids, and also, the things Jenny had shared with her. It seemed that both her mom and Jenny had learned that the blame can't be put on just one person when a relationship fails. It takes not just being in love but a lot of time, discipline, and effort to make a marriage work. But most of all, it takes doing things God's way, having your priorities right, and being willing to forgive.

Was she willing to do that in her relationship with Aaron? Did she want to just remain friends? Did she want more? She had a lot to think about!

Chapter 11

With school starting up in two weeks, April was busy getting things ready in her classroom, attending meetings with the principal and other teachers, and talking to Missy about possibly taking over the lease when it expired at the end of October. Missy actually sounded excited about the idea and thought there was a friend of hers, a nurse at the hospital, who may be interested in rooming with her. She had even gone to the secondhand store and looked at some used furniture that might look good and fit her style. She definitely seemed anxious to decorate and have a place to call her own.

April called Aaron to let him know that she'd made it home safely and had a great time with Jenny and her kids. April also told Aaron she would be busy for a few weeks getting ready for school and wouldn't be able to do any kayaking for a while. She said she would see him at church on Sunday and at their Thursday-evening Bible study but wasn't ready to spend one-on-one time with him yet. However, April wasn't able to get what her mom and Jenny had said out of her mind, so she had been reading over the verses they'd mentioned, praying about her relationship with Aaron. However, she hadn't come to any conclusions yet.

The first week of school was a busy one. She had twenty-eight students in her sixth grade class that year and was enjoying getting to know them. Their first writing assignment was to tell her about themselves—their families, what they had done during the summer, and what they liked or disliked about school. She learned a lot about her students that way and found that there were a lot of hurting children in her class, and that divorce and pain were a big factor in many of their homes. She would definitely have to make it a point to pray for her students on a daily basis.

The Saturday after Labor Day, Aaron had invited April and her mom to go on a boat cruise of the Apostle Islands with him. He had made it so enticing that they'd accepted.

"I promised your mom that I would show her some of the sights that she hasn't seen yet in the area, April. We'd also talked about the Apostle Islands when we were kayaking, and I thought this would be a good opportunity for you to see them as well. I can make reservations for the eleven o'clock tour, which would take about two hours. We can have lunch afterward, walk around Bayfield, and see some of the sights before we head back. I checked the weather, and it looks to be a perfect day to be out on the water."

Aaron was being so kind but not pushy, and he'd talked about the Apostle Islands so much that she was really excited about the trip, as was her mom. She checked out the cruise information online and learned that along windswept beaches and cliffs, they would experience where water meets land and sky, culture meets culture, and past meets present. The twenty-one islands and twelve miles of mainland have a unique blend of cultural and natural resources; the lighthouses shine over Lake Superior and the wilderness areas; and people can hike, paddle, sail, or cruise to experience the "jewels of Lake Superior." The cruise would provide views of most of the islands, as well as close looks at dramatic sandstone cliffs and historic lighthouses. And the main attraction were the sea caves that were formed by the waves as they hit the north side of the islands.

On Saturday morning, Aaron picked them up and said, "I'm so glad you ladies agreed to go on this cruise. I have some brochures that I thought you might want to look at before we get there."

He passed them out and they looked them over while Aaron drove. It was about an hour drive to Bayfield, Wisconsin, from Ironwood, so he answered many of their questions along the way. They also talked about their visit with Jenny and how much they enjoyed spending time with her and the kids.

Aaron seemed very interested in their visit and commented, "I'm glad you were able to spend some time with them. Family is very important, and I'm sure she appreciated you coming to support her and the kids. It can't be easy for her."

"No, it isn't," April replied. "But Jenny has come a long way over the last few months and shared with me some of the things she's learned from the experience. I was surprised at how well she has adjusted and that she and the kids are going to church again and praying for Brent. Jenny said she has even asked Brent to forgive her for her anger and bitterness against him."

"It sounds like God is really doing a work in her heart," Aaron said. "God will really make a difference in a family through prayer and willingness to forgive."

When they arrived at Bayfield, April and her mom were awed by the view of Lake Superior and the marinas with all the boats, quaint shops, and beautiful gardens throughout the unique town.

"I will definitely have to come back here again. I can't believe I've lived an hour from this place but have never been here before," Barb exclaimed with amazement.

"We'll stop later at the visitors' center and get you some brochures about some of the other amazing things they have here. I know that the first weekend in October, they have an apple fest. They have a lot of fun activities, and many of the orchards have their produce for sale. People come from all over for their apples, pears, and peaches in the fall, as well as berries, jams, and pies in the summer. But right now, let's head to the cruise building and get our tickets, as it's almost boarding time."

They got their tickets and headed to the cruise boats that were docked nearby. It was a little windy, so they decided to stay inside on the lower deck as it would be cooler once they got out onto the lake. The tour was narrated, so they learned a lot about the various islands.

"Centuries of wave action, freezing, and thawing have sculpted shorelines throughout the Apostle Islands National Lakeshore," the guide told the tourists. "People often come to the Apostle Islands' lakeshore in the summer and winter to visit the sea caves and witness Lake Superior's ever-changing handiwork. In the summer, the sea caves are best seen by boat. Raspberry Island is the most popular, and the lighthouse is the 'showplace of the Apostle Islands.' It began operation in 1863 and marked the entrance to the West Channel.

The lighthouse served as home to several lighthouse keepers until 1947, when the light was converted to automatic operation.

"Devil's Island, which is the northernmost island, has two lightkeeper's houses on it and has the most amazing sea caves of them all, since it's most susceptible to the wind and waves. The most spectacular scenery occurs where the wind and waves interact with the sandstone of Devil's Island and creates extensive sea caves. Nature has carved delicate arches, vaulted chambers, and honeycombed passageways into cliffs on the north shore of Devil's Island."

"It is truly amazing to kayak in those caves and see all that the wind and waves did to the rocks of the island," Aaron informed April and her mom.

"Devil's Island would not be my choice of sea caves to kayak to for the first time. The water is much rougher out here and it's very far from the mainland," April cautioned

"Well, there are some that are closer and also wonderful to see. In fact, we're planning a group trip to Sand Island next weekend. You should come along," Aaron invited.

"You adventuresome young folks can do all the kayaking and exploring you want, but when it comes to Lake Superior, this cruise boat is the smallest I want to be on," April's mom informed them.

On the way back to the mainland, Aaron pointed out where Sand Island was and informed her that from where they would set out on their kayaks, it would only be an hour paddle to the island.

"It will be a two-day trip, so we would be camping overnight. We set up camp on the south side where we'd have a wind break from the hills and trees, but the lighthouse and sea caves are on the north side. You would enjoy exploring the rest of the island as well."

"I'll have to think about it, but after seeing all the beauty of the islands and sea caves on this cruise, I just might try it," April said to Aaron with a smile.

They had a delicious lunch at the Pier Plaza when they returned from the cruise and still had a great view of the bay. After lunch, they walked through some of the shops and past the well-manicured gardens of some of the homes and inns in town. Aaron even took them to the ice cream and candy shop.

"This is a must stop whenever you come to Bayfield," Aaron said and ordered an ice cream cone of their favorite flavor for each of them. They also purchased some fudge to take home.

Their final stop was to the visitors' center where they picked up brochures for some of the sights they'd like to check out the next time they came to Bayfield. When they left, Aaron drove past some of the other popular places in the area—the famous Rittenhouse, Windsor Inn, more of the amazing houses in the area, and, finally, some of the orchards on the outskirts of town.

"This is definitely a place I want to come back to," announced April's mom.

"Me too," April agreed. "There are so many different things to see and places to shop and eat—you just can't do it justice in one visit."

"Well, ladies, anytime you want a driver, just let me know. It would be my honor to chauffeur you any time," Aaron announced.

April knew that her mom was impressed with Aaron, who was being a perfect gentleman. Even she had to admit that he wasn't being pushy but seemed to be content to just be her friend and give her the time she needed to decide where she wanted their relationship to go. She liked that.

Chapter 12

April gave Lori, her mom's realtor friend, a call and made an appointment for after school on Friday so they could talk about available houses she would be able to look at. She looked forward to meeting with her and sharing what she was looking for in a home. Lori recommended that before their meeting, she figure out what she wanted to pay for a house, how much she could put down, and talk to a banker to get the financing started. This was definitely going to be a new experience for her.

When April met with Lori on Friday, she filled out the necessary paperwork and expressed to her that she was looking for an older home in town that had character.

"I would really like hardwood floors, nice woodwork, possibly arched doorways, and a fireplace, as well as an enclosed porch that has windows all across the front to bring in lots of light. I would like three bedrooms, as I need to use one as an office, and I prefer two bathrooms, one on each floor. I'm okay with it needing some updates. That way, I can fix it up and make it into my dream home. Hopefully that would keep the price down also so I'd have money for the renovations. I have twenty thousand dollars to put down on a house and am working with the bank to get a loan approved, but they don't perceive a problem."

Lori thought that that would be doable, as there were many older homes in the area, and she would contact her when she had some houses for her to look at very soon.

The next day was the kayak trip to Sand Island. April had agreed to go but was nervous and excited at the same time. There were twelve people going, and some were from their young adult group. Even Missy was going, so it looked to be a fun weekend.

Whitecap Kayak was guiding the trip and supplying the kayaks and life jackets for those who needed them. They were to meet them at the start-off point just past Bayfield where they would have a straight shot to Sand Island. April and Missy rode with Aaron, and he had two others from their young adult group in his Jeep as well.

When they arrived, the guides made sure each of them had their lifejackets on properly and went over some basic instructions and safety precautions. April was grateful for Aaron's previous instructions and the experience she had kayaking so far, as it made her feel more confident. The guides stored all their food items and camping gear in the kayaks. April was surprised at how much storage was available in the kayaks; however, April could tell the guides had done this before and knew what they were doing. Soon, they were ready to set off.

Aaron stayed close to April to make sure she wasn't too nervous as they got farther out on to Lake Superior but was impressed with how well she was doing. April was grateful she had remembered what Aaron had taught her and was even looking around and enjoying some of the views. She noticed that the new youth pastor, Mike, was paddling close to Missy and keeping her company, though Missy looked like she knew what she was doing and much more proficient than April.

"So what do you think of kayaking on Lake Superior, April?" Aaron finally asked. "You look pretty relaxed and are handling your paddle very well."

"Well, you taught me well," April said as she smiled at Aaron. "But the waves aren't too bad today. I'm glad of that."

"You're doing great, and I'm proud of you!" Aaron affirmed.

He smiled at her, and it helped her relax even more as they conversed back and forth. Before she knew it, they were approaching Sand Island. They all worked together to set up camp on the south side of the island. They put up tents, collected dry firewood, and prepared their lunch.

After lunch, they were all excited to do some exploring, so they set out again in their kayaks to the north side of the island to see the lighthouse and sea caves. They learned that the lighthouse was built in 1881. The forty-four-foot tower and lighthouse were made from locally quarried brownstone. Over the years, the park service had performed needed renovations to the lighthouse, which housed volunteers during the summer to welcome visitors, give them a tour, and allow them to climb the tower. They learned a lot of its history and the struggles the keepers and their families had to deal with. They also learned that in the early 1900's, several Norwegian families lived on the island year-round, farming the land and fishing Lake Superior. It was a hard life, and after the Depression and the fishing business closed down, they moved back to the mainland.

Then they kayaked through the sea caves. April was so amazed by the caves that she was in awe and couldn't say a word.

"So what do you think, April?" Aaron asked as he watched April try to take in everything around her.

"I don't know what to think, except that it's more wonderful than I ever expected. Seeing the caves from a distance last week on the cruise doesn't compare to being right here in the caves, kayaking through the channels. Seeing the different colors in the sandstone and the moss clinging to the walls of the caves is simply awesome! It's like the verse in the Bible that says that 'creation displays God's glory and majesty.' I'm just amazed that the wind and waves of Lake Superior, in all its power and strength, could cause such beauty. Oh Aaron, thank you for encouraging me to come on this trip. This is one I will never forget."

Again, April was quiet, as if worshiping God in all His glory, in a sanctuary He created for her to enjoy, so she could get a glimpse of who He is and always will be. Aaron too was quiet as they kayaked through the various caves, taking in the beauty, majesty, and awe of what they saw as they worshiped God, the Creator of all the beauty around them.

When they returned to their campsites, they were all subdued and reflecting on what they had seen. They built a campfire and, after eating their supper, sang songs of praise to God. Some shared thoughts of how they were impacted by what they had seen, and then they gradually left quietly to their tents, not wanting to disturb the worshipful atmosphere they sensed was in their midst.

The next morning, they woke up excited to go hiking on the island. So after a hearty breakfast and devotions led by Mike, they were ready to see what else the island had to offer. They found old stone foundations from the homes of the early settlers of the island, as well as fossils, driftwood, and seashells near the shore. April and Aaron climbed up the hill to some of the other campsites on the island and were amazed at the view of Lake Superior and the mainland from there.

"You know, this island seems so small and insignificant from the mainland, but now that we're here, with all the beauty that it has to offer, I can see why the settlers preferred the quiet and tranquility of island life rather than the crowds and hectic lifestyle of the mainland," April said with a sigh.

"I'm sure life was hard and the mainland had its advantages even then. Like a doctor, grocery store, and other necessities. But I see what you mean. It's very peaceful here," Aaron agreed as he stood by her side, looking at the vista before them.

When they climbed back down the hill and joined the others, they all decided to go for a swim. The water was cool but refreshing, and they had a lot of fun, laughing and splashing each other.

But soon it was time to prepare lunch, pack up, and return to the mainland. The wind had picked up a little, but the guides said it was nothing to worry about and would give them a little push back to the mainland, making it easier to paddle. That was a good thing as they all had much to reflect on as they kayaked back to the mainland. April had seen things she hadn't seen before, slept in a tent overnight for the first time, and cooked over an open fire. What an adventure this had been!

She had even seen Aaron in a different way as well. As time progressed that weekend, she hadn't viewed him as her kayak instructor or Bible study teacher but as a man who was very caring and receptive to her needs but not overbearing. He was friendly, kind, and concerned for her but wasn't smothering. He respected and listened to her and was truly interested in what she thought and felt. He was definitely a godly man whom she could learn to trust.

That was a new concept for her to digest and think about. Aaron said he loved her. Even her mom had noticed that Aaron cared for her in a special way. Could she one day come to love and trust Aaron enough to consider marriage some day? Only God knew.

Chapter 13

April had lunch with Bonnie at school on Monday and shared some of the experiences she had on her kayak trip.

"I never believed how much fun kayaking could be and how much more you can see from the water. I even find it relaxing," April beamed. "You and Brad are going to have to come kayaking with me and Aaron again before it gets too cold. The trees are starting to turn, and it would be amazing to kayak along the shore and take in the view."

"Boy, you really are getting into this kayaking aren't you, April? Or is it Aaron who's the main attraction?" Bonnie teased with a grin.

"Come on now, Bonnie. You know I don't think of Aaron that way. We're just friends."

"Well, that's how Brad and I started out too, remember? Feelings can change, and I really think Aaron has been good for you. You were never this adventurous before Aaron came along."

"Speaking of adventure," April said, hoping to change the subject, "I have put in my notice to vacate my apartment, and Missy will be taking over the lease, along with a friend of hers who works at the hospital. I've even talked to a realtor and am going to buy a house, fix it up, and make it into the home of my dreams."

"Wow, that is exciting! So what brought this on?"

"Well, helping you get your home fixed up, seeing how nice it looks and how happy you and Brad are living there, I thought it was time for me to set down some roots and have a home of my own."

"Just remember," Bonnie cautioned, "it's not the house that makes people happy but the people who live there. Brad makes me happy, not the house and the things in it."

"Oh, I know. But now that I've struck out and tried new things, I feel like it's awakened something in me that makes me want to go after my dream of having a home of my own. I'm getting tired of apartment living where everything looks the same."

"I think that's great, April. So what are you looking for in a house?"

"Well, I told the realtor that I want an older home in Ironwood that has three bedrooms, two bathrooms, has character and charm, but needs some updating. That way, I can make it my own and design it the way I want it."

"Well, it just so happens that Aaron works for a contractor in Hurley, Wisconsin," Bonnie said with that matchmaking grin again. "Maybe they can give you an estimate on how much it would cost to fix it up once you find the house you want. Aaron could then work with you on your house this winter, since you won't be able to kayak then."

"Oh, quit it! Your matchmaking isn't going to work with me. Not everyone can be as happy as you and Brad."

"You know, I think God brought Aaron into your life for a reason. Why don't you just face it? I think he really cares for you."

"Maybe he does, but I don't care for him that way."

"You *don't* or *won't*? This divorce thing has really got you spooked, hasn't it? You know, God can break the chains of your past. Just because your parents' and sister's marriage didn't work out doesn't mean you can't have a marriage that will last. It's all about letting God be the center of your marriage and allowing Him to work through you, being willing to forgive one another, communicate, and share openly with one another."

"Just because you and Brad are happy doesn't mean it's for everyone."

"But you could have it too, you know."

"Lunchtime is over. I have to get back to my class," April said as she picked up her tray.

"April, I'm sorry. I didn't mean to upset you. I'll be praying for you. Can we talk later?"

"Sure," April replied.

She gave Bonnie a hug and returned to her classroom.

Lori called April the next day and told her she had two houses to show her. She set up a time on Wednesday evening so Barb could look at them with April. The first house was a two story with three bedrooms and a front porch, but it didn't have the charm and hardwood floors she was looking for. The front porch had a closet but not the windows she wanted. The price was good, as it had just been reduced. But it was on a busy street, and she wanted a quieter location. The second one was long and narrow and again didn't have the charm she wanted.

"Well, this is a start and gives me more of an idea of what you're looking for. I'll keep looking and let you know when I find a house that will work better for you. We have a lot of charming older homes in our area, but when they hit the market, they don't last long," Lori informed her.

As April took her mom home, her mom asked, "So, April, when you find the house you're looking for, it will take time to do the renovations that will be needed. If you move out of your apartment when your lease is up, where will you live while the renovations are being done?"

"I guess I planned on living in my house and redoing one room at a time."

"That could take a long time, and you'd be living in constant chaos, a lot of dust, and, when they redo the plumbing and electrical—which they usually need to do in an older home—a lot of inconvenience."

"I guess I never thought of that. This is all new to me," April admitted as they arrived at her mom's home.

"Why don't you move in with me while you have the renovations done? You've been approved for the money needed to do the work, and you'll need a contractor for most of the projects anyway. Maybe you can do some painting or small things yourself, but you have no knowledge of carpentry and your furniture would just be in the way. If you move in with me for a few months, it wouldn't drag on so long, and the house would be done sooner."

"Boy, that sounds like a good idea. Are you sure you wouldn't mind?"

"Of course, not! Why do you think I mentioned it?" April's mom answered with a smile.

"Well, I have to be out of the apartment by the end of October, so that would give me a place to go. Do you think I'll be able to find what I'm looking for?" April asked.

"Nothing is impossible with God! Remember that."

"Thanks, Mom, you're the best. What would I do without you?" April said as she gave her a hug, laughing a little. "And when did you get so smart?"

"Oh, life has taught me many lessons over the years, though some take longer than others to learn. But since you started talking about buying an older home and renovating it, I've been watching some of those home improvement programs. They can be pretty helpful, and they definitely recommend not living in the house while it's being renovated. It causes a lot less stress, and with you teaching full time, it would be much easier if you lived with me."

"Well then, I'll take you up on your offer. Thanks again. Maybe we can watch some of those home improvement shows together."

"I'd like that. I just may get some ideas to fix up my home next summer too. It could use some sprucing up. Thanks for letting me come along, and have a good night, dear," Barb said as she got out of the car and went into her home.

April sensed that her mom was lonely and was looking forward to her moving in with her for a while. She would definitely have to make an effort to spend more time with her.

Chapter 14

April was invited to Bonnie and Brad's home for dinner after church the following Sunday. Brad had also invited Aaron, and they went outside while April and Bonnie got dinner ready. This gave April and Bonnie a chance to talk, though April knew she couldn't stay mad at Bonnie for long. She wasn't really angry, just frustrated with her pushiness.

"I want to apologize again, April, for being so pushy. You have always been there for me, and I just want you to be happy," Bonnie stated. "I understand that you need to take things at your own pace, and I respect that. I promise I won't be so pushy from now on. I'll continue to pray for you, your relationship with Aaron, and leave the rest in God's hands."

"Thank you for understanding, Bonnie. And I'm sorry I got so upset the other day."

April and Bonnie hugged each other, and all was forgiven. They soon had the food ready and called Brad and Aaron in for dinner. Conversation flowed more easily, and it was nice to have things cleared between them.

Brad and Aaron watched the football game while April and Bonnie did up the dishes and put the food away. They soon joined the men, but April didn't understand much about the game. Not having any brothers growing up, like Bonnie did, they had to explain much of what was going on to her. She cheered when someone made a touchdown, no matter which team they were on, and was happy for Brad and Aaron when their team won.

Once the game was over, they went to sit on the porch. Brad and Bonnie sat in the swing, Brad with his arm around Bonnie, and April and Aaron took the two chairs.

"Boy, the weather is pretty nice for the end of September. I hope it lasts a while longer. The leaves are turning, and it should peak in about another week," April said as she sat looking out at the yard around them. "I was mentioning to Bonnie the other day that we should go kayaking together again before it gets too cold. Maybe go along the shore of Lake Superior at Black River Harbor and enjoy the colors. We could even have a picnic if it stays nice like this."

"I think that's a great idea," Aaron agreed. "Are you and Bonnie available on Saturday, Brad?"

"Well, what do you think, Bonnie? Are you up to going kayaking again? I know I'd have to work the morning, but I could check with Kevin to see if he could handle the afternoon by himself."

"Sure. I enjoyed it last time we went, and the colors should be perfect by Saturday. I love fall when the leaves turn, and a picnic sounds great too. We need to enjoy this nice weather while we can."

"Good. Then I'll check with Kevin and let you know what time I can get away, Aaron." Brad replied. "It would be nice to get out on the water again. I don't get out as much as I'd like to. It's been pretty busy at the shop."

"Well, that means business is good. That's a good thing," April commented.

"Yes, it is. I need to be thankful. We're getting in all our winter stock, so it keeps us busy this time of year. Molly has been coming in to help out. I don't know what we'd do without her."

"She is such a sweetheart," Bonnie acknowledged. "She was so helpful with our wedding plans and fixing up the house. We get along very well, and she's almost like a second mom to me."

"And she's a lot of fun to have around too. Remember when we went shopping for curtains and how much fun we had, Bonnie? I've never laughed so much and had so much fun on a shopping trip," April added.

"Yes, that was a fun time," Bonnie agreed. "Profitable too. We got a lot done."

"Well, speaking of getting things done, I need to go and get some things ready for my class tomorrow," said April.

"Well, thank you so much for coming for dinner. You know you're welcome any time," Bonnie said as she gave April a hug. "And thank you for forgiving me and being my best friend."

"Always," April whispered. "Well, I'll see you, Brad, hopefully on Saturday. Don't work too hard. And, Aaron, I'll see you on Thursday evening at Bible Study."

They all said their goodbyes, and April went home. She was very thankful to have such great friends. She truly felt blessed.

April got a call from Lori when she got home on Monday after school, saying she had another house for her to look at. She called her mom to see when she would be available, and she said she could go right after work, probably by five-thirty. April then called Lori back to see if that would work for her. It did, and April was really excited. Lori seemed pretty sure that April would like this house.

When April saw the house, the outside wasn't really impressive, but she thought new siding would make a big difference. It was in a good location and on a quiet street, so that was good. However, when she got inside, she knew this was her house!

The front porch had windows on three sides, with blinds for privacy if she wanted them closed, and valances across the top, which allowed the light to shine in. The walls were painted white, and everything was so bright and clean looking. When she opened the door, she saw the hardwood floors and the wide wooden staircase that went to the second floor. It had the same wide, dark trim on the windows and wide entryways that led to the living room and dining room. There was a closet under the stairs, and the kitchen was down the hall.

"The house was built in 1909," Lori said, "and it has the original hardwood floors and woodwork. It basically is in pretty good shape but will need some upgrades. But wait until you see the window in the dining room."

She took April's hand and led her through the living room and into the dining room. The bay window was extended out three feet with windows on all three sides. It had a radiator underneath, but

April could just picture herself sitting on a bench that hopefully could be built under the window, with a cup of hot chocolate in the winter or bird-watching in the summer.

"This is just what I was looking for!" April exclaimed. "You nailed it with this one."

"Oh, April, this is perfect!" her mom agreed. "For being as old as it is, it's really in pretty good shape and wouldn't take a lot to fix up."

"Well, let's take a look at the rest of the house," suggested Lori. "It has the old radiators and will need upgrades on the electrical, plumbing, and in the kitchen."

They continued to walk through the house, and Lori continued, "Otherwise, just some fresh paint in the other rooms. The three bedrooms upstairs have old carpets but may have hardwoods underneath. There is a bath on the first floor and another one upstairs. The basement isn't finished, but there's a laundry area down there, and you can always redo that later."

After they looked at everything on the first floor and the basement, they went to the second floor to look at the bedrooms and bathroom.

"Because the second floor extends all the way up and the roof doesn't cut into the bedrooms, they are very roomy and have nice windows—two in each room," Lori pointed out.

"Yes, they really let in a lot of light," April observed. "The closets are fairly good sized too. I would use one bedroom for an office, one for a guest room, and the other for myself. I might need a little more closet space in that one, but it's workable."

When they checked out the bathroom, April was impressed with the claw-foot tub, wainscoting, big window, and the unique character of the room. It didn't have a shower, but April thought that could be worked out.

When they went back downstairs, Lori gave them some more information.

"This house is new on the market, but it won't last long. As I said, old houses with this kind of character don't last. The woman who lived here is a widow and had to be moved to a nursing home due to medical issues, so the family is anxious to sell it as soon as possible, in order to help pay for her expenses. She and her husband purchased this house after they were married back in the fifties and raised their family here, so as you can see, it was a house filled with love."

"So what's the asking price?" April said hesitantly, hoping it wasn't out of her reach.

"This is well within your budget, April, but the upgrades needed will be costly," Lori advised. "You're getting in early, and the family is eager to sell, so I think you can negotiate even a little lower and see what they say. You can always go up if they reject your first offer."

"Okay. I have a friend who's a carpenter and would like him to take a look at it too so he could give me an idea of what it may cost to do the renovations and upgrades. Could I get back to you in a couple of days?"

"Yes, I think that would be okay. But don't wait too long. This house won't be on the market for long," warned Lori.

Her mom invited April over for supper so they could talk about the possibilities of April purchasing the house. They were both excited about what they saw and talked nonstop while they prepared and ate supper together. Then April called Aaron to see when he would have time to take a look at the house.

"Well, I work on houses, but Ed does the estimates. How about I give him a call and see when he'd be available to take a look at it with us? It would be a lot more accurate then," Aaron advised.

"Okay, but I don't have a lot of time. Lori said I need to act fast on this house, as it won't be available for long."

"If Ed can't look at it soon, I'll come tomorrow evening and give you a rough idea of what it will need. Does that work for you?"

"Yes, that will be fine. I told Lori I'd get back to her within a couple of days."

"All right, let me give Ed a call, and I'll get back to you in a little while."

"Thanks, Aaron. I really appreciate it," April said as she hung up.

"Aaron is sure a wonderful man," April's mom said. "He's always so kind, helpful, and thinks of others before himself. He's a wonderful Christian and really loves the Lord. He's a man worth hanging on to."

"Careful, Mom, you're pushing again."

"Sorry, dear. How about if we watch one of those remodeling programs on TV while we wait for Aaron to call back? I think it's about time for one to start, and it may give you some ideas when you look at the house again."

They sat down and started watching the program, but it wasn't long before Aaron called back. He said Ed couldn't come the next day but that he would be there at seven. April gave Aaron the address and set it up with Lori for them to see the house again the next evening. They finished watching the remodeling program, and then April went home. She was so excited she didn't know if she would be able to get much sleep that night.

Chapter 15

April didn't get much sleep but still woke up early and grabbed her Bible to read her devotions. She was still in the Book of Psalms and was enjoying reading how David and the other writers dealt with different issues in their lives. Today she would read chapter 33 and was anxious to see what it would teach her.

After reading the passage, she knew it was just what she needed for that day. It challenged her to keep things in the right perspective and not put getting this house first in her life. She knew God must always be first. He was the Creator of all things, all powerful, all knowing, and had a plan for her life; and she needed to trust in Him for that plan. When she prayed, she asked God for His leading in her decision regarding the purchase of this house and concluded with the last three verses of chapter 33:

> We wait in hope for the LORD; he is our help and our shield.
> In him our hearts rejoice, for we trust in his holy name.
> May your unfailing love be with us, LORD, even as we put
> our hope in you. (Psalms 33:20–22, NIV)

After praying, she felt ready to face her day and knew that whether she got the house or not, she would rejoice in the Lord.

That evening, when April, Barb, and Lori got to the house, Aaron was waiting for them. As they took another tour of the house, April noticed things that she had overlooked the day before. She was still very impressed with the house, and from the look on Aaron's face, he was as well.

"Wow! This house has some nice woodwork and it looks original," Aaron admired. "I would really like to work on this house. Do you have any idea as to what you would like to do with it, April?"

"I love the hardwood floors, but I'm not sure if I like the color, so may have it sanded down and refinished. Is it possible to take out the radiators and switch the hot water heat to forced air so I can have air conditioning? And I would really like to have a bench under the bay window in the dining room and redo the kitchen. Do you think there are hardwood floors in the bedrooms also? They have carpeting now."

"Whoa, slow down. You have been giving this a lot of thought I see," Aaron said with a laugh. "Since you want to refinish the floors anyway, it would be a good time to remove the radiators, but it would be very expensive and more cost effective to keep the hot water heat and just put in a new boiler. I'm sure the electrical would need to be updated and probably the plumbing too. But the wood trim, windows, and staircase are gorgeous, and this pocket door in the living room is very old style and unique."

"Lori suggested I put in a bid for the house, but it would depend on how much I need for the renovations."

"Well, your kitchen is always your most expensive room in the house, so I would say about twenty-five to thirty thousand dollars for that. Electrical and plumbing about ten to fifteen thousand. Replacing the boiler, another ten thousand. New siding, possibly a new roof, new windows, and a door for the front porch, another thirty thousand. Then another twenty thousand for all the other miscellaneous things that would need to be considered. These are rough estimates now, but I would say about a hundred thousand dollars by the time you're done."

"Wow! That's more than I was expecting."

"Whenever you talk about redoing an older home, there are always extra costs in updating everything. But this house has good bones and is definitely worth the investment," Aaron assured.

"Oh, and you were so interested in the inside yesterday, April, that we didn't get a chance to look in the backyard. There is a concrete patio and a newer garage in the back. The yard isn't really big, but it's good sized," Lori informed her.

"Well, the garage increases the value of the property, and I definitely like the idea of being able to put my car in a garage, especially in the winter. Is there anything that you could think of that I could put off and do later, Aaron?"

"I haven't looked at the roof, but there doesn't seem to be any leaks in the ceiling, and the current siding isn't pretty, but you could do the inside now and the outside later," Aaron suggested.

"Well, that gives me something to think about. Thank you, Aaron, for coming out and giving me an estimate on the renovations," April said discouragingly.

She knew she should be more grateful, but it seemed like her dream home would not become a reality.

As they walked out, Aaron tried to encourage April.

"You know, April, I could have been a little high on my estimates and there may be other ways we could cut some of the costs. Most of it would have to be contracted out, but some of it I could help you with."

"I know what you're trying to do, Aaron. Maybe it's just not meant to be." April walked to her car and thanked Lori for coming out again. "I'll let you know of my decision by the end of the week. Who knows, maybe it will be sold by then anyway."

Barb asked her daughter to come to her home and talk before going to her apartment.

"So are you going to just give up?" she asked after they sat down on the couch. "Why don't you go back to the bank and see if they will loan you more money? Did you specifically ask for a certain amount or was that all they said they would give you?"

"That's all I asked for. I never dreamed it would cost so much to renovate a house."

"Well then, go back to the bank tomorrow and see what they say. It would be easier to have it all in one loan than two separate ones anyway. It may not make that much difference in your payment. I really think this is the house for you and don't want to see you give up so easily."

"But, Mom, you've always said we should live within our means and be grateful for what we have."

"Yes I did. But I also saw the look on your face when you were in that house. I want you to pursue your dreams, sweetie. You have worked hard, have paid off your school loans, and I don't want you to quit before you've checked out all your options. That's all I'm asking."

"All right, Mom. I'll talk to the banker tomorrow and see what he says."

"That's my girl!" Barb gave April a hug and a kiss on her forehead.

April felt like she did when she was a little girl, and her mom would come and make everything all better after she had fallen and hurt herself.

"Thanks for giving me hope again, Mom."

"That's what I'm here for. And remember, nothing is impossible with God!"

"You say that a lot lately."

"That's because it's true. I've learned some things over my years of walking with the Lord. I just wish I would have learned them earlier. But now I can pass on that wisdom to you."

April went home with a lighter heart and prayed as she drove home—that if it was God's will, she would be able to get the money needed for the house.

Aaron felt bad for April and wished he could have found a way to be more of an encouragement to her instead of crashing her dream. He prayed there would be a way for her to get that house.

Maybe I could lend her the extra money, Aaron pondered. *But would she take it? I'll need to seek God's wisdom to find a way to help her.*

The next day at school, April sat with Bonnie during lunch and told her about the house, the cost for the house, and the renovations needed, and that she would be going back to the bank after school to see if they would loan her the extra money she would need. They prayed together, and Bonnie promised to ask Brad to pray also.

After school, April talked to the banker and was surprised when the banker was so helpful and encouraging.

"I will have to get it approved, but I don't think it will be a problem. With the extra money you need for the renovations, we can add another five years to your loan, so the payment will be about the same. Again, if you can pay extra on your loan payments it will be to your advantage, as it will decrease the amount of interest you pay and the number of years it will take to pay it off. I should be able to get back to you by Friday since the original loan was already approved."

"Oh, thank you very much. That would mean a great deal to me."

"Not a problem. That's why we're here," the banker said as he stood and shook her hand.

April left with a much lighter heart and a prayer of thanks to God. She would have to thank her mom too for encouraging her not to give up.

Chapter 16

The rest of the week went slowly for April as she waited to hear from the bank. On Friday, April and Bonnie decided to eat their lunch in April's classroom so it would be quieter and she could make a phone call to the bank later. They ate their lunch quickly, and then April called the bank and asked for the loan officer with whom she'd worked.

When the banker picked up the phone, he said, "Oh, I'm glad you called. I was just going to leave for lunch and planned to call you when I got back. The additional money you asked for has been approved."

"Oh, thank you so much for doing this for me!"

April hung up and with an excited squeal, turned to Bonnie, and said, "They approved the loan!"

Bonnie gave her a hug and said, "Thank the Lord! Oh, April, I'm so happy for you."

"Now I can put in my bid on the house and pray that it's accepted. I'll call Lori right now and let her know the money is approved so she can place my bid on the house and see what the family says."

April called Lori, and Lori said she'd contact the family and let her know as soon as she found out anything.

"Now it's a waiting game again," April said. "I didn't realize how much stress it was to purchase a home."

"Let's pray and ask God to help you through this time," Bonnie said.

April and Bonnie both bowed their heads as Bonnie prayed, "Lord, we thank You for answering our prayer about the approval of April's loan for this home and renovations that are needed. You are an awesome God, and Your Word says that we have not because we ask not, so we're asking that April's bid be accepted by this family. You know April's desire to purchase a home that she can make her own, and we ask that if this is Your will that You will make it a reality for her. But, Lord, we'll give You all the praise and glory that is due You, whatever Your answer. For we know that Your will is better than our will. In Jesus's name, amen."

"And, Lord, help me keep things in the right perspective," April added. "Help me not to place my desires above Your desires but to accept whatever Your will is for me. Amen."

As April raised her head, she felt a peace that God was in control and that she needed to trust Him to work out His best for her life. Now she could go through the rest of her day with the assurance that God knew what was best for her.

April took her mom out for supper to celebrate God's answer to prayer.

"Thank you, Mom, for being such an encouragement to me. It has meant so much to have you share your wisdom and come alongside me during this time. This is all so new to me, but after Bonnie and I prayed this afternoon at lunch, I felt a real peace that God is in control of this situation."

"God teaches us to trust in Him through our everyday experiences. It's often a hard lesson to learn, but He's faithful, patient with us, and ready to pick us up when we fall," Barb said as the waitress brought their food. "So have you told Aaron the good news yet?"

"I left a message on his phone, but he hasn't called me back yet. Oftentimes he's out of cell range or he could be busy and not able to call back."

April and her mom enjoyed their meal, and the rest of their conversation was lighter and more about plans for the weekend.

"In fact, Aaron and I are going to go kayaking with Bonnie and Brad tomorrow since the colors on the trees are so beautiful right now. This may be our last chance to go kayaking for a while."

"Oh, that sounds nice. I'm glad you've found something you really enjoy doing and can do it with Aaron, Bonnie, and Brad. It's important to have good Christian friends to have fun and fellowship with. By the way, I got a call from Jenny this week, and she said she's gotten involved in a Bible study at her church and that they've been a real encouragement and prayer support to her. I'm so glad she's found a good church family and has the support of good Christian people. It's so important when you're going through a difficult time."

"Amen to that!" April agreed.

After they finished their meal, they went their separate ways. April started a load of laundry, and she and Missy baked some cookies for her kayak trip the next day. Then they put in a movie to unwind, and April folded the clothes when they were dry. Aaron called around eight to congratulate her on the approval of her loan.

"I'll be praying that your bid will be accepted on the house. It would be awesome if you'd get it! It really has a lot of great character, though the house needs some updates. But I've had a long day and am pretty tired, so I'll let you go. But I'll pick you up at one-thirty tomorrow for our kayak trip, and I'll bring some chips and drinks for our picnic."

"Good! Bonnie said she'll make sandwiches, and I'm bringing fruit and cookies that Missy and I just baked," April added.

"Sounds good. I'll see you tomorrow then," Aaron said before he hung up.

Saturday turned out to be a great day for kayaking. The temperature was in the sixties, the wind was calm, and there were only a few puffy clouds in the sky. They started out kayaking in the river by the boardwalk of Black River Harbor to give Bonnie a chance to practice again, as this was only her second time out.

Then they went along the Lake Superior shoreline, admiring the yellows, oranges, and reds of the leaves, enjoying the gentle ripples of the water and the soft breezes. They kayaked for about an hour and then decided to go for a walk and stretch their legs.

They walked up a path through the woods and came to Rainbow Falls. The water was lower than earlier in the summer, so the water wasn't rushing as fast but was still a sight to behold, as was the colorful leaves in the background. They all commented how creation definitely proclaimed God's glory and proved that He was worthy of their praise and trust. For if He could put all this together, they could certainly entrust Him with their everyday lives.

After their hike, they were all hungry, so they found a table to enjoy their picnic. There were many families also enjoying the colorful, warm fall day; so as they ate, they enjoyed watching the children run and play. April also noticed Brad and Bonnie's looks of love to each other, quick kisses, winks, and acts of courtesy to each other. They were definitely a picture of a married couple who were madly in love. April prayed it would last a lifetime.

April also noticed Aaron watching her whenever she looked his way. He would smile at her and ask if she wanted something more to eat or drink. She said she didn't want anything but appreciated his thoughtfulness. She knew he cared for her and was being very patient, waiting for her to return his affection.

However, her resolve to never marry was beginning to waver. She wanted what Bonnie and Brad had. She had always dreamed of one day having a family, playing and laughing together in the grass, but thought it was a dream she had to let go.

What does God want for my life? April wondered. *Can I trust Him with my future? He helped me follow my dream of learning to kayak and answered my prayer for the approval of the money needed to purchase the house of my dreams. Will my bid on the house be accepted? Could I have a marriage with Aaron that would be long lasting? Mom and Jenny both said that it takes a lifetime commitment, a willingness to forgive, and relying on God's help to make a marriage last, which was what their marriages lacked. Can I release my fears and trust God to give me a marriage that will last?*

So many questions ran through April's head.

Chapter 17

The following Monday, as April was getting ready to leave the school, she received a call on her cell phone from Lori.

"April, I just received a call from the family selling the house you put the offer on. I'd told them that you were an elementary school teacher, that this was your first home, and how you'd fallen in love with the house. I found out that their mother was also a schoolteacher and that they wanted the house to go to someone who loved children and would love her home as much as she did. They'd loved growing up in that house but have no use for it, as they all have homes of their own. Since nothing has been done to the house in a long time and it needs a lot of upgrading, they have agreed to accept your offer. They wish you the best and hope you'll be as happy in that home as they were. Congratulations, April, you got the house!"

"Oh, thank you, Lord! And thank you, Lori, for telling them about me and letting them know how much I love that house. I appreciate you letting me know right away. This means so much to me!"

"I knew it would. I'll draw up the papers for you to sign and let you know when the closing will be. The son who is taking care of his mother's estate doesn't live too far from here, so that makes things easier. Again, congratulations, April. I know you'll be very happy in that house."

When Lori hung up, she went to see if Bonnie was still in the building. When she found out Bonnie had already left, she called her mom and told her the good news. Then she called Aaron. She was able to reach him right away, and he offered to take her and her mom out for supper to celebrate.

"I'm so happy for you, April!" Aaron cheered. "I know how badly you wanted that house. And if it's okay with you, I'd like to recommend the company I work for to do the renovations. We're finishing up some of our current projects, so by your closing date, we could have a good crew to work on it. Maybe you could even move in shortly after the first of the year. The outside would have to wait 'til spring, but we can work on the inside over the winter. It would be my honor to work on that house for you."

"Wow, this is really going to happen! Just listening to you talk about the house gets me excited! I would love to have your company do the renovations. I don't have a key yet, but I'm sure Lori would let us in for you and Ed to take a look at it and give me some suggestions and an estimate on the time and cost of everything. I know you and your crew would do an excellent job and make sure everything is done right. What time works good for you to have supper?"

"I'm just finishing the job I'm at now, and then I'll go home and clean up. How about if I pick you and your mom up around six?"

"That sounds good. I'll meet you at Mom's house to save you a stop."

"Okay, I'll see you at six."

At the restaurant, April was so excited that when their food came, she could hardly eat it.

"Oh, this soup smells so good, but my stomach is tied up in knots. I don't know if I can eat it," April commented as she sat back on her chair.

"Okay, take a deep breath, April," her mom instructed. "This is an exciting time for you, but it will be a stressful time as well. You'll have a lot of decisions to make, and you need to learn to pace yourself and relax."

After April took a deep breath and let it out slowly, she did feel better.

"You'll also need to make a list of things that need to be done first, then second, and so on so you can keep things in perspective and see the progress that's being made," April's mom added.

"You're right. Thanks, Mom. I remember that's what Bonnie did when she was planning her wedding. It was really helpful."

April took another deep breath before she went on.

"Let's see, Aaron already offered his company to do the renovations, and I suppose the next step is to pack up my things and move into Mom's house since I need to be out by the end of the month. Missy has already found someone to share the apartment with her and is excited to make it their own and decorate it according to their tastes. So I'll start packing and move things over to Mom's house. I can rent a storage unit for the bigger items and should be able to cross all that off my list by closing time."

"Very good! Sounds like you have a good start on your list already," Aaron interjected. "I'll talk to my boss and let you know when Ed can come and look over the house, find out what you want done, make his suggestions, and give you an estimate. Once you've had your closing, have the key to the house, and sign the contract with my company, we can get started. I can't wait! I'm anxious to get started on that house myself. The woodwork is gorgeous, and I'm anxious to hear what renovations you plan to make on the house."

"I have a few ideas, but since I'm new at this, I'm open to any ideas you and Ed can give me," April said as she finished her soup. "And, Mom, I'm glad I have you during this process to coach me and help me relax and keep things in perspective. I think we'll be watching more of those home improvement shows together for ideas."

"Just remember, when you watch them, you have a budget to stay within so you may have to make some compromises. Also, the programs only last an hour, but renovations take months to complete," Aaron cautioned.

"Okay, I'm starting to realize that this house project may be my biggest challenge yet. Learning to kayak was easy compared to this."

"Just remember to take one step at a time and keep the goal of having a home you can move into and be proud of in mind," Aaron suggested. "It was the same with learning to kayak, getting your education, or anything else in life worth working for—take one step at a time and trust God to help you through each step of the way."

"You're right! You may need to remind me of that from time to time though."

"It will be my pleasure," Aaron said with a smile. "I'll be here for you throughout this process, whenever you need me."

April could see from the look in his eyes that he meant it but also that he wanted to be with her, not just for this project but for a lifetime. She would have to take one step at a time with that challenge as well.

When April got home, she realized she had a message from Bonnie on her cell phone. With the noise at the restaurant and the fact that they had been so engrossed in their conversation, she hadn't heard the beep on her phone. When April called Bonnie, she was very excited for her and offered to help in any way she could. They planned to get together Saturday morning to pack some boxes, have lunch, and then April would make arrangements with the realtor to show Bonnie and Missy the house at one-thirty. They were both anxious to see the house and were excited for April's new adventure.

On Saturday morning, April, Bonnie, and Missy packed her summer clothes, some of her dishes, knickknacks, and extra bedding and linens that April could get by without and took them to her mom's house. Her mom had cleared some space in her basement and laid down boards on the floor so no moisture would damage April's things. April had put her clothes in totes but used boxes for items that weren't delicate or would mold.

"Well, that's a start. I'll keep packing up boxes and bringing them over as I get a carload. Aaron asked the young adults on Thursday evening if they would help with the bigger items the last Saturday in October. With someone's pickup, I think we can get them to the storage shed I'll be renting. Missy decided to keep the end table, coffee table, and couch and just get a slipcover for it, which would save her some money right now. She also wants to keep the dining room table and chairs, as I'll be getting a bigger one for the dining room in my new home."

"Well, if you're eliminating most of your big items, why rent a storage unit?" her mom asked. "You might as well bring it all here, then it won't be in the cold and will be all in one place. There is plenty of room in my basement. I only use it for storage, laundry, and my sewing table."

"Are you sure, Mom?"

"Of course I'm sure! Any money you save can go toward your house."

"Well then, I think we're through here. You want to join us for lunch, Mom? Then we're going to meet Lori at the house so I can show it to Bonnie and Missy."

"Since you're going to look at the house again, I think I will. I've been watching some of those home improvement shows, and I wanted to know what you think of possibly making that kitchen bigger. It's awfully small."

"All right, let's go. I'm hungry!"

April, Bonnie, Missy, and her mom ate a quick lunch and met Lori at the house. Bonnie and Missy were a little leery when they saw the outside, but when they saw the woodwork on the inside, they knew why April fell in love with it.

"It will need some work to update everything, but it has good bones, and the woodwork is amazing! But I do agree with your mom, April, the kitchen is small. So what are your ideas, Barb?" Bonnie asked.

"Well, you would have to check with Aaron to see if it's a possibility, but they're doing a lot with open-concepts in houses now, and I was wondering if you could remove some of these walls in order to open up the kitchen to the dining room. Then you would have room to put in an island. It would give you a lot more storage and workspace."

"I like that idea," April affirmed. "Bonnie, you have an open concept in your house, and it really seems bigger and works so well for entertaining. But that would mean taking out some of the woodwork, and that's why I bought this house."

"But maybe you could use some of it elsewhere, like for that bench you want to build under the dining room window," April's mom suggested.

"Yes, that definitely gives me something to think about. And I like the idea of an open concept with more storage and work space in the kitchen. I meet here with Ed and Aaron next Tuesday after school for their recommendations. I'll see what they have to say."

Chapter 18

Tuesday morning started out with three inches of snow on the ground, their first snow of the season. She had hoped it would hold off for another month, but then she had to remember she lived in the UP of Michigan where the winters are long and have lots of snow. April's students were excited about the snow, and some came in soaking wet from their snowball fight during recess. She wished that her students would dress better for the colder weather, as many didn't have warm-enough coats or mittens when they came to school. She knew some didn't have the money, but others had parents who didn't care or weren't home to notice if their children had dressed properly before they left for school. She would have to stock up on scarves, mittens, and extra coats to keep in the supply closet of her classroom for those who didn't have warm outerwear for the winter.

This was something she'd started last winter, and they came in very handy for some of her students. She thought her young adult group would be interested in helping her collect some items, since the cold and snow were coming earlier than she'd hoped. She would talk to Aaron about it when she saw him later.

That afternoon, she found herself looking at the clock quite frequently and was disappointed at how slow the hands were moving. But eventually, four o'clock struck; and April left to meet Ed, Aaron, and Lori at the house.

"The closing is scheduled for next Friday at four-thirty, but the family sent me an extra key so you could come and look at the house whenever you'd need to, but no work can start until after the closing," Lori said as she handed April a key to the house. "I've enjoyed working with you, April, and I'm so glad I was able to find you the house of your dreams. I'll see you next Friday."

And with that, Lori gave April a hug and left.

"Okay, so when was this house built?" Ed began with his questions.

"In 1909," April answered.

"Any recent renovations done to the house?"

"No."

"That means we'll need to redo the electrical and plumbing to bring it up to code. Well, let's take a look at this house you're purchasing so you can fill me in on what you'd like us to do for you," Ed stated as they walked up to the porch door.

"As you can see, it needs new siding, porch windows, a new door, and I would like wider steps and a new railing of some kind," April began. "Also, with the winters here and the roof so high up, I'd like to replace the roof with a metal one so I don't have to worry about the snow accumulating up there and having it scraped off."

April opened the door, and they walked into the porch.

"The inside of the porch is in pretty good shape, so I was planning on just paint and new flooring," April added.

Ed nodded, wrote on his pad of paper, and motioned for her to continue inside the house.

"The woodwork is in good shape, and I love the stairs and the hardwood floors. But I was wondering if the radiators could be removed and put in forced air and air-conditioning or if we should just have a new hot water boiler put in."

"Removing the radiators would be very expensive," Ed confirmed, continuing to write on his pad. "I would recommend you leave the radiators and put in a new boiler, which would be much more cost effective. Then you'd have more money for the other renovations."

As they walked into the dining room, April pointed out that she'd like a bench under the bay window but was wondering if it would be possible with the radiator there.

"Yes, as long as you keep it open in the back since they must remain unobstructed. And I assume you want to keep the corner china cabinet in here since it matches the woodwork?" Ed asked.

"Yes."

"And where does this door go?" Ed asked, pointing to a door in the dining room.

"It goes to the concrete patio outside. I'm not sure what I'm going to do with that yet."

Ed opened the door and looked out at the patio.

As Ed moved on into the kitchen, he said, "The kitchen is pretty small. Did you have any ideas as to what you want to do with that?"

"My mom mentioned the idea of taking out some walls to open up the dining room and kitchen and put in an island, which would give me more storage and counter space."

"That's a thought," Ed said while looking around the kitchen, the hallway, and the bathroom off the kitchen, as well as the area that went to the basement and back door. "What would you think of taking out all the inside walls, except for the partial wall for the china cabinet in the dining room and a partial wall by the front door into the living room. We would have to put in a support beam for the second floor, but that is the only way you would have enough space for an island, in which you could have a stove top, work space, and some storage.

"Since this downstairs bathroom needs to be gutted anyway, you could make that area into a pantry and work area. We could then use the pocket door in the living room for the door for your new pantry, which would go into the wall space on the left. And on the other side, you could have a built-in oven and microwave."

"Wow! I love the open concept, the pantry, and large island idea, but then I wouldn't have a bathroom downstairs. I really would hate to have to go upstairs all the time and only have one bathroom."

"Is there a laundry room in the house?"

"There's a washer and dryer in the basement, but it's not finished. I'm not really happy with that, but I can work with it for now."

"What if we would build a room where your patio area is and make it into a main-floor half bath and laundry? It would be close to the plumbing and you already have a door for it. I can draw up some plans with the different options for you, then you can take some time to think about it."

April looked at Aaron, and when he nodded, April said, "Okay."

"All right, let's head upstairs."

While going through the hallway, Ed took notice of the closet under the stairway and checked the sturdiness of the stair railing and seemed satisfied. There were three bedrooms upstairs and a full bath.

"Looks like the bedrooms mainly need fresh paint and new carpeting. What about the closet space, are they sufficient?"

"I will be using one bedroom for an office, the second will be a spare bedroom, so they will be fine. The one I would use as a master could use more closet space though."

"Do you know which one you'll use as your master?"

"Probably the one facing the backyard and across from the bathroom," April informed him.

"And what about the bathroom? What changes in here?" Ed asked as he walked in.

"It needs more storage. I like the claw-foot tub, but I wish it had a shower and more counter space."

"Okay, I think I have what I need. I'll take some pictures, and Aaron can help me with the measurements. I'll get back to you in about a week with some options for you, the costs, and time frame it will take to do the job. Any questions?" Ed asked.

"Not offhand, but I'm sure I'll think of some later. Do you have a card with your number so I can contact you if I need to?"

"Of course," Ed said as he handed April one of his cards.

Ed then started taking pictures upstairs while Aaron started measuring the bedrooms and bathroom.

April decided to go downstairs so she wouldn't get in their way and tried to visualize what Ed was suggesting. The more she thought about it, the more she liked it. She even contemplated adding a gas or electric fireplace in the front corner of the living room, with a mantle and television above it. She would ask Ed about it when he came downstairs.

"A fireplace would be doable," Ed said after April asked about the fireplace. "It would look very nice there. Just remember that everything you add to the design costs more money."

Yes, it always came down to the money, April thought. She would wait to see Ed's designs and cost estimates before she ruled out the fireplace. It took about another forty-five minutes for Ed to get the pictures and measurements he needed on the main floor, looked at the siding and roof, and then he left. By then, it was six o'clock, so Aaron offered to take April out for supper.

"It's kind of overwhelming for you, isn't it?" Aaron observed after they ordered their food.

"I'll say! I didn't realize there would be so many decisions to make or so much involved in a renovation project. I don't know if I'm up to this," April admitted.

"That's why you're hiring us. We'll take care of the permits, dumpster, subcontractors, and all the messy stuff. You get to do the fun stuff like picking out your paint colors, kitchen cabinets, flooring, furniture, and accessories."

"That's all? That's pretty overwhelming for someone who's never done it before," April said as her voice got higher and louder.

"Hey, take it easy," Aaron said as he took her hand in his, speaking softly and assuredly. "I can help. And your mom and Bonnie said they would help too. I'll get some catalogs of kitchen cupboards and countertops and some sample paint colors and carpet swatches, and you can look on the internet for whatever else you need. You need to breathe deep and take one step at a time, remember?" Aaron said with a smile.

"Yes," April said after she took a deep breath. "And do you also remember that I told you that you would have to remind me of that many times before this is over?"

"And I said it would be my pleasure, and I meant it," Aaron promised with a smile. "But don't worry, it will all be worth it when your house is done and you can move in."

Chapter 19

The snow didn't last long, as it warmed up again and melted. It must have been a teaser, warning them of what was to come. But April wanted to be ready for it, and since she'd forgotten to talk to Aaron about getting help with collecting winter coats, mittens, and scarves on Tuesday, she went to Bible study a little early on Thursday to discuss it with him.

Aaron asked April to present it to the group, and she was surprised at the overwhelming support. They even suggested that the information be put in the church bulletin so others could help as well. That way, they could expand the project to all sizes and not just her class, for children in the other grades could benefit from the project as well. She would pick up some totes to put the supplies in as they were brought in. She was excited to see how God would supply.

The next week went by fast. April packed more of her belongings in the evenings and took them to her mom's home. Her pile in the basement was growing, but she'd also taken a load to the secondhand store. She couldn't believe all the stuff she'd accumulated and wasn't using. This was a good time to go through everything and get rid of things she didn't need. Some of the things Missy said she could use, so April left them in the apartment for her.

Soon it was Friday, the day of the closing on her house. They met at the realtor's office, and she was introduced to the previous owner's son. He was really nice and happy to hear that she loved the house and was going to fix it up.

"That house has been neglected for some time. Our dad had a bad heart and wasn't able to do much around the house. After he died, Mom didn't want to change anything, so she refused to let us make the improvements it needed. The last few years, she hasn't been well, and it was difficult for her to go up and down the stairs. Then she had a stroke, so we had to put her in the nursing home."

"Is she in a local nursing home?" April asked.

"Yes, she's at the Villa Maria in Hurley, Wisconsin."

"Would you mind if I visited her?"

"That's very thoughtful of you. She's in a wheelchair now as her left side was affected by the stroke, but yes, she enjoys getting visitors."

He then gave April his mom's room number, and April looked forward to meeting her.

Ed called April the next Monday, saying he had the proposals for the renovations ready for her. She wanted Aaron and her mom to be at the meeting too, so she scheduled it to be at her mom's home on Tuesday at six-thirty. April was nervous about the results but tried to take her mom and Aaron's advice to breathe deep, take one step at a time, and put her trust in God.

When Ed arrived, she felt more at peace and remembered that God was in control of her situation, knowing the beginning and the end. She needed to trust Him with her home and her life as well.

"Okay," Ed began, "I've broken the proposal into different groups and subgroups. The first group is the heating, plumbing, and electrical updates, since they're nonnegotiable and need to be brought up to code. The second group is the main floor renovations, with a subdivision for each area. The third is the upstairs. The fourth are the outside renovations of the porch, siding, and roof. And the last is the addition for the laundry and main floor half bath."

He proceeded to lay out the first proposal on the kitchen table. April grabbed Aaron's hand as she looked at the paperwork. As Ed went over each proposal, she realized that she was going to be overbudget and would have to choose which renovations she'd be able to do.

After going over the proposals, Ed showed her the drawings for the new kitchen/pantry option and the laundry/half-bath addition. They were very functional and would really make her home what she wanted. The upstairs would have minor changes, except for the bathroom. He gave her the option of removing the tub and putting in a tub–shower combination with added storage or keeping the tub and putting in a small shower unit; however, that meant she'd lose the extra storage space.

The outside proposal included the new windows, door, and steps for the porch; the metal roof and premium vinyl siding, with an option to use faux stone on the bottom part of the porch for contrast; and the raised sides of the new wider concrete steps, which would slant down to work as a wide railing. The same stone could also be used for the fireplace option in the living room, to pull it all together. April had some important decisions to make.

"Can you give me some time to think and pray about all this?" April asked.

"Of course, it's a big decision. Do you have any questions about any of the proposals?"

"No, you did a very thorough and wonderful job, Ed, thank you. You laid everything out so well that it's easy for me to understand and will help me choose the options I want to go with."

"Well, I hope you'll allow us to do the work for you. This will be a lovely home for you once the renovations are completed," Ed said, as he shook her hand and let himself out.

"So what do you think, April? her mom asked.

"Everything is so amazing. His proposals are wonderful, and I can picture myself living in this beautiful home. And it will be so much more functional with the changes he suggested. At first, I thought removing the walls would take away from the look of the house, the woodwork, and the charm I liked about it. But really, it will open it up and enhance it, not take away from it. What do you think, Aaron?"

As April looked at Aaron, she realized that she was still holding his hand. His presence and touch had given her a calmness that she hadn't expected.

"Ed definitely did a great job. It's going to be difficult to choose what to wait on. I wish you could do it all. I'm sorry if I got your hopes up and led you astray on the renovation costs. I'm used to doing the work, not the pricing."

"Oh, I don't blame you, Aaron. Actually, you were very close. It's all the extras that added to the cost. Thank you for being here and for your support," April said as she looked at their clasped hands.

"You're more than welcome," Aaron said with a smile as he squeezed her hand. "Anytime I can be of service, I'm more than willing."

Aaron held her gaze, and she knew that he appreciated her taking the initiative to reach out to him, to need him, and to allow him to meet that need.

April's mom had cut some cake and brought tea and coffee to the table, which broke the spell between April and Aaron, and they moved apart.

"Thanks, Mom, but you didn't have to do all this."

"I needed something to do with my nervous energy. Besides, you two were busy," she said, winking at April.

April blushed and started eating her cake, avoiding Aaron's eyes.

"Well," she said after preparing her tea, "I'll definitely have to pray about all this. There's a lot to consider."

"I think it would be a good idea for us to pray together right now," suggested Aaron.

"That's a wonderful idea, Aaron," Barb affirmed.

They all bowed their heads and prayed together, with April's mom concluding by saying, "Lord, not our will, but Thine be done. Please give April Your wisdom in the decisions she needs to make, and we will give You the honor and glory in whatever the outcome is. Amen."

April left with a lighter heart, knowing that she had the prayer support of Aaron and her mom and that she wasn't alone in this process. God would help her make the right decisions.

Chapter 26

On Saturday, some of the young adults helped April get the last of her things moved out of the apartment; and Missy's new roommate, Beth, moved in. When she closed the door of the apartment for the last time, it was like one chapter in her life was ending. April had already taken on the challenge of learning to kayak, she had just purchased her first home, and now she was embarking on a large renovation project. She was eager to see how this new chapter would turn out. It was definitely a big learning experience and was teaching her to not rely on her own wisdom and abilities but to lean on God, trust Him, and be thankful for the support of her Christian friends and family.

After April got settled into her mom's spare bedroom that afternoon, she realized how anxious she was to have her home finished and be able to move in. She needed to make a decision soon about the renovations so they could get started. The weather would be turning colder, and though the snow had held off so far, she knew it wouldn't be long before the workers had snow to contend with. She decided to go over to the house, look it over again, and spend some time praying and seeking God's wisdom.

Two hours later, she called Aaron and asked if he could come over to the house.

"Is it too late to have the roof done before the snow flies?" April asked when Aaron arrived.

"If the weather holds out, it should be okay. It was in the low fifties today, and the forecast is predicted to stay mild for another week or so. Things are slow at work right now, so we could get a crew here and be done in about a week."

"Good. I'd like to get the new metal roof done in brown then as soon as possible. I'd hate to go through the winter and worry about all that snow on the roof or it leaking and causing damage after the renovations are started. I would like to go ahead with the demolition on the inside of the house as well. It would be nice to get that going before we get several feet of snow and it gets colder. And what about the new boiler system? Once you take out the old one, it'll take a while to get heat back in the house. You can't work here in the cold, and I don't want my pipes to freeze."

"Whoa, slow down! We'll bring in heaters so your pipes don't freeze. We do this all the time. Just leave the details to us, okay?"

"Okay," April said, taking a deep breath. "So I've decided to go ahead with all the inside renovations, except the new laundry/half bath option, since you can't do all the outside stuff now anyway. Then we'll see where I'm at with money for the siding, steps, and new porch windows and door in the spring. That way, I can move in once the inside renovations are done and do the outside stuff later. What do you think?"

"I think that makes sense. You'll have to come to the office on Monday to sign the contract, and then we can get started as soon as we have the permits and roofing supplies."

April gave a long sigh and said, "Good."

She felt a real peace about her decision and was glad she could now move forward.

Aaron put his arms around her, held her close, and said, "Congratulations! Your dream of living in this house is going to become a reality. And you didn't even need me to remind you to take a deep breath and relax."

No, in fact, April felt very relaxed with Aaron's arms around her. She felt cherished, safe and protected, and like she could do anything as long as Aaron was by her side. What was changing in her? Was she learning to let go of the past and trust again? Whatever it was, she liked it.

As she rested her head on Aaron's chest, she heard his heart beating rapidly and prayed silently, *Thank you, Lord, for bringing Aaron into my life.*

April signed the renovation contract on Monday after school, and by Friday, they had the building permit, the dumpster in place, and began working on the new roof the following week. Some of the men even started on the demolition inside. April wanted to take pictures of her home's renovation process, so she took pictures before any work started and planned to take pictures through each stage of the renovation.

Bonnie often asked her during lunch how it was going and seemed as excited as she was.

"I didn't get to see the process when Brad and Joe built our home, but now I'll be able to see the changes of your house as it develops into the home of your dreams," Bonnie said. "I love the designs you've shown me of the open concept and kitchen with the pantry. It's going to be great for entertaining and so functional."

"Yes, I'm getting excited to move in, and the renovation is just getting started. Aaron said I should go ahead and start looking at cupboards, countertops, paint colors, and carpet swatches. I think he's trying to keep me busy so I don't come over to the house.

"He wants me to stay away until the roofing and demolition are done. He says it's too dirty and dangerous right now for me to be there. Aaron and I picked up some kitchen cupboard and countertop catalogs, as well as some paint and flooring samples. Are you available to come over on Saturday to Mom's house and help me choose cupboards and colors for the house?"

"I should be able to. Brad will be busy at the shop most of the day. I'll check with him just in case things have changed, but it shouldn't be a problem. He won't be going skiing since there's no snow." Bonnie paused a while and smiled. "It's kind of weird. Brad is praying for snow so business picks up and he can go skiing. You're praying that the snow will hold off so you can get work done on your house. Looks like God is answering your prayers right now, and Brad's answer is to wait."

"Well, once they get the demolition done and are working on the inside, tell Brad that I'll join him in praying for it to snow. I know a lot of businesses in the area rely on the snow and skiers for their livelihood.

Besides, now that the leaves are off the trees, it looks pretty dead and drab outside right now. Some snow would brighten things up."

"I'll tell him," Bonnie said, laughing. "And plan on me for Saturday. If anything changes, I'll let you know."

She started gathering her lunch containers and putting them in her bag.

"Looks like lunchtime is over and time to get back to our classes. I'll see you Saturday."

At first, looking through the cupboard catalogs and seeing all the options were overwhelming for April and Bonnie. Then April's mom helped them put things in perspective.

"April, you need to think of your kitchen in light of what it will look like with the walls removed and opened up to the rest of the area. You like the woodwork in the house and want to highlight that, so then your kitchen cupboards should be a similar color and style. And since that kitchen wall that the cupboards will go on is so small, how about if the cupboards go all the way to the ceiling? That would give them some height and accent the woodwork around the bay window and the bench you want to have built in the dining room, as well as the rest of the woodwork in the house."

"I like that, thanks, Mom! Now we have some direction of what to look for."

They soon found a style they liked for the wall cupboards and the island. It was the Bennet style, which had the wide trim on the top and went all the way to the ceiling and came in maple and a sorrel color, similar to the color of the woodwork already in the house. They would go with the same-style cupboards in the pantry but in French vanilla color, since it was such a small area. Now they could move on to the countertops, or so she thought.

"The color of the countertops will depend on the color you choose for the walls and the flooring in the kitchen, since the hardwood floors aren't in the kitchen or pantry," Bonnie pointed out. "Do you know what color you plan on painting the walls? Since you'll only have the outside walls, the same color will be throughout the main floor."

"Okay, let's switch to the paint samples then," April said as she moved the catalogs and pulled out the paint samples. "I definitely want to go with a lighter neutral color and will be using the furniture and accessories for accents. There are a lot of browns with the floors, woodwork, and cupboards, so let's pick a color from this brown pamphlet. It says here, 'Lighter and brighter browns are reassuring and friendly in living rooms but are also welcome practically everywhere in the home.' So a lighter neutral brown should do the trick."

They decided on the dusty dawn color. It was light and would blend with anything April would put in the rooms, as well as the hardwood floors.

"Now for the flooring in the kitchen and pantry. It would have to go with the colors of the cabinets in both the kitchen and the pantry, as well as look good butted up to the hardwood floors," April began. "It needs to have some brown tones in it, but I think we're getting too much brown in the room. What if we would go with something a little different? I picked up some sample flooring, and the salesman said this Bastille flooring is very popular right now. It is a floating vinyl tile that comes in large squares and is easy to install."

April showed them the samples she had. One was in a beige marble color called Parisian Cream, and the other was a gray marble called Castle Gate.

"I personally like the Castle Gate color the best," April said.

"Oh, I like the gray one better too. I agree, we're getting too much brown in the room. And it looks really nice with the paint color and cupboards we already picked out," Bonnie exclaimed. "Good choice, April."

"Before we go to the countertops then, I have something else to show you," April said as she pulled out a faux stone sample. "When Ed talked about the siding for the outside of the house, he mentioned putting a faux stone on the bottom part of the porch as an accent to the tan siding and also along the outside of the concrete steps going up to the porch. I found this stacked stone with a mixture of tan and gray tones in it. He said it could also be used for the fireplace I wanted to put in the corner of the living room. It would add an additional cost to my budget, but I think it would really be a great addition to the house. What do you think?"

"Oh, April, I think it's a great idea!" April's mom said excitedly. "And a fireplace in the corner of that living room would make it look so cozy. How high were you thinking of going with the stone?"

"All the way to the ceiling, but I would keep it flush, without a base, as I don't want to take up any more floor space. A gas fireplace would be on the bottom, a mantle above it—hopefully made with the wood that has been taken out—and then a set-in TV above that."

"That would be wonderful, April! It would be worth the extra money to do it. I know Brad and I really enjoy our fireplace, especially on these cooler nights. You would get a lot of use out of it, and it would really pull the whole room together, especially with the color of the flooring we just picked out for the kitchen," Bonnie assured her. "I can just picture you sitting in your living room on a light gray sectional sofa with lots of colorful pillows, watching the fire in your fireplace or a romantic movie on your TV."

"A light gray sectional sofa—I like that, Bonnie. It would help break up all the browns in the room, and the pillows would add a pop of color. Okay, I think we're ready to pick out the countertops now. I was given a catalog that explains the different types of materials, such as: granite, quartz, high-resolution laminate, and standard laminate. After looking it over, I've decided to go with the high-resolution laminate. It's very durable, easy to take care of, provides a natural stone appearance, and is also more cost efficient and easy to install. The money I save would help pay for the fireplace. So all we have to do is pick out the color."

It didn't take them long to pick out one that had the same tone as the wall color, with streaks of tan and grays in it, looked awesome with the cabinet colors, and wouldn't clash with the flooring.

"Well, I think we've accomplished quite a bit today, and now it's time for lunch," April's mom announced.

As she got the food ready, April thanked them both for all their help and wonderful suggestions. She felt like she was really moving forward with the house plans and that everything was coming together nicely. It was fun working with her mom and Bonnie, and the decision-making was much more productive and less stressful. She was feeling more confident and looking forward to whatever step came next.

Chapter 21

On Sunday, April was eager to show Aaron the items they had chosen for the house, so she invited him over for dinner after church.

"I would never turn down a home-cooked meal. It beats my cooking any day," Aaron acknowledged.

After dinner, April and her mom showed him everything they'd picked out, and he was very impressed.

"Wow, you gals really accomplished a lot! The colors and choices you made will really look nice in the house too. We should finish with the roof and demo this week and get the support beam up. We're saving the bigger pieces of wood trim that we've taken out to use for your bench—or anything else we may need it for—and putting it in the garage. We put the stove and refrigerator in there also. You probably won't be using them, but you can decide what you want to do with them later.

"The new boiler system is scheduled to be put in next week, and then the electricians and plumbers will be able to do their thing. Since you have the cupboards and countertops picked out, you can show me what cabinets you want where, and we can get them ordered. That way, they'll be ready when the electricians, plumbers, and inspections are done. Do you have the design for the kitchen with the measurements?"

"Yes, right over here. And I want to go with the pullout drawers. Those I've talked to say it makes it so much easier to find what you need."

Aaron made a list of the cabinets and countertops that needed to be ordered for the kitchen and pantry.

"Okay, we'll get these ordered for you. Also, we need to know what you've decided for the bathroom upstairs before the plumber comes. Do you want to keep the claw-foot tub or go with the tub–shower combination?"

"You know, as much as I liked the idea of keeping the claw-foot tub, it would be more practical to go with the tub–shower combination and more storage space. I can sell the tub, as well as the stove and refrigerator, and put the money towards things I need to buy for the house. I'll keep the washer, dryer, and freezer in the basement for now, until I decide what to do about the addition."

"Okay, that sounds like a good idea, and I'll let Ed know. If things go as scheduled, we may have you in your house by Christmas."

"That would be so wonderful! It would be the best Christmas present ever," April said with a huge grin on her face. "Thanks to all your support and encouragement, this is really going to happen."

April gave her mom and Aaron both a hug of gratitude.

The next couple of weeks went by swiftly. The three totes that April had placed at her church for winter coats, mittens, and scarves for the children at school had been filled. At their Thursday evening Bible study, the young adults helped her sort them according to sizes, and she took them to the appropriate classrooms the next day. They would definitely be put to good use, as it had turned colder and they now had a foot of snow on the ground. She was very pleased with the response of her church family, and more were still coming in. The winter was just beginning, so there would be many cold days ahead of them, and mittens and scarves had a tendency of getting lost or forgotten.

April also went to see the woman at the nursing home who had lived in her house for so many years. Her name was Lydia, and she was eighty-three years old. She wasn't able to walk since her stroke so she was in a wheelchair, but they were giving her therapy on her left arm and leg to strengthen it. Lydia was still pretty alert, happy to meet the person who bought her home, and was glad that April loved it as she had.

"That was the house my husband and I moved into after we were married. My husband was a banker, and I was an elementary school teacher. We raised our three children in that house. Are you married?"

"No."

"Do you have a special someone?"

"Well, there's Aaron, but he's just a good friend. He's one of the carpenters working on the house. He's been a big help and encouragement to me during this process. So have my mom and friend, Bonnie. Bonnie and I shared an apartment for about a year, but she got married in August. She teaches third grade in Ironwood, and I teach the sixth grade."

Lydia was easy to talk to and they visited for an hour. April promised to come back and see her again.

Aaron informed April of some delays with the electrical and plumbing, as there was more that had to be replaced than they'd expected, which is usual with an older home. Also, they needed to add outlets in the kitchen for the island, wall oven, and microwave, as well as in the new pantry. The ceiling fan/light above the table in the dining room required more amps and support, and more plugins for the fireplace/TV in the corner of the living room and in the floor were needed, since there were only outside walls now and she would need outlets for lamps by the sectional sofa, which would be opposite the fireplace. Of course, that would all cost more money. Once the electrical and plumbing were completed, then it would have to pass inspection before they could go any further.

This disappointed April, but she was learning that it was part of the renovation process. She was trying to keep busy by getting other things done for the house like deciding on and pricing appliances for the kitchen. She decided to go with new stainless-steel appliances, as it would go well with the gray tones they were adding to the main floor design and would also update the look of the kitchen.

April had been talking to her sister, Jenny, on the phone, and she was excited that April was able to buy her first home and was anxious to come and see it. Jenny was hoping to come for Christmas, as the kids would be with their dad. She'd asked April if she would be moved in by then, but there was still so much left to do that April didn't think that would be possible.

April had been in the house after the demolition was done and the new boiler was installed. It looked so different with the walls removed and so much bigger. They still had to patch the ceiling and floors, but it was a big improvement. In fact, it enhanced the woodwork she loved, even though there was less of it. The way Ed designed it made the staircase, window trim, china cabinet, and bay window stand out even more. She took more pictures and had started a photo album so she could show it to Jenny when she came.

Jenny had also shared that her ex-husband, Brent, had started going to church with them and was spending more time with the kids. Nick and Arietta had really missed their dad after the divorce. Divorce was always so hard on children, as April well remembered. She had seen it in some of her students as well. They say that children are resilient and will get over the separation quickly, but it's not true. That feeling of rejection stays both with the child and parent for a long time.

However, Jenny had made a lot of progress spiritually in the last year. She'd found a good church, had gotten right with the Lord, found a good Bible study and support group, and even asked Brent for forgiveness. She realized that she was probably much of the problem with all her nagging, complaining, and high expectations. April was proud of her big sister but wished she didn't live so far away. They talked on the phone, but it just wasn't the same. With Jenny coming for Christmas, it made her look forward to it even more.

Thanksgiving came, and with it more snow. They had gotten twelve inches of snow on Tuesday and another six inches the previous night. But the wind had died down, so it wasn't drifting now, and the plows were able to get out to clear the roads. Bonnie and Brad had invited April, her mom, and Aaron for Thanksgiving dinner. It was Bonnie's first big dinner since they'd gotten married, and she was excited to use some of her new wedding dishes and linens.

April's mom made two pies, one pumpkin and one cherry; and April made a salad. Bonnie had everything looking so festive. The fireplace was lit; and the mantel was decorated with fall gourds, pumpkins, and candles. The table looked very inviting with her new tablecloth with matching napkins and a floral arrangement in the center. The aroma made everyone anxious to sit down and enjoy the delicious meal of turkey with dressing, mashed potatoes, sweet potatoes, and green beans, along with April's salad and her mom's pies for dessert.

They all shared what they were thankful for, and Brad asked the blessing for the food. The food tasted delicious, and the conversation was of varied topics. However, they all decided to wait and have their dessert later. Brad and Aaron went to watch the football game; while Bonnie, April, and her mom put away the food and cleaned up the dishes. Once the kitchen was cleaned up, they joined the men and watched the rest of the football game. When the game was over, Bonnie suggested they go for a walk before they had their dessert.

"I've been in the kitchen all day and am eager to get out and enjoy our new snow," Bonnie announced.

So they bundled up and went outside into the bright sunshine, which glistened on the snow. The air was crisp but refreshing after being inside most of the day.

Brad had made a path into the woods with his tractor plow, and as they walked into the woods, Brad said with a teasing smile, "Bonnie likes walking through the woods in the snow, so I try to keep a path plowed so I don't have to worry about her getting stuck in the deep snow."

She returned his smile and gave him a quick kiss as they walked hand in hand. Bonnie and Brad had met the previous winter while she was out walking in the woods, and Brad had bumped into her, literally, while he was cross-country skiing. He helped her up out of the deep snow, and the rest was history. It was a wonderful love story.

When they returned from their walk, they were ready for their pie. It was hard to choose between the two kinds, pumpkin or cherry, so they decided to have a small piece of each. It was a great choice, as both were delicious. Then they played games for a couple of hours and ate turkey sandwiches and leftovers for supper. It was a very relaxing and enjoyable time, and they almost hated to see the evening come to an end.

But Brad and Aaron planned to go downhill skiing in the morning, since it was opening day at the ski resorts and were anxious to hit the slopes. April had never gone skiing and Bonnie only went a few times last winter, so she decided to let Brad go without her this time and let him enjoy it without having to stay with her on the easier slopes. There would be other opportunities to join him. Instead, April and Bonnie were going shopping for appliances for her new kitchen. The hardware store in Hurley, Wisconsin, was having a big sale, offered free delivery, and also did repairs when needed. Besides, April liked giving the local stores her business.

Chapter 22

April and Bonnie had a successful morning at the hardware store, as April was able to purchase a refrigerator and dishwasher to be delivered when they were ready to install them. The wall oven, microwave, and range top would have to be ordered but would also be delivered when the kitchen was ready for them.

"It's almost like the list you had for your wedding, Bonnie. As things get crossed off, it gives me a real sense of accomplishment and the feeling that things are progressing."

"Yes, it was really helpful to keep me on track and make sure I didn't forget anything. So what's next on your list?"

"The living room furniture and dining room table. And I also need to pick out the paint colors for the bedrooms and bathroom on the second floor, as well as the carpet. Ed said carpet would make the bedroom floors quieter and warmer. Right now, they're concentrating on the main floor, but it would be nice to get that upstairs bathroom done, since we don't have one on the main floor anymore," April informed her.

"Yes, that would be very helpful, especially since the construction workers have to use a porta potty outside, and it's getting colder. Let me know if I can be of any help."

"I definitely will. It made it so much easier to have you and mom help me think through the other colors and choices. Thanks again for your help."

"It was my pleasure! Besides, it gives us more time to spend together," Bonnie said as she gave April a hug before they went their separate ways.

Brad and Aaron had an enjoyable time skiing as well. April was glad Aaron was able to get a break from the house and have some fun.

He'd been working hard to keep the house on schedule by filling in replacement flooring where the walls were removed and patching the ceilings. Aaron recommended that they hire a painter who could spray the ceiling with a one-coat paint and then use an orange peel texture for the walls, which would cover up any blemishes on the old plastered walls but wouldn't be too rough. The process would be quick, more uniform, and would give the house a nice look. April was grateful for all his helpful suggestions.

When April's students came back to school after their Thanksgiving break, they continued practicing for their Christmas program, which would be in three weeks. The first through third grades were doing a winter theme, while the fourth through sixth grade classes would again have the nativity story. Her class would portray the shepherds and the angels that gave the message of the Christ child that was born in a manger in Bethlehem. She was grateful their school still allowed the true Christmas story to be told, though there were some parents who disagreed with it. The children were excited to act out their parts and were learning their songs as well. They had a good director who loved working with the children each year.

They also continued working on making Christmas presents for their parents, and some wanted to make something for their brothers and sisters as well. April decided to do something different this year and asked some of the women from her church to come and show those interested in learning to crochet, making simple projects with yarn. The women said they had extra yarn they would bring that the children could choose from.

She also ordered some simple wood projects from a catalog so the children who didn't want to crochet could choose from one of them, as well as some coloring books that had been popular lately. Then the children could color and frame their drawings once they were completed. The children were excited about their Christmas projects, and it helped them stay motivated to complete their assignments so they would have more time to work on their special Christmas gifts.

The weeks before Christmas went by quickly. The children were progressing on their studies, Christmas program, and projects. But April was seeing things progressing in her home as well. It passed the electrical and plumbing inspection; the hardwood floors were patched, sanded, and refinished; the painters painted the walls and ceilings on the main floor; and the new flooring was being installed in the kitchen and pantry. Soon the cupboards would be installed and the appliances could go in. She took pictures after each phase was completed and put them in her photo album. It helped her to realize that progress was really happening, she needed to be patient and let things get done correctly, and not rush the carpenters or contractors.

She also visited with Lydia again at the Villa Maria. Lydia had made progress with her therapy as well. She was still in her wheelchair but had gained some strength in her left arm and leg and was being fitted with braces for her arm and leg so she could begin using the parallel bars to try and walk. April brought her some cookies, so they sat at a table in the dining room and visited over coffee and cookies.

"So how is the house coming along?" Lydia inquired. "I'm sure it looks much different from when I was there. My husband had a bad heart so wasn't able to do much over the last twenty years or so. And I just didn't have the energy or knowledge of what to do. I guess I was just content to leave it as it was. But I know it needed some work, especially on the outside."

"Well, I'm saving the outside for spring when we have warmer weather. But I did replace the roof with a metal one so I don't have to worry about the snow accumulating on it. They're working on the inside right now, mostly on the main floor," April said cautiously.

She wasn't sure how much she should tell her about the changes she was making as it may upset her.

"Yes, we do get a lot of snow here in the UP. A lot of people in the Ironwood area are going with metal roofs. I'm sure it's a good idea, especially with that high roof. I was always frightened when my husband talked about scraping the snow off the roofs. He just did the ones over the porch and the bay window but hired the main roof done if it needed it. Do you have any pictures of the inside? I would love to see them."

"Why, yes. I started a photo album of the before and the different stages of the renovation process. And I'll take pictures of the house when it's completed."

"Oh, I would love to see them," Lydia said with a smile. "You're doing what I was unable to do. I'm so glad that you love the house. I was always very happy there."

April didn't know how to respond. She would have to talk to her son before she brought any pictures to show Lydia. She decided to avoid the request and filled their coffee cups instead.

"And how is that young man of yours?" Lydia asked, changing the subject.

April was unsure how to answer this question as well.

"Aaron is keeping very busy working on the house. But he's not *my* young man. We're just friends," April corrected.

"I'd like to meet him sometime. You'll have to bring him with you the next time you stop by for a visit," Lydia suggested. They visited a while longer, and then April took her back to her room.

"Don't forget now, bring your young man with you next time," Lydia reminded April when she left.

April returned her smile but didn't respond.

Why is everyone trying to match me with Aaron? April wondered. *Yes, he's a wonderful Christian man, even handsome, hardworking, kind, and considerate. But I have resigned myself to stay single—at least, that's the plan. Do I still even want that? Is God somehow changing my plans? Am I willing to trust God with my life?*

April's mind was filled with so many questions! She would really have to pray about it and listen to what God had to say to her through His Word.

At their school's Christmas program, April was very proud of the way her students remembered their lines, sang their songs, and performed for their family and friends. As she listened to the familiar Christmas story, she was reminded of how the shepherds were willing to change their plans and go to Bethlehem to see the baby about whom the angels had told them. Would she be willing to change her plans if God asked her to?

Aaron asked April to marry him months ago, but she turned him down. He had been very patient with her and hadn't been insistent by asking her again. She knew he still loved her, and she knew she cared for him too. But was it enough to take a chance on being hurt like her mom was when her father left or when Brent and Jenny divorced? Her mom and Jenny had both said that they were part of the fault and that it takes two people to make a relationship fail or succeed. Was she willing to make that kind of commitment in order to make a marriage work?

April and Bonnie planned on getting together the following Saturday to finish their Christmas shopping and look for furniture for her new living room and dining room. They would also pick out carpeting for the bedrooms upstairs. April had picked out colors for the upstairs rooms already.

She decided to go with a Holly Glen color for the office walls, as it was a balance between blue and green and would promote energy and induce calm. She would have the trim and closet doors painted in Delicate White, which would be a nice contrast to the walls and brighten up the room. The bathroom would be Midsummer's Dream, an aqua color, with the same Delicate White for the trim in there, as well as white subway tiles and an aqua mosaic strip around the tub/shower and sink areas. The master bedroom walls would be painted in Sterling Silver, which was a blue-gray color, known for stimulating feelings of tranquility and had a calming and relaxing effect. She chose Pacific Pearl for the trim in the master bedroom, as they had added to the closet space and were putting in new doors. The spare bedroom would be in Caribbean Green, but she'd leave the brown trim as it was and make it a fun, beachy room that her guests would love to spend time in. April was happy with her choices and would enjoy accessorizing them when the time came.

Now that she had the colors picked out, choosing the carpet would be much easier, so they decided to start with Floors N' Mor in Ironwood. The staff was very helpful, and they didn't take long picking out a light gray carpet that would feel soft on her bare feet in the morning for the master bedroom; a light tan Berber for the office, which would be durable; and a soft, sandy color for the spare bedroom, which would add to the beachy theme. The carpets were on sale, and they also gave her a good deal on a large area rug for between the couch and fireplace.

They would install the new padding and carpet in the bedrooms after the New Year, as the painters still had to paint them. She wouldn't be able to move in by Christmas as she'd hoped, but at least the main floor was almost done. The cupboards, countertops, backsplash, and appliances were installed that week in the kitchen and pantry, and they started on the fireplace in the living room and the bathroom upstairs. April's house was starting to look like the home of her dreams. Now she needed to furnish it. The next stop they would make was the furniture store.

"So what are you looking for in a sofa?" Bonnie asked as they started looking around. "We might as well start with the biggest piece and work from there. They definitely have a lot of choices."

"Well, I really liked your idea of a gray sectional sofa facing the fireplace. Let's see if we can find something like that," April suggested.

A saleswoman soon came, and after April explained what they were looking for, she and Bonnie were directed to several choices. April was also looking at the prices and found one that fit her budget very well.

"I like this one, and it's very reasonably priced too."

"Yes, it's one of our clearance items so it's marked down quite a bit but is a very nice option. We have it in brown or this platinum color, and you can switch the lounge sectional part to either side."

The saleswoman demonstrated how it worked, and April thought it would work very well. The sofa didn't have the recliner she was hoping for, but the lounge idea was just as good and, at that price, was great.

"What about the ottoman? Does that come with it?"

The saleswoman looked at her price sheet and said, "It's available for an additional three hundred dollars and has a lid that lifts up for storage inside, which is a very nice option too. It's very soft, so it would feel comfortable to put your feet up on or you could put a tray on it for drinks or food."

April looked at Bonnie, and they both smiled.

"I'll take the one in the platinum color, along with the ottoman. Just $1,500 for a sectional sofa and ottoman? I couldn't pass that up!" April stated with confidence. "And I also need a dining room table."

The saleswoman took them to the dining room section, and it didn't take long for April to find one she liked. It had six chairs with padded seats and was in her price range too. Their shopping trip was going better than she'd expected.

"Anything else that I can help you with?" asked the saleswoman.

"Well, I need some end tables, a bookcase, and a few other items for the living room, but I don't want to spend a lot of money on them."

"Well, we do have a lot of unfinished furniture downstairs that you could look at and finish yourself. That would save you some money. Why don't you look downstairs while I write up your order for the sofa and dining room set?"

April and Bonnie went downstairs and were amazed at the large selection of unfinished furniture that were very reasonably priced.

"You know, I think this would really work well for me. I could finish the furniture in Mom's basement, and then the color of the pieces would all match."

She found a long, narrow table for behind the sofa and an end table she liked, a bookcase that had similar trim on top as the kitchen cabinets, and a bench and small table for the foyer. She even found some stools for the kitchen island.

"This is going to be perfect and saves me a lot of money as well," April said, very pleased with their progress.

"And, April, for your Christmas present, I'd like to buy some decorative pillows for your sofa and benches. So you pick out whatever pillows and colors you'd like and let me pay for them," Bonnie said as she took her hand and smiled.

"But that's too much!"

"No, it's not," Bonnie insisted. "Besides, we can enjoy them together when I come over to visit," Bonnie said with a laugh.

"Okay. The sectional comes with two pillows that have a pattern on them and are the same color as the sofa. So now I need some with bright colors that will pop and be more fun."

"All right, let's go add these unfinished furniture pieces to your order and go find your fun pillows," Bonnie stated as they laughed all the way up the stairs.

The sofa and dining room set would be delivered to her new home before Christmas; while the unfinished furniture, which she would stain, would be sent to her mom's home the first part of the following week.

Chapter 23

April and Bonnie had fun picking out colorful pillows. April picked out two red, two blue, one green, and one yellow pillow. It would definitely add a lot of color to her home. April also picked out the stain and polyurethane for the furniture she would finish, and her mom volunteered to help her.

"I would really enjoy doing something like that," her mom admitted happily.

April appreciated her willingness to help as it would get them done sooner.

April invited Aaron over for dinner after church on Sunday and made his favorites—lasagna, green beans, garlic bread, and pumpkin pie cake for dessert. After dinner, Aaron went with her to visit Lydia at the Villa Maria. When they arrived at Lydia's room, she was very pleased to meet Aaron.

"So you're April's special man who's doing all that hard work to fix up the house for her," Lydia said as she smiled up at him. "And quite handsome too, I might add."

April blushed and didn't know what to say, but Aaron grinned and said, "Why thank you, ma'am. But I have had some help. There are four of us working on the house, plus the other contractors who did the heating, plumbing, electrical, and painting. It's quite a project April has taken on, but it's coming along nicely."

"Well, it did need a lot of work. I hadn't been able to do much to the house for a long time. I want to thank you for all you're doing for April. She's a very special young lady."

"I would have to agree," Aaron said as he smiled and looked at April.

They visited for a while longer, with Lydia asking a lot of questions and April and Aaron asking Lydia about her family as well. She showed them pictures of her children and grandchildren, and they could tell she was very proud of them. Then Lydia asked Aaron if he minded stepping out for a few minutes so she could talk to April alone. He stepped out, and Lydia asked April to pull her chair closer to her.

"Aaron is a fine young man, and I can tell he cares for you a great deal. And you care for him too, don't you, dear?"

"Yes, we're very good friends."

"Oh, I think you're more than friends. He's in love with you, you know."

"Yes, I know. He asked me to marry him back in August, but I told him no. You see, my mom is divorced, and so is my sister. I saw the pain they went through and just don't want to go through that. My family has a long history of bad marriages, and I don't want that for myself," April said with tears in her eyes as she looked down.

"Oh, honey, don't let your fears steal your joy! That man loves you, and I can tell you love him too. Yes, there are good times and bad in a marriage. It takes a lot of hard work and commitment to make a marriage work because we're naturally stubborn and selfish people. But God can help you through those difficult times, and when He does, it often makes your marriage stronger. You believe in God, don't you?"

"Oh yes. I accepted Christ into my heart as a teenager."

"Then quit trying to be the boss of your life, and let God give you the abundant life He wants for you! Satan is ruling your heart when you're controlled by fear. Kick him out and let God rule instead. For when He rules, He gives you the power to conquer anything, even your family's past. The Bible says, 'I have chosen you and have not rejected you. So do not fear, for I am with you; do not be dismayed, for I am your God. I will strengthen you and help you; I will uphold you with my righteous right hand' [Isa. 41:9–10, NIV].

"April, I was very selfish and wanted my own way when I was about your age, and I had to learn that God designed life for companionship, not isolation, for intimacy, not loneliness. Please don't isolate yourself and try to go it alone. The Bible says that two are better than one, and when we add God to the equation and entwine our lives with Him, then we have a cord of three and it's not quickly broken. My husband taught me that. And we had over fifty wonderful years together.

"We weren't perfect, but we learned to communicate and forgive one another. Our relationship grew stronger through the difficult times because we knew the Lord was our strength. Grab on to that strength and break free from your fears. Then you'll have the joy, peace, and love God wants for you and can share that with others, especially Aaron. He's waiting for you, so I'll stop preaching and let you get going. But you will think about what I said, won't you, dear?"

"Yes, I'll think about it," April agreed.

"Come see me again soon. I so enjoy your visits and know that I'll be praying for you."

"Thank you, Lydia. I enjoy our visits as well and really appreciate your prayers."

With that, April gave Lydia a kiss on her cheek and joined Aaron.

"Lydia is quite the lady. I'm glad you brought me to meet her," Aaron said as they walked to his Jeep.

"Yes, she is," April replied.

But she was quiet the rest of the way back to her mom's home as she contemplated on what Lydia had shared with her.

Is Lydia right when she said that I'm being controlled by my fears? April pondered. *Does God want more for my life? Am I keeping God at a distance and not allowing Him to guide me? Am I depending on this house to give me the joy and peace I am searching for?*

The last day of school before Christmas break was hectic as her students wrapped the gifts they made for their families and were excited about the upcoming festivities. April was also excited about her sister, Jenny, coming to visit. She was to pick her up at the airport on Saturday morning, and they would be able to spend a week together. She was looking forward to talking with her sister. Maybe she would be able to shed some light on the many questions she had running through her mind.

When Jenny arrived, she was anxious to see April's new house once she got settled in, so April gave her a tour. The main floor was almost finished, and the sectional and dining room table and chairs had been delivered, so it was starting to look like she'd hoped it would. The upstairs bedrooms still needed to be painted and the carpet installed, but the bathroom was done. So now April would be able to spend a longer time at the house, cleaning and putting things in the cupboards. Jenny was impressed with the openness of the main floor, the beautiful woodwork, the colors she'd chosen, and the hominess she felt as she walked through the house.

"I haven't seen what it looked like before yet, but I really like what you've done to it!" Jenny exclaimed. "I love the pantry with all the cupboards and storage. And the island is very handy and gives you a lot of counter space and storage too. Your new dining room set looks awesome in this dining room, and I can just picture you entertaining in this space."

As Jenny walked again into the living room area, she sat on the sofa and said, "This sectional is very comfortable, and I can't wait to try out your new fireplace. I love the stonework you chose and that it goes all the way to the ceiling, with the mantel that matches the wood trim. I take it you're putting a flat-screen TV above that? You'll definitely enjoy sitting here and watching the fire or a movie on a cold winter night. I can't believe how much colder it is here and all the snow you have."

"Well, you've been away for a while. But I haven't purchased the TV yet. There were so many other things that were more important. I've found that it's quite expensive to remodel an older home and furnish it, but I was able to get a lot of good deals, and it will be worth it once it's all done."

"It really looks amazing on the inside. Are you going to do the outside in the spring when it warms up?"

"That's the plan. But I'll have to wait and see what the cost of the new siding and windows for the porch will be. I already replaced the roof, so that's done."

"You have really done a great job, April. I'm so proud of you," Jenny said as she gave her sister a hug. "We'll have to have a slumber party here, just you and me. We can sit here on the couch, make some popcorn, watch the fire, and just talk and catch up on things. I have some things I'd like to share with you."

"I'd really like that. I have some things I want to talk to you about as well."

April, Jenny, and their mom went to church on Sunday morning and then spent the rest of the day visiting and relaxing. Jenny showed them pictures of Nick and Arietta and shared with them some of the things the kids were involved in. April showed Jenny the photo album of her house before and during the renovation process.

"Wow, what a difference from what it looked like before and now after all you've done to it. I can't wait to see it after it's all done. It's going to be amazing! Do you know what you're going to do with the outside?" Jenny asked.

"Well, as I said, I need to replace the windows on the front porch, I want to widen the steps and replace the door with a bright color to make it more inviting. The bottom part of the porch will have the same stone as the fireplace and the sides of the steps. And I'm thinking of a tan color for the new siding."

"It will be as beautiful and inviting on the outside as it is on the inside," Jenny concluded.

The next day was Christmas Eve, so April and Jenny helped their mom make Christmas cookies, fudge, and a chocolate torte for their Christmas festivities, as well as putting the final coat of polyurethane on the furniture April was finishing in the basement. April was hoping they would be dry and ready to add to her home on Christmas Day. They were going to have Christmas dinner at her mom's home but agreed to have dessert later in the afternoon at April's new home. Aaron had spent the weekend with his parents but would have Christmas dinner with them. Bonnie and Brad were spending Christmas in Minnesota with Bonnie's family, so it would be just the four of them.

Christmas morning started with the opening of their gifts. They oohed and aahed over each gift. April asked that the family get her things she could use in her new home and was overwhelmed with the abundance of wonderful gifts she received. Her mom had gotten her a set of silver candlesticks with wide, red candles to go on her fireplace mantel, a floral silk arrangement that would look nice on the small table in the front entry, and six green cloth placemats for her dining room table. Jenny gave her a beautiful lap-sized afghan that a woman in her church had crocheted for the back of her new sofa. Jenny also brought a gift from Nick and Arietta, which was inscribed "*For our favorite aunt*," and was a beautifully framed eight-by-ten picture of them for her wall.

"Oh, this is wonderful! I will definitely have to find the perfect place for this. Please tell Nick and Arietta that I really love their gift. I love all my gifts, and they'll look just wonderful in my new home. Thank you both so much," April said as she gave them each a hug.

April had gotten her mom a new necklace and matching earrings, Jenny a couple of women's Bible study books she said she wanted, and gift certificates for Nick and Arietta so they could each get what they'd like, as Jenny said she had limited space in her luggage to take back with her.

Then they had a light breakfast, and afterward, Jenny called Brent to see how the kids were doing and talked to Nick and Arietta. They were excited to tell her all about their Christmas presents and what they'd been doing while spending time with their dad. Jenny had tears running down her cheeks by the time she hung up but had stayed strong while talking to them. April held her sister in her arms and let her cry until she gained control again.

"Oh, I miss them so much," Jenny said. "I haven't been away from them this long before. But it's good for them to spend time with their dad. Brent says he's missed them and has even been spending more time with them on the weekends lately.

"Did I tell you he's been coming to church with us the last several weeks? We then go out for lunch together afterward. It has been so nice to do things together as a family again. Please pray for us, April. I still love Brent and sense that he loves me too. I'm praying that we can become a real family again. I've grown so much since

I've gotten right with the Lord, and I think Brent has noticed the difference and likes what he sees."

"I'm already praying for you and can see how God has been working in your life. You have so much more peace and joy than you used to. I'm sure Brent must see it too," April assured her sister.

"I pray he does." Jenny went to freshen up, and then April and Jenny helped their mom finish the dinner preparations.

They had decided on ham with pineapple, cheesy potatoes, scalloped corn, buns, and a lettuce salad. When everything was about ready, April and Jenny set the table and used April's new candles for a centerpiece, and it looked very festive. When Aaron arrived, April's mom asked them to all go into the living room before they ate, where Aaron read the Christmas story out of Luke 2 from the Bible. Then they each shared a special Christmas memory and sang "Joy to the World" together. It really put them in a festive mood as they dished up the food and sat down at the table. Mom asked Aaron to give thanks, and then the food was passed around. It tasted as good as it smelled, and they all enjoyed the food, as well as the fellowship.

After the leftover food was put away and the dishes were done, they got ready to go to April's home. Since Aaron had his Jeep, he suggested they bring some of the furniture up from the basement and take them to the house as well, as he'd put the back seats down to make more room. April's mom drove her car too and brought their dessert, paper plates, cups, and drinks, as well as April's Christmas gifts to her new house. They even put a few of April's totes that had her dishes and other kitchen items in the trunk.

When they entered her home, April was surprised to see that the window bench under the bay window was there with a colorful cushion and her new green and yellow pillows on it. It looked very inviting and really enhanced the space.

"Merry Christmas, April!" Aaron said as April stood staring at the beautiful bench.

"This wasn't here the other day when I was here."

"No, I wanted to surprise you, so I brought it over yesterday. I made the frame from some of the wood trim we took out of the house, and your mom made the cushion. Do you like it?"

"Do I like it? I love it! It's exactly what I was hoping for. Thank you, Aaron," April said and gave him a kiss on the cheek. "Thanks, Mom. The cushion is beautiful, and the pillows just make the flowers in the material pop."

April gave her mom a hug and wiped the tears that had started to make their way down her cheeks.

"Oh, this is so wonderful!" April said as she sat on the bench.

"Well," Jenny began, "I don't think your surprises are over yet. Look over by the fireplace."

As April turned and looked across the room to the fireplace, she saw a fifty-inch flat-screen TV in its designated place above the mantel.

"How did that get there?" April asked.

"I got a really good deal on it, so I had the cable hooked up and installed yesterday. That way, it would be here and ready to go when you moved in. The bench didn't cost much, since I used mostly the wood that was already here, and I really wanted to get the TV for you. Merry Christmas, April!" Aaron said as he stood next to her and looked into her eyes.

April couldn't look away; it was as if he was looking into her heart and soul, begging her to let him in. His eyes spoke of the deep love he had for her and how much he cherished her. It was truly a romantic moment that she hadn't expected. Finally, she forced herself to look away, remembering that her mom and Jenny were in the room with them.

"Wow, I don't know if I can take any more surprises. Thank you again, Aaron," she said and kissed his other cheek. "Let's unload the Jeep and put the rest of the things where they belong."

After the furniture items were placed in their designated places, April put her new floral arrangement on the front entry table, the candlesticks on the mantle, the afghan on the back of the sofa, and the placemats on the dining room table. It made her home look even more inviting and complete and April more anxious to move in. She had wiped out the kitchen cupboards and hutch earlier, so they emptied the totes they'd brought and April put the dishes and other kitchen items away. It was beginning to feel like home.

"Anyone ready for dessert?" Barb asked after the empty totes were put back in her trunk.

Everyone answered with an exuberant *yes,* so Barb dished up their cherry–chocolate torte onto the paper plates she'd brought, handed out napkins and silverware, and they all sat at the dining room table, enjoying the comfort of April's new home.

Chapter 24

April and Jenny decided to have their slumber party at her home that night. So they went back to their mom's home to get a few items and were then ready for a relaxing evening on her comfortable sofa, with the fireplace and her new candles lit. It really added to the atmosphere, and April was so glad she had added the fireplace feature. It was definitely worth the extra cost. And since Aaron had the TV hooked up, they started their evening by watching a Hallmark Christmas movie while they ate ham sandwiches, leftover salad, and Christmas cookies.

When the movie ended, April commented, "I love movies with happy endings."

"And how is your story going to end? Will we be hearing wedding bells soon for you and Aaron?"

"No, we're just good friends. I don't plan on getting married, you know that," April answered as she looked at her sister sternly.

"Oh, April, I saw the way you two looked at each other earlier today. That man is in love with you, and I think you're in love with him too. What's holding you back?"

"I just can't commit to a marriage when I don't know how it will turn out. I don't want to go through the rejection and pain that you and mom have. It hurts too much!" April said with a determined sigh.

"April, there are no guarantees in life, and we all go through difficult times—some of our own making, like the situation with Brent and me. But that doesn't mean we give up. I really believe that Brent and I may get back together, and I'm going to keep praying that God will allow that to happen. But we have to do our part too. Asking for forgiveness, forgiving ourselves for our mistakes, and by responding to each other in loving and kind ways, instead of nagging and being demanding. A successful marriage takes a lot of hard work. It takes a strong commitment by both the husband and wife to be willing to respect, communicate, and forgive one another, as well as be willing to compromise and not be selfish or demand our own way."

"That's what Mom said too as we drove to your house in August," April began. "But our family has had such a long line of divorce and bad marriages. How do I know that I'll be the kind of person Aaron needs in a wife?"

"By relying on God and not yourself." Jenny grabbed her Bible from the bag of things she'd brought for the evening. "The Bible says in First John 4:16–19 (NIV), 'God is love. Whoever lives in love lives in God and God in Him. In this way, love is made complete among us…There is no fear in love. But perfect love drives out fear…We love because He first loved us.'

"April, when we rely on God's love and not our own, we can love more perfectly and completely. Yes, we'll make mistakes, but God's love also offers forgiveness. You and Aaron are both Christians and have God's love and His Word to guide you. Mom and Dad didn't have that, and I forgot it and put my career and my own desires ahead of Christ and my husband. You don't have to make the same mistakes we did."

"But I already told Aaron that I'd never marry. He's probably given up on me."

"Look around you," Jenny said as she swept her arm to the room around them. "This looks like a labor of love to me. Everything he did to renovate this home has been out of love for you. It's seen in every detail, every area he's touched. That bench you wanted, the fireplace, the TV he installed—it was all to show you that he loves you very much. I think he's just waiting and giving you time to realize how much he loves you and that you love him too."

"I don't know. I have everything all planned—I'll stay single, continue teaching, live in my newly renovated home, and live the life of my dreams."

"And I think that's where the problem lies. It's all *your* plans. Have you prayed about all this? Have you asked God to take away your fears and trust Him with your future? Or are you trying to make things go according to your plans? Trying to play it safe? But in the meantime, you're lonely and missing out on what God has planned for you. Are you willing to give up your plans for His? To put your complete trust in Him?"

April had much to think about as they prepared to go to sleep on her sofa that night. Jenny soon fell asleep, but April lay awake and spent time praying silently, asking God what His will for her life was.

Lord, what do you want for me? I've allowed my past pain and fears to dictate what I do. But I'm tired of living that way and don't want that for my future. I've surrounded my heart with protective walls to keep out the hurt, but it's also kept me from being able to love completely and to accept the love of others.

Please tear down those walls and fill my heart with Your love. Take away my fear that if I marry, it will end in rejection, divorce, and pain. Break that destructive cycle in my family and help me to put my trust in Your love and strength. Help me love like you loved me—unselfishly giving of Yourself, forgiving, and keeping Your promises. And, Lord, I desire to lay my plans aside, surrender everything to You, and follow Your plan.

I've seen You work things out for my good so many times, and I know that You desire me to have the abundant life You've planned for me. You even designed marriage and said that it was good. Aaron wants me to marry him, and if You want Aaron and I to get married, I pray that You will make that very clear and give me the peace I need to accept his love. Help me trust in You and give me Your perfect love that endures, even through difficult times. Thank You for loving me, saving me, making me Your child, and for not rejecting me, even when I go my own way. You've been very patient with me, waiting for me to come to my senses and drawing me to Yourself. Thank You, Lord! I love You and yield my life totally to You! Amen.

After April prayed, she felt a real peace come over her and a great weight had been lifted from her heart and now was full of God's love—love she could now share with others, even Aaron.

She remembered that Jenny said Aaron was giving her time to realize how much he loved her and that she loved him too. That's what God had done with her also. He patiently waited for her to release her fears and put her trust in Him. She smiled as she fell asleep and was looking forward to sharing with Jenny that she had released her fears and was ready to follow God's plan for her life.

Jenny was very happy for April and reminded her of the words that the angel had shared with Mary after he told her that she'd be the mother of God's Son: "For nothing is impossible with God" (Luke 1:37 NIV).

"You need to take one day at a time and remember that God has chosen us to accomplish His purposes," Jenny advised. "He gives us the strength we need for each day and each task. When we face unexpected circumstances, there is no need to fear, for God is with us and will walk with us through each challenging situation. So relax in His presence and trust in His strength."

That was good advice, and April promised to follow it, with God's help.

Jenny flew back home on Friday morning and was anxious to see her children again. She'd also been having long talks on the phone with Brent, and he said he wanted to talk about their relationship when she returned home. Jenny asked them to really pray that they'd become a family again. She knew they'd have to make some changes in their lives in order to make it work, but she still loved Brent and knew that her children needed their dad's love as well as hers. April was again reminded that "nothing is impossible with God," so assured Jenny that she would indeed pray.

On Friday afternoon, April went to the house with a few more totes to empty and found Aaron there working. She asked him to join her for supper at six-thirty that evening in her new home, just the two of them. She wanted to fix Aaron a special dinner so she could give him his Christmas present and talk to him about the miracle God had done in her heart on Christmas night. She knew he'd be happy to hear that she'd finally released her fears.

He seemed surprised by her invitation but pleased and said, "I would love to. I'll quit a little early so I can go clean up and be back by six-thirty. What is the occasion? We already had Christmas dinner at your mom's house, and it's a little early for New Year's."

"With everything happening on Christmas day, I didn't have a chance to give you your Christmas present, and I also want to talk to you about something. So I thought it would be good to have some time alone."

"I'll look forward to it," Aaron said with a big grin.

After April emptied her totes into the cupboards and china hutch, she went to the grocery store to get the supplies she needed for their special dinner. By the time she got back, Aaron was gone. She'd decided on a menu of sirloin steak, baked potatoes, broccoli, coleslaw, and a French silk pie, which she bought for dessert. She'd never learned to bake pies like her mom but knew she couldn't go wrong with something chocolate.

She got things going right away and by the time six-thirty arrived the table was set with her best dishes, she'd changed into her favorite dress, the fireplace and candles were lit, and the food was ready. Then Aaron knocked on the door.

She opened the door and had never seen Aaron look so good. He was wearing black dress pants and a white shirt with a red tie. His hair was slicked down since it was still wet from his shower, and he was holding a bouquet of red roses.

"Wow, don't you look handsome! Are those flowers for me?"

"They sure are! You seemed pretty mysterious when you invited me for dinner, and I wanted to bring my special lady flowers for our special dinner."

"It's a good thing I unpacked a vase today. Thank you for the flowers. I'll go put them in water and they can be our centerpiece for the table."

As Aaron followed April into the dining room, he noticed that she'd unpacked some of her special things and set them around the house. The table was beautifully set, and the dinner smelled delicious.

"You've really been busy this afternoon. The house really looks nice and dinner smells wonderful."

"Well, everything is ready, so why don't you just sit down at the table and I'll dish things up," April instructed.

After Aaron said grace, they enjoyed the food April had prepared and talked about the house and how pleased April was with the way everything looked. Aaron told her when to expect the painters to be there to paint the upstairs and when the carpet would be laid, but Aaron knew that April hadn't invited him over just to talk about the house.

"So you said there was something you wanted to talk to me about. Do you want to tell me what's on your mind?"

"Why don't we go into the living room? I think we'll be more comfortable there and you can open your Christmas present," April said nervously. She was having a hard time knowing how to say what she felt.

Once they sat down, Aaron took her hand in his and said, "Look, April, we've been friends for a long time. You know you don't have to be afraid to tell me anything. Just come out and say what's on your mind."

"But that's just it. I've always been afraid and let my fears stop me from doing and saying what I really feel in my heart," she said as she began to open up. "But on Christmas night, when Jenny and I stayed here, Jenny told me I needed to release my fears to God, tear down the walls I've put around my heart to protect myself from getting hurt, and not be afraid to accept God's love, your love, and realize how much I love you. That night I prayed, and God tore down those walls and set me free from my fears and filled my heart with His perfect love."

"You said you love me?"

"Yes, Aaron, I do love you and am ready to accept your love for me as well."

Aaron didn't waste any time but drew April close and kissed her with a passion he'd been holding inside for a long time.

"You've just made me the happiest man alive! I love you with all my heart!" Aaron confessed.

"I know! And I realize that you've been waiting for me to accept your love, just as God has been waiting for me to release my fears. And they're finally gone."

"I can tell. Your face truly shines with love, and you've never looked more beautiful," Aaron said as he kissed her again.

Aaron held April close as they enjoyed each other's presence, the fire in the fireplace, the lighted candles on the mantle, and the joy of knowing that they were loved.

After some time, April lifted her head and said, "Oh, you haven't opened your Christmas present yet."

April got up and pushed a large box, wrapped in red Christmas paper and topped with a large, green bow over to Aaron.

"Wow, whatever is in there is heavy. I wonder what it is?" he said as he knelt on the floor and started ripping the paper off. "Oh, it's a DeWalt miter saw! I sure could have used this when I made your bench. I used Ed's so I'd get nice clean cuts. How did you know I needed one?"

"When I was here a few weeks ago, I heard you talking to Ed and saying you needed one. I didn't know what for or even what it looked like, but I knew I wanted to get it for you. A man at the hardware store helped me pick it out."

"It's perfect! Now I'll be able to make you all kinds of nice things. Thank you, April, but you didn't need to do that."

"They say a carpenter needs his tools, and you've been working so hard on this house, I wanted to make it a little easier for you."

"You are too sweet," he said as he kissed her.

"Oh, that reminds me," April said as she broke off the kiss. "We haven't had dessert yet. I bought a French silk pie for dessert. Can I get you a piece?"

"I'd rather have you in my arms than dessert."

"But it's chocolate, and if you don't help me eat it, I'll have to eat it all myself. I'll get fat, and then I won't fit in your arms anymore."

"That could never happen," Aaron said with a smile. "But all right, I'll have some pie with you, but hurry back."

April came back soon with two pieces of pie, and they took turns feeding each other. Sometimes Aaron got whipped cream on her cheek on purpose so he could kiss it off. They spent the rest of the evening laughing and sharing all the things they loved about each other.

"I really need to get going. I need to finish the trim on the master bedroom closet tomorrow so the painters can get in here and paint the walls after the first of the year. I'll even be able to use my new saw, thanks to you," Aaron finally said as he kissed her again. "And by the way, do you want to join the young adult group on Sunday afternoon? We're getting a group together to go skiing at Indian Head after church."

"Oh, I don't think so. I've never skied before."

"Remember last year? Brad taught Bonnie to ski, and she did really well. You will too! Besides, didn't you say that God had removed all your fears and you wouldn't be a slave to them any longer?"

"Yes, He removed my fears, but that doesn't mean He gave me the talent to ski."

"Well, we got another ten inches of snow yesterday, so you'll have a nice soft cushion if you do fall."

"Oh, that's real comforting! Just remember, if I fall, I'm taking you with me!"

"You'll do fine," Aaron assured her, gave her a kiss good night, and left with a smile on his face.

On Sunday, during the worship service, the worship team led them in a new song that really touched April's heart. It was called "No Longer Slaves." She was really touched by the words, as they were a confirmation that she was truly a child of God and was no longer a slave to her fears. The tears ran down her face as she listened to the words, especially the chorus, and praised God for His goodness.

> "I'm no longer a slave to fear, I am a child of God
> I'm no longer a slave to fear, I am a child of God."
> (Written by Brian Mark Johnson, Joel Case, and
> Jonathan David Helser)

Aaron stood with his arm around April as the tears flowed, handed her his handkerchief, and rejoiced over the freedom God had given her and the love He'd filled her heart with.

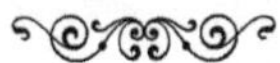

April agreed to go downhill skiing with the young adults' group that afternoon. She was still leery of trying it – sure she would break her leg, arm, or both. But Aaron assured her that he'd stay with her and help her as long as necessary. And he did. Aaron was an excellent teacher, and it wasn't long before she left the beginners' hill and moved on to a longer one. She even discovered that she enjoyed it.

Now April was even more determined to not let her fears keep her from trying new things. She'd learned to kayak this summer, purchased a home and the renovations were nearly completed—at least, on the inside—and now she'd gone downhill skiing for the first time. She wondered what God had for her next. She was looking forward to the New Year.

Chapter 25

New Year's Day came with more new snow on the ground, so everything looked fresh and clean, just like the New Year and how her heart felt. April had asked her mom, Aaron, and Brad and Bonnie, as well as Missy and Mike, the youth pastor at their church, to come to her new home for an afternoon of relaxing, playing games, watching movies, and of course, eating. They were to arrive at noon, so she was up and going by six-thirty so she and her mom could start putting together some snacks and other foods and games to take over to April's home.

Bonnie and Missy said they would bring food and games over as well, Aaron said he'd bring drinks, and Mike said he'd bring chips so they wouldn't go hungry, thirsty, or run out of things to do. She purchased a large supply of candles, as she'd burned down most of what she had. April found it enjoyable setting up her home the way she wanted it, and now, most of her boxes had been emptied and put away, except for the things that needed to go upstairs, as it wasn't finished yet. She was really looking forward to entertaining in her new home.

As her guests arrived, she had them put the food on her new island in the kitchen. It was so nice to have the extra counter space and the stools she'd finished. Since it was the first time Brad, Bonnie, Missy, and Mike had seen the downstairs since it was done, she let them look around; and they all exclaimed how wonderful everything looked.

"I love the open design, the fireplace, and the pantry really gives you a lot of extra storage and working space. And look, a sliding door that matches the woodwork. This is so cool!" Missy commented as she opened and closed it.

"Yes, it originally came from the living room, and we moved it here for the pantry," April informed them.

"I love your new bench by the bay window, April," Bonnie said as she sat on it. "It adds such a nice, cozy feature. And your new green and yellow pillows with the flowery fabric on the cushion looks really great and inviting. It's just the right pop of color you needed for this spot."

"It was a Christmas gift from Aaron and my mom, and yes, I love it. It's just what I wanted but is more beautiful than I ever dreamed it would be. I can just picture myself sitting there in the morning, drinking my juice or tea, watching the birds or reading my devotions."

"Yes, I know I really enjoy the bench Brad made me for our bedroom window. And are you still planning on doing the addition for the bathroom and laundry room?" Bonnie asked, pointing to the door that would go to the proposed addition.

"Well, I hope to. But I'll have to wait and see how much money I'll have by spring. In the meantime, I'll be using the washer and dryer in the basement, and you'll have to use the bathroom upstairs. It's finished, but the bedrooms aren't done yet."

Once everyone had looked everything over and got their questions answered, Mike said grace; and they enjoyed a wonderful lunch. Then it was game time. They got two different games going, one at the dining room table and one in the living room. Snacks were left on the island, and perishables were put in the fridge. Everyone helped themselves whenever they wanted something. It was a relaxing and fun time.

About three o'clock, they played a game of charades. Missy and Mike went first, and then Bonnie and Brad wanted to go next. They smiled the whole time they did it, and it didn't take Barb long to figure out that they were telling them they were going to have a baby. Everyone congratulated them and were very excited for the couple! April could tell that marriage had definitely been good for Bonnie, and she literally glowed with happiness—even more so now, knowing that she and Brad were going to have a baby.

"So when is the baby due?" April asked.

"Well, we just got the results of the pregnancy test, so it's early yet, but I'm guessing it won't be until around August."

"Well, I think we should have a prayer of blessing for Brad and Bonnie and that Bonnie will have a healthy pregnancy," April suggested. "Also, I would like to share with you all that this past week, I asked God to release me of my fears and control I had over my life. Now I want to trust Him for each day and let Him guide me and show me His will for my life. I really enjoy having you all in my home, and I want it to be a place for more gatherings like this. So could we have a time of prayer together for Brad and Bonnie and to dedicate my new home to the Lord? I'd also like to ask you to keep me accountable, so I'll stay close to Christ and on His path for my life."

They all agreed and formed a circle, holding hands. Each took turns praying, and it was a blessed and uniting time. What a marvelous way to start the New Year!

"Oh, April, I'm so proud of you," Barb said as she gave her daughter a hug after their prayer. "You've done a good thing, both in surrendering your life to God and in dedicating your home to the Lord. It will be exciting to see where He leads you from here and how your home will be used for God's glory. It truly has been a blessing from the beginning."

"Thanks, Mom, that means a lot," April responded.

Others in the group shared how God was working in their hearts and teaching them from His Word, promising to pray for each other. April felt truly blessed to have such wonderful friends who encouraged one another and would keep each other accountable.

The evening ended by eating more of the food that remained, and then they started to leave, except for Aaron.

"This was a great afternoon, April, and you were a wonderful hostess. This house has truly been a blessing, and now you've made it into a welcoming home for others to enjoy as well. I love you even more than before," Aaron said as he wrapped his arms around her. "And as I watch you bloom with God's love, you're even more beautiful. How about if we watch a movie together before I take you back to your mom's house? I don't want this day to end yet."

"Sounds good to me. You pick out a movie, and I'll light the candles," April said as she left his arms.

But she was looking forward to cuddling up again on the sofa. Being in his arms made her feel very warm, comfortable, and loved.

School started up again the next day. It was hard to go back to the old routine after having such a wonderful time off with Jenny, Aaron, her mom, and friends. But it didn't take long to see that her students needed her love and attention also. Some of them shared some of their exciting holiday experiences, while others had to split their time between divorced parents or single parents who didn't have much money for presents or special activities. April would have to see what she could do to reach out to more of her students. She decided to pray about it and would ask her young adult group to pray with her.

Jenny called the next evening and shared with April and her mom that she and Brent had a long talk, and Brent said he wanted what Jenny had. So Jenny and Brent had prayed together, and Brent turned his life over to the Lord and asked for forgiveness for his selfishness and pride. They would both go for counseling with the pastor of their church, and if he agreed, they wanted to get married again.

"Probably in the spring," Jenny said. "But I need to know when you have spring break, April, so we can plan it for then. I want you and Mom to be able to come, and I'd like you to stand up with me, April."

"Oh, Jenny, I'm so happy for you! That's wonderful news. And yes, of course I'll stand up with you. It would be my honor and pleasure! Let me check the school schedule, and I'll get back to you."

"It will be a simple wedding, just for family and close friends. We already had our big wedding, but this one will be even more meaningful, as we'll be committing our marriage to God and allowing Him to lead our lives and family."

Jenny talked to her mom also, and when she hung up, they both cried tears of joy and thanked God for answering their prayers. When April shared the good news with Aaron, he asked if she would share her testimony and Jenny's answer to prayer with the group on Thursday evening. April did, and she included her prayer request of ways she could help her students who needed extra help and love that they weren't getting at home. They spent a lot of time praying together, and April really felt that God was doing a mighty work among them.

In fact, one of the young adults came up to her afterward and asked if she could tutor one or two of her students after school and spend some time with them, just to get to know them on a personal basis. She said she would even like to take them out for a burger or ice cream once in a while. April thought that was a great idea but wondered if that could be done on a larger scale with more volunteers. She decided to talk to the principal and see if it would even be a possibility. The principal said they had a tutoring program in place, and those interested in tutoring would just have to fill out an application and go through a background check.

So the principal gave her applications to be filled out, and the parents would need to sign permission slips for the students who desired to participate in the tutoring program. More young adults and other adults from April's church volunteered to spend time tutoring children in the elementary, as well as teens in the high school. It would make a real difference in those kids' lives as they helped them with their studies, but also as they built positive relationships with them and showed them the love they desired and hungered for.

April moved into her home at the end of January. The bedrooms were done two weeks earlier, but the fresh paint and new carpet smells were pretty strong, so she waited a while for it to air out a little. It also gave her time to get her bedroom organized and office set up. She didn't have furniture for the extra bedroom, but that would come in time.

When April went to visit Lydia again, she brought her photo album of the before, during renovation, and after pictures, with her son's permission. Lydia had shared with her son how she'd asked about the house and was excited that April was making it her own and doing the updates that she was never able to do. He felt that his mother was now ready to see the pictures. And as April showed her the photo album, Lydia got tears in her eyes but also had a big smile on her face.

"Oh, April, what you've done to the house is more amazing than I could have ever imagined," Lydia marveled with a smile. "It's just beautiful, and so charming! I'm surprised to say that I even love the openness, as it still has the classic look with the old wood-trim, staircase and doors. And I love the stone fireplace and mantel. It looks like it was always meant to be in that corner of the living room. And that bench by the bay window is so lovely and inviting. We must have similar tastes, for I always wanted one there.

"And what you've done with that kitchen and adding that pantry is something I wish I'd done years ago. That kitchen was always so small, but now you've made it more functional. I had to store so many things in the basement as I didn't have enough storage space. Now you won't have to go up and down those basement stairs so often like I did. Of course, it was good exercise. My husband always said it kept me fit and trim. Oh, you'll be able to entertain your guests so much easier with the way you've designed it."

"Actually, I didn't do it all myself. Aaron, my mom, my friend Bonnie, and the designer from the construction company helped quite a bit with the plans and ideas. And even though I wasn't moved in yet, I already had guests over on New Year's Day. They loved it too, and we had a prayer of dedication for the house. I want it to be used for God's glory and hope to have other occasions when I can use it to encourage and share God's love with others."

Lydia looked at April closely and then said, "You seem to be more at peace since your last visit, April. Is there something else you'd like to share with me?"

"Yes, as a matter of fact, there is. When my sister was here at Christmastime, she said some of the same things you shared with me at our last visit. That I was letting my fears rule my life and not letting God be in control or trusting Him with my future. So on Christmas Day, before I went to sleep, I prayed and asked God to remove the walls of fear from my heart and fill it with His love. I told Him I wanted to follow His plan for my life and not mine."

"Well, I can see that God answered your prayer, my dear. Your face glows with His love. And what about your young man? What was his name again?"

"Aaron," April said with a smile.

"Ah, yes, Aaron. I liked that boy. So have you told him that you love him yet?"

"Yes," April admitted as her cheeks turned a blushing pink.

"Good! And I want to be invited to your wedding, don't forget."

"He hasn't asked me yet."

"Well, he will. And be sure you give him the right answer this time," Lydia advised.

"I will, Lydia. I promise!" April kissed her on the cheek and promised to visit her again soon.

Chapter 26

Jenny and Brent's wedding was scheduled for March 17. April and her mom would stay after the wedding to take care of Nick and Arietta while Jenny and Brent went on a five-day honeymoon to St. Lucia. April was excited for them and so glad God had brought that family back together again. God was so good!

In the meantime, April was looking forward to Valentine's Day. She'd gotten something special for Aaron and was anxious to see his response. Aaron said he planned to take her out to dinner and then they'd come back to her home for some quiet time together.

April and Bonnie went shopping in Duluth for a new dress for April to wear on Valentine's Day and Jenny's wedding. She chose a black A-line dress with cap sleeves and a scooped neckline that would be easy to accessorize for either occasion. For her dinner with Aaron, she purchased red jewelry and a wide red leather belt that really dressed it up. She also picked out green and black jewelry and a green cropped cardigan to wear with the dress for the wedding. Then they looked at maternity clothes for Bonnie. Bonnie didn't need them yet but would soon, so they found a few outfits she could wear to start out with and would shop later for more summery outfits.

Valentine's Day came, and April was glad that it was warmer than normal and not snowing. It had been a busy day at school, with much excitement during the student's Valentine's Day party. When she got home, she tidied up the house a bit, took a relaxing shower, and was ready when Aaron arrived. He looked very handsome in his black dress pants, gray shirt, and red tie while he handed her a bouquet of red roses.

"Thank you, Aaron. They're lovely!"

"Not nearly as lovely as you," Aaron said as he leaned down and gave her a kiss and a big smile.

"Let me put these in water, and I'll get my coat."

The restaurant was busy, and April was glad Aaron had made reservations. Dinner was delicious! They both had ordered a steak dinner but decided to pass on dessert. Aaron had been all smiles and full of compliments all evening, even as they went back to the house and sat on the sofa.

"You're so beautiful!" Aaron began as he took her hand in his and looked into her eyes. "And not just tonight when you're all dressed up, but I think you're beautiful all the time, inside and out. You have such a sweet spirit and are kind and thoughtful to your family, to me, to your friends, and your students. April, I love you very much, and I've been waiting all evening to ask you if you will be my wife."

With that, he reached into his pants pocket, pulled out a ring box, opened it, and waited for April's answer.

He didn't have to wait long as April smiled and, with tears running down her face, replied, "Oh, Aaron, yes! I would be honored to be your wife!"

With that, she gave him a kiss that told him she had no more reservations or fears and loved him very much.

"You've made me so happy with your answer, and you'd make me even happier if you would agree to a short engagement," Aaron began with a nervous smile. "I know you're busy with school and Jenny's wedding coming up, but what do you think of getting married sometime this summer?"

"I think I've made you wait long enough. I want to thank you for your patience, understanding, and prayers, but I don't want to wait long either. I've always thought a June wedding would be nice. Would that be soon enough?" April asked with a big smile.

Aaron wrapped her in his arms and gave her his answer with a passionate kiss.

"And I don't want a fancy wedding with a lot of expense," April began after he released her. "I've put a lot of money into this house, and I'd prefer a simple wedding that's meaningful to us, and then invest in our life together instead."

"I couldn't agree more. You pick the date and we'll plan it together. It will be wonderful, just knowing that you'll be my wife and we'll be building a life together, with God as our guide."

"Amen to that!" April agreed and sealed it with a kiss. "Oh, but with all the excitement, I almost forgot I have a gift for you too. It's not as glamorous as a ring, but I hope you'll like it. But it was too big to bring in the house, so you'll have to go out to the garage to see it."

"Now you've made me curious. Lead the way, oh lovely one," Aaron said as he waved his hand to allow her to go ahead of him.

When they got out to the garage, Aaron saw a large item covered with a red cloth and a big white bow on it.

"Wow, I wonder what that could be?" Aaron asked as he gazed at it.

"Well, take the cover off and you'll find out!"

When Aaron did, he gasped with surprise as he looked at a large outdoor grill.

"Wow, I've really wanted one of these," Brad said, putting his hand on his chest.

"I know. While I was putting things away in January, I heard you talking to someone and you'd said you wanted one and hoped to get it before summer. So I checked at the hardware store to see if they had one in the back, and they did. So they delivered it here so I could surprise you with it."

"Well, you definitely did that. This is amazing! And it has all the features I wanted," Aaron said as he looked it over.

"The salesman at the hardware store said it was one of their most popular grills from last summer, so they kept it and were going to put it out in a few months at a discount, since it was last year's model. But they gave me the discount now since I bought all the appliances, paint, and a lot of other things from them. I think they like seeing me come into their store."

"I would like to see you in my arms so I can give you a proper thank-you."

April went willingly into his arms and was rewarded with a kiss that let her know how much he liked her gift.

"That was a very nice thank-you," April said when he released her. "I guess you liked it, huh?"

"I liked you in my arms even better, especially since it's cold out here. Let's go back inside where it's warmer, and if you don't mind, I'll leave the cooker here, as I'll probably use it here more than at my place anyway."

April agreed and they went inside. April offered to make him some coffee and cut the chocolate chip cheesecake she'd gotten for their dessert, and she put cherries on top. It was a nice finale to their romantic evening.

April and Aaron chose June 24 for their wedding date and enjoyed working on wedding plans during their free time together. They reserved the church and set up counseling appointments with their pastor. Aaron asked his brother and Brad to stand up with him, and when April called Jenny, she was very excited about the news. She happily agreed to be her matron of honor, and Nick and Arietta were thrilled to be their aunt's ring bearer and flower girl.

When April asked Bonnie to be her bridesmaid, she said, "You know I would be honored to be in your wedding, but I'll be over seven months pregnant by then and as big as a house. Are you sure you want a pregnant woman as your bridesmaid? I'd be just as happy with another job if you'd rather ask someone else."

"Are you kidding? I don't want anyone but you. You'll be beautiful, and I'd be proud to have you stand up with me. We've been through a lot together, and I want you to be a part of my wedding as well."

"Well then, I'd consider it an honor to be your bridesmaid!" Bonnie said as she gave her a hug. "We better enjoy these hugs while we can because by June, this baby will be getting in the way."

Barb was very happy for her and knew that this was a great victory for April, for she had released her fears and now loved the man God had provided for her. To have both her daughters in love and happy was truly a blessing and answer to her prayers.

When April and Aaron went to visit Lydia and told her the good news, she was overjoyed and said, "I hate to say this but, I told you so!"

Then she laughed and gave them both a hug.

April showed her the ring and said with a smile, "I'll be sure and listen to you next time. We've set the date for June 24, and you can consider yourself invited, though we'll bring you an invitation once we get them printed."

"I'll be there, God willing!" Lydia said with a smile.

March had warmed up and the snow was melting fast, so the construction company said they would be able to start the renovation process on the outside of her home soon, and they needed to know what she wanted ordered. April had enough money to do the siding but not the addition. However, Aaron offered to pay for the addition so the house would be completed by their wedding day.

"You've invested a lot of money into this home, and we'll soon be a married couple, so let me do the addition. I've been putting money away, as I was hoping to build a house for us some day. But when I saw the house you chose, I knew that I wanted it to be our dream home together. I loved it from the moment I saw it, just as you did. The colors and choices you've made in finishing and decorating this home has really made it lovely and inviting, and it also brings out your personality. I will love living in this home with you, and besides," Aaron smiled, "it will be nice to have a bathroom and utility room on the main floor."

"I couldn't agree more, so I accept your generous offer. But I want you to know that I also realize how much love and effort you've already put into this house. This has been a labor of love by both of us from day one. And it will continue to be a home that is filled with love for us, our friends, and, one day hopefully, our family."

"Yes, that would be another dream come true for me—you and me and a family of our own living in this house. So now we need to pick out the color for the siding so they can get it ordered, as well as the windows and new door for the porch. Any ideas?"

"Well, I know I want the same faux stone as the fireplace to be put on the bottom part of the porch and on the sides of the new steps, as Ed suggested. And I think a tan color for the siding. What do you think?"

After looking at the different colors, they chose a khaki color as it would make the stone a nice contrast to the house, and would also go well with the brown steel roofing that was already installed. They would go with the premium vinyl insulated siding and an insulation vapor wrap to make the house more energy efficient. Then they picked a thirty-six-inch steel entry door in Colonial Red, with twelve-inch sidelights on each side to add a pop of color to the front of the house. They had windows on the top half in order to match the windows around the porch. Then they chose new double hung windows in white for the porch but wider than the current ones. A window for the addition was also chosen, but April wanted that one to be a slider.

"Okay, I'll have them order the supplies we'll need then. We should be able to start on the addition soon, so it can all be sided at the same time," Aaron informed April. "The only other decisions will be the color for the inside of the addition and what items you'll want to purchase. But we have some time before we need to do that. Let's not talk business anymore tonight. How about I order us a pizza and we relax with a movie?"

"Oh, that sounds like a wonderful idea!" April agreed with a sigh.

Chapter 27

The addition and outside renovations began, and April was excited to see them happen, for that meant they were going to have their home finished before the wedding. The freezer, washer, and dryer that were in the basement were still in good condition; so April and Aaron decided to move them upstairs when the room was finished. They chose a sienna red for the walls and delicate white for the trim. They purchased the same flooring, style of cabinets, and countertops as the pantry but added a tall cabinet for storage, a table for folding laundry, and a new sink and toilet. They'd have to add electric heat for that room as well.

Now that those decisions were made, April could concentrate on packing for Jenny's wedding in Lansing. They decided to fly rather than drive and were able to get good prices on the tickets. It would save a lot of time, and Aaron would fly home after the wedding so he could continue to work on the house. April and her mom would stay and watch Nick and Arietta while Jenny and Brent were on their honeymoon.

The wedding was simple but very special, with only family and close friends in attendance. The minister read verses from Ephesians 5 and shared that Brent and Jenny were making a new commitment to love each other as Christ loved the church, for He willingly gave His life for His bride, the church. As they said their vows, which they'd written themselves, you could see the genuine love they had for each other on their faces, and there wasn't a dry eye in the room. April looked on with thankfulness to God for answered prayer and a smile on her face.

After the ceremony, they went to a restaurant for dinner where Brent had reserved a room for their guests. It was a joyous celebration, and everyone enjoyed visiting and congratulating the couple.

April and her mom enjoyed their time with Nick and Arietta, as the kids were on spring break as well. Jenny and Brent came back excited about their trip and shared pictures of things they'd done and seen in St. Lucia but were also glad to be home to see their children again.

When April came back to Ironwood, she was excited to hear how her students had spent their spring break and see the progress made on the front porch. They had to replace some of the boards that were rotted, but now the new windows were in and the new door was also installed. And it was none too soon—as the following week, it turned colder and they had a snowstorm with ten inches of new snow, which was not unusual for the month of March. But it soon melted, and they were able to begin work again and started on the footings for the new addition.

Aaron's family said they would come for Easter so they could meet April and get to know her and her mom before the wedding. They lived in Minneapolis, and Aaron's mom was also a teacher. April hoped they would get along well. Aaron's younger brother, Jeff, who would be his best man, was coming as well. Jeff would stay with Aaron, and his parents would stay with April's mom, since April didn't have furniture in her spare bedroom yet.

The month of April brought warmer weather, so they were able to get the shell up on the addition. Easter weekend turned out to be sunny and in the sixties, so they had a pleasant time with Aaron's family. They split their time between April's home and her mom's, but Easter dinner was in April's home. Aaron's mom kept raving about how wonderful the house had turned out after April showed them her album of the before, during, and after renovation pictures. Aaron's parents were very proud of the part their son had in doing the renovations.

"Aaron always loved building things, even when he was a boy," his mom informed. "This will be a wonderful home in which to build your life together. We can tell that you love each other, so it will be an honor for us to welcome you into our family, April."

With that, Aaron's mom and dad presented them with a plaque that said, "What I love most about my home is who I share it with."

"We'll be praying that you always keep this as your focus," Aaron's dad said. "This home is lovely, but working on your relationship is even more important than all the improvements you've made on this home."

"Thanks, Mom and Dad," Aaron said as he accepted the plaque and hugged them both. "This means a lot to us, and we'll find a special place for it and be reminded of it often."

April thanked them as well and was enveloped in a welcoming hug.

Her family was growing, and she knew she would enjoy getting to know Aaron's family more in the future. God was truly blessing her with people who loved and accepted her.

After Easter, the April showers began, but they were able to work on the inside of the addition. It progressed quickly; and by May, they began working on the siding, front steps, and sidewalk. The steps and part of the sidewalk would be widened to the edge of the porch on the left and go just beyond the sidelight on the right side of the door.

The three steps would have concrete risers that would go up to the bottom of the windows, with cheek walls in white that would slant down and replace the iron railings on each side of the steps. However, April wanted the top step to be deeper so there would be a longer landing in front of the door. The faux stone would be put on the bottom of the porch and the interior and exterior of the step risers, which would give the house a nice, inviting entrance. April was very pleased with how the outside of the house would look when it was finished, for though it would look very different, it would still have a classic charm to it.

Aaron had decided that since they were coming with concrete for the steps, he also wanted them to pour concrete in the backyard where he'd prepared a spot for a covered outdoor patio off the side of the garage, which would be sixteen by twenty-four feet. It would replace the patio they'd turned into their addition but with a larger area to enjoy the backyard and for entertaining.

By the end of May, with the outside of the house and back patio done—and to follow the tradition that Bonnie and Brad had started the year before—April and Aaron invited Bonnie and Brad over on the Saturday afternoon of Memorial weekend to plant a flowerbed in front of the house. Aaron had prepared the ground and put in an edging ahead of time, but since April wasn't the gardener that Bonnie was and the area was much smaller, they decided to keep it simple. They planted two burning bush plants in the middle, some boxwoods on each end, and a few annuals in between for a pop of color. Then they put redwood cedar mulch down to keep the moisture in, have less weeds, and hopefully, keep the deer out.

"Well, I'd say this is a job well done," Brad said as they stood back to take in the finished look. "April and Aaron, you've done a fantastic job with this house. You've revived the old style of the house with a modern twist, and it looks really great! We hope you'll enjoy this home for a long time to come."

"Thank you, Brad," Aaron responded. "It's been a lot of hard work, but I think the end results are well worth it. We had good bones to start with, and April added great ideas to really make it turn out beautifully."

"Well, I didn't do it alone. This was all new to me, so without Ed's suggestions, as well as Aaron's, Mom's, and Bonnie's help, it certainly wouldn't have come out this well. So thank you all for your support, suggestions, and encouragement."

She gave Aaron a kiss and Brad and Bonnie each a hug.

"Now I'm sure you've all worked up an appetite, so let's move to the backyard. We can put things away, get washed up, and Aaron will get the grill going. Bonnie and I will get the food ready and set the table. I don't know about you guys, but I'm getting hungry."

"Me too," Bonnie replied as they walked toward the backyard. "Since I've been pregnant, I always seem to be hungry."

"You're eating for two now," Aaron said.

"The doctor says that's not really true, and I have to be careful not to gain too much weight or it'll be hard to take off later," Bonnie informed.

After they washed up, Brad took the meat out for Aaron to put on the grill while April and Bonnie stayed inside and got the rest of the food ready.

"I'm so glad I haven't had morning sickness like so many others I've talked to, but I sure have been tired," Bonnie said as they worked together. "It seems I always have to take a nap after school before I can make supper. I'm glad school is almost done, and I'll be able to rest when I need to this summer. Brad doesn't want me helping him in the shop this summer as he thinks it will be too much for me. He's even planning on putting air-conditioning in the house. It would sure make it more comfortable. But I'll need to do something with my time besides getting the nursery ready, so I'm thinking of learning to sew. Molly said she'd teach me."

"I'm sure air-conditioning will be a big help. By the way, how are you coming with the nursery?"

"I think I've found the crib and furniture I want to order. I'll bring the pictures to school next week to show you. And we've decided to go with a baby animal theme for the decorations. That way, it will work whether it's a boy or a girl."

"That would be really cute. But don't you want to find out if it's a boy or a girl?" April asked.

"We really don't care, as long as it's healthy. Even if it isn't, we'll love him or her anyway."

"That's a good attitude to have. I'm so happy for you, Bonnie. This is an exciting adventure for you, even more so than renovating a house."

They carried out the dishes, food, and drinks and soon everything was ready for them to eat. Aaron asked the blessing on the food, and the conversation turned to April and Aaron's wedding.

"So how are the wedding plans coming, April? It's only four weeks away now," Bonnie began.

"Well, I have my dress, you have yours, and Jenny called to say that she found her dress in Lansing last week and that it will look really nice with yours, even though they won't be matching. Nick will wear the black pair of dress pants he wore at his parents' wedding with a white shirt and gray vest, and Arietta will wear a white dress with pink and purple flowers on it. Arietta's favorite colors are pink and purple, so she's very happy about that," April said with a chuckle. "That girl is obsessed with purple, so when Mom and I ordered the flowers two weeks ago, I had her put some purple flowers in the arrangements. We ordered from the same flower shop you went to and are renting the white archway as well. So we're set with that part of the wedding."

"We mailed the last of the invitations this week, so that job is done too," Aaron added. "And, Brad, you'll be happy to know that April has conceded to let us men wear black dress pants with a white shirt and gray vest instead of a suit. But she did insist on the pink ties. But as you well know, in a marriage, we have to learn to compromise and give in to some things."

"Well, I think I can handle that for a few hours," Brad agreed with a smile.

"I really would have liked to have an outdoor wedding, but you can't depend on the weather, so I'm hoping to give the platform a summery, outdoor feel. And if the weather is nice, we'll have the reception outside," April chimed in.

"That sounds nice. Is there anything you need help with? You know I'd love to help with anything I can," Bonnie volunteered.

"Well, you were a great help with the decorating ideas for the house. Maybe you can help me think of ways to give the sanctuary a summery, outdoor feel."

"All right, I'll think about it and let you know what I come up with," Bonnie agreed.

It was a beautiful day, and they enjoyed the afternoon outside, as well as the fellowship with great friends. The covered patio with the new patio furniture was definitely a nice addition as it gave them a nice shaded area and an entertainment space in their backyard. They hoped to have many more opportunities for entertaining friends and family in their home and their backyard during the coming months.

Chapter 28

The last week of school was always crazy. It had warmed up into the eighties, so the kids were anxious to be outside, and April was glad they'd planned some outdoor activities. Their class picnic was a lot of fun, and many of her students came up to her and said how much they'd enjoyed having her for a teacher and wished her much happiness with her marriage to Mr. Matthews.

Matthews—I will have to get used to that last name, as it will soon be mine, April realized. For in a few weeks' time, she would become *Mrs. Aaron Matthews*. She liked the way that sounded.

After school was done, books put away, bulletin boards taken down, and report cards turned in, April could concentrate on finishing up things for their wedding. The first thing on the agenda was her bridal shower. Bonnie and Missy had planned it for Saturday, but instead of having it at the church, it would be in April's home.

So many of the ladies at church, and her coworkers, were anxious to see the house now that it was completed, so she thought it would be a good way to do both at the same time. April's bridal shower would be at eleven, so Bonnie and Missy were there by nine to get everything ready. Barb came also to help where needed. They set up folding chairs they'd brought from church for extra seating, hung pink and white decorations on the staircase and around the house, and arranged the food on the dining room table, which they'd pushed back against the wall, with drinks on the island. The gifts would be placed around the fireplace. They had everything ready by the time the ladies started arriving.

Everyone commented on how beautiful the house looked. It was transformed from an old, tired house to a unique, warm, and inviting home, but still had a lot of character. They loved the colors she chose for the walls and cupboards, as they pulled everything together and were very welcoming. April was very pleased, for that was what she'd hoped for in the design.

After everyone had their tour and punch, they started with the games, and everyone seemed to have a good time, with much interaction and laughter. Bonnie then gave a devotion on love and marriage; which April thought was very thought provoking and asked for a copy of it to read again later. For lunch, they served different kinds of salads—pasta, lettuce, coleslaw, broccoli, and fruit salads—along with breads and buns. For dessert, they had vanilla ice cream with all kinds of toppings. It was simple but very delicious. Everyone raved about it.

Then April opened her gifts. She was amazed and grateful for all the lovely items she received. There were colorful sheets and blankets; beautiful, fluffy new towels; items for the kitchen, and candles for her home, as well as decorations and personal items for the bride-to-be. She couldn't stop oohing and aahing over each one. Saying thank you just didn't seem like enough.

Aaron came toward the end and also expressed his thankfulness and visited with the ladies. She was so proud of him! Not every man would be so brave and considerate.

After things were put back in place and everyone left, April and Aaron looked over their gifts again and decided to begin writing thank-you cards right away, washing things up, and putting them away, in order to get a sense of order back to their home. They got part of it done and would finish after church the next day.

When they finished the thank-you cards at four o'clock on Sunday, April asked, "What about the wedding service? We told Pastor the scripture passage and general items we want for the service, but are there any particular songs that you'd want for the wedding ceremony, Aaron? I want it to be worshipful and meaningful to us but also have a good message for those who attend."

"Well, for a worship song, I really like 'Ten Thousand Reasons.' I think it has a lot of meaning, but I wouldn't know about any other songs. Did you have some in mind?"

"Not really, but maybe we can go on YouTube and pick out some we'd like."

So they listened to music the rest of the afternoon and evening, then picked out songs they felt were meaningful to them as a couple and decided who to ask to sing them or if they would be played from YouTube. Then they decided where the songs would be most appropriate in the service. April was getting more and more excited for their special day.

April met with Bonnie the next morning at her home. Bonnie showed her the ideas she had for the nursery.

"I found this material with baby animals all over it and will use it for making curtains for the windows. Isn't it cute? It really goes well with our theme. And I found this soft flannel material for blankets. Molly will be coming over later this week to help me sew them. She said simple paneled curtains and receiving blankets would be something easy for me to start with. I ordered the crib and dresser I showed you, and Brad is going to get me a rocker for the nursery too."

"Oh, Bonnie, it's going to be adorable! I'm so happy for you and Brad. You're going to be wonderful parents! So are you getting more rest now that school is done?"

"Yes, Brad makes sure I lay down every afternoon. I don't always sleep, but just resting makes a big difference. And now that it's getting warmer, my legs are starting to swell if I'm on my feet too much. But the baby is getting more active and doesn't always rest when I try to." Bonnie grabbed her stomach. "Ooh, there he goes now. Do you want to feel him kick? He's really quite strong."

Bonnie placed April's hand on the side of her stomach, and April felt the baby's movement.

"Wow, that's amazing! But you said 'he.' Do you think it's a boy?"

"Oh, I don't know. But I don't like calling the baby 'it,' and I think Brad really wants a boy. He says it doesn't really matter, but we'll have to wait and see."

"So do you want your baby shower before or after the baby's born? We should really be thinking about it soon."

"Since I don't have a lot of baby things yet, I suppose it would be better to have it before. But it makes it harder for people to know what to get without knowing the gender."

"There are still many things that you'll need that don't depend on gender like diapers, among other things. Besides, many people now give gift receipts so you can always exchange it if you need to. You let me know which you prefer," April suggested.

"Well, you have enough on your plate right now with your wedding coming up. So why don't we get going on that? Have you come up with any ideas on decorations?" Bonnie asked.

"Well, the wedding is at two in the afternoon, and we should be able to have the entry doors open, so I want something on that wall in the entry as people walk in. The stained-glass window is there, and I plan on putting a stand with the guest book underneath it.

"Then I was thinking of maybe getting two tall vases and putting silk flower arrangements in them to put on each side of the stand with the guest book. I could always use the vases and arrangements in the house after the wedding so they'd have a double purpose. The gift table will be by the staircase on the left with a pink cloth covering on it and clear lights draped around the railing of the staircase."

"Oh, that will be beautiful! What about inside the sanctuary? Any ideas there?" Bonnie asked.

"That's where I need your help. We can use the trees that are already in the sanctuary and puts lights on them as well, and I'll have the white arch from the flower shop that I'm renting. But I'd really like some flowers in there too, but they can get expensive. So I need some ideas that would be cost effective."

April and Bonnie put their heads together and came up with some great ideas that would work well for the service, as well as the songs she and Aaron had chosen. April was now even more excited for her wedding day to occur.

Chapter 29

Aaron's parents and brother Jeff arrived the Wednesday before the wedding to help with preparations. His parents again stayed with April's mom, and Jeff stayed with Aaron to help him get his apartment packed up and emptied. Brad helped them move his living room furniture into the porch, moved his bedroom furniture into their spare bedroom, his clothes into their closet, and all other items into the garage to sort through later. Then Aaron and Jeff stayed with Mike, the youth pastor of their church, until the wedding day.

Jenny, Brent, and the kids flew in on Friday morning and were staying at a nearby hotel that had a swimming pool for the kids.

"It will be easier not to have the kids underfoot and give them something to do," Jenny said.

Brent stayed with the kids while Jenny helped decorate.

When the day of the wedding finally came, April was nervous but excited to become Mrs. Aaron Matthews. She was so grateful that God had released her from her fears and she'd learned to trust God with her life. She knew it would be a continual learning process, but she no longer felt alone—for now she'd have God and Aaron by her side. And today, she also had her mom, Jenny, and Bonnie to help her get ready.

It was chaotic at times, but they all got ready on time, and everyone looked beautiful. Her mom would be walking her down the aisle and was wearing a pink crinkle sheath dress and jacket set. Jenny wore a pink lacy fit and flare dress, and Bonnie wore a solid-pink pleated fit and flare dress. Bonnie was seven months pregnant, but April had never seen a more beautiful and glowing pregnant woman. Arietta loved her flared white dress with pink and purple flowers on it. She enjoyed twirling in it and showing off her favorite colored flowers.

April's dress was white Victorian lace over satin, with cap sleeves, a V-neckline, and a silver beaded belt at the empire waistline and had covered buttons down the back from the neck to the waist. It flared out at the bottom with a long train. The veil was attached at the back of her head and flowed down to her hips. She felt beautiful in it and was sure Aaron would think she was as well.

"You are a beautiful woman and a beautiful bride," Barb said as she hugged her daughter before they left the room to go out to the foyer. "I am so proud of you. You've released your fears and have learned to trust your life into God's hands. You've chosen a godly man to love and cherish, and I know God will continue to lead and guide you in your life together. I love you so much!"

"I love you too, Mom! Thank you for your prayers and for being willing to say the hard things that I needed to hear. And thank you for all your support this past year with the house and the wedding. You've been my rock and a great encouragement."

With that, they released each other and headed out to the foyer of the church.

April was pleased with the way they'd decorated the foyer and the sanctuary the day before. Her mom and Jeff, Aaron's brother, had surprised her with a two-by-six-foot cloth banner to hang above the stand and guest book that read, "Dreams Do Come True!" Under the words were their names, *April and Aaron*, with entwined wedding rings in between.

On the left side of the banner was an eleven-by-fourteen picture of April and Aaron kayaking together, and on the right, a picture of their new home they had worked so hard to renovate. She didn't know Jeff was so artistic, as the banner and the pictures were beautifully done and very thoughtful. They really depicted the three dreams they'd accomplished in the last year, with their wedding being the most important.

The trees in the sanctuary had been draped with clear lights and glowed with expectancy. The steps going up to the platform had a plant stand on each side with Bonnie's large potted pink geraniums on them to give the added color and life April had hoped for.

"I knew I planted pink geraniums for a reason. I planted red last year, but God prompted me to plant pink this year," Bonnie had said with a smile when she brought the plants the day before.

On the right side of the platform, they put the white archway, covered in pink artificial climbing roses, with a white wedding bell hanging from the center. A small table was placed under it, draped with a white cloth, and on it was their pink unity candle on one of her wide candleholders she'd gotten for Christmas, with a white tapered candle in clear glass candleholders on each side.

On the left side of the platform, they had draped a light blue cloth over a large blackboard stand to depict a summer sky and a slightly darker blue cloth over the bottom of the stand and the floor in front of it for the lake. On the darker blue cloth, they had put Aaron's kayak, signifying that this was when their relationship began and April's first dream accomplished. However, Aaron had surprised her at the rehearsal the evening before with another kayak for a wedding gift. It was the yellow one she'd admired the previous summer. He'd put a large white bow on it, so now they had two. On the center of the back wall of the platform hung the quilt that Jenny and Brent had given them for a wedding gift. It was a wedding-ring pattern in blues and pinks with a cream background, made by the ladies from their church.

April and Aaron had chosen the song "Dreams Come True" to be played from YouTube as the bridal party entered the sanctuary. Then April walked down the aisle on her mom's arm while the wedding march was played and she met Aaron at the front. As she looked into his eyes, she knew today would be a day to remember and cherish; for they were to be united in marriage with God, their family and friends as witnesses.

The pastor used 1 Corinthians 13:4–13 as a challenge for them to love each other as God directed them. He ended his talk with the verses that were on their wedding bulletin: "'And so, we know and rely on the love God had for us. God is love! … There is no fear in love. But perfect love casts out fear' (1 John 4:16, 18 NIV).

"April and Aaron have learned this lesson together and released their fears to God, and now He has replaced that fear with His perfect love," the pastor added. "May they continue in this love for many years to come. In celebration of this love, they've asked that we give God the glory and entrust their lives to Him by singing together one of Aaron's favorite songs, 'Ten Thousand Reasons.' The worship team will lead us, and the words will be on the screen."

After the song, they repeated their vows, exchanged rings, and while the song, "This Is the Day (A Wedding Song)" was played, along with the video on the screen, they lit their unity candle with the individually lit tapered candles and blew them out, leaving only their unity candle aglow. What a great illustration of two lives becoming one!

Once the pastor pronounced them as husband and wife, Aaron kissed April with a kiss that she knew was a promise of his undying love, and she returned it with her promise as well. As they walked down the aisle, two of their friends, along with the worship team, sang the closing song, "All of the Above." It was a very meaningful service for them and, they hoped, for others as well.

The weather turned out to be a perfect summer day with a soft breeze, so they were able to have the reception line outside and serve the wedding cake and ice cream on the lawn of the church. It worked out perfectly and gave them time to visit with their guests. One of her favorite guests was Lydia, whom she had given the honor of being her adopted grandmother, since April didn't have one, and was wearing her corsage proudly.

Her son had brought her in her wheelchair, and she said, "I wouldn't have missed this day for the world. You've become very special to me, and I hope you'll continue to visit me. I'm honored to have you as my new granddaughter."

After the pictures were taken and before they prepared to go, April threw her bouquet. She was glad when Missy caught it, since that was who she'd aimed it for. Missy had become a good friend, and she wished her all the happiness that she'd found.

April and Aaron spent five days honeymooning on Madeline Island, near Bayfield, Wisconsin. They enjoyed visiting all the unique shops and restaurants, taking walks on the island, and relaxing on the beach. They'd brought their kayaks, so they were able to go kayaking along the shore and to other neighboring islands as well. It was very relaxing after all their hard work renovating the house and getting things ready for the wedding. But they also looked forward to getting back home and beginning their life together.

April knew she would need to make some changes. She knew it would no longer be *her* home but now would be *their* home. Life would be full of challenges but also new dreams to look forward to. Her summer dreams had come true, and now she and Aaron would make new dreams and enjoy making them become a reality, with God's guidance.

She wondered what God had in store for their future. Whatever it was, she knew she could trust God with knowing what was best and that He would be with them each step of the way.

Book III

Autumn Discoveries

"For I know the plans I have for you," declares the Lord,
"plans to prosper you and not to harm you, plans to give
you hope and a future. Then you will call on me and
come and pray to me, and I will listen to you.
You will seek me and find me when you
seek me with all your heart."

—Jeremiah 29:11–13

Chapter 1

"Here are your new glasses, Mrs. Cooper. Please put them on, and I'll see where we need to adjust them for you."

After adjusting the temples and nose pads, Missy gave them back to Mrs. Cooper. She put them on and looked in the mirror.

"Oh, they look lovely! You were so right about the color and shape of these new frames. They really do bring out the color of my eyes and even make me look younger. Thank you for taking the time to help me pick them out. I feel like a new woman."

"You're more than welcome, Mrs. Cooper. But I have to agree with you, I think you look ten years younger. And now, let's see how you can see with your new prescription since your cataract surgery," Missy said as she handed her a card to read from.

"My goodness, I can see all the way to the smallest print on the bottom, and everything is so much clearer and brighter when I look across the room. This is amazing!" Mrs. Cooper exclaimed with a smile.

"I'm so glad. Here's your new case and a cleaning cloth for your new lenses. They have the antireflective coating that I recommended for you, so it will cut down the glares from the fluorescent lights and night driving. Your frame and lenses come with a two-year warranty against breakage or scratches, so let us know if we can help you with anything. We've billed your insurance, and this is the balance that you owe today," Missy said as she pointed to the amount due.

"All right, I'll give you my debit card for that amount. And thank you again, Missy. I really dreaded the thought of picking out a new frame and lenses, but you made it so easy and fun. I really appreciate all your help," Mrs. Cooper said as she handed Missy her card.

"It was my privilege, and I enjoyed working with you. Stop by anytime if you need any adjustments or cleaner for your lenses," Missy said after swiping her card, giving Mrs. Cooper her receipt and card.

"Well, my grandchildren will be coming to visit in a few weeks. They can get kind of wild sometimes, so I may need them adjusted again. Goodbye, Missy, I may see you again soon."

"You have fun with those grandchildren and stop in anytime," Missy assured her.

She watched as Mrs. Cooper left and then went to help the next patient who had just come from seeing the doctor and had a new prescription. The technician introduced them and handed Missy his file, explaining what the doctor recommended. He was a teenager who was getting his first pair of glasses.

Missy enjoyed helping people find frames that would look good on them and make them feel good about themselves, as well as choosing lenses that would help them see better. It was a rewarding job, though at times challenging when she had to troubleshoot problems or had patients who had a difficult time making decisions. But it was never boring, as there was always new technology to learn about and frame styles to check out.

Missy had worked as a nurse's aide part time while in high school and brought a resident to the eye clinic to pick up her new glasses. After seeing how happy she was with her new glasses, how much better she could see, and how it had changed her whole attitude—Missy decided to check it out. There was an opening the summer after she graduated from high school at the eye clinic, so she applied, and they were willing to take her on part time and train her for the position.

She continued working there while she got her two-year accounting degree at Gogebic Community College, and when they offered her a full-time position after graduation, she decided to stay on. Her accounting degree came in handy when she dealt with balancing at the end of the day, working with the different insurance companies, and figuring out patients' coverage and balances. But her father was disappointed that she hadn't pursued a BA degree and wished she'd "do something more with her life." He was a loan officer at one of the local banks. It was a good job but also had more stress.

By the end of Missy's day, she felt good about the people she'd helped and the sales she made, though tired and glad to go home. Home was a two-bedroom apartment which she shared with Beth, a friend from high school, who was now a nurse at the local hospital. Missy and Beth had shared the apartment for a year now, but it hadn't worked out as Missy had hoped. They didn't work the same hours, so often weren't at the apartment at the same time. Also, they didn't have a lot in common, so they hadn't really bonded or done much together. However, Beth would be moving out soon as she was getting married the Saturday after Thanksgiving.

Missy usually kept busy with activities at her church and with friends and family. But it seemed many of her friends were either married, engaged, or had serious boyfriends. Missy was twenty-two years old and didn't even have a steady boyfriend. When she did go out, it was usually with friends from her young adult group at church, which was the case that evening.

She had plans to go kayaking with Emma and Julie and was to meet them at Black River Harbor at 6:30 p.m. So when she got home, she quickly changed clothes and put her long, dark-blonde, curly hair into a ponytail to keep it out of her face. Then she made a chicken sandwich and cut up some apple slices, which would give her quick energy. After eating, she grabbed a sweatshirt and headed out the door, glad that her kayak was still on top of her car.

Missy, short for Melissa, had lived in Ironwood, Michigan, all her life, which was in the Upper Peninsula of Michigan. It was a great place to live and grow up, for it offered many beautiful sights to enjoy. One could go hiking in the rolling hills and kayaking down the rivers, inland lakes, and, the most challenging, Lake Superior. It was the middle of September, and soon it would be the beginning of Autumn, her favorite season. She loved the changing colors of the leaves, less humidity, and more comfortable temperatures.

Missy parked her car close to the boat landing and noticed that Emma and Julie had just arrived as well. They unloaded their kayaks and carried them to the edge of the water.

"I'll stay with the kayaks while you get the lifejackets and paddles from our vehicles," Missy offered. "I can lock my car with my ignition key from here."

Emma and Julie went to get their life jackets and paddles and locked their vehicles. They planned to kayak out of the harbor and along the coast of Lake Superior so they could enjoy the colors of the leaves that had started to change. The water was fairly calm, the sun was shining, and it was a perfect evening to be out on the water.

"Oh, I've waited all day for this!" Emma said as they started out. "I had such a stressful time at work today. It seemed nothing went right, and the kids were either crying or fighting.

Emma worked at a daycare center, and though she loved working with children, there were days when she wondered if she'd chosen the right career.

"Oh, but you love it," Julie reminded her. "Tomorrow you'll be telling us how wonderful it was to have those babies' soft cheeks rubbing against yours or how those three-year-olds gave you kisses and said, 'I wov you, Miss Emma.' And then at story time, you'll pretend you're Sleeping Beauty and are kissed by your Prince Charming when you read to them from a storybook."

"Yes, I do love my job. But I think it would be even better if there were a real Prince Charming who would kiss me and carry me away to his castle. Then after a few years, I'd have my own baby to cuddle and a toddler who'd say, 'I wov you, Mama.' That would be my ideal job—just being a wife and mother," Emma said with a sigh.

"In God's time, Emma! In God's time," Missy reminded her as she came alongside.

"Well, I'm ready anytime God wants to send Prince Charming my way."

Will God send me a Prince Charming? Missy wondered. *Not that I'm looking for one, but I know I want to get married someday. What would he be like? Would I recognize him when I saw him? Oh, these are too many questions for an evening meant for relaxing and less stress. To be continued at a later date.*

They paddled offshore and enjoyed the beauty of the colored leaves on the trees. There were yellows and reds—but still some greens—so they'd be able to enjoy them for a few more weeks. If they got heavy rains or winds, they'd come down sooner, but Missy hoped that wouldn't be the case. They could see Porcupine Mountain off in the distance, and Missy hoped she'd be able to go hiking there soon.

Autumn was the best time to go hiking as it was cooler and not as many bugs. But Missy knew she needed to do it before too many leaves fell and got soaked by the rains, as then they'd become moldy and she was very allergic to mold. Missy was also allergic to dust and grasses, as well as gluten. She'd only found out about her allergies a few years prior and had wondered why she got sick so often. Now that she knew, she was learning what to watch out for and trying to be more careful. She'd also learned that there were many others who had similar allergies and was more sympathetic toward them.

After they turned around and headed back, they could see the beginning of a lovely sunset, which was even more beautiful than the leaves. The sky was lit with pinks, lavenders, and yellows against the blue skies and the few clouds that had appeared. By the time they got close to the entrance of the marina, the sun had sunk lower and the sky had more of a red, orange, and golden glow to it. It was true what the Psalmist said, "The heavens declare the glory of God; the skies proclaim the work of His hands" (Ps. 19:1).

The three of them stopped paddling to take in the grandeur of the sunset but couldn't gaze too long, as they wanted to get their kayaks loaded onto their vehicles before dark.

"This was definitely a good way to end our day," Julie said after they got everything loaded. "It was a beautiful evening, the leaves are starting to turn colors, we saw an awesome sunset, and the kayaking really helped me relax, so I'm sure I'll sleep good tonight. Thanks for agreeing to do this, Missy and Emma, I really enjoyed it. When can we do this again?"

"Well, I promised my mom I'd help her with some canning tomorrow after work, we have our young adult Bible study on Thursday evening, and on Friday, I promised Beth I'd help her with her wedding invitations. I have this weekend off but was hoping to do some hiking. So I don't have anything open for a while. How about you, Emma?"

"I'm pretty booked too. I have an Awana leadership, planning meeting tomorrow evening at church, and I promised my sister I'd help with my nephew's birthday party on Saturday, so I'll be making a birthday cake and helping with the decorations on Friday and Saturday."

"Well, thanks for tonight anyway. I guess we all have busy lives and it's not always easy to get together. Call me when we can do this again," Julie said as she waved to her friends and got into her car.

As Missy drove home, she thought about what Julie had said. It was true—they all lived busy lives. They had work commitments, family obligations, and personal things that needed to get done as well like laundry, cleaning, grocery shopping, and other obligations. Was she too busy? Did she have time to do what she wanted and enjoyed? Or was she always doing what others expected of her? More questions to contemplate.

Chapter 2

Missy brought her laundry when she went to her parent's home the next evening after work. She figured she might as well get two things done at the same time—laundry and making pickles. After Missy started her laundry, her mom put her to work scrubbing a sink full of cucumbers she'd picked earlier. They were going to make dill pickles out of the smaller ones and bread-and-butter pickles from the larger ones.

"I washed the jars and put dill and garlic in the ones for the dill pickles. You can add the smaller cucumbers into those after they're scrubbed. The larger cucumbers leave on the towel on the counter, and we'll slice them later. I'll get the pickle brine and hot water bath heating on the stove," her mom instructed.

Her mom had Christian music playing on the stereo, so Missy hummed along. They worked well together; and soon the dill pickle jars were filled with the brine, covered, and put into the hot water bath for fifteen minutes. Then Missy started slicing the larger cucumbers while her mom cut the onions for the bread-and-butter pickles. They'd have to soak in a large roaster pan with salt and ice cubes for three hours before draining and rinsing them, then they'd be heated in a brine-and-spice mixture. The house was smelling strongly of vinegar, spices, and onions.

"Smells like my gals are making pickles today," Missy's dad said when he got home from work.

After setting his briefcase down, he gave his wife a kiss and Missy a peck on the cheek.

"Looks like you'll be busy for a while. How about if I take care of supper and cook some burgers on the grill? I'll even put together a salad to go with it."

"Oh, I was hoping you'd say that," Missy's mom said with a smile and a wink as she took the dill pickles out of the hot water bath and tightened the lids on the jars. "Emily won't be home until later. She's working tonight."

"Okay, I'll just change my clothes and get the grill going."

Missy was very grateful for her family. Her parents, Ken and Liz Andrews, were both Christians and loved each other and their three children. Missy's dad worked at a local bank. Her mom worked as a high school English teacher and was grateful to have summers off so she could work in her flower and vegetable gardens. Her brother, Tony, was twenty-six and lived in Green Bay, Wisconsin, with his wife, Shari and their three-year-old son, Josh. He was an assistant manager at a retail store and was enjoying living in a larger city. Her younger sister, Emily, was nineteen and a freshman at Gogebic Community College and planned on becoming a teacher, just like their mom. They were raised with Christian values, went to church every Sunday, and were taught to respect their elders and work hard.

Missy and her mom ended up with seven quarts of dill pickles and had the sliced cucumbers and onions in the roaster pan, along with the salt and ice cubes, by the time Missy's dad had supper ready. So Missy quickly put her first load of laundry in the dryer and started the second load washing before sitting down at the table on the deck. Supper was simple but delicious, and it was nice to take a break from the pickle making. They visited while eating, sharing with each other how their day went.

"Have you thought any more about going back to school and getting your BA degree?" Ken asked his daughter after they'd visited for a while. "They offer a lot of classes online, and I know you could make a lot more money than you do now once you got your degree."

"No, Dad, I haven't."

Missy noticed her mom discreetly shaking her head at her dad, trying to change the subject.

"Missy, I think the dryer has stopped," her mom said. "Why don't I help you fold those clothes and you can put your last load in the dryer? I also have some zucchini that needs shredding. Would you mind helping me with that?"

"No, not at all."

So while Missy and her mom folded laundry, her dad went to clean the grill.

"Thanks, Mom. I know Dad wants me to go back to school, but I really like what I'm doing and don't know if getting my BA degree in accounting and punching numbers all day is what I want to do."

"I know, dear. Your Dad means well and just wants what's best for you. He's the only one in his family who went to college, and he wants to see you succeed and be the best you can be."

When they finished folding the clothes, Missy began shredding the zucchini while her mom packed two cups into each freezer container. Missy didn't mind shredding zucchini as she enjoyed the delicious zucchini breads, muffins, and cakes that were made from her labor.

"Thank you so much for helping me with the pickles and zucchini this evening, Missy," Liz said as they folded Missy's last load of laundry together. "Why don't you go on home and I can finish up the bread-and-butter pickles when they're ready. And please take a couple of containers of zucchini home with you. I have quite a lot in the freezer already."

"Gladly! I may even make some zucchini bread this weekend. Thanks for supper, Dad," she said as she gave him a hug. "I'll see you both at church on Sunday. Love you!"

Missy grabbed her laundry basket full of clean clothes. She enjoyed helping with the garden produce and had gotten her laundry done as well, so it was a productive evening. Since Missy lived in an apartment, she often went to her parents' home to help with the gardening, canning, and freezing the many vegetables her mom grew. She was always sent home with some of the produce, which was a nice bonus. Everything tasted so much better when picked fresh from the garden. Plus, the canned or frozen produce was much better than what she could purchase in the stores.

The young adult Bible study group, at the Community Bible Church where she attended, met on Thursday evenings and were studying the Beatitudes in the Gospel of Matthew. Their leader, Luke Williams, was doing a great job teaching them how important it was to follow Jesus's example and display a godly character toward others. He'd taken over the leadership of their group in June since Aaron Matthews resigned after getting married to Missy's friend April. Now April and Aaron were hosting a young married couples' group in their home. Missy had enjoyed Aaron's teaching, but she liked Luke's also. Luke was more laid back; and many of the young adults asked questions, shared their thoughts, and how they were applying what they were learning. Missy especially enjoyed the study, interaction, and fellowship.

Mike Reeves, the youth pastor at their church, was single, twenty-six years old, and also attended their young adult group.

"I have a proposition for you, Missy," Mike said as he approached her after the meeting. "We're taking the youth group to Lake Gogebic on Saturday, and I was wondering if you'd like to come along and help chaperone? A retired couple, who are friends of my family, have a cabin on the lake. He and his wife have offered to take the youth group on a boat ride around the lake, if they would agree to help bring in their boat and dock afterward, with a picnic to follow. They live near Milwaukee, Wisconsin, and won't be coming up again until next summer. I thought it was too good of an opportunity to pass up. I have about sixteen youths who said they can go, plus two other leaders, but I would feel more comfortable with another adult. What do you think? Are you available?"

"Well, I was hoping to go hiking at Porcupine Mountain on Saturday, but I haven't been to Lake Gogebic in quite a while, and a boat ride sounds like fun. So yah, I'd love to," replied Missy.

"Good," Mike said with a big smile. "Actually, we're planning on going hiking at Porcupine Mountain in a few weeks. It should be about peak time for the fall colors. You're welcome to come along with the youth then too, if you wouldn't mind chaperoning again."

"Sounds good to me. I've never done anything like that before. But if you think I could do it, then yes, I'd be happy to go along. What do I have to do?"

"Spend time getting to know the teens, keep them from wandering off, be a good Christian example, and just have fun," Mike explained.

"I guess I could do that," Missy affirmed. "What time are you leaving on Saturday?"

"We're going to meet here at the church at 12:45 p.m. We'll take the church van and any other vehicles needed."

"Okay, I'll meet you here about 12:30 p.m. then. I can drive my car, if you need me to. Thanks for thinking of me, Mike."

Missy then went to get some refreshments and visit with Julie and Emma before she left for home.

"So what was that about?" asked Julie. "Did Mike ask you out on a date?"

"No, he asked me to help chaperone a couple of youth events coming up," Missy explained.

"Men don't smile like that when they ask you to chaperone. I think he likes you and is just too afraid to ask you out," Julie countered.

"Oh, please, he's the youth pastor. There's no way I'd date a pastor."

"Why not?" Emma asked. "You're a Christian, good with people, fun to be with, and pretty. Why not you?"

"Because people expect more from a pastor's wife. I'd never be able to measure up or be good enough."

"Missy, pastors and their wives are human too," Emma said. "They're not perfect, and people shouldn't expect them to be."

"Well, I don't want to be put in that position. Besides, Mike doesn't think of me that way. We're just friends."

"Time will tell," Emma said as she looked at Julie, and they both smiled. "Time will tell."

Missy just shook her head and left for home.

Sometimes, I think Emma has her head in the clouds, Missy scoffed. *Me and Mike? No way!*

After work on Friday, Missy agreed to help Beth, her fiancé Kurt, and Beth's mom, Judy, address Beth and Kurt's wedding invitations at their apartment. Kurt brought Chinese from the Golden Dragon, so they set the food on the counter and each filled their plates with whatever they wanted. There was fried rice, sweet-and-sour pork, chicken and broccoli, chicken and cashew, pepper steak, and egg rolls. They definitely weren't going to go hungry. But they had a hundred invitations to address, so it would be a long evening.

The wedding was going to be at the Zion Lutheran Church, as that was where Beth and her family attended. They'd planned it for the Saturday after Thanksgiving so Beth's relatives from out of town could attend. Beth grew up in Ironwood and came from a family of four children and had lots of aunts, uncles, and cousins, plus friends from college and the hospital, so she was expecting about two hundred people to attend the wedding. She chose cabernet and yellow for her colors, so it would be a beautiful fall– holiday wedding.

Beth's mom brought the addresses for their family members and a roll of stamps, and Kurt brought addresses of his family and friends. Kurt had moved to Ironwood for his job two years prior, but most of his family lived in Missouri. They cleared off the table and got to work as soon as they finished eating. Since the women's handwriting was better than Kurt's, they did the addressing; and Kurt was tasked to stuff the envelopes, put on the stamps, and seal each invite.

"Yuck! These envelopes taste terrible!" Kurt complained, slamming down the second envelope. "There has to be a better way of sealing these. I'm not going to lick a hundred of these envelopes."

The women just laughed, and Beth's mom got him a wet sponge to swipe the envelopes on to seal them.

"How long were you going to make me suffer and lick these envelopes?" Kurt asked.

"Oh, not much longer," Judy said with a smile. "I just wanted to see how dedicated you were and what lengths you'd go to please my daughter."

"See what I've had to put with all these years?" Beth asked. "My mom and her family like to pull pranks, so beware when we attend family functions in the future."

"Thanks for the warning," Kurt said with a smile. "Just remember, what goes around, comes around. I've been known to pull a few pranks of my own. But thanks, Judy, for the sponge. This works so much better."

Kurt was more at ease as he continued sealing the envelopes, and with all of them working together, by nine, they finished all the invitations. Kurt took them with him and said he'd mail them in the morning on his way to work.

"Thank you so much for helping with our wedding invitations, Missy and Mom. This was a big help. And, Kurt, thanks for bringing supper. It was delicious!" Beth said as she gave Kurt a kiss and Missy and her mom a hug.

"I was glad to help," Missy said. "Besides, many hands make the work much easier and more fun."

Missy hadn't spent a lot of time with Kurt, so she was glad to have the opportunity to get to know him better. She could see that Kurt really loved Beth and would be good for her. He had strengths where Beth was lacking and encouraged and complemented her in areas where she excelled. So they looked to be a good match. Missy was happy for Beth but would miss having a roommate when she moved out. She didn't think she could afford to keep the apartment on her own. But she'd deal with that at a later date.

After Kurt and Judy left, Missy and Beth sat on the couch for a while before getting ready for bed.

"Well, invitations are done, and we've reserved the church for the wedding and the Legion Hall for our reception. I've got my dress, the bridesmaids' dresses are ready for the last fitting, and Mom found a caterer. So I'm getting more things ready for the wedding. I'll be glad when this is all over and Kurt and I can settle into our home and be a married couple. I didn't realize there was so much work in putting together a wedding," Beth commented with a sigh.

"Just remember to put as much effort into your marriage," Missy added. "A wedding is one day—a marriage is for a lifetime."

"That's for sure. But don't you think Kurt's wonderful? He's so sweet and thoughtful, fun to be with, hardworking and smart, but not arrogant. It's like he completes me and makes me so happy. We've talked about having a family but want to wait a few years so we can save up some money first. We've both recently started our careers, so we want to get that established first."

"That sounds smart," Missy agreed. "And yes, Kurt's pretty wonderful. And I'm so glad you both agreed not to live together before you got married. So many couples are doing that now, but I don't think it's a good way to start a marriage."

"Well, both our parents were against it, and being with you this last year and listening to what you've said about what the Bible says made me think it would be more romantic to wait. Besides, it will make our wedding night much more special. I guess some of your Bible talk is rubbing off on me," Beth said.

"I gave you a Bible. I wish you'd read it for yourself."

"I will, when I'm not so busy," Beth insisted.

"But when will that be? You'll always be busy and find other things to do. Beth, I care about you, and I don't want you to keep putting off a relationship with Christ.

"I'm tired. It's been a long day, and I'm going to bed," Beth said as she got up and started toward her bedroom. "I know you care about me, Missy, but I'm just not ready."

Beth then went on to her bedroom.

You're being too pushy, Missy, she realized, reprimanding herself. *You need to be more patient with Beth. The way you're going about it isn't working—in fact, it's pushing Beth further away. We rarely see each other anymore. Of course, Beth's spending a lot of time with Kurt and getting ready for her wedding. But there has to be a better way.*

Chapter 3

Missy was excited about going with the youth group to Lake Gogebic on Saturday. She arrived at the church at 12:30 pm. Mike was already there, checking out the van and putting some life jackets in it.

"Do you need any help?" Missy asked as she approached him.

"No, I was just making sure the van was clean of all paper and other garbage," Mike said as he got out of the van. "And I had a couple of life jackets at home, so thought I'd bring them along in case we need them. Thanks again for agreeing to come along today. I really appreciate it."

"Actually, I'm looking forward to it. It sounds like a fun afternoon, and it would be a good opportunity to get to know some of the youth better. I know some by name, but not much else."

Then the other leaders and youth started arriving or getting dropped off. Missy, Mike, and the leaders, Ron and Sue, interacted with the youth and their parents while they waited for the rest to arrive. Mike informed the parents that they would make sure their teens had a ride home, as they weren't sure what time they would get back, but that it would be after dark and promised to keep in touch. The teens who wanted to travel in the church van got in and picked their seats while others got into Ron and Sue's van, as they'd offered to drive. They all seemed excited to spend time at the lake on a beautiful autumn day, for the sun was shining, and the temperature was in the upper sixties. Soon they were all loaded and ready to go.

It took about forty minutes to get to the cabin, which was on the south side of Lake Gogebic. The owners, Harold and Millie Jacobson, were there to welcome them when they arrived.

"Thank you so much for coming," Harold said as he patted Mike on the back and smiled at the rest of the group. "I know you're all anxious to get out on the water, but we can only take six of you at a time in the boat. So while you're waiting for your turn, there's a volleyball net, horseshoe, and croquet set up in the yard.

"The first six can follow me to the dock, and we'll get started. I'll take you for a spin around the lake for about twenty minutes, and then we'll come back for the next group. You must all wear a life jacket while in the boat, so grab one and make sure they're fastened properly," Harold said as he started for the dock.

Mike followed him with the two life jackets he'd brought and made sure each teen had on a life jacket that fit and was properly fastened. Missy stayed behind with Ron and Sue, and each went to one of the other activities. Missy introduced herself to Millie as they walked toward the croquet game.

"Hi, I'm Missy Andrews. You have a lovely place here. And it's such a beautiful day to be on the lake. Thank you so much for inviting us."

"It's our pleasure. Our children couldn't come up this weekend, and Harold couldn't get the dock in alone. We probably wouldn't have been able to come up again before the snow started flying, so when Mike offered to help—well, it was a real answer to prayer. And we enjoy seeing so many young people here."

"I'm sure the boat ride and food had something to do with that," Missy said with a smile. "Do you need any help with the food?"

"No, not yet. But I'll let you know when I do. Right now, I just want to see everyone enjoy themselves."

Missy and Millie each grabbed a mallet and ball, along with the others who decided to play croquet. Sue joined those getting lined up at the volleyball net, while Ron joined the group starting to play horseshoes. Everyone was going to have a good time.

Missy went with the last group for the boat ride and made sure she took her jacket, as she knew it would be cooler on the lake. As they got going, Harold regaled them about Lake Gogebic as they started out while Mike drove the boat.

"Lake Gogebic is Michigan's largest inland lake and covers 13,380 acres and thirty-six miles of shoreline," Harold began. "The south half of the lake—where we are—is in Gogebic County and in the central time zone. The northern half is in Ontonagon County and in the eastern time zone. It's a really good fishing lake, great for water sports, and has a state park, as well as several county parks along its shoreline. It's a great place for year-round family fun, as the wooded areas that surround the lake are great for hiking, bike riding or ATVs, viewing wildlife and wildflowers, or hunting. We've had the cabin on this lake for twenty years now and our family and friends have had a lot of fun here. We see beautiful sunsets in the evenings and sometimes even the northern lights. Maybe you'll see them tonight if it stays clear."

Missy truly enjoyed the ride but was glad she had brought her jacket along. Some of the girls didn't, but Harold had small blankets in the boat they could wrap up in. When they got back, Missy, Sue and the teen girls went inside to help Millie with the food.

Harold and Mike supervised bringing the boat and dock onto shore while Ron supervised taking down the volleyball net, croquet game, and putting away the horseshoes. The boys seemed to be a great help. The women and girls were able to watch some of the outdoor activity from inside the cabin, and it looked to be quite a process and definitely a group effort.

Missy knew they'd be hungry when they got done. Millie had made a large bowl of potato salad and had a large Crock-Pot full of baked beans simmering. Harold had grilled chicken earlier and it was warming in the oven. Missy and Millie had shucked corn before Missy went on her boat ride, and it was now washed and cooking in a large pan on the back of the stove. Sue and Isabelle were making a lettuce salad while Sarah and Katie were getting silverware, dishes, and napkins laid out as Millie directed. Missy, Lexi, and Brianna were getting the cookies and bars trayed up; and Jill and Alice were slicing the buns. Their food was all smelling and looking very good.

Soon the boat was on the trailer, rinsed off, and parked in the garage; the outside play equipment was put away; and part of the dock was on shore. They decided to eat when the food was ready and would finish the dock after supper. As Missy had expected, the food was enjoyed and devoured quickly. With the fresh air, fun activities, and work efforts, they were all hungry.

"I love to cook, and it's so satisfying to see people enjoy eating the food I prepare," Millie said after everyone was done eating. "And thank you, Missy, Sue, and young ladies, for all your help in getting everything ready. I enjoyed working with you and having you in our home."

"Well, now it's time for the ladies to help get things cleaned up in the kitchen and us guys to get the rest of the dock brought onto the shore," Mike announced. "When we're done, we'll have a bonfire, do some singing, and I'll share a thought from God's Word. That's always my favorite part of coming to the Jacobsons' cabin. So let's get going, and hopefully we'll get done before dark."

Just as the sun was beginning to set, the dock was on shore, the bonfire was lit, and everyone was grabbing chairs or blankets to sit around the fire. The sunset was gorgeous, which was an added bonus to their evening. Mike played his guitar while they sang some praise songs about God's love, His willingness to sacrifice His Son on the cross, and the fellowship we can have with Him. Harold then thanked the teens for their hard work and help with the boat and dock, and Mike gave the teens an opportunity to share about their afternoon. The boat ride, food, and fellowship ranked high on their list of good times. But for Missy, it was getting to know the teens, leaders and Millie, and seeing them all work together so willingly and without complaining.

Then Mike read from 1 John 1:1–5 and commented, "Now, none of us have personally seen Jesus, as the apostle John had, but we have the Word of God, which gives us this and many other eyewitness accounts, as well as God's promise that His Word is true. And for those of us who have accepted Jesus Christ as our personal Savior, we're also His witnesses of the forgiveness God offers because of Jesus's willingness to pay the penalty for our sins on the cross. And because He rose from the dead, we also have victory over sin and fellowship with God and other believers. That's what we've enjoyed today—the joy of fellowship with one another, caring for, and helping another believer in Christ, as well as enjoying the wonderful food that Millie and Harold provided," Mike said as he smiled and pointed toward Millie and Harold.

"This is what God wants for us—to be an example to the world around us, make the burdens of others lighter, share with others the joy we have when we accept Jesus Christ, and find the forgiveness, peace, and joy that we all long for. God wants us to be His lights in our world. Just as the fire before us dispels the darkness around us, so sharing Christ and His love with others will dispel the darkness of our sin-ridden world. So let's be lights in our homes, our schools, and among our friends, just as the stars tonight light up the dark sky."

Mike closed their time in prayer; and they all said their goodbyes to Harold and Millie, got their things into the vehicles, and headed back to the church or their homes. Those who lived on the way back to the church were dropped off, and those with cars at the church offered to take the others home. Their parents were informed that they were on their way. It was much quieter on the way back, but all said they had a great time and found that it was fun to help others.

"I want to thank you again, Missy, for coming along and helping with the youth yesterday," Mike said as he spoke to Missy after church the next day.

"Oh, it was my pleasure," Missy responded with a smile. "I enjoyed getting to know some of the teens, especially the girls, as we played croquet and helped with supper. And I enjoyed getting to know Millie as well. She's a real sweetheart."

"Yes she is. Harold and Millie have been friends of my family for a number of years. They are true saints and real prayer warriors who have really helped me in my growth in the Lord. They even helped me in making my decision to be in full-time ministry."

"Wow, that does make them very special then," Missy replied.

"Yes it does. So do you still want to come with us to Porcupine Mountain in two weeks? You were great with the teens, and we could really use you."

"I would love to!" Missy said. "They're really a great bunch of teens, and I love hiking at Porcupine Mountain, so it's a great opportunity on both counts. Is there anything you'd like me to bring or know ahead of time?"

"Sue is in charge of the food for the trip, so you can talk to her about what she'd like you to bring. I'll be bringing the first-aid kit and bug spray, as well as a good supply of water bottles, so we're set that way. We'll be leaving on Saturday, October 6, from the church at nine and should be back by about four."

"Okay, I'll look forward to it," Missy said with a smile and started to turn and walk away.

"Ah, Missy," Mike said to stop her.

Missy turned around to face Mike.

"I was wondering, do you have plans for lunch? Could you join me for a quick bite?" asked Mike.

"Oh, I'm sorry. My parents are expecting me at their home. Maybe another time," Missy replied, glad she had an excuse.

She left quickly and got in her car. She took a deep breath and gave a sigh.

Are Emma and Julie right? Missy asked herself. *Is Mike interested in asking me out on a date? No, he probably just wants to talk about the hiking trip in two weeks.*

She started her car and drove to her parents' home.

Chapter 4

The next week went by quickly. Missy was busy working at the eye clinic during the day and helping her mom in the evenings with canning tomatoes that had ripened, as well as shredding more zucchini. It seemed her mom had a bumper crop of zucchini this year, so she'd been giving away zucchini to people at church and teachers she worked with at school. She also gave Missy zucchini and tomatoes to give away to staff at the eye clinic.

On Saturday morning, Missy went to help her mom pull up plants in the garden that were done producing, and when they stopped for a break, she asked her, "Can I talk to you about something?"

"Of course," her mom answered. "Have a seat at the table on the deck, and I'll get us something to drink."

Missy sat down and took off her garden gloves. She looked around and realized how much she enjoyed helping her mom with the garden, working outside in the cooler autumn temperatures, listening to the birds, and watching the squirrels and chipmunks running around the yard. She missed not having a backyard to enjoy since moving into her apartment. Soon her mom came out with two glasses of iced tea and a plate of bars.

"Mmm, this goes well," Missy said after taking a drink. "And gluten-free oatmeal chocolate chips bars? Thanks, Mom! You didn't have to make these for me."

"I wanted to. It's the least I could do after all your help these past few weeks with the canning and garden work," Liz said as she took a drink. "Now what was it you wanted to talk to me about?"

"Well, as you know, Beth will be moving out of the apartment after she gets married in November, and that will leave me without a roommate. It's really worked out well to share the expenses, but

I don't know of anyone who's looking to share an apartment right now. Emily has hinted that she'd like to move in with me, but I don't think she's in a financial position to help much, with going to college and only working part time. I stayed here at home while I was in college, and it really saved me a lot of money. I was then able to use what I earned at the eye clinic for tuition and books."

"And that was very wise. Your dad and I enjoyed having you home while you were in college. It made good financial sense, especially since it was right here in town. And you're right—Emily can't afford to pay for housing now. She's just in a hurry to grow up. I'll have a talk with her."

"No, maybe it would be better if I talked to her, sister to sister," Missy said. "She might take it better from me than you."

"Yes, you may be right. I keep forgetting you're an adult now. And as hard as it is for me to see my children grow up and leave the nest, I realize that's the way God designed it." After a short pause, her mom continued, "Have you asked Pastor Mike or your young adult group if they know of someone who's looking to share an apartment?"

"I guess I'm a little afraid of getting someone just to share the expenses. When I agreed to take the apartment a year ago, there wasn't anyone in our young adult group who was interested, so I was in a hurry to find a roommate and asked Beth. But it didn't work out like I thought it would. We got along okay, but we didn't really bond or have much in common. I guess I was expecting more. This time, I want someone who knows the Lord, I can have a good relationship with, we can do things together, encourage one another, and maybe even pray with. Like April and Bonnie did."

April and Bonnie had rented the apartment before Missy took over the lease. They were close friends and had a strong relationship. Now they were both married, and Bonnie just had a baby in August. They all attended the same church, and Missy had become good friends with them.

"Well, it sounds like you learned something from your experience and now have a better criterion for choosing a roommate. That's all part of growing up," Missy's mom stated. "So have you prayed about finding a new roommate? That would be the best place to start. The Bible says that we should ask God for wisdom, and He will give it to us generously. I know God will guide you to the person He has for you. We could pray together right now, if you'd like."

"Yes, I'd like that very much."

Missy and her mom prayed together, and afterward, Missy felt less anxious and more at peace. She knew God would lead her to the right person and that she was no longer in this alone. Having God and her mom on her team was a strong combination.

Missy went kayaking with Emma and Julie again on Sunday afternoon. This time, they went to Gile Flowage, which was a small lake in Wisconsin, as it was too windy to kayak on Lake Superior. The colors of the leaves were much more vibrant since the last time they'd kayaked, and they enjoyed the afternoon together.

Missy mentioned to them that she'd be without a roommate after November and asked them to pray with her about finding a new roommate. Emma lived with her sister, who was a young widow, and needed help with her four-year old son and expenses. Julie already shared an apartment with her cousin and didn't know of anyone else who was looking to share an apartment. But both agreed to pray about it with her.

"So how did the chaperoning go with the youth group last weekend?" Emma asked as they loaded up their kayaks.

"Oh, it went really well. I enjoyed getting to know the teens, Sue and Ron, and Mike's friends. They were an older couple who had a cabin on Lake Gogebic and needed help getting their boat and dock in before winter. Everyone had a great time. We were able to play games and take turns going for a boat ride before the work started. Millie and Harold provided a wonderful supper, and after the work was done, we sat around the fire, sang songs, and Mike shared a devotional. It was a nice ending to a wonderful day."

"So are you going out with Mike again?" Emma asked.

"Yes, as a matter of fact. I'll be chaperoning again Saturday when they go hiking at Porcupine Mountain."

"I wasn't referring to the chaperoning. I meant, did Mike ask you on a date with him?" Emma corrected.

"He did ask me to get something to eat with him after church last Sunday, but I told him I'd already planned on going to my parents' house for dinner."

"Let's see, a date with a handsome man or dinner with my parents. I don't know if I'd have made the same choice you did," Emma said with her hands held out like a balance scale.

"I'd already told my parents I'd come over for dinner. It's not right to go back on my word."

"No, but maybe you could have invited Mike to come along. I'm sure your parents wouldn't have minded," interjected Julie.

"I'll keep that in mind," Missy said.

After everything was loaded, Missy gave Emma and Julie each a hug and said, "Okay, I'll see you two on Thursday night at young adults. Have a good week."

Then she got into her car.

Those two are really the matchmakers, Missy thought as she shook her head and drove away.

Missy contacted her sister, Emily, and invited her over Monday evening for supper, since Emily didn't have to work and Beth was scheduled to work at the hospital. Missy thought it would be a good opportunity to talk to her and explain why it wouldn't be a good idea for her to move in with her after Thanksgiving. She planned a simple menu of gluten-free spaghetti with meatballs and a lettuce salad, with Moose Tracks flavored frozen yogurt for dessert—Emily's favorite.

Emily came in exclaiming how she loved Missy's apartment and the way she'd decorated it.

"You're so lucky to be on your own," Emily went on. "I can't wait to move out of Mom and Dad's, and since you won't have a roommate soon, it would be the perfect opportunity for me to move in with you. Don't you think?"

"That's why I had you come over tonight for supper, Emily. We need to talk. Sit down, I've got supper just about ready. I just have to dish it up."

Missy put the food on the table, asked the blessing, and started passing the dishes to Emily.

"So you're going to tell me I can't move in with you, aren't you?" Emily stated sadly as she dished up the food on her plate.

"Emily, I would love to have you move in with me, but I just don't think it's the right time. You said I'm lucky to be on my own, but, Emily, luck had nothing to do with it. I worked for three summers as a teenager to save money for college. I received a scholarship and grant that helped pay for my tuition. Then I worked while I was in college—and the summer after that—before I moved out of Mom and Dad's home."

"I couldn't work while I was in high school because I was in sports, and it took too much of my time. But I'm working now while I'm in college. And I received a scholarship too, you know."

"Yes you did. And I'm very proud of you. And I'm not saying you should have given up sports. You're very good at them, and it will help you later if you want to coach while teaching. But I just don't think you have the financial stability right now to handle anything besides college. If you would move in with me, I'd need you to pay half the rent, utilities, plus help with the groceries. Right now, you don't have to worry about any of that."

"I thought the utilities were included in your rent," Emily said hopefully.

"Only the water, garbage, and heat. I have to pay the cable, internet, and electricity, plus extra for the garage."

"Oh. Well, how much does half of all that come to?"

"Finish eating, Emily. After we clear the table, I'll get some paper and a pen to write down the figures for you. It will make much more sense if you see it written down. I bought your favorite frozen yogurt for dessert. We can have that later while we sit on the couch and relax."

They were soon done eating, the table was cleared, and Missy started writing out the monthly expenses that Emily would need to be responsible for in order to share her apartment.

"Wow, that doesn't leave any money for clothes, eating out with my friends, or buying books for school."

"No, it doesn't. And I don't want you to miss out on spending time with your friends and having some fun. Emily, you're only nineteen years old. Don't be in such a big hurry to grow up and move away from home. Mom and Dad love you and are willing to let you stay at home while you're in college so you don't have such a financial strain. Be thankful for that because not everyone has that option. When you're done with college and have a full-time job, then you'll be able to handle the extra cost of living expenses."

Emily gave a sigh and said, "You know, sis, maybe you're right. Now, how about that frozen yogurt?"

Missy hugged her sister, smiled, and said, "Coming right up."

She dished up their dessert, and they sat on the couch, talking about much lighter things than money concerns before Emily had to go home and do schoolwork.

At their young adult meeting on Thursday evening, they studied the third beatitude, which said, "Blessed are the meek, for they shall inherit the earth" (Matt. 5:5). Jesus's explanation of that beatitude was in Matthew 5:38–48, where it talked about initiating a radical kindness to others, even those who oppose you. Matthew 5:46 said, "If you love those who love you, what reward will you get?" which then ended with a challenge that said, "Be perfect, therefore, as your heavenly Father is perfect." (Matt. 5:48).

They had quite a discussion about showing kindness to people who weren't kind to them. They all agreed that it wasn't easy or normal for people to do that and could only be done with God's help. For only when we have an intentional and growing relationship with God can we do what He asks of us and become like Him.

This really challenged Missy to think about her life and how she treated people, especially Beth.

Oh, Lord, Missy prayed intently. *I've really messed up. I realize that I've been selfish and comparing my relationship with Beth to what April and Bonnie had. I've been trying to force Christ on Beth instead of being kind and just loving her. And really, how much time do I spend reading, studying, and applying the Bible to my everyday life? How often do I pray for others and not just ask for what I want You to do for me? Lord, help me to do better with Beth and be a true friend. And on Saturday, when I'm with the teens, help me follow your example and be kind to them, showing them how much You love them. But, Lord, I know I can't do this in my own strength. Give me Your love and help me follow Your leading to be more kind and loving to others. I do want to be more like You, Jesus! Amen.*

Missy knew she had a lot of growing to do and was far from perfect. She vowed to spend more time, not just reading her Bible but studying it and applying it to her life, as well as making her prayer life a time of truly communicating with God and opening her heart. For she needed to not just talk to God, but listen to what He wanted to teach her. In her heart, she knew she had a long way to go, but with God's help, she'd press on.

Chapter 5

Missy talked to Sue about what food to bring for the hiking trip and was asked to bring an assortment of fruits, veggies, and gluten-free bread and cookies and bars, as some of the youth were also allergic to gluten. Missy also brought her camera and made sure she had Benadryl and her albuterol inhaler along, just in case.

Fifteen teens arrived at the church on Saturday for the hike, and two of her friend Bonnie's brothers would join them when they arrived at the Summit Peak trailhead. Bonnie's family were visiting from Minnesota and camping at Porcupine Mountain, so Bonnie asked Mike if her teen brothers could join the hike. Ever since they had come the previous summer for Bonnie's wedding, her brothers had wanted to come back in the fall to go camping. Mike agreed, and Bonnie offered to provide the chips for their picnic lunch. So now they'd have a total of twenty-one people for their hike and picnic.

With seventeen teens, Mike was grateful that Missy agreed to come along. They split the teens between the church van (which Mike would drive) and Ron and Sue's van. Mike introduced Missy to the teens she hadn't met at Lake Gogebic, and they left the church shortly after nine. They were all excited to get to Porcupine Mountain.

Porcupine Mountain covered sixty thousand acres and was Michigan's largest state park. The park was comprised of almost thirty-five thousand acres of what is considered the best stand of virgin Northern Hardwoods and Hemlock in North America. This makes for some very attractive color during the fall. The park also had many attractions and hiking trails, but the leaders decided on a route that combined three hiking trails and provided a variety of scenery and a doable day hike.

They would park at the Summit Peak trailhead and take the trail to the peak first, which had a 1,958 feet elevation, the highest point of the park. It offered quite a panoramic view of the area, and they'd get some of the best fall foliage pictures in the Upper Peninsula. Then they'd have lunch and take a side trail that would lead down the hillside to Mirror Lake, which then joined up with the Little Carp River Trail for 1.5 miles and intersected with the Beaver Creek Trail. That trail would then return them to the Summit Peak parking lot. The estimated length of the hike was 5.5 miles, so they'd definitely have a good workout.

The hour-long ride to Porcupine Mountain was loud, with eight teens in the back. Mike and Missy frequently looked in the mirror of the van's visors to keep track of what was happening in the back. Missy observed that one girl seemed quiet and kept more to herself. Missy recalled that her name was Rose and decided to try and connect with her during the hike.

When they arrived at the parking lot of the Summit Peak trailhead, Bonnie's dad was there with her two brothers. They all got out of their vehicles, were introduced, and everyone was excited to get going. Mike laid out the ground rules, and they headed out. The boys went ahead, setting a strong pace, which Missy assumed was to impress the girls. But Mike soon slowed them down.

"Hey, slow it down a bit and save some of that energy. It's a long way up, and we have a long hike ahead of us," Mike cautioned them.

The slower pace allowed Missy to take in the views, and she took out her camera. She noticed that Rose also had a camera with her.

"Do you like taking pictures, Rose?" Missy asked as she came alongside her.

"Yah," Rose answered but said nothing else.

Missy realized it would be a challenge to get Rose to warm up to her and open up.

But she wasn't going to give up and asked, "What do you like to take pictures of?"

"Mostly animals, flowers, and stuff," Rose replied.

Missy got a few more words out of her, so she continued, "So what kind of camera do you have there?"

"It's a Nikon D3300," Rose showed it to Missy. "It's compact, easy to use, and comes with a zoom lens."

Missy looked it over and was very impressed.

"Wow, it's really nice. I just have this Nikon that I've had for a while, but it takes nice pictures. I really don't know a lot about taking pictures—I just aim and shoot. But I can zoom things up if I want a closer picture. I'm sure you could give me some tips on taking pictures though."

"Maybe. I'm not that good," Rose said as she walked away, putting distance between them.

Missy could tell that no one had ever affirmed or encouraged her interest in photography and that she didn't have a lot of self-confidence.

Maybe that's a good place to start, Missy analyzed. *I'll have to be careful not to be too pushy, and look for opportunities to connect with her during our hike.*

When they got to the top of the hill, they were all enamored by the colorful fall scene before them. The combination of reds, yellows, and oranges of the hardwoods mixed with the greens of the pine trees was breathtaking. They could even see Lake Superior in the distance, so adding the blues of the sky and water to the colors of the leaves, it really added to the colorful panorama before them. Missy noticed that Rose was taking pictures with her camera, as were others, though she knew it would be difficult to capture the true wonder of what they saw and were experiencing.

They then climbed the observation tower and were again awed by the splendor of all that God had created. After they looked around for a few minutes, Mike asked that they all bow their heads in a moment of thanksgiving for the beauty that God created for them to enjoy. A few teens prayed out loud, and then Mike closed their time of thanksgiving.

"Lord, we are in awe of Your majesty and creativity displayed before us. We thank You for all this beauty that You have created for us to enjoy. I pray that as we enjoy Your nature today, that it will remind us of how awesome you are, how much You love us, and how much You want to have a relationship with us. Keep us safe and let us be mindful of one another, be considerate, and enjoy each other's fellowship today. In Your Name, amen."

Then they went down the tower, descended the hill, and went back to the vans to prepare for their lunch. Ron and Sue started getting food out of their van, and Missy got the food she had brought, as well as the bags of chips Bonnie had sent along for their lunch. The girls helped put tablecloths on the tables and set out the food. Mike and the boys brought out the water bottles. The water would quench their thirst, and the chips would replace the salt they would lose during their hike. Ron asked the blessing on the food, and it wasn't long before their plates were heaping with food.

Sue had brought both white and wheat bread, meat, cheese, and other sandwich fixings; so with the chips, veggies, and fruit that Missy brought, as well as a variety of bars and cookies, they had a feast before them and no one would go hungry. Missy found out that Rose and two other teens also had a gluten allergy. They were grateful for the gluten-free products from which to choose.

"So, Rose, did you get enough to eat?" Missy asked as they were finishing up their lunch.

"Oh yes. Everything was very good. You're allergic to gluten too?" Rose asked.

"Yes. I found out a few years ago. I wondered why I'd get so sick after eating, so I got tested. I found out that I'm allergic to gluten, dust, molds, and grasses. So I have to stay inside when people mow the grass, and I can't rake leaves anymore or go walking in the woods when the leaves get wet after it's rained and get moldy. So today is a good time for a hike when most of the leaves are still on the trees. How about you?"

"Very similar. I'm allergic to gluten, dairy, dust, and molds," Rose informed.

"So did you get some good pictures up on the peak?" Missy asked, eager to keep the conversation going.

"Yes I did. But then with that view, how could you not?"

"May I see them?" Missy asked.

Rose brought up the first picture she'd taken and handed her camera to Missy.

"Rose, these are really good!" Missy remarked. "You should have some of these blown up and framed or copied on canvases. They do that a lot lately. I've seen them in clinics and other professional buildings. You could probably even sell some of them."

"No, they're not that good. I just take pictures for myself."

"Believe me, they are that good! The colors are so vibrant, rich, and lifelike. You have everything centered so well. Even your closeups are unique, especially this shot with the bee sitting on a daisy. I would pay to have some of your photos blown up and framed."

"Really?"

"Yes really!" Missy answered.

Missy wanted to look at more of Rose's pictures, but Mike announced that it was time to pack up the food and continue on their hike. So Missy and Rose helped pack the food away, and they were soon ready to continue their hike.

The colors of the leaves and the variety of undergrowth and flowers were spectacular. As the sun came through the trees. it made the leaves and flowers glow. When they arrived at Mirror Lake, they all stood in awe at how blue the water was and took in the glimmer of the sun sparkling on the water. Ron started singing "How Great Thou Art," and others joined in or stood silently in reverence to the Creator of all that was around them.

When they continued down the trail, they heard the trickling of water from Little Carp River and saw signs of deer and other wildlife that had come for a drink. Missy jumped when a grouse flew up from the tall grass along the trail as she walked by. Some of the other teens were startled as well.

"Wow, what was that?" asked Missy, holding her hand to her chest.

"That was a grouse," Mike informed. "They can really scare a person when they fly up like that. They're birds that forage on the forest floor for seeds and insects."

"It scared me too," Katie exclaimed.

As they walked along, some of the boys saw some brook trout swimming in the river. Soon they came upon some fishermen.

"Any luck?" Kyle asked.

"Yah," said one of the men, as he pulled a string of fish out of the water. "Good fishing today."

Going a little farther up the trail, the river became rough, and they could hear the sound of a waterfall up ahead. When they came upon it, they felt a spray of water as it cascaded down the rocks and to the river below. What a sight to behold.

Missy had seen many waterfalls around the Ironwood area but was always fascinated with each one. She took pictures of the waterfall, as did others in the group. She noticed Rose was taking a number of pictures as well.

As they went along, they came to some wetlands along the Beaver Creek Trail. The area was alive with a variety of birds flying around the various grasses. However, Missy had some trouble breathing due to the molds of the marshy grasses along the creek. She took a Benadryl and her albuterol inhaler, then offered it to Rose as well.

"I'll take a Benadryl, but I have my own inhaler," Rose informed her.

Missy was glad they were nearing the end of the hike as the Benadryl would make her drowsy. Mike noticed that Missy and Rose had stopped to use their inhalers and went to check and make sure they were okay.

"Is everything all right? Are you able to make it back to the parking lot?" Mike asked.

"Yes," Missy said. "It's just that the molds in the grasses and marshy areas along the creek make it difficult to breath. The albuterol and Benadryl will help, and I don't think it's too much further back to the vehicles, is it?"

"No, it's not much further. I'll stay back and walk with you two to make sure you don't have any more problems."

"Oh, that's not necessary," assured Missy. "Once we get where it's more open and not so marshy, it will get better."

"I insist! Ron and Sue are with the others, and they're all doing fine. You two are a part of our group, and I want to make sure you get back safe and sound."

"Well, thank you, kind sir," Missy said as she smiled and looked at Rose. "We appreciate you being such a gentleman and helping two damsels in distress."

"I'm at your service," Mike said as he bowed and directed them to go ahead of him down the trail.

This even brought a smile from Rose, so Missy locked arms with her and they walked down the path together.

They all made it back to the parking lot safe and sound, though tired from their long but enjoyable hike. Bonnie's dad was there to pick up his two sons, and Mike informed him that they enjoyed having them along. The boys thanked him for allowing them to go on the hike with them and said goodbye to the new friends they'd made.

After using the restrooms and getting refreshing drinks of cool water, they got loaded up into the vans and headed for home. Missy decided to sit in the back with Rose so she could look at more of her pictures, so one of the boys sat in the front with Mike. It was definitely a much quieter ride home and wasn't long before some nodded off to sleep.

As Missy looked at more of Rose's pictures, she was very impressed with her talent. She set up a time the following Saturday to get together with Rose to decide which ones she would like to have printed and which ones Rose could put on Facebook to get people's reactions. Missy was sure there would be a good response. But the Benadryl soon took effect, and Missy and Rose both fell asleep also.

Chapter 6

That evening Missy was surprised to get a call from Mike. "Are you feeling better after the allergy reaction you had this afternoon?" Mike asked.

"Yes, I am. Thank you for asking. I'm still tired, but that's normal after an allergy reaction and taking Benadryl."

"I'm glad to hear you're doing better."

Then there was a pause, and Missy was beginning to wonder where this conversation was going.

"I wanted to ask if you would have dinner with me after church tomorrow," Mike continued, breaking the short silence. "I know the last time I asked, you had plans, so I wanted to be sure to ask you ahead of time. You don't already have plans, do you?"

"I was really hoping to grab a quick lunch after church and take a nap. Usually it takes a lot out of me after an allergic reaction and I need a few days to recover and rest. So tomorrow wouldn't be a good day," Missy answered with a tone of regret.

Mike had truly been a real gentleman that afternoon, and she hated to keep turning him down.

"Okay, how about Tuesday evening, about six or six-thirty? That would give you a few days to recover. I have some things I'd like to talk to you about."

"All right, Tuesday should work okay. I think six-thirty would be better so I'd have time to get ready after work. Did you have a place in mind?" Missy asked.

"I was thinking of Breakwater. It's usually pretty quiet on a Tuesday evening and would give us an opportunity to talk."

"Is there something specific you want to talk about?" Missy asked, getting concerned that maybe she had done something wrong.

"Well, I've been watching how you interact with the teens. Ron, Sue, and I are impressed with the way you connect with them and draw them out, and they seem to really like you. So we were wondering if you'd like to help us with the teens on a regular basis on Wednesday evenings, as well as other scheduled activities. You can pray about it, and we can discuss it further on Tuesday evening."

"Oh, okay. I appreciate your confidence in me, and I'll definitely pray about it. I'm sure I will have questions for you on Tuesday, so I look forward to seeing you then. Should I meet you there?"

"No, I'll pick you up at six-thirty. After all, I am a gentleman, remember? Will that give you enough time to get ready?"

"Yes, that should be fine."

On Tuesday after work, Missy tried on several outfits before she decided on her tan, thin cords and a turquoise sweater with her low brown leather boots. She'd worn her hair in a ponytail for work that day, but she let her hair down for dinner, with combs in the sides to keep it off her face. Then she added a little mascara to highlight her eyes, a little blush to give her cheeks some color, and pink glossy lipstick to moisten them. She knew this wasn't a real date as it was to talk about her working with the youth at church, but she still wanted to make a good impression. After all, it was kind of like a job interview.

When Mike arrived, he was wearing a pair of black jeans with a tan sweater under his black leather jacket, which accented his brown hair and blue eyes. He looked very handsome and definitely an example of a true gentleman when he handed her a bouquet of yellow and orange gerbera daisies.

"Flowers for me? What is this for? I thought we were going to have dinner to talk about me helping with the youth group," Missy said as Mike handed her the flowers.

"Yes we are, but I wanted to let you know how much we appreciated all your help for the last two events and how much I hope you'll say yes to our offer to work with the youth on a regular basis."

"Isn't that called bribery?" Missy asked with a smile.

"No, I just appreciate you finally accepting my invitation to dinner. I figured every beautiful woman likes flowers."

"Thank you for the compliment, and yes, I do like flowers. Let me just put these in a vase of water, and we can get going," Missy said as she went into the kitchen for a vase.

Missy had always considered herself ordinary with her five-foot-five height, mousy blonde hair, and brown eyes—but she never considered herself beautiful. She was taken back by his compliment, but it was rather nice to be called beautiful by someone, especially someone like Mike, whom she respected and considered a good friend.

Does he want to be more than a friend? Missy pondered. *Do I want to be more than friends with Mike?*

After putting water in the vase and adding the flowers, she went to the closet to get her jacket. Mike helped her with it, and then they left for the restaurant. When they got to his pickup, Mike opened the door for her, and Missy continued to be impressed with his good manners.

At the restaurant, Missy found Mike easy to talk with and was glad that he kept the conversation light while they waited for their food to arrive. He told her a little about his family and background. He said he grew up in Brookfield, Wisconsin, with his parents and one sister, Linda, and got his training at Moody Bible Institute in Chicago. Mike then asked Missy how her family was doing, as well as her job.

When their food arrived, Mike looked at his bacon cheeseburger with fries and then Missy's grilled chicken salad without croutons.

"I forgot about your gluten allergy. Is it difficult to find foods to accommodate your allergies when you eat out?" Mike asked.

"Sometimes. I can usually find a salad that's pretty safe, but it's definitely limiting. It forces me to eat healthier though, so it's really not that bad. I've gotten used to it, and as long as I stick to it, I feel so much better that I don't really mind."

"Does it bother you when I eat this in front of you?" Mike asked, pointing to his burger in the large bun.

"No, you go ahead and enjoy your food. I'm fine.

Mike asked the blessing on their food, and they both dug in. Missy didn't realize how hungry she was. She was by herself in the optical shop that day, as her coworker had called in sick. She'd cut up her apple and ate that between patients, but the rest she ended up taking home. While they ate, Missy began asking questions about what they did on Wednesday evenings with the teens and what would be expected of her.

"We usually start with some games and snacks, which gives us a chance to interact with the teens. Then we have a time of Bible study and are currently going through a series called, 'How to Find True Joy in Life,' using the Book of Philippians. For most studies, we keep the group together, but there are times when we separate the boys from the girls for gender-specific topics that need teaching and discussion on a more personal level. Ron and I work well with the guys, but it would be helpful if Sue had another woman to relate to the girls. Since you're already connecting well with the girls, we thought you'd be a great asset to our leadership team," Mike explained.

"I'm very interested and appreciate that you'd consider me. I've really enjoyed getting to know the teens. They're a great bunch of young people. In fact, I'll be meeting with Rose on Saturday to look over some of her photographs. She's very talented, but I don't think she gets much encouragement at home. I don't know a lot about photography, but I just want to encourage her to pursue her talent and see where it will take her.

"If you know of someone who knows something about photography or how to market some of her pictures, I think it would really boost her confidence and help her come out of her shell. She said she doesn't come to youth group but came on Saturday because one of the girls invited her. Also, she wanted to get away from her home and have a chance to take some pictures," Missy informed Mike.

"Well, I've done some photography and have framed some of my pictures as gifts for family and friends. I'm definitely not a professional, but if you feel Rose would be comfortable with another person, I'd be more than happy to help if you want to frame some of her pictures. I'll keep my ears open though for someone who may be better able to assist in giving her direction."

"Oh, that would be great! I know a little encouragement would really help her. But even more important, I just want to be her friend and let her know how much God loves her and wants to truly care for her heart."

"Yes, that's what's most important," Mike agreed. "And because you understand that and have a real passion for our teens, that's why I'd like you to pray about joining our leadership team. Ron and Sue are in agreement with me, and I've talked to the church board as well. If you agree, they'll want to talk with you and hear your testimony, but I'm sure they'll see your love for the Lord and passion for the youth as much as we do."

"All right, I'll pray about it and let you know by Sunday. But would it be okay if I come and observe tomorrow night, just to see what goes on?" Missy asked.

"Absolutely! I think that's a great idea," Mike said as he grabbed the bill. "And if you're ready to go, I have another idea. I've enjoyed our time together and hate to have our evening end so soon. Would you be willing to take a walk with me?"

"I think that would be lovely. We need to enjoy these nice evenings while we can. Where did you have in mind?" Missy asked as she got up and Mike helped her with her jacket.

"Well, it's getting dark, but I thought we could go to Norrie Park and watch the stars come out while we walk. They do have some security lights out there, so it won't be totally dark. And since the wind has died down, we could walk along the river and probably see some fireflies too."

"That sounds great. I haven't done that in a long time," Missy said excitedly.

She didn't want the evening to end yet either. She'd enjoyed their time together. Mike was easy to talk to and so kind and gracious to her. And since they may be spending more time together as youth leaders, she wanted to get to know him better.

Can it become something more? Missy wondered. That was something else she needed to pray about.

Chapter 7

Wednesday evening, Missy observed the youth meeting and was even more convinced that working with the youth was what she wanted to do. But she would continue praying to be sure that was what God wanted for her and not just her own desire. She promised Mike an answer on Sunday, so she prayed until then.

Thursday evening, the young adults continued their study on the Beatitudes and were on the fourth, which was, "Blessed are those who hunger and thirst for righteousness, for they shall be filled" (Matt. 5:6). They also read Matthew 6:1–18, which went on to explain how to put it into practice. She learned that when doing for others, we need to take no thought of recognition; when praying, we need to give God praise and trust in Him alone for our needs; and that spending time with God nurtures our soul and helps us grow in Him.

Wow, that surely gives me more to think about! Missy reflected. *What is my motive in wanting to work with the youth or in helping Rose? Is it for recognition or is it because I really care for them? Do I really trust God to meet my need of finding the right roommate? In finding the right helpmate? And when I spend time reading God's Word, do I do it out of duty or to nurture my soul and desire to grow in my relationship with God?*

She decided she really needed to evaluate her motives in all aspects of her life.

Missy prayed often the rest of the week; and on Saturday, when she met with Rose, Missy knew that she truly cared for Rose and the youth. Missy wanted to be an unselfish friend to Rose, not expecting anything in return. She wanted to help Rose come out of her shell and develop her gift of photography and, most importantly, know that God loved her and wanted to have a loving relationship with her.

Rose didn't feel comfortable inviting Missy into her home, which was a beautiful, large craftsman-style house, so they went to Missy's apartment since Beth was spending the day with Kurt. Rose had saved her recent pictures to her computer where she had separated them into categories. She had a category for flowers; wild animals; insects; pets; general nature pictures; and waterfalls, river, and lake pictures. She was very organized, but Missy noticed she didn't have any pictures of people.

As they started looking through Rose's pictures, Missy asked, "So which pictures would you say are your favorites?"

"I really like some of the flower pictures, especially the close-ups. But I also like the waterfall pictures I took on our hike and some I've taken of Lake Superior when the water was so calm and peaceful."

"Okay, why don't you show me those first?" Missy suggested.

As Rose brought up the pictures to show Missy, she was impressed again with Rose's talent and the way she was able to capture the beauty of each intricate flower, the power and magnificence of the waterfalls, and the serenity of Lake Superior on a calm day.

"These are really good, Rose! I'd like to have some of these framed and hung on my walls."

"You're just saying that to make me feel good," Rose stated shyly, not even looking at Missy.

"No, I'm not," Missy said as she put her finger on Rose's chin, lifting her head up so she'd look at her. "I really mean it. In fact, I think you should pick ten to twelve of them and post them on your Facebook and see what kind of response you get. And if you add me as your friend, I'll share them on my Facebook as well. I'd even like to have the peaceful Lake Superior picture copied onto a large canvas to hang on the wall above my couch. And that close-up picture of the pink rose I'd like to frame and hang in my bedroom. This waterfall picture would be great blown up and framed to give as a wedding gift for my roommate, Beth, who's getting married in November. It would be perfect, and I know she'd love it!"

Rose was speechless and didn't know how to respond to Missy's excitement about her pictures. So Missy continued.

"Let's go to Walgreens and have them printed. Then I want to take you to the Z-Place Gallery in town so you can see what they have on display. Your photos are as good, if not better than what they have there."

"You really think so?" Rose asked, with a smile on her face.

"Yes, I really think so," Missy affirmed.

They printed the pictures that Missy wanted, then went to the Z Place Gallery. After walking through the store, Rose admitted that her pictures were as good as some of those she saw displayed.

"But I'd need help with the framing and matting. I've never done any of that before," Rose admitted.

"I may know someone who could help you with that. Of course, you'd have to add the framing into your cost when you sell your pictures. Or you could make some prints available for those who want to frame it themselves. I noticed they had some of those available at the gallery. But you'd want some of your pictures framed in order to draw people's attention to your work."

"That makes sense and would also help keep my cost down to start out with," Rose agreed. "So who do you know that does framing?"

"Pastor Mike told me that he's framed some of his pictures for family and friends. He could maybe get you started and then recommend someone who does it professionally later on. Why don't you come to church with me tomorrow? We could show him these prints and then see what he says," Missy suggested.

"I'll have to think about it," Rose said. "Can I let you know?"

"Sure. You have my number. How about we grab something to eat, and then I'll take you home?" Missy suggested.

"Sounds good. I'm starving!" Rose acknowledged.

"Then I guess you're a typical teen," Missy said, laughing. "They're always hungry. Let's go."

Missy and Rose had a nice conversation over their salads at Subway, but Rose always seemed to change the subject when Missy asked any questions about her family. Missy knew she would have to be careful how she approached that subject and give Rose time to build trust in her before bringing it up again. In the meantime, Missy would pray for Rose and her relationship with her family.

Missy got a call from Rose Sunday morning saying that she'd like to go to church with her, so she picked her up. Rose seemed to listen attentively to the service but didn't make any comments about it. Missy didn't want to push her too soon. They took Mike to Missy's car after the service was over to show him the pictures they had printed, and he was very impressed.

"These are really good, Rose," Mike commented. "I'd love to help you frame these, but I'm by no means a professional. I know the Ben Franklin store in town does framing, and there's another framing store in town also. We could look at some framing supplies and maybe get some suggestions, but if you want to display them at a gallery, you may want to have them framed professionally."

"I appreciate your advice, and that sounds smart. But I know I couldn't afford to have very many pictures framed professionally," Rose said, sounding discouraged.

"Well, I'll tell you what. Why don't we work together and do the ones you have here to start with? Then we can talk to the framing places and find out their pricing and go from there. How does that sound?" Mike suggested.

"Okay, if you think you have the time."

"I'll make the time and would enjoy doing it," Mike affirmed. "When would be a good time to get together?"

"Next Saturday would work for me," suggested Missy. "Does that work for you Rose?"

"Yes, but I don't want to take up too much of your time," cautioned Rose.

"You'd be doing me a favor. Last night I hung this canvas picture of Lake Superior on my living room wall above the couch, and it really gives the room a relaxing feeling. I can't wait to get the rose print framed so I can hang it in my bedroom. And I want this waterfall print framed for Beth's wedding present. So I'll pay for the framing supplies."

"Okay then," Mike added, "Rose, bring your computer next Saturday, and I'll take a look at some of your pictures too. I may choose some as well that I'd like framed for Christmas presents. But let's do it at the church so we can have the room to lay everything out. Then we can figure out what we'll need and go to Ben Franklin for the supplies. I'll bring my tape measure and a utility knife for cutting the matting. Shall we meet here, say at ten on Saturday morning?"

"That works for me," Missy said. "Does that work for you, Rose? I can pick you up at 9:45 a.m."

"Yes, that's fine. I sure appreciate all you're doing for me. No one has ever taken an interest in what I do before," Rose said with tears in her eyes.

Missy gave Rose a hug and said, "You are a very special and talented girl, Rose. I want to be your friend, and that's what friends do. They help each other."

"Thank you!" Rose said, as she stepped back from Missy. "I'd like for you to be my friend too."

"Well, may I take you two friends out for lunch and celebrate this new friendship?" Mike asked.

"Are you able to go, Rose, or do you need to get home?" Missy asked.

"I can go. There won't be anyone at home anyway."

"Well then, let's go!" Mike said.

They had a great time over lunch. Rose even smiled and began to open up a little more. Missy and Mike could tell Rose was enjoying having someone care and show an interest in her. It was sad to realize that such a wonderful girl was so lonely, starving for attention and someone to care and listen to her. How many other teens just needed someone to be their friend and care about them?

After they dropped Rose off at her home, Missy turned to Mike and said, "Mike, I've decided that I'd love to work with the youth with you, Ron, and Sue. God has given me a love for Rose and the other teens whom I've met, and I want to use it for His glory. These teens need our love, direction, and the chance to realize how much God loves them. And if we can show them how God wants them to live from His Word and by our example, they can have a greater chance at a future of serving Him in whatever way God leads them."

"I'm so glad. I know you'll be a great asset and encouragement to the teens. You're already making a real difference in Rose's life. I'll talk to the board, and like I said, they'll want to talk with you and hear your testimony and why you want to work with the teens. I'll let you know when and where, but I'm very excited that you've decided to join our team," Mike said with a large smile.

Chapter 8

Missy was busy at the optical shop that week, so the days went by quickly. She'd gotten a call from Mike on Tuesday evening to say that the church board would meet with her after the second worship service on Sunday. They wanted to hear her testimony and why she felt God was calling her to work with the youth. After that, the board would talk together and let her know if they approved of her being a youth leader. So in the evenings, she worked on writing out what she would say to the board.

On Saturday, when Missy and Rose arrived at the church, Mike was already there and had everything set up for their framing projects. He even had cardboard laid out on the table, so when he cut the matting, it wouldn't damage the tabletop.

"Okay, let's lay out the prints you have and decide what size frames and matting we'll need," Mike began. "Then, Rose, I'd like to look at your pictures to see what I may like to have printed and framed, and you should probably choose a couple of pictures to frame and use as a sample of your work."

Mike chose two pictures that he wanted for Christmas gifts and one for his own apartment, and Rose chose two pictures to show her work to businesses in the area. They made a list of items they'd need to purchase and then went to Walgreens to have the pictures printed to the sizes they wanted. At the Ben Franklin store, they got the framing items they needed. They chose some frames that already had the matting cut to size and others that needed a more unique frame and matting to enhance the pictures they chose. They also purchased the hardware to put on the back of the frames for hanging them on the wall. Then they stopped for lunch at Subway before heading back to the church.

After two more hours of work, they leaned the pictures up against the wall and stood back to admire them.

"Well, I would have to say that we did a pretty good job today," Mike said excitedly as they looked at the pictures.

"I would have to agree," Missy said with a big smile on her face. "Rose, with your great photography and, Mike, with your wonderful suggestions of frames, mattings, and sizes of prints, they look like masterpieces."

"I never imagined my pictures could look like this! I can never thank you enough," Rose said through tears in her eyes. "Thank you so much for believing in me and for all your help."

"You are very welcome!" Missy said as she gave Rose a hug.

Mike extended his arms, and Rose welcomed his hug as well. They had made a real breakthrough with Rose that day. She now had a beautiful smile on her face and felt cared for and loved. Missy sent up a quick prayer of thanks and was grateful that God had chosen to use her to reach out to this wonderful girl.

Rose again went to church with Missy on Sunday and seemed to listen with great interest. After the service, Missy met with the board, and they approved her to work with the youth as a leader. This made her very happy; and Mike, Ron, and Sue were pleased as well that she'd be working with them.

"I've enjoyed working with you already," Sue said as she gave Missy a hug. "You will be a great addition to our team. Besides, it will be nice to have another woman working with the girls, and you seem to fit right in. I've really appreciated your willingness to help wherever needed."

"Welcome to the team, Missy," Ron said as he gave her a hug also. "These teens are a great bunch to work with, and we know you'll come to love them as much as we do. We've seen you interact with them already and are glad you're joining us in sharing Christ with them."

"Thank you both so much! I look forward to working with you also," Missy said. "I count it a true honor and privilege."

As they left the church, Missy noticed some of the teen girls talking to Rose. She was grateful that Rose hadn't been left alone, feeling awkward while Missy met with the board. As Missy drove her home, Rose asked questions about what was shared in the message. Missy tried to answer her questions as clearly as possible, praying for wisdom and that God would help Rose open her heart to the truth. She also invited Rose to youth group on Wednesday evening.

"It would be a great opportunity for you to get to know some of the teens better and learn more about the Bible in an informal setting. They also have a lot of fun," Missy shared.

"I think I'd like that," Rose agreed.

"Good. It starts at 6:30 p.m., so I'll pick you up at 6:00 p.m. Since I'll now be one of the leaders, I need to be there a little early. Is that all right?"

"Yes, that's fine. I'll look forward to seeing you then, and thanks for inviting me," Rose said as she got out of the car.

Missy's heart went out to the girl. She seemed so troubled and lonely. She would continue to pray that Rose would come to know the Lord in a personal way and receive Christ as her Savior.

Missy was excited for Wednesday evening, both since it would be her first evening as an official leader and because Rose agreed to attend. Mike had informed her that they'd be studying Philippians 3:1–11 that week, so she read it over several times and was excited to see what Mike would bring out about the passage and how the teens would interact with it.

In the verses, Paul was giving a warning for the believers not to put confidence in their own selves but only in Christ. Paul shared part of his own testimony and admonished, "But whatever were gains to me I now consider loss for the sake of Christ. What is more, I consider everything a loss because of the surpassing worth of knowing Christ Jesus my Lord" (Phil. 3:7–8 NIV). What a challenge for herself, as well as the youth.

Missy had met many of the teens during the two events that she'd participated in, as well as the previous Wednesday evening.

They all greeted her warmly and welcomed her to their group. During game time she enjoyed interacting with them, discovered some of their personalities, and watched how Rose interacted with the other teens. She was still shy and reluctant to participate, but with the encouragement of two of the girls, Katie and Lexi, Rose got involved and seemed to enjoy herself.

Then they grabbed some snacks, which Sue had provided, and settled down for their Bible study. Mike read the scripture and asked a lot of thought-provoking questions that got the teens to really think and talk about the struggle they faced with putting confidence in Christ rather than themselves. With the peer pressure teens had to face and the push to "be somebody," life was not easy for them. They needed a lot of prayer and encouragement, as well as time in God's Word to stay strong in their faith.

They spent time praying for specific requests that several teens shared, and the leaders spoke words of encouragement to other teens they knew were struggling with issues before leaving for the evening. Missy discovered that being a youth leader involved more than just being prepared and attending the meetings; but also praying for the teens on a daily basis, getting to know them, and being an encouragement to them whenever possible. It was a big commitment and one she prayed God would help her follow through and be faithful to.

Chapter 9

By the end of October, the leaves had all fallen from the trees, leaving their branches bare. Missy's dad had been kept busy trying to keep their yard cleared of the leaves that had blown down. Missy used to enjoy helping her dad rake leaves before her allergy to molds had become a problem. Now the youth group was getting involved in raking yards for some of the seniors in their church who needed help with the task. Since Missy and Rose weren't able to help due to their mold and dust allergies, they prepared the refreshments for the group. Everyone was hoping that the snow would hold off until the leaves were all bagged and hauled away.

Missy also took Rose to the Z Place to show them some of her work. They were willing to put one of her framed pictures in the gallery and a couple prints to see what kind of interest there would be in her work. Mike had also made an appointment for Missy and Rose to visit a new frame shop in town. Rose was fascinated with all the different types of frames that were available and what was entailed in the framing process.

The owner really liked some of Rose's pictures and was willing to make her an apprentice and let her display some of her pictures in the shop.

"I can't afford to pay you more than minimum wage, but I'd be willing to provide the materials and teach you how to frame your own pictures. Then you could display them here and get a 30 percent commission from any that are sold. Would that be agreeable to you? You could come in after school, say two or three days a week, and I'm usually here on Saturdays until noon," said Gloria, the owner.

"Oh, that would be wonderful! Thank you very much!" Rose said with a big smile on her face. "I could walk over after school, and my mom could pick me up when she gets off work."

"Well, you'll have to make sure it's okay with your parents first. So why don't you talk to them and get back to me?" Gloria advised. "Here's my card with my phone number."

When they left the shop, Rose thanked Missy many times over for her help in making this possible. Seeing Rose so excited and having the opportunity to display her talent was thanks enough for Missy. But as they got closer to Rose's home, her excitement seemed to dwindle.

"Do you think your parents will allow you to work at the frame shop?" Missy asked hesitantly.

"I hope so," Rose began hopefully, staring out the window. "They think I waste too much time taking pictures and should use my time doing something more constructive. But maybe if they saw some of my pictures in frames, they would realize that it's not a waste of time, that people actually want to purchase them."

"I think you may be right," Missy assured her. "You have one framed picture left, and I could bring the large canvas print of Lake Superior and my rose picture to church tomorrow. Then when I take you home, we can show your parents how wonderful your photography is."

"I don't know," Rose said doubtfully as they arrived at her home. "Can I think about it and call you later?"

"Sure."

Rose got out of the car and went inside her home.

Why can't Rose's parents see what a wonderful girl she is and accept her talent? Missy thought.

She would have to keep Rose in her prayers and ask God to do His work in that family. She would ask Mike, Sue, and Ron to pray also.

After church the next day, Missy took Rose home and, per her request, brought along the pictures they had printed and framed. As they approached her home, Missy sensed Rose's nervousness.

"Do you mind if we pray together before we go in?" Missy asked.

"No, please do," Rose affirmed.

They both bowed their heads, and Missy prayed, "Lord, we ask that You guide our steps, our words, and the hearts of Rose's parents. We know that You have given Rose her talent of seeing the beauty You created, and, Lord, she wants to share that beauty with others. Thank You for this gift, and we pray that Rose's parents will be able to see her gift as well. We leave their decision in Your hands and will give You praise, whatever the outcome. In Your Precious Name. Amen.

"Okay, let's go in," Missy said as she opened her car door.

They grabbed her pictures from the back seat and went inside the house. The interior was immaculate and very tastefully decorated. Rose's parents were waiting for them in the living room, and her dad spoke first.

"Good, you're here. We're to be at a meeting in half an hour, so say what you have to say so we won't be late," her dad demanded.

"Mr. and Mrs. Simms," Missy began, in as confident a tone as she could conjure up, "my name is Missy Andrews, and I have become a good friend of Rose's and am one of the leaders of the youth group at the Community Bible Church. Rose is a very gifted photographer, and we had some of her pictures printed. This scene she took of Lake Superior was enlarged and printed on this canvas. I also had this beautiful pink rose picture framed to put in my apartment.

"She has been offered an apprenticeship at a frame shop in town so she can learn to frame her own photographs and have them on display to sell in Gloria's shop. One of her framed pictures and some of her prints have also been placed at the Z Place Art Gallery."

"I would really like to do this, Dad. It would be a good learning experience for me, and I may even sell some of my pictures," Rose added.

Rose's mom looked more closely at the pictures.

"You took these pictures, Rose? They're really good! I would say they're as good as some of the pictures we have in our office. I don't see any problem with you doing an apprenticeship, as long as you keep your grades up at school," she said, looking at her husband for approval.

"So how much time at this frame shop are we talking about?" asked Rose's dad.

"Just two or three days after school and some Saturday mornings, so I would still have my evenings free for schoolwork," informed Rose.

"All right, you can do this apprenticeship for three months, and we'll reevaluate it again then. Is that agreed?" her dad asked.

"Agreed," Rose answered.

"All right then. Your mom and I have to get going," Rose's dad insisted.

"There's food in the fridge. I'm sure you can find something for your lunch," Rose's mom said as she put on her coat and grabbed her purse.

After they left Rose said, "Thanks, Missy, I couldn't have done this without you. Can you stay for lunch? It's the least I can do after all you've done for me."

"I'd love to!" Missy said with a smile.

After they prepared lunch together, Missy asked Rose if it was okay that she thanked God for the food and for answering their prayer.

"Of course," Rose replied and bowed her head.

"Lord, I want to thank You for this wonderful food that we are about to eat. But most of all, I want to thank You for all your goodness to us, for answering our prayer so that Rose can work at the frame shop and for the chance I've had to get to know Rose better. Bless our time together and may our friendship continue to grow. In Jesus' Name, amen."

When they finished eating, Rose showed Missy her room. Everything was neat, clean, and in its place. However, Rose had printed several different pictures that she'd taken and displayed them around her room. Missy walked around the room admiring each print. She even noticed a few pictures of cute cocker spaniels above her desk on a bulletin board that looked as though they'd been printed from the internet.

"Did you used to have a cocker spaniel?" Missy asked.

"No, but I've always wanted one. I'm an only child, and it gets lonely since Mom and Dad are gone so much for work and other activities. But they say a dog would mess up the house and chew on things, so they won't let me have one."

"So what do you do with your time when you're not taking pictures?"

"Schoolwork, since I'm expected to get good grades. But I also like watching movies, especially old classics, movies that have great scenery, or National Geographic documentaries. I have a bunch over here if you want to take a look."

They picked out a movie and watched it on the large sixty-five-inch-screen TV in the family room. It was almost like being at the movies. Rose even made popcorn. It turned out to be a very fruitful and relaxing afternoon.

When Missy got home, she called Ron and Sue and shared with them the good news and thanked them for their prayers. Then she called Mike. He was just as excited about the good news as she was.

"That is so awesome! God is good! I think it will really help Rose develop her talent and promote her pictures. She really has started to open up and blossom since you started working with her. I really appreciate the time you've spent with her," Mike commented.

"I just pray that she'll come to know the Lord as her personal Savior. She has really been listening to the messages on Sundays and the Bible studies on Wednesday evenings and asking a lot of questions. She seems really interested but confused. I gave her a Bible, and I think she's been reading it. Please continue to pray for her and her family. They all need to know the Lord."

"I surely will," Mike confirmed. "By the way, my sister, Linda, wants to come up and visit me on Thanksgiving weekend. She's been hearing me say how much I love it here and now is thinking about maybe moving here also. She's been applying for jobs in the area. You don't know of any apartments for rent, do you? Anything available in your building by any chance? It seems to be pretty nice."

"Well, it depends on what she's looking for. Does she want a one or two-bedroom apartment, one to share, or does she want her own space? Why don't you give me a little more information about your sister?" Missy asked.

"Well, Linda loves the Lord. She recently turned twenty-four and graduated this last spring from the University of Wisconsin in Milwaukee and is an occupational therapist. She sent her résumé to Aspirus Hospital here in Ironwood, and since Ashland and Minocqua aren't too far away, she applied to those hospitals as well. She likes to kayak, hike, ski in the winter, and just enjoys being outdoors, which is the main reason she wants to move up here. She's currently living in Brookfield with our parents but would like to move to a smaller town that's near a lake and skiing. She has a beautiful singing voice and is an amazing person, though I may be a little biased since she's my younger sister."

"I'll definitely keep my eyes and ears open. She sounds like a wonderful person. I hope I'll get a chance to meet her."

"Oh, I'll make sure of it. That's why I mentioned her. I'm sure you two would get along really well. It would be a great help if she could meet some people her own age while she's here," Mike informed. "Do you know anyone who has an extra room where she could stay while she's here? My extra bedroom isn't available right now."

"I might. Let me check it out, and I'll get back to you."

Missy had an idea and called her mom after she hung up with Mike.

"Hi, Mom. I was just talking to Mike on the phone, and he said his sister is coming to visit over the Thanksgiving holiday. Since Tony, Shari, and Josh won't be coming this year as they're going to Shari's family for Thanksgiving, what would you think of allowing Mike's sister, Linda, to use your extra bedroom and inviting her and Mike to spend Thanksgiving with us?"

"Well, I'll talk to your Dad, but I think that's a fine idea. No one should spend Thanksgiving alone. But what are you not telling me?" Missy's mom asked.

After Missy explained to her about Linda wanting to move to the area and may be looking for an apartment, her mom said, "This may just be the answer to your prayer. Is she a Christian?"

"Yes, and she enjoys all the things that I do. I didn't say anything to Mike yet, as I want to keep praying about it and meet her first."

"Okay. I'll keep praying too," her mom assured.

Chapter 10

Missy was now really looking forward to Thanksgiving. She informed Mike that his sister, Linda, could stay at her parents' home and that they were both invited to Thanksgiving dinner. Rose started her new job at the frame shop and was really enjoying it. And Beth's wedding was only two weeks away.

Beth was getting pretty nervous, but things were well set, as her family was handling a lot of the final preparations. Because of all the relatives coming for the wedding, Beth would not be moving her things out of the apartment until she came back from her honeymoon. This was okay with Missy, as she didn't have anyone moving in right away anyway. But she was praying about Linda's visit and her possibility of moving to the area. Missy would leave the results in God's hands and wait for His leading.

The eye clinic decided to be closed on the Friday after Thanksgiving, so Mike and Missy planned to show Linda around the area, take Linda to see her apartment, and several other sites. It would give Missy time to get to know Linda and see if they would connect or not.

"I'm so grateful for your help. I think you and my sister will be great friends," Mike said to Missy. "I plan on taking Linda skiing on Saturday. Since we've gotten ten inches of snow this week, the ski resorts will be opening the day after Thanksgiving. More snow is in the forecast, so it should be good skiing. I wish you weren't busy with Beth's wedding on Saturday or you could come with us."

"The season is just beginning. I'll go another time," Missy assured him.

They got another six inches of snow the Monday before Thanksgiving, but the rest of the week was supposed to be just flurries or possibly an inch or two, but nothing to stop those who would be traveling for the holidays. Beth was grateful that most of her relatives would be able to attend her wedding, Mike was excited about his sister coming, and Missy was busy helping her mom with the baking. Emily was to help with the cleaning—although not happily—but it was getting done, nonetheless.

Linda arrived on Wednesday evening around 9:00 p.m., and Missy's parents received her graciously.

"We are so glad to have you stay with us, Linda. My name is Liz, and this is my husband, Ken. He'll take your bags to your room. I'm sure you're tired from your long drive," Missy's mom said as they followed him to the guest room. "We hear you might be moving to the area. You'd love it here. And we love having Pastor Mike at our church. He's great with the youth. Our daughter, Missy, works with the youth too."

"Yes, I've heard. He speaks very highly of her. And I've fallen in love with the area just by all Mike says about it and the pictures he sends. I can't wait to see it for myself. And thank you for allowing me to stay with you. It was so nice of you."

"We're glad to have you. You make yourself at home. There's room in the closet if you need to hang anything up, and I emptied a couple of drawers for you in the dresser. The bathroom is right next to your room, and I've set out towels and extra blankets for you here on the dresser. If you need anything else, we usually stay up to watch the news before we go to bed. You're welcome to join us or you can call it a night if you're tired. We certainly understand."

"Thank you, and I am tired. I think I'll just get settled in and have an early night," Linda said.

"That's fine. Our daughter, Emily, should be getting home soon. She had to work this evening. She's a freshman at Gogebic Community College and waitresses at a local cafe. Missy will be here tomorrow, so you can meet them both then. We plan on having a continental breakfast in the morning whenever people want it, so there's no specific time you have to be up. Dinner will be at 12:30 p.m., and Mike will be joining us," Liz informed her.

"Sounds good. And thank you again, you've been most kind," Linda said.

Linda unpacked her suitcase and freshened up a bit before getting ready for bed. She heard Emily come in, talk to her parents a few minutes, and then go to her room. Linda read in bed for a while to unwind, but it soon got quiet as Ken and Liz also went to bed. It wasn't long before Linda set her book down and fell asleep, as it had been a long day.

When Linda woke up the next morning, she heard voices in the kitchen. She got dressed and followed her nose to the kitchen and the coffee.

"Good morning, Linda, I hope you slept well," Liz greeted.

"I certainly did. Is that coffee I smell?"

"Yes. Here, let me get you some," Liz poured Linda a cup of coffee and handed it to her with a smile. "My husband can't do anything until he gets his first cup of coffee in the morning. Emily is the same way, but Missy and I never liked the taste of it. Though I do love the smell. Do you take cream or sugar?"

"No," Linda said as she took a sip and sighed. "Just black is fine. This got me through college and late-night studies. I don't think I would have made it without it – and the Lord, of course."

"Of course! Do you want something to eat with that coffee? I have some cinnamon rolls, gluten-free zucchini bread, and fruit on the table. I can also get you some milk or juice. My husband and I were just about to sit and have something to eat. Would you like to join us?"

"Yes, thank you. Those cinnamon rolls look and smell delicious. Did you make them yourself?"

"I wish I could take the credit, but no. I bought them at the bakery yesterday. Rigoni's have the best baked goods. They're right downtown. You'll have to have Missy and Mike take you there tomorrow. I did make the zucchini bread though. Missy is allergic to gluten, so I always try to have something that she can have."

They sat at the table, Ken said grace, and they began to get acquainted.

"So Missy said that you're an occupational therapist. Where did you go to school?" Liz asked.

"I went to the University of Wisconsin in Milwaukee. It's a great school, especially for careers in the medical field. We learned to design plans to help people who have life-changing illnesses or injuries to dress, eat, and even drive. It's a very rewarding job, though it has its challenging moments at times. I'm working at a hospital in Milwaukee right now, but I'd like to live in a place that is less crowded and has a slower pace of life. The traffic in Milwaukee is crazy, though I do like having shopping and coffee shops handy. I'm sure I won't have that here, but I'm willing to make the sacrifice for less traffic and a quieter and slower lifestyle. Of course, having Mike close by would be a great bonus. We were always close, and I've missed him since he moved up here. My parents live in Brookfield, just fifteen miles west of Milwaukee, so I've been able to live at home while going to school and work. But now, it's time for me to be on my own, and I want to see if Ironwood could be that place for me," Linda explained.

"Well, we hope you like it here. We do have a couple of coffee shops in the area and several good restaurants. We have some good stores in town too but not much for clothes. Most people go to Duluth for their clothes shopping. It's two hours away, so when we go, we usually make a day of it and take in some of the other sites as well."

"Emily works at Mike's Café. They have really good food there," Ken informed. "You'll have to check it out while you're here. A lot of their food is made from scratch."

"Sounds good. I think I'll have a lot to check out while I'm here. Mike has a long list of things for me to do and see. Maybe I should have planned a few more days here or I just may have to come back again. For a small town, you have a lot to offer."

"Well, with the ski season opening this weekend, it gets a lot busier. We have five ski hills in the area, and since Duluth doesn't have snow yet, the skiers all come here," Ken said.

Just then, Missy came into the kitchen and sat at the table.

"Good morning, everyone!" she announced her entrance. "You must be Linda, Mike's sister. Hi, I'm Missy." Missy extended her hand to Linda and they shook hands. "We're so glad you were able to come for Thanksgiving weekend. I know Mike is really excited that you're here."

"And I'm happy to be here and finally meet you, Missy. Mike has told me so much about you that I feel like I know you already," Linda said with a smile. "And your parents have made me very welcome and comfortable."

They continued talking and getting acquainted while Missy helped herself to some fruit, zucchini bread, and juice.

It didn't seem long, but an hour had passed when Liz looked at the clock and said, "My goodness, I need to get the potatoes peeled and our dinner going if we're going to eat on time. I put the turkey in the oven at six-thirty, so I know that will be ready."

Missy and Linda offered to help, and they worked well together while continuing their visit. Ken went into the living room and turned on the TV. Emily came out to the kitchen at about eleven, but things were pretty much on their way by then, so she was asked to set the table. She did so willingly, glad not to have to be in the kitchen, and then sat in the living room with her dad afterward.

Mike arrived at noon, gave his sister, Linda, a warm hug, and visited with Ken and Emily in the living room until dinner was ready. Liz, Missy, and Linda soon got the food dished up and called everyone into the dining room. They each shared something they were thankful for, and then Ken asked Mike to say the blessing on the food and their fellowship. The food was delicious, and the conversation was lively and full of laughter.

After everyone had eaten and decided to save dessert for later, Liz got up to clear the table and asked, "Why is it that we spend hours preparing a Thanksgiving dinner and it's devoured in less than thirty minutes?"

"Oh, but we get to enjoy the leftovers for several days, and it's always so good. Thank you, dear, for a delicious dinner. And, Missy and Linda, thank you for helping her," Ken added. "We appreciate all your efforts."

"Amen to that," put in Mike. "It was the best dinner I've had in a long time."

"Yes, thanks, Mom," Emily added. "It was delicious! And you made all my favorites."

"Well, you're all very welcome!" Liz said. "Now I have a turkey to debone and a kitchen to clean up."

"You debone the turkey, Mom. Emily and I will clean up the dishes, right, Emily?" Missy volunteered.

"Yeah, I guess. Since I didn't have to do any of the cooking, it's the least I can do."

"And I will help clear the table," Linda offered. "Many hands make light work after all."

So the women cleaned things up and put the leftover food away, while Ken and Mike went to the living room to watch the football game. The women joined them when they were finished. After the game was over, Liz and Missy served the dessert. They had made several pies, including cherry, chocolate cream, and pumpkin, which were enjoyed by all.

"I don't know about you guys, but I need to go for a walk after all this good food and get some fresh air. Anyone want to join me?" Missy asked.

"I will," replied Mike. "I could definitely use the fresh air and a chance to walk off some of this good food. Again, Liz, everything was very delicious. Thank you for inviting me."

"You're most welcome! You know you're welcome here any time," Liz replied.

"I'll join you for that walk," Linda said as she stood up. "It was dark when I arrived last night, so it would be nice to see what it looks like in the daylight. Let me get my coat."

"I'll come too," Emily joined in as she grabbed her coat.

"And I'm going to take a nap," Ken said as he stood up. "You young folks enjoy yourselves. You going to join me, Liz?"

"Yes, I think I will. It was an early morning, and I'm tired," Liz said as she followed her husband.

Missy, Mike, Linda, and Emily enjoyed their walk. The cool air was refreshing, and Linda enjoyed seeing the neighborhood and listening to Missy and Emily tell about some of their neighbors and things they liked about the community. Mike talked about some of the places he wanted Linda to see and said they would need to get an early start in the morning.

They had a relaxing evening visiting, ate leftovers, and watched a movie together. Then they called it a night, for a busy day lay ahead of them.

Chapter 11

Missy and Mike met at her parents' home for breakfast at 8:00 a.m., went over their plan with Linda, and were ready to leave by 9:00 a.m. They started by showing her the church, some of the shops around town, and then the hospital. They had lunch at Mike's Café, and Linda agreed that the food was phenomenal. Missy then took them to her apartment, as Beth was with her family decorating the church for the wedding on Saturday.

"So this is my apartment. All the two-bedroom apartments are pretty much laid out the same. I believe they have a one-bedroom apartment available but no two-bedrooms. They also have garages available to rent for an additional cost. Beth is moving out in a couple of weeks. I don't know if you want your own place or are willing to share, but I'm looking for a roommate to share the expenses," Missy informed.

"I guess I hadn't really thought about sharing an apartment, but it would definitely cut down the cost, so I wouldn't rule it out at this point. Right now, my plan is to rent something for a few years until I get settled in and get used to the area and my new job. But eventually, I'd like to buy a house, if I decide to make the move permanent," Linda explained. "It's really quite cozy and homey in here. I like the way you've decorated it. I especially like the picture above the sofa. Is that Lake Superior?" Linda asked as she took a closer look.

"Yes. A girl who recently started coming to our youth group took that picture, and I had it enlarged and printed on that canvas. Rose is a great photographer and recently started an apprenticeship at a frame shop in town. She's showing great promise and becoming more active in our youth group," Missy said with admiration.

"She definitely has a good eye and is very talented," Linda agreed.

"Yes she is!" Missy remarked as she took Linda to see her bedroom and the bathroom. "Both bedrooms are the same size and have a nice-sized closet, but there is only one bathroom. Beth wasn't here much, and we worked different hours, so it wasn't really a problem."

As they entered the living room again, Missy added, "There are several other apartments to show you, so if you're done here, we can move on."

"I'll definitely keep this in consideration, but yes, I'd like to see other options," Linda responded.

Missy had made arrangements with the manager to show her the one-bedroom apartment that was available, so they saw that next. It was a lot smaller and, of course, unfurnished, so was not as homey looking, but Linda could then put her own touches on it. Then they went to two other apartment buildings in town that had vacancies. One was a one-bedroom unit and the other a two-bedroom. They both came with a garage, which Linda liked.

"Well, you've given me a lot to think about and consider. I still have to wait and see if I get hired for a job here, but I really like the area. How about if we check out that bakery your mom told us about before we go back to the house? We can bring your mom some fresh bread for supper and maybe some more rolls for breakfast. They were really good!" Linda concluded.

Linda bought a loaf of French bread and six caramel rolls, Missy got a loaf of gluten-free bread, and Mike bought some apple fritters.

"Well, over all, I think it was a fruitful day," Mike said. "Tomorrow, Linda, I'll take you to the scenic Black River Road and Lake Superior, though it will be frozen close to shore. Then we'll be able to do some skiing in the afternoon while Missy is busy with Beth's wedding. Is there anything else you're interested in seeing before I take you back to the Andrews home?"

"No, I think I've seen enough for one day. It would be nice to spend some time relaxing this evening since it sounds like I'll have another busy day tomorrow. On Sunday, I plan on going to your church in the morning, and then I'll need to head home after lunch.

It is a five-hour drive back to Brookfield after all. But I'm glad I came. The more I see, the more I like it here."

After supper that evening, Emily had invited Missy and Linda to watch a chick flick in her room while Liz and Ken sat and read in the living room.

"I even cleaned my room this afternoon so we could watch this movie together," Emily informed them. "I've been wanting to watch it for a while now and thought this would be a good time to do it. I'll make some popcorn. You guys get comfy, and I'll be right back."

Missy and Linda grabbed some pillows and got comfortable on Emily's bed.

"I never had any sisters as it was just Mike and me," Linda said. "It's been a while since I had friends over for a girls' night, being so busy with studies. This is going to be fun!"

"It's been a while since Emily and I have done this too. I'm glad she thought of it!"

Soon Emily came back with a large bowl of popcorn, three empty bowls, and three cans of diet soda. She started the movie; and they all dug into the popcorn, enjoying the movie, laughing, and commenting on some of the scenes and characters. It was a night of fun, laughter, and bonding—one Linda wouldn't soon forget.

Missy slept in the next morning; ate a simple brunch of scrambled eggs, toast, and juice; and took her time showering, doing her hair, and dressing for the wedding. She wanted to be at the church by 2:00 p.m., as she was to greet the guests and have them sign the guest book. The wedding would start at 3:00 p.m., followed by a reception at the Legion Hall at 5:30 p.m.

The Lutheran church was beautifully decorated with white calla lilies and yellow and cabernet roses with cream-colored ribbons down the aisles. Similar arrangements were on the platform in large vases in front of a candelabra on each side of the platform. When the processional began, the four bridesmaids came down the aisle dressed in floor-length, cabernet chiffon A-line dresses and carried four white calla lilies with a cream-colored ribbon. The groom and groomsmen were in black tuxes, the groomsmen each had a cabernet rose in their lapel, and the groom had a yellow rose.

Beth looked absolutely beautiful as she walked down the aisle with her father. She was dressed in a satin ball gown, with a V-neckline and long, lacy sleeves, carrying a bouquet of yellow and cabernet roses. It was a wonderful, traditional service, and Missy thought she'd never seen Beth happier. She was glad she could share this time with Beth and Kurt and their family and friends.

The reception line was in the foyer of the church following the ceremony, and then people made their way to the Legion Hall in Hurley, Wisconsin. Punch and hors d'oeuvres were served while they waited for the dinner, and it gave the guests time to mingle and visit with the bridal party and other guests. Rigoni's Inn catered the dinner with a selection of different pastas, green beans, lettuce salad, and garlic bread—a family favorite—followed by the wedding cake. A dance followed. Missy stayed until about 9:00 p.m. and then left.

On Sunday morning, Missy went to church and was anxious to hear how Linda's skiing afternoon went. The three girls had a great time on their Friday evening movie night and seemed to really bond together. Missy liked Linda and hoped she'd get a job in the area and decide to move to Ironwood. She knew Mike wanted her to move to the area too as they seemed pretty close.

"Hi, Missy!" Linda said as she came up to her. "How was the wedding?"

"Oh, it was very nice. The church was beautiful, and the service was really nice too. Beth looked so happy! She was so afraid something would go wrong, but everything went very well, and everyone had a great time! How was the skiing? Did the hills have enough snow?"

"They didn't have all the hills open, but they'd made some snow on top of what was on the ground, so the hills were in good shape. We had a great time! Mike and I haven't skied together in a long while. It was nice to be together and just have fun. With going to school and work, I haven't been able to do that in a long time," Linda said.

"I'm glad you were able to do that yesterday. So you heading back today after lunch?"

"Yes, but I'm so glad I came up here. It was really nice to see the area, meet you and your family, and spend time with Mike. I really hope everything works out because I think I'd love to live here."

"I'm glad. But we better head to a Life group. I think it's about time to start," Missy said as she led her to the meeting room.

Linda enjoyed the Young Adult Life group and discussion time, as well as the church service after. Mike again joined them, and as they visited over lunch at the Andrews home, they talked about the church service.

"You have a great worship team, and the congregation really gets into the singing and worship time. In many churches, you have a hard time getting people to sing. Sometimes the instruments are so loud, you can't hear the words. You have a nice balance at your church," Linda expressed. "And I enjoyed the pastor's message as well. It was very biblical and practical for daily living. And the people are very friendly."

"Yes, we've really enjoyed our church," Ken agreed. "Every church has its issues, but we strive to work through them and be diligent in following the scripture's teaching."

"Well, it shows. And I have really appreciated your hospitality and getting to know you all. And, Liz, thank you for such wonderful meals. You have really outdone yourself. This lunch is delicious."

"It was just something simple, as I knew you wanted to get on the road," Liz stated.

"Turkey divan is my favorite dish after Thanksgiving. And this salad is delicious. I like the strawberries, mandarin oranges, and cashews in it. It gives it a nice sweet and crunchy texture," Linda said.

"Well, I hope you save room for dessert," Liz added. "I made a zucchini chocolate cake, which is Missy's favorite. It's gluten free, by the way, but you wouldn't know it. It is so moist and good."

They finished their lunch, and Linda finished packing her things and Mike put them in her car.

"I'm going to miss you, sis. It was so nice having you here. Hurry back!" Mike said as he gave Linda a hug.

"I enjoyed spending time with you too, and I'm praying it works out that I can move up here. You take care. I love you, big brother!" Linda said and kissed him on the cheek. "And take care of Missy too," she whispered in his ear, winking at him after. "She's pretty special!"

Mike looked at her with a shocked look on his face, smiled, and then said, "I will."

As Linda said goodbye to Missy and her family, she gave them each a hug and then got into her car and drove off. What an adventure she had over the last few days. Linda was glad she'd decided to come and hoped she would be back again soon.

Chapter 12

December was always a busy time at the eye clinic, as people were trying to use up their HSA money or order glasses before their insurance benefits expired. But Missy enjoyed keeping busy and helping their patients find the best possible solution to meet their needs. Sunglasses were very popular this time of year, as the sun glaring on the white snow made it difficult to see while driving or being outside. So Missy sold a lot of polarized sunglasses, especially after she showed them the difference between polarized lenses and just tinted lenses. It was an easy sale!

And as for easy sales, when Missy talked with Rose on Wednesday evening at youth group, she informed her that she had sold two pictures that she'd framed—with Gloria's help, of course. She was so excited for her young friend!

"And the Z Place sold a couple of my prints and would like more, as well as a couple more framed pictures," Rose cheerfully said. "They've had several people looking at the one they already have but thought a larger variety would draw more attention and bring more sales."

"With Christmas just around the corner, it's a great time to display your pictures. I am so proud of you," Missy said as she gave Rose a hug.

"I really like working at the frame shop, and I'm learning so much. Not just about framing but also about what makes a good picture. Thank you for making it possible."

"I can't take all the credit. Pastor Mike is the one who made the contact and suggested it, "Missy said.

"Did I just hear someone say my name?" Mike asked as he joined Missy and Rose.

"I was just thanking Missy for helping me get the job at the frame shop, but she reminded me that you were the one who made it possible. So thank you very much! I've even sold some of my pictures," Rose informed him with a smile.

"Well, congratulations are in order! I knew you'd do good. Your pictures are awesome!" Mike exclaimed.

"Thanks!" Rose said again with a smile. "Will you excuse me for a minute? I need to talk to Katie about a picture she wants to have framed."

As Missy and Mike watched Rose leave and talk to Katie, they both were amazed at the change in this shy and reclusive girl.

"What a difference in her," Mike stated. "It's nice to see her interact with the other teens too."

Rose and Katie went to the refreshment table and continued talking after they sat and enjoyed the food Missy and Sue had brought. Other girls joined them, and Katie was introducing Rose to them.

"God is still working on her heart, but her coming to church and youth group is really making a difference. She's able to see that people do care about her," Missy said.

"And it all began because you took the time to care for her," Mike commented. "You are a great addition to our leadership team. I don't know what we did without you, Missy."

"Oh, please. You were doing just fine before I came along," Missy said.

"No I wasn't. I like having you around," Mike said, giving her a smile. "And Linda said she really enjoyed getting to know you and your family. You all made her stay very enjoyable."

"We enjoyed getting to know her as well. I like your sister and hope she finds a job here soon."

"Me too," Mike said and left to talk with some of the other teens.

Missy asked Emily to come over on Sunday after church to help decorate her apartment for Christmas. She was looking forward to having some sister-sister time. Ever since Beth came back from her honeymoon and moved her things out of the apartment, it seemed so quiet and lonely. Missy had enjoyed spending time with Linda and Mike when she was here over the Thanksgiving holidays. And Emily had made their girls' movie night very special and a lot of fun. Missy needed some fun time, companionship, and laughter again. Emily was good at providing both.

Missy cooked the meat for sloppy joes the day before; and when they got to her apartment after church, she just had to heat it up in the microwave, add the buns, chips, and some carrot sticks for a quick lunch. Missy then turned on some Christmas music, and they started in on the boxes she'd set out.

"So what do you want to do first, the tree or the other decorations?" Emily asked.

"The tree. That's the biggest project and takes the longest," Missy decided.

They worked together setting up her five-and-a-half-foot artificial tree with the attached clear lights.

"I picked up some new decorations this year as I wanted to go with red and gold. I think it should look pretty festive. What do you think?"

"I'll let you know when we get it all done," Emily smiled and said as they started hanging the balls. "Mom and I put up our tree at home yesterday morning. Your suggestion to come here today got me in the Christmas decorating mood. Dad helped get the boxes up from the basement but then just sat in his chair and watched us do all the decorating. He hasn't been himself lately."

"Yeah, that's what Mom said at church this morning. She's pretty worried."

"So am I. Grandpa had a heart attack when he was in his midsixties, and Uncle Ray had one a few years ago. Do you think Dad could have a heart attack?" Emily asked.

"I hope he doesn't, but it's definitely in the family genes. Mom said she talked to his doctor about getting a referral to see a cardiologist. Hopefully he can get in to see one soon and they'll check things out to find out if there's anything wrong," Missy said, trying to assure her sister. But she was just as worried.

"Well, what do you think?" Missy asked after they finished decorating the tree and turned on the lights.

"I think it looks very festive. The red and gold balls really look nice, but now you need to get rid of that old skirt and get a shimmery gold one instead," Emily suggested.

"I think you're right. What would I do without my great decorating consultant?" Missy said and gave her sister a hug. "I'll pick one up tomorrow after work. And now you can help me set out the rest of the Christmas decorations. I've got some artificial poinsettias, battery candles, and a nativity scene.

When they were finished, Missy said, "And to reward you for all your hard work, I made some fudge. I thought we could have some while we watch a Christmas movie and enjoy all our hard work."

"Bring it on, sister! I hope you made my favorite."

"Chocolate walnut? Of course. You pick out a movie and turn on the battery candles while I cut up the fudge and make some hot chocolate."

After the movie was over, Emily had to go home to study for one of her finals the next day. It was a busy time for her, but Missy was glad Emily had taken the afternoon to spend with her. The rest of the evening, Missy decided to make a list of Christmas gifts she still needed to purchase for her family, special friends, and coworkers.

She had picked up a few things already but definitely didn't want to wait till the last minute with her Christmas shopping this year. She would have to keep things simple and watch how much she spent since she no longer had a roommate and now had to pay the rent and utilities all herself. But she knew that the cost of a gift wasn't as important as the thought and love one puts into it. So she spent extra time thinking of gifts that would say "You're special to me" or "I thought of you."

On Monday evening, Missy got a call from Mike, asking if she could stay later on Wednesday evening after youth group so they could go over the last-minute details for their youth Christmas party on Saturday evening. They would be going caroling at the nursing homes this week, and Missy was in charge of providing the refreshments when they got back to the church. She was making Christmas cookies when he called and would make some bars the next evening.

"That shouldn't be a problem," Missy responded. "I'm looking forward to going caroling on Wednesday. I enjoyed doing that when I was a teenager and seeing the smiles on the residents' faces. They get so lonely and really like to have children and teens come to visit and sing to them."

"Yes they do. And I think it's important for teens to realize that serving others is important and not just think about what they can get out of something. We've done a few service projects, but if you think of any other ideas, please let me know," Mike said.

"I will, but maybe some of the teens might have some ideas as well. It wouldn't hurt to ask them. If they make suggestions, they'll be more interested in participating in the service project."

"You're right, and that's a great idea. Teens don't like to be told what to do but want to be part of the decision-making process. And if they come up with the idea, we can have them take part in organizing the project and they'll learn leadership and responsibility as well. It also shows them that we value them as a person, as well as their ideas."

"Yes, that's important. I guess we need to remember what it was like when we were teens. I know I liked it when people listened to my ideas and thought I had something constructive to contribute. It builds trust and respect both ways," Missy added.

"I agree. I like your ideas, Missy," Mike acknowledged. "By the way, I heard from Linda today. She said she got a call from Aspirus Hospital in Ironwood, and they want her to come for an interview. She'll be coming up again in a week or so, whenever she can work it out with her schedule."

"That's wonderful! She must be so excited! It would be so nice for her to get a position close by so she doesn't have to drive so far, especially in the winter," Missy said. "Will she want to stay with my parents again?"

"Linda said she'll call and talk to you once she has a date set up for the interview. I'm sure it's best to leave it up to you ladies and not have me in the middle of it."

"Probably so. She has my number, so I'll look forward to hearing from her," Missy said.

Chapter 13

Missy got a call from Linda on Friday evening. She scheduled her interview at Aspirus Hospital for the next Friday morning, but had also heard from the hospital in Ashland, Wisconsin, so she would also interview with them in the afternoon. Since it would be the Friday before Christmas, she planned on driving to Ironwood the next Thursday and would leave the day after Christmas back to Brookfield.

"However, my parents have decided to come up also and will arrive next Friday evening so we can spend Christmas together as a family and do some skiing. They booked a room at the AmericInn," Linda informed Missy. "You had mentioned that your brother and his family were coming for Christmas. That would mean they'd need your parents' spare bedroom. I was wondering if you'd mind if I stayed with you in your apartment for those few days."

"But I don't have a bed in the second bedroom. Beth moved all her furniture out, so it's empty right now," Missy informed.

"I figured that," Linda began. "I'd be willing to sleep on the couch if that would be okay with you. I really liked your apartment the best of what we saw when I was there. And when you mentioned sharing an apartment and the expenses, well, that really appealed to me too. It would help us both out. You wouldn't have the full expense of the apartment, and neither would I. If I were to stay with you next week, it would give us a chance to get to know one another better."

"If you want to stay with me, that's fine. But as my guest, you can have the bedroom and I'll take the couch," Missy insisted.

"No, I won't do that. I will be living out of a suitcase anyway and all your things are already in your bedroom. It will be much easier for me to take the couch. That's the only way I'll do it. I don't want to put you out—that's not why I asked to stay with you. All I'll need is a place to hang up some of my clothes so they won't get wrinkled," Linda said.

"Are you sure?" Missy questioned.

"I'm sure. As a matter of fact, I'm looking forward to it. I've never had a sister, and the evening we spent together in your sister's room for that movie night was the most fun I've had in a long time. It will be like when I was a teenager and had sleepovers with my friends. And I hope we can be good friends, Missy."

"I would like that too, Linda."

"Good, then it's settled. I'll arrive next Thursday evening about nine-thirty. I'll be busy on Friday, but I'm hoping we can have some time to get to know each other. When my parents arrive, I'd like to introduce them to you. Maybe you can even join us when we go skiing," suggested Linda.

"Sounds good. I'll look forward to you coming next week then," Missy said as they both hung up.

Wow! Is this God's answer to my prayers? Missy wondered. *Is Linda the one God is providing to be my new roommate? She is Mike's sister, a Christian, and we seemed to get along well when she was here earlier. This might just work out. But I will still continue to make it a matter of prayer.*

The youth Christmas party on Saturday afternoon was a lot of fun. They went sledding, then came back to the church for food and games. Missy and Sue both made a Crock-Pot full of chili, and the kids loved it. They also had breadsticks, crackers, a veggie tray, pickles, and all kinds of Christmas goodies to go along with it. They had about twenty-five youth out, and Missy was happy to see Rose mingle and have fun with the rest of the teens. Mike gave a devotional and talked about the greatest gift we could ever receive—God's Son, Jesus Christ. It was simple but very clear. He concluded with a challenge:

"If you have not received God's gift of eternal life, provided by Jesus Christ, I hope you will do it today. Jesus was willing to leave

His glory in heaven and be born as a baby, live as a man, and die in *our* place to pay for *our* sin. If you have received Jesus Christ as your Savior, what are you doing with God's gift of His Son? Have you stuck Him away in a closet, only bringing Him out when you think you need Him? Or are you building a relationship with Him every day, entrusting your life to Him and letting Him guide your steps and decisions? He doesn't force Himself on you. It's your choice. What will you do with God's gift this Christmas?"

It was quiet in the room when Mike finished, and Missy knew he had spoken to many hearts.

After Ron closed their time in prayer, Rose came up to Missy and said, with tears in her eyes, "Can I talk to you?"

"Of course," Missy said, guiding her to another room where they could talk in private.

"I want to accept God's gift. I don't know how, but could you help me?" Rose asked.

"I would love to!" Missy answered.

Missy explained that accepting God's gift was acknowledging that she was a sinner and realizing that the penalty for sin was death. Jesus paid that price by dying on the cross for our sins because He was the only One who could since He was without sin.

"If we believe that Jesus died for us and rose again from the dead, we can pray and ask Him to forgive us of our sins," Missy added. "He then washes our sins away and we become a part of God's family. Is that what you want?"

"Oh yes! I've seen the difference in your life and Pastor Mike's, as well as many others in this church. I want that peace and joy that you have," Rose affirmed.

They prayed together, and when they finished, Rose looked up with a smile on her face and said, giving Missy a hug, "My heart feels clean and so light and free. I didn't think I'd feel so different. Thank you, Missy, for helping me!"

"You're so welcome. Now we're sisters in Christ, for we're both children of God. We'll have eternal life and will be together in heaven after we die. But for now, God's Spirit lives within us, so we can communicate with God, and the Holy Spirit helps us live the way God desires us to. You've been reading your Bible I gave you, right?"

"Yes, but I don't always understand it."

"Well, how about if we get together once a week and study it together? That way, you can ask me any question you may have, and I'll try to explain it to you. If I don't know the answer, I'll get it for you and share it with you the next time we get together. Would that be all right?"

"That would be wonderful!" Rose answered with a smile.

"All right then, what would be a good day for us to study together?"

"I work at the frame shop on Tuesdays, Thursdays, and Fridays. Would Mondays work for you?" Rose asked.

"Yes, that would work fine. I get off work around five. How about if I come to your house about seven so we can study for an hour? That way, you'll have time to do any schoolwork you have and still get a good rest."

"That should be okay, but I'll check with my parents and let you know," Rose said.

"Sounds good." Missy gave Rose another hug. "I'm so happy for you, and I'm glad we're sisters in Christ. You're very special to me."

"You're special to me too. I've never had anyone care for me like you."

"Now you have a large family who cares for you and loves you very much!"

"Do you think my parents will notice a difference in me? Do you think they'll want to accept Jesus into their hearts too?" Rose asked.

"I've been praying for you and your parents to accept Jesus. You just did, and now we can pray together that your parents will too."

"Good! It can't hurt to have too many people praying."

"No it can't," said Missy. "Come on, let's go tell the others that you are now a child of God."

"Yes, let's."

Mike, Sue, and Ron were thrilled with the news and each gave Rose a hug and welcomed her into the family of God.

Katie also came up to Rose and said, "Rose, I'm so glad that you've accepted Christ into your heart. It's the most important decision you'll ever make. I've been praying for you, and God answered my prayer. I hope we can be good friends and sisters in Christ."

And with that, she gave Rose a hug. Others who hadn't left yet also came and welcomed Rose into the family of God. Rose had never felt so loved and accepted.

Missy went home that evening very happy and blessed to be a part of the youth group's leadership team. She was also glad that God used her to share God's love and salvation with Rose. Missy prayed that God would now use Rose's newfound joy to help her parents come to know the Lord too.

As Missy was getting ready for bed that night, she got a call from her sister.

"Missy, we brought Dad to the emergency room. He was having chest pain and trouble breathing. They did an EKG right away, gave him some nitro tablets, and are putting in an IV. The doctor ordered blood work and will be in soon. I'm really scared! Can you come?"

"Of course! I'll get dressed and be on my way," Missy said as she hung up.

"Lord, help my Dad! I don't want to lose him!" Missy prayed as she quickly got dressed, grabbed her car keys, and headed out the door.

Chapter 14

When Missy got to the hospital and found out where her dad had been taken, they had just finished doing a chest x-ray. Her mom looked very worried, and Emily's face was filled with fear and she had tears in her eyes.

"They're going to find out what's going on and will do everything they can to help him," Missy said, putting her arms around her sister.

The nitro tablets seemed to have eased their dad's chest pain, and he was breathing easier with the oxygen. Now it was the dreaded waiting time for the results.

"The X-ray and blood work didn't show any heart damage, so that's good," the doctor began when he finally came in. "However, his blood pressure is high, and with his family history, it's probably heart related. I'm recommending that we transfer him to Wausau where they can further evaluate him. Being a smaller hospital, we don't have the capability to deal with heart issues, and we send all our heart patients down to Wausau. They'll probably do an echocardiogram, which will give them a better picture of how his heart is functioning, and possibly an angioplasty to check for blockages. We can keep him here overnight and transfer him in the morning, or we can transfer him by ambulance tonight. Which would you prefer?"

"Is he in any danger? What would happen if we waited 'til morning?" Missy's mom asked.

"He's stable, and they probably wouldn't do anything until morning anyway. Since it's almost midnight, I would recommend everyone get a good rest and leave in the morning. I wouldn't want anything to happen to any of you on the way, and we'll keep a close watch on your husband, Mrs. Andrews."

"Will we need the ambulance? If Dad is stable, why can't we drive him down to Wausau ourselves?" Missy asked.

"Because he still needs the oxygen. I highly recommend that he go by ambulance, just in case he needs any extra help," suggested the doctor.

"Yes, that would make me feel better too," Liz agreed.

"All right, I'll see if they have a room ready for your husband upstairs, and we'll get him settled in for the night. I'll get the transfer papers ready, and he'll be taken by ambulance to the hospital in Wausau first thing in the morning," said the doctor.

Liz thanked the doctor, and they started making plans for their three-hour drive to Wausau in the morning.

Missy didn't get much sleep that night but was grateful they were driving to Wausau in the daylight and not in the dark, as she'd never been to the hospital in Wausau before. Her mom was packed and at the hospital by seven-thirty in the morning so she could be there when the doctor made his rounds. She'd called and said their dad slept okay and had no issues during the night. Missy and Emily would be packed and ready to go once they heard their dad was being transferred to Wausau.

Missy called Mike to let him know what had happened.

"I don't know how long we'll be there, but being it's Sunday, they probably won't do much until Monday," Missy said. "I probably won't be here on Wednesday evening for youth group. And would you pick Rose up for church this morning and let her know that our Bible studies will have to wait until I see how my dad is doing?"

"Of course. And know that I'll be praying for your dad and family. Do you mind if I share your dad's condition at church this morning so the church family can be praying also?"

"No, that would be great! We would appreciate everyone's prayers. I know God is watching over Dad and will hear our prayers. I'm just glad it wasn't a heart attack, and if there are blockages, they can be fixed before his heart is damaged."

"Yes, that's good. Well, I better finish getting ready so I can get to church on time, but know that we'll be praying for you and your family."

"Thanks, Mike, I really appreciate it," Missy said and hung up

She finished packing and was at her parents' home by 8:15 a.m. Emily had her suitcase ready also, so they had breakfast together and waited for their mom to get home.

By 9:00 a.m., she was home, and they loaded Emily's suitcase into their mom's car.

"I think I'll drive myself, Mom," Missy said. "That way if I need to get back before you're ready to leave the hospital, I'll have my car. I'll follow you down to the hospital."

"Okay, that's probably a good idea. I called your brother, and he said to keep him informed. If Dad needs surgery, he'll come earlier. Otherwise, he was planning to come on Saturday anyway for Christmas. I don't know what kind of Christmas we'll have if your Dad is in the hospital, but we'll have to wait and see," her mom said. "I'm going to let Emily drive my car. I'm pretty tired and don't feel up to driving. Maybe I can get some sleep on the way. Emily has Google maps on her phone so she shouldn't have any trouble finding the hospital. We'll meet you there."

They all got into their vehicles and were on their way.

When they got to Wausau, Missy's dad was already settled into his room in the cardiac unit, and they were told that the doctor would be in to see him soon. They visited for a short while. The doctor came in, asked a lot of questions, and looked over the reports of the testing that was done in Ironwood. The doctor then informed the Andrews he was ordering an echocardiogram to be done shortly. After the echocardiogram was completed, the doctor would let them know the results.

The test showed that his heart was working harder than normal, which was a sign that there could be a blockage, so the doctor ordered an angioplasty to be performed the following day. Ken was very tired and wanted to rest, so Missy and Emily talked their mom into going to the cafeteria for something to eat. Liz had slept about two hours on the way there, so she felt a little more rested.

When they got back to the room, Ken was still asleep, and the nurse suggested they take the time to get settled into the hotel where they would be staying. She recommended one that was only a few blocks away and gave a 50 percent discount for families with patients in the hospital. They found it to be very nice and the staff very accommodating.

Missy called her boss at the eye clinic to inform her that she wouldn't be in for a few days, due to her dad's heart issues. Missy's boss understood and asked Missy to keep them informed as to when she would be able to return.

Monday morning came, and the surgeon came in and said he would be doing Ken's angioplasty at around eleven that morning. They would have more information after the procedure. The waiting time was difficult; and they did a lot of praying, pacing, and holding each other's hand, trying to encourage each other. When the surgeon finally came in to talk with them, he said he found one blocked artery, but also that the main aorta was 70 percent blocked, which was what was causing his heart to work so hard and resulted in his chest pain, high blood pressure, lightheadedness, and fatigue. Ken would need to have open-heart surgery, which would be scheduled for the next morning.

The doctor said he was very close to having a heart attack and was glad he was brought in when he was. So was Missy. They all held hands around Ken's bed and thanked God for allowing Liz to notice the signs and get him into the ER before there was serious heart damage. Ken felt blessed to have his wife and family around him and expressed his love and gratitude for them.

"I love you all and thank the Lord that He has given me more time to be with you. Thank you, Liz, for insisting that I go to the ER. I know I can be stubborn at times. I love you very much and am so thankful that you are my wife. Missy and Emily, you are both a ray of sunshine to me, and I am so proud of you both. I know I've been a bear lately, and for that, I apologize. I promise to make an effort to be more understanding. I don't want to take you for granted and am so thankful I have the opportunity to make things right."

Liz hugged and kissed her husband and, with tears in her eyes, said, "I love you too. And I'm so glad we got you here on time. I don't know what I'd do without you."

She then made way for Missy and Emily to give their dad a hug too.

"I love you, Dad," both girls said with tears in their eyes as they gave him a hug.

After they each dried their eyes, they visited a while longer. Soon, dietary brought him his supper, which was a liquid diet in preparation for surgery the next morning.

"Looks like I might lose a few pounds with this diet. This isn't enough to feed a bird," Ken commented.

"We'll definitely have to eat and cook differently now. But that's okay. It won't hurt either of us to lose a few pounds," Liz said thoughtfully.

After Ken finished his supper, he encouraged the three of them to get something to eat and let him rest. "Maybe I'll see if there's some football on TV later."

They left and got some supper. Afterward, their dad was resting comfortably. Missy and Emily went to the hotel, but Liz stayed at the hospital with her husband. She was still very worried and wanted to spend as much time as possible with him.

Missy was surprised to get a call from Mike that evening, asking for an update on her dad. When he found out about the open-heart surgery, he asked what time it was scheduled for, as he wanted to be with her and her family during the procedure.

"Oh, that's not necessary. It's quite a long distance, and I certainly don't expect you to drive down here. Mom has Emily and I with her," Missy explained.

"I want to be there—for you *and* your family. You all mean a lot to me, and I would consider it a privilege to be there during this difficult time you're going through," Mike explained. "My dad had heart surgery a couple of years ago. I know it's not an easy thing to go through."

"All right then, we'd really appreciate it. Thank you," Missy said as she informed Mike of the time and looked forward to having him with them.

The next morning went by slow. They were at the hospital two hours before the surgery was scheduled for all the prep procedures and were told by the doctor that the surgery would take about three to four hours. Mike arrived and had a time of prayer with them before her dad was taken into surgery. He kept them occupied in the waiting room by asking questions about family times they had enjoyed together.

Mike enjoyed hearing more about Missy's family and shared fun times his family had enjoyed as well. It was a good way to pass the time in an upbeat manner. Mike and Missy also took some walks to stretch their legs, went to the chapel to pray, and got drinks for the others.

Finally, the doctor came and reported that everything went well.

"I was able to bypass the blockages and cause good blood flow again. Ken will be in the recovery room for about another hour or so before they take him back to his room. He'll be on medicine to control the pain and will need to adjust his diet. But Ken should have a good recovery, and his blood pressure has gone down to normal already."

"Thank you, Lord," Mike said, noticing the tears of joy and relief in the three women.

Liz thanked the doctor, Emily put her arm around her mom, and Mike did likewise to Missy and let her cry tears of relief and thankfulness.

After Missy wiped her eyes and nose, she looked up and said, "Thank you, Mike, for being here. It meant a lot to have your support, prayers, and company."

"Yes," Liz agreed. "The time would have passed much slower without you. You reminded us of the many blessings we've shared together, instead of thinking about what we may have lost. Your prayer gave me real peace, and I was able to put Ken in God's hands. Tony wasn't able to get away until tomorrow, so God sent you instead. Thank you!"

Mike gave Liz a hug, and she rewarded him with a wide smile.

"It was my honor to be here with you. My dad had open-heart surgery, so I know what it's like. I didn't want you to go through this alone."

"Can I have a hug too?" Emily asked, with tears in her eyes and her arms open.

"Of course," Mike said, giving Emily a hug.

They all formed a circle, with their arms around each other, while Mike gave a prayer of thanksgiving for God's presence with them, for watching over Ken and giving the doctor wisdom to perform the procedure and praying for Ken's time of recovery.

They went to the cafeteria for some lunch, and when they got back, Ken was being taken to his room. Before the family was able to join him, Mike tried to prepare them for how he would look, the machines that would be monitoring his heart, and the pain he would be in. It was difficult for them at first, but they realized he had been through a lot and the pain would subside with time and medication.

They stayed with him for a while, but the nurses stressed that he would sleep most of the day and evening due to the medicine he was on. The nurses encouraged them to go and get some rest too. Liz wanted to stay with Ken, but Mike followed Missy and Emily back to the hotel. The nurses would bring a pillow and blanket for Liz later, and she would sleep in the recliner in Ken's room for the night.

Chapter 15

Wednesday morning came; and Missy, Emily, and Mike got to the hospital around ten to find Tony there talking to his dad.

"Dad, you have to listen to the nurses and do what they say," Tony implored his father.

"I just had open-heart surgery yesterday, and these nurses expect me to get up and walk?"

"They just want you to stand by the bed first, walk a little in the room later, and maybe tomorrow down the hall. They don't want you to just lay in bed and get pneumonia. It's for your own good, dad," Tony argued.

"You feel the pain I have and see how quickly you jump out of bed, my boy," Ken countered.

"Honey, please," Liz spoke softly. "Just do what they ask. They do this every day. I'm sure they wouldn't have you do this unless it was to help you get well."

"I know it sounds impossible, Ken," Mike added. "My dad struggled with it after his open-heart surgery too. But it really does help to move around as much as you can tolerate."

"All right," Ken conceded. "Missy and Emily, you step out for a minute, and I'll see if I can stand for a bit. These hospital gowns don't exactly give a person the best covering."

Mike went with Missy and Emily to the family waiting room. Then the nurses continued with some instructions.

"Now we're going to help you sit up, and we want you just to sit on the edge of the bed first, as you may be a little dizzy. We're going to place this heart pillow on your chest, and we want you to hold it tight when you cough to help with the pain. When you're ready, we'll have you stand at the edge of the bed, just for a few minutes, then you can lay back down again."

The two nurses helped Ken sit up on the edge of the bed. When he started coughing, they helped him press the heart pillow to his chest.

"Pressing the pillow to your chest helps cushion the pain," one nurse said. "Your lungs are trying to get rid of the fluid that collected there during your surgery, so it's important to cough, take deep breaths and walk, in order to prevent pneumonia from settling in, as well as prevent blood clots."

After Ken sat for a while on the edge of the bed and his dizziness subsided, he nodded that he was ready to try and stand. The nurses helped him stand for just a minute and then let him sit back down again.

"You did very well," Ken's charge nurse said once Ken was lying down and they made him comfortable. "I know it doesn't seem like it now, but before you leave here, you'll thank us for insisting that you walk, cough, and breathe into this breathing apparatus. This heart pillow will go with you wherever you go. You'll need to continue doing this once you get home as well. It will make your recovery go much quicker."

"I'll have to take your word on that for now," Ken said as he closed his eyes and sighed deeply.

Liz gave her husband a kiss on the cheek and said, "Thank you, dear. You did good."

"Good job, Dad," Tony added. "I'm going to check on Shari and Josh in the waiting room. Mom, you let us know when Dad is ready for visitors, okay?"

"I will. Thanks, Tony."

Tony went to the waiting room and saw Shari and his son, Josh, visiting with Missy, Emily, and Mike.

Missy stood when she saw him and asked Tony, "How's Dad doing?"

"He's doing okay. The coughing and moving was pretty painful. I think we should give him some time alone with Mom for a while. Getting up for the first time was pretty hard on him."

"That's to be expected. Hi, I'm Mike," Mike said as he stood and shook Tony's hand. "I'm the youth pastor at the church your family attends. My dad had heart surgery a couple of years ago, so I understand what your dad's going through is very difficult."

"Well, thanks for being here. Mom said she really appreciated you coming, and it meant a lot to her. I know Dad can be pretty stubborn at times, but he's in a lot of pain. It will get better with time."

They all visited for a while, and when Liz came into the waiting room, she said, "They gave your dad some more pain medicine and he's sleeping now, so we should just let him rest. Josh, why don't you come here and give Grandma a hug?"

After hugging him, Liz looked at him and said, "My goodness you have grown since I saw you last. What has your dad been feeding you?"

"I like hot dogs and french fries," Josh announced, holding three fingers up. "I'm free."

"Yes you are, and getting to be such a big boy. I'm so glad you came to see Grandma and Grandpa. But Grandpa isn't feeling too well right now, so we're going to let him rest."

"Okay," Josh said and went to play with his toys again.

They continued to visit for a while, and then Liz went to check on Ken again. He was still asleep, so Tony suggested they go for lunch.

"We left early this morning to get here, and I know Josh is hungry. We can all go together or we can do it in shifts. What do you prefer, Mom?"

"As long as your dad is sleeping, let's all go together," their mom suggested.

"And after lunch, I should be heading back to Ironwood," Mike informed them.

"Thank you again for coming, Mike. It really meant a lot to have you here with us," Liz said giving Mike a hug.

"It was my pleasure."

They all went to the hospital cafeteria for lunch, said goodbye to Mike, and then went back up to the family waiting room. Liz checked on Ken. He was still asleep, so she went back to the waiting room to visit with the family.

"Since Tony is here now, I think I'll go home tomorrow, as Linda will be arriving at my apartment in the evening," Missy informed them. "I can take Shari and Josh to the house and they can get settled in as well, if that's okay with you Tony."

"Yes, I think that would be a good idea. In fact, I think I'll get them settled into the hotel now while dad is resting. Then I can come back later and sit with him for a while."

"That sounds like a good idea," Liz agreed. "There's a wading pool at the hotel, so it would be much better for Josh there. By tomorrow, hopefully, your Dad will be up for some company and Josh and Shari can see him before they go to the house."

Missy and Emily also went to the hotel, showing Tony the way and giving their mom some time alone with their dad. Tony got his family settled into their room, changed Josh into his swimming suit, and they took him to the wading pool. Shari watched Josh and visited with Emily while Tony took Missy aside and talked to her privately.

"I know dad can be stubborn at times and has high expectations for each of us kids. That's one of the reasons why I went away to school so I could do my own thing. I also know he's been pushing you to go back to school, but you need to do what's right for you. Dad loves us—there's no doubt in my mind about that—and I love him. He's worked hard to provide for us, and I appreciate that more and more, especially now that I have a family of my own. So be patient with Dad. He might come around eventually. Oh, and I like your Pastor Mike. Mom's been telling me about him and that you're working together with the youth group. Is there something going on between the two of you?" asked Tony.

"No, we're just friends and coworkers."

"He doesn't look at you like a friend would. Are you sure he doesn't want to be more than friends?"

"Why does everyone keep saying that? He's the youth pastor. I'm me. I'm not pastor's wife material."

"What's that supposed to mean? I might be biased, but I think you're pretty special and could do anything you set your mind to. Don't sell yourself short, Missy."

"Thanks, big brother, I think you're pretty special too," Missy said as she gave her brother a hug.

"Well, I suppose I better get back to the hospital and check on Mom and Dad," Tony said as he went to check on his family first.

Missy visited with Shari and Emily and watched Josh enjoy the pool. But Tony's words weren't far from her mind.

When Tony got to the hospital, his dad was awake, so they were able to visit for a while. After receiving the pain medicine and resting, Ken was more cooperative and found that holding the pillow to his chest when he coughed, as well as using the breathing apparatus, made his breathing easier. He was also pleased that his blood pressure was so good. He was able to go for a short walk in the room but was then ready for more pain medicine and a short nap before supper.

While his Dad slept, Tony went back to the hotel to spend time with his family, and Missy went back to the hospital. Liz and Missy ate their supper with Ken and visited for a while, watched a little TV, and left by eight so they could all get some rest. Missy knew her Mom was exhausted and needed a good night's sleep.

Thursday morning, Liz and Missy were at the hospital by eight so they could be there when the doctor made his rounds. The doctor was pleased with Ken's progress and said that he may be able to go home by Saturday, as long as he continued to walk and do his breathing and coughing exercises. He would have to follow a strict heart-healthy diet once he went home. The nurses would go over that with them and give Liz information to take home with her. Then after about three weeks, he would need to go to cardiac rehab to gradually increase his activity and build up his strength.

Liz gave a sigh of relief and said, "Thank you, Doctor. We'll do whatever needs to be done to make sure he recovers and stays healthy once he goes home."

"Good. That's all I ask," the doctor said.

Turning toward Ken, he said, "You should be just fine, Ken. We caught it in time before there was any serious damage to your heart. I'll check in with you again tomorrow, but you're doing as well as can be expected. Do you have any questions for me?"

They all shook their heads no, and the doctor left the room.

"Well, you may go home on Saturday. That's good. We'll have a happy Christmas after all. We may not have a big Christmas dinner on Monday, but we'll be together. That's the important thing," Liz said with a smile, holding her husband's hand.

Missy visited with her mom and dad; the nurse helped Ken get cleaned up a little; and by ten, Emily, Tony, and his family arrived. Their dad enjoyed seeing Shari and Josh but tired quickly; so by ten-thirty, Missy left with Shari and Josh, put their things in her car, and then they were on their way to Ironwood.

They stopped for lunch at Minocqua, and when they arrived in Ironwood, Missy helped Shari unload the car and get them settled into the spare bedroom of her parents' home. Since Josh had taken a nap in the car, they then went to Super One to get some grocery items that were needed. The milk in the fridge was outdated, Josh wanted to pick out his favorite cereal for breakfast, and Shari wanted to pick up some simple things she could fix for just the two of them for the next couple of days. Shari was grateful they wouldn't have to stay in the hotel room any longer, though Josh enjoyed the wading pool. But at least now he would have the house to play in and could get back to a more regular schedule.

"I'm not going back to work until after Christmas, so I can come over tomorrow and take Josh sledding if you'd like so you won't be cooped up in the house all day. I need to finish some Christmas shopping in the morning. You're welcome to come along if you have anything you need to get," Missy offered.

Shari shook her head. "No, I finished my shopping before we left and thankfully have everything all wrapped, but I'm sure Josh would love to go sledding. What do you say, bud? Do you want to go sledding with Aunt Missy tomorrow afternoon?"

"Yah!" Josh yelled with eagerness and raised arms.

"I guess that's an enthusiastic yes," Shari said with a chuckle. "Thank you, Missy, for being so helpful. What time do you want us to be ready?"

"I'll get my shopping done and then why don't I pick up some burgers and fries for you two and a salad for me, and be here by noon. We can eat and go sledding for an hour, and then Josh can still get a nap in."

"Sounds good. I'll let Josh play for a while, and then I'll make some supper. We'll probably watch one of his movies that I brought after supper and call it an early night. We'll see you at noon tomorrow."

Shari and Josh gave Missy a hug, and then she left.

When Missy got home, she felt exhausted and decided to take a nap. Linda wouldn't be arriving until after nine, so it would be later before they'd get to bed. She was looking forward to seeing Linda again but wished she was able to spend more time with her while she was here. Her mom would need help with her dad, and she didn't know what they'd do for Christmas dinner. But that was the least of her worries. Now she just wanted to get some sleep.

Chapter 16

Missy awoke to her phone ringing. By the time she got to it, it had stopped ringing. She noticed it was Mike, so called him back.

"Sorry I missed your call. I'd fallen asleep, and it took me a while to get to my phone."

"I'm sorry I woke you. Are you home now or still in Wausau?"

"I'm home. I left the hospital about ten-thirty this morning and brought Shari and Josh to Mom and Dad's. It will be much easier for Shari to have him there than at the hotel. Tony and Emily stayed in Wausau with Mom. The doctor said Dad will probably be able to come home on Saturday," Missy informed him.

"That sounds good. How is he doing with the pain?'

"He's doing better. The medicine helps, though makes him kind of groggy. But he's more cooperative and is realizing that what the nurses said is helping. When I called earlier, Mom said he even went for a walk down the hall today."

"That's great! He's making progress then. What an answer to prayer."

"Yes, God has been answering our prayers through this whole difficult time. I'm so grateful Dad is going to be okay. There will be adjustments he'll need to make in his lifestyle and diet, but he's alive and there's no heart damage. God is good!"

"All the time, that's for sure! I'm glad you're home, but I don't imagine you feel much like cooking after all you've been through. I'm about ready to leave the church. How about I pick up something for the two of us and bring it over? What are you hungry for?" Mike asked.

"Oh, since you're in Hurley, I could go for Iron Nugget's grilled chicken with mashed potatoes and coleslaw, since you're asking."

"All right, I'll call it in right now and be there in about thirty minutes."

"Thanks, Mike. I really appreciate it," Missy said before they hung up.

It's sure nice to be cared for and thought of—even pampered. Mike is so thoughtful and a real gentleman. Just the kind of guy I was hoping for. Too bad he's a pastor. I could never be a pastor's wife, Missy thought.

Missy took a quick shower to help her wake up, then got dressed in a comfortable pair of jeans and a sweatshirt with snowflakes on it, as she noticed it was snowing outside. The fresh snow would make it nice for Josh when they went sledding the next day. But she said a prayer for Linda that she would have a safe trip and the snow wouldn't make it too difficult for her to see while driving up from Milwaukee.

Mike soon rang the buzzer to be let into her building, and once she opened the door and smelled the food, she realized how hungry she was.

"Come on in. I set some plates, glasses, and silverware on the table, so let me take those bags and you can throw your coat on the chair for now. The food sure smells good."

They sat down at the table, and Mike asked the blessing on the food. They both dug right in and took several bites before they spoke.

"I guess I was hungrier than I thought," Missy acknowledged. "I didn't have much of an appetite the last few days, but now that the worst is over, this food really tastes good."

"Yes, it does. I talked to Linda on the phone while I was waiting for the food. She left Milwaukee at 3:00 p.m., so she should be here about 9:30 p.m., as planned. It wasn't snowing where she was, but it's snowing here now. Not heavy though, so she should be fine."

"Oh good. I prayed she would have safe travels when I noticed it was snowing," Missy said as they were about to finish eating. "I have some ice cream in the freezer, if you'd like dessert."

"Sure, that sounds good. I'll clear off the table while you get it," Mike offered.

My goodness, he loves the Lord; is a gentleman, thoughtful, caring, and even helps in the kitchen. Do I really want to let him get away? Missy debated with herself.

"Do you have time to stay for a movie or do you need to get home?" Missy asked.

"It's Thursday night, so I don't have any plans," Mike said with a smile. "Relaxing with a pretty woman sounds like a winner to me."

"Flattery will get you an extra scoop of ice cream," Missy responded with a grin.

"All right! I win all the way around."

"Pick out a movie from the bookshelf by the TV, and I'll bring the ice cream and napkins over."

When Missy set their bowls of ice cream on the coffee table, she noticed Mike had picked the movie, A Christmas Prince.

"That's an interesting choice," Missy commented.

"Well, it's almost Christmas, and it sounded like a light and relaxing story after the stressful week you've had. Besides, I thought it would be nice to see what the life of a prince would be like."

"All right, push Play and let the movie begin. I may even make you some popcorn later."

"Sounds good, but first the ice cream before it melts," Mike said after he pushed Play and Missy handed him his ice cream.

They both enjoyed the movie, and Mike was right—it was a good movie to relax to and the scenery was beautiful. Missy even thought that Mike would make a very good prince. He definitely had the integrity and charm, and she thought he was as handsome as the prince in the movie.

Missy's mood was light and, after she picked up their ice cream bowls, said with a curtsy, "Well, my prince, would you like me to make that popcorn I promised you?"

"That would be very nice, my lady," Mike replied, continuing the light bantering and bowing his head.

"And some hot chocolate to go with it?"

"That would be most appreciated."

As they ate their popcorn and sipped on the hot chocolate, they talked about Christmases past and what they enjoyed most about Christmas as they grew up. The time passed quickly, but soon the entry door buzzed and they realized that Linda had arrived.

They both jumped off the couch and Mike said, "I better go help Linda carry her things in."

"And I'll get the blankets and pillows for her to use on the couch tonight," Missy said.

After Mike and Linda had everything brought in from her car, Linda gave them each a hug and said, "I didn't expect to see you here, Mike, but I appreciated the help carrying things in."

"Well, I brought Missy some supper, ended up staying to watch a movie, and we spent time talking after. But I suppose I should get going so you ladies can get some sleep. You've both had a busy week and another busy day tomorrow. Nice to see you, sis. I'll be praying that your interviews go well tomorrow," Mike said as he gave his sister a kiss on the cheek.

"Thanks, big brother. I'll let you know how it goes. And Mom and Dad should be here tomorrow evening. They booked a room at the AmericInn."

"Good. All right, I'll check in with you ladies tomorrow then," Mike said as he left the apartment.

"So how was your drive up?" Missy asked as she helped Linda put her things in the extra bedroom.

Missy had put a small table and chair in the room for Linda to set her things on, and Linda put her hanging clothes in the closet and her small case in the bathroom.

"It started snowing about an hour away, but the roads were still good so it went fine. It was a long drive, but I listened to Christmas music all the way here, so it made the time go by quicker. I was so sorry to hear about your Dad. How's he doing?" Linda asked, as they went back into the living room to make up the couch for Linda to sleep on.

"He's doing better. The bypass surgery went well, and the doctor thinks he might be able to come home on Saturday."

"That's great. So did your brother make it for the surgery?"

"No, he came the day after. I brought his wife, Shari, and son, Josh, to Mom and Dad's with me today, but Tony and Emily stayed in Wausau with Mom."

"That's good that he can be there with them. I'm sure they appreciate it. I hope my staying here hasn't caused you too much inconvenience," Linda said.

"No, not at all. I have some Christmas shopping to finish up tomorrow morning, and then Shari and I are going to take Josh sledding in the afternoon. A hotel room was no place for an active three-year-old, so it worked out good for us to come back to Ironwood today."

"Well, if there's anything I can do for you after my interviews, just let me know. But right now, I think I'm going to get ready for bed. I've got a big day tomorrow."

"Of course. You get a good rest, and I'll see you in the morning. I'll give you a key to the building and apartment, so if I'm not here you can get in whenever you need to."

"Okay, that will be helpful. Good night, Missy. And thanks for letting me stay with you."

"You're more than welcome. Good night."

Missy and Linda ate a quick breakfast the next morning, and then Linda was off to her first interview and Missy to finish her Christmas shopping. It would be a different Christmas this year, with her dad needing quiet and rest. She sure hoped her dad would be able to come home on Saturday, as Christmas was on Monday. It would be a simple celebration this year, but a celebration nonetheless.

Missy called her mom after she finished shopping, and she confirmed that their dad would be discharged on Saturday morning. He would need a walker for a while, so Tony had bought one on Thursday afternoon. That way, he could use it for his walks in the hospital and when he arrived home. He would also need to be on a low-salt, low-fat diet.

"Why don't you let us girls worry about the meals for a while - even Christmas dinner. You just concentrate on taking care of Dad," Missy suggested.

"Oh, that would be a big help, but I don't want you to go to a lot of fuss," Mom said.

"No fuss. But it's the least we can do after all you and Dad have done for us. We'd be happy to do it."

Missy picked up their lunch at McDonald's, Josh's favorite, and started thinking about the menus for their Christmas dinner and the remainder of the weekend. When Missy got to the house and talked to Shari about menus over lunch, she was more than willing to help. Even Josh got excited.

"I wanna make cookies!"

"That's a great idea, Josh," Missy said excitedly. "Tomorrow morning we can make some Christmas cookies together. Let's write out some menus, then I can get the groceries we'll need when Josh takes his nap later."

They decided on turkey, which was low fat and heart healthy, mashed potatoes, green beans, cranberry sauce, lettuce salad, and buns for Christmas dinner. Shari thought mint chocolate chip ice cream would be a nice, simple touch at the end of the meal and would go nicely with their Christmas cookies.

"Good idea," Missy agreed. "That would keep the prep down and easy to serve too. Okay, if everyone is done eating, I'll take a quick look through the cupboards to see what I'll need to pick up, then we can put our stuff on and go sledding."

"Yah, sledding!" Josh said, jumping up and down.

All three of them had a great time sledding and rolling in the snow. It was nice to have fun and laughter after the stressful week they had. After going up and down the hill several times, Missy knew Shari wouldn't have any trouble getting Josh down for his nap when they got back to the house.

Missy had brought dry clothes to change into, so after changing, she went to the grocery store and got everything they would need for their cookie baking in the morning, as well as some simple meals for the weekend and their Christmas dinner.

Chapter 17

Saturday morning, Linda had decided to join them for their Christmas cookie baking. Now that her interviews were done, she could relax and enjoy some Christmas festivities. They arrived at Missy's parents' house by nine, as she wanted to get the baking done and things cleaned up before her parents got home. Linda thought her interviews on Friday went well, and after a tour of each facility, felt she would be happy with either position. Both hospitals said they would decide in a week or two and let her know. She would leave it in God's hands. In the meantime, it was time to make cookies!

They made cutout cookies in the shapes of trees, angels, snowmen, stars, and bells. They also made peanut butter cookies with chocolate kisses in the middle and Rice Krispies bars with green frosting and Christmas sprinkles on top, which Josh put on. And of course, everyone's favorite, chocolate fudge, one pan with walnuts and one without. Missy wasn't sure who had the most fun—the adults or Josh.

Missy ordered pizza for lunch, and while they waited, Shari and Linda cleaned up the kitchen while Missy vacuumed the rest of the house and straightened things up. After lunch, Mike picked up Linda, and they went to the hotel to connect with their parents and would go skiing for the afternoon.

Missy's parents, Tony and Emily, arrived home about two that afternoon. Tony helped his Dad into the house while Liz went ahead of them to open up their bed so Ken could lay down. He was tired after their long drive. Missy, Shari, and Emily carried in the suitcases and bags from the car. Josh was still taking his nap, so everything went smoothly and fairly quiet.

Missy thought her dad still looked kind of pale but was glad to see him up and walking. However, she could tell that seeing their dad so weak was going to be an adjustment for all of them. They were used to seeing him active, in charge, and the leader of their home. Now he looked frail, tired, and needing their help. She knew he would get stronger, but there would still be a lot of changes.

On Sunday morning, their mom insisted they all go to church while she stayed home with her husband. She asked them to thank their church family for all their prayers and cards that were sent. Missy had bought a roast for dinner, so Emily just had to put the roast, along with potatoes and carrots from their mom's garden, in the Crock-Pot to cook while they were in church.

At church, Missy and her family were introduced to Mike and Linda's parents.

"It's so good to finally meet you," their parents both expressed. "Mike and Linda have told us so much about you, Missy and Emily. And, Tony, it's good to meet you and your lovely family. We are sorry to hear of your dad's heart issues. I know it's difficult to see him like he is now, but he'll get stronger and more like himself again. We went through this a couple of years ago, so we know how difficult it can be," Mike's mom, Lisa, said.

"Just remember, he's the same person, just not as strong right now," Mike's dad, Jonathon, added.

That sounded like good advice to Missy. It helped her put things in the right perspective. Though her dad needed time to heal and build up his strength, he didn't want to be treated any differently. He needed their love and understanding even more now, not their pity. He needed to feel like he was still the head of their home, not a burden. She needed to remember that.

After a nice family dinner, Ken decided he wanted to watch a little football before lying down, so Tony and Josh joined him in the living room while the ladies put the food away and cleaned up the dishes.

"So what are Mike, Linda, and their parents doing this afternoon?" Liz asked.

"I think they're going skiing again. Linda said they had a good time yesterday. We've had plenty of snow, so the hills are in good shape," Missy informed.

"Why don't you kids go join them? You've been cooped up in the hospital and under a lot of stress. It's time you got some fresh air and had some fun. I can watch Josh while you're gone, and we'll probably all take a nap later anyway," their mom insisted.

"Oh no, we couldn't leave you with Josh," Shari objected.

"And why not? We haven't seen him in a while. That's one of the reasons we wanted you to come for Christmas—to spend some time with our grandson. He's growing up so fast, and we don't get to see him very often, with you living in Green Bay."

"Well, let me check with Tony and see if Dad is up to it first," Shari countered.

She talked to Tony privately in the bedroom, and then Tony talked to his dad.

"Oh sure, you kids go have some fun. You don't need to babysit me. Me and Josh will watch some football together, and maybe Grandma will make us some hot chocolate later. How does that sound, Josh?"

"Yah! Me and Grandpa like football," Josh said, standing next to Grandpa's chair with his hand on his arm. "And cookies too?"

"Sure, you can have some cookies too," Grandma replied with a smile. "So I guess that's settled. You kids go have some fun, and I'll have hot chocolate and cookies ready for you when you get back. And while you're at the ski hill, why don't you invite Mike, Linda, and their parents over for Christmas dinner tomorrow. I'm sure all the restaurants will be closed, and we would be more than happy to have them."

"Are you sure, Mom? Do you really want four more people in this house?" Missy asked.

"Why not? You girls said you were doing the cooking, didn't you?" she said with a teasing smile. "And I would love to meet Mike and Linda's parents and have a chance to get acquainted with them."

Tony, Shari, Missy, and Emily went skiing and had a great time with Mike's family. It really was nice to get out for some fresh air and exercise. They found it a great way to relieve some of the stress that had been building up for the past week. They also realized that their parents needed some time alone, to process some of the changes they would need to make and sort through some of their priorities.

When they returned home and changed clothes, Missy and Emily made sandwiches from the leftover roast beef, cut up some fruit, and added them to the hot chocolate and cookies their mom had ready. Mom turned on the Christmas tree lights and battery candles in the living room, while Tony and Josh picked out a movie for the family to watch together. Soon, the family was settled down for a quiet, relaxing evening.

All seemed well with the Andrews family that evening. They were all together and had much to be thankful for. There was a real sense of "peace on earth and goodwill toward men" that Christmas Eve.

Christmas morning, Missy and Emily got up early to put the turkey in the oven, as Missy slept in Emily's room the night before and Linda had spent the night in her parent's hotel room. The Reeves family would join them at noon for dinner, but each family wanted time alone for opening presents and spending Christmas morning with their families.

After Josh had gone to bed the night before, the adults had brought out the Christmas presents and put them under the tree. They were all excited to see his face when he came out and saw the presents, for at age three he would be old enough to really enjoy Christmas this year.

By seven-thirty, Josh was up and excited, as expected. Tony had the camera ready and captured Josh's face, with his eyes as big as saucers and his mouth open wide when he saw the presents under the tree.

"Wow, look at all the presents!" Josh exclaimed. "Can we open them now?"

"Well," Grandpa said, "why don't you sit down here by my chair first and let me read to you about the best Christmas present ever. The one that God gave to us many years ago. Then we can open the ones under the tree."

Josh sat down very quietly, but so he could still see the presents under the tree, to make sure they would be there when Grandpa finished his story. When everyone was seated and ready, Ken took his Bible and read from Luke 2:1–20. Then he had Liz lead them in the song, "Away in the Manger," with Josh and Shari doing the motions. They also sang, "Joy to the World," and after a short time of prayer, Grandpa announced that it was time to open the presents.

Emily and Josh, being the youngest in the families, were elected to pass out the presents. It was a joyous time, and each gift was oohed and aahed over, appreciated, and thanked for. Once all the paper and bows were cleaned up, Missy and Emily set out a simple continental breakfast for those who wanted it. Josh was too involved with his new toys to be concerned about food, and they all enjoyed watching him play, as well as admiring the gifts the rest of the family had received.

By noon, their Christmas dinner was ready, the Reeves had arrived, and Ken had gotten up from his nap. He welcomed their guests and asked Mike to say the blessing on the food. There was much interaction during the meal and appreciation offered by the Reeves for the Andrews hospitality. They found they had much in common and enjoyed getting to know one another.

After the meal, Ken and Jonathon Reeves sat together in the living room and talked while the ladies cleared the table, put away the food, put the dishes in the dishwasher, and cleaned up the kitchen. Tony took Josh into the bedroom, read him one of his new storybooks and put him down for a nap. He knew his dad needed some time alone with Jonathan, since he had gone through heart surgery himself recently. Tony was sure his dad had questions he needed answers for, as well as some encouragement and support.

Tuesday morning, it was back to work for Missy and Emily; and traveling back home for the Reeves, as well as Tony and his family.

It certainly wasn't the Christmas their families had planned, but was one that made them grateful and appreciate their family and friends. Most of all, they were thankful for God's hand on their lives, for answering their prayers, and for helping them realize what was really important in life. For as Jesus had told his disciples, the most important thing in life was to "love the Lord your God with all your heart and with all your soul and with all your mind. This is the first and greatest commandment. And the second is like it: Love your neighbor as yourself" (Matt. 22:37–39).

Missy was reminded of this and recommitted to love God with all her being, and to live each day loving others so there would be no regrets, for we never know what the day, or tomorrow, will bring. She was so thankful for friends who were praying for them, for the Reeves family being there to help them through this difficult time, but especially for Mike. He had been there when she needed him most. He was her "Christmas prince," and her knight in shining armor. However, she had to be careful not to take him for granted. For she was realizing that Mike cared for her as more than a friend, which Emma and Julie, and even Tony, had implied.

Could I care for him that way too? Missy wondered. *He did bring me flowers and said I was beautiful. He treats me like I'm special. I enjoy spending time with him, and we both love the Lord and working with the teens.*

She would have to evaluate her feelings and really pray and ask God how she should respond to Mike.

Linda had promised to let her know when she heard from the hospitals she'd interviewed with. Missy hoped it would be within a few weeks. In the meantime, they would keep in contact. She'd like to have Linda as a roommate. Even though they weren't able to spend a lot of time together while she was here, they had enjoyed the cookie baking, skiing, and Christmas dinner. Linda seemed like part of the family. But the greatest bond was that they both loved the Lord.

Another six inches of snow fell that week, and Emily had taken over the job of clearing out the driveway with the snowblower and shoveling the sidewalks—a job that needed to get done in order for her to get to work, and one their dad was not able to do now. Their mom had also taken a leave of absence from teaching 'til the end of January. There definitely were changes happening in her family's lives.

Chapter 18

Missy didn't see Rose until the Sunday after New Year's as she'd been away visiting family with her mom over the holidays, so Rose was anxious to connect with Missy after the Sunday service.

"I was so sorry to hear about your Dad's heart problems. I've been praying for him and your family, but that had to have been so scary," Rose said as they walked outside together.

"Yes, it was. But he's doing better now. Thanks for your prayers. I know they made a big difference. We could really sense God was helping us through it."

Then Rose grabbed Missy's hand and led her to a red car.

"My parents got me this 2012 Chevy Impala for Christmas. Now you won't have to pick me up for church and youth group anymore. I have my own car! But I think it was mostly because Mom didn't like me walking from school to the frame shop in the wintertime, and it was hard for her to get away from work to pick me up at closing time. But isn't it great? And I just love the color—red! And look, it even has a spoiler on the back!" Rose said excitedly as she walked to the back of the car.

"This is great, Rose! I'm so happy for you."

"Oh, and I talked to my parents about studying the Bible together on Monday evenings, but they said that with me working at the frame shop three days a week, youth group on Wednesday evenings, and church on Sundays, I shouldn't add anything more to my schedule. They don't want me taking any more time away from my schoolwork, and they think I have enough Bible and church as it is."

"Well, you keep reading your Bible and write down any questions that you have. We can always talk about them when we get together on Wednesday evenings or Sundays. And pray too that the Holy Spirit will help you understand what you're reading."

"I'm still trying to understand all that Holy Spirit stuff," Rose said with a puzzled look on her face. "But I do know that I don't feel alone like I used to. I feel more at peace, and things that I've read, you've told me about, or we've learned in youth group—God reminds me of when I need it the most."

"That's the Holy Spirit working in you. He's your comforter, teacher, and is there to encourage and guide you in your everyday life. He's always with you wherever you are because He lives in your heart."

"Wow! That is so cool!"

"Yes it is," Missy said with a grin.

Missy was also excited about a mission trip that the leaders were planning for the youth on July 14–19 called, Week of Hope. This would be Missy's first mission trip, and on the second Wednesday in January, Mike presented the program to the youth with information and videos. Many of the teens were excited about it as well. They would be joining other youth groups in Kenosha, Wisconsin, and be involved with serving in food distributions, visiting with residents in a nursing home or assisted living facility, general yard work, home repairs, and volunteering at a community center and day camp.

The cost per person was $266, plus transportation costs, so they would need to plan fundraisers for the trip and asked the youth for some suggestions. They came up with a car wash, Sunday morning breakfast at church, a bake sale, a yard sale, and even a silent auction. Ten teens said they were interested in going on the mission trip right away, but they were hoping more would decide to go as well.

Those going would need permission slips signed by their parents, but everyone would be involved in the fundraising process to encourage and support those who were going. More information would be available, and a presentation to the parents and church body would be given at a later date. But it was good to know that the teens were already getting excited about it.

Mike approached Missy after the meeting and asked, "Missy, with your accounting background and organizational skills, would you be willing to do the bookkeeping for the fundraising events and keep track of how much is raised, spent, and who works at each event? I know you'd be very good at it. Of course, you'd be working with the church treasurer also, giving her the money that comes in, receipts for any purchases for events, and so forth, as she'll be the one making the payments to the Week of Hope."

"Wow! That's quite a responsibility," Missy acknowledged. "I'm excited about the mission trip, but handling the bookkeeping and responsibility of all the money is a huge undertaking."

"Ron, Sue, and I would help, of course, but we need someone to oversee it, be the go-to-person, and make sure that the money, receipts, and those who worked at each fundraiser is kept track of."

"Well, if you think I can do it."

"I have no doubt," Mike assured her.

"Let me pray about it and talk to the church treasurer to see what will be required, and what she'll need."

"That's fine. I understand it's a big responsibility, but I wouldn't have asked you if I didn't believe you could do it."

"All right, I'll get back to you within a week with my decision," Missy promised.

Missy prayed about the responsibility of the bookkeeping for the fundraising events, and talked to the church treasurer to see what she would require. She was very helpful in offering information and a notebook for Missy to keep an accurate record of money raised and receipts of items purchased. Then she would need to give all the money and receipts to the treasurer so she could keep track of and pay the required payments from the youth group's account. She even provided her with a money bag to keep the money and receipts in.

Missy knew it would be a big responsibility. But when she talked to her dad, Missy was surprised at how encouraging and supportive he was. He really believed she could do it.

The next Sunday, Missy told Mike, Ron, and Sue that she would do the bookkeeping, as long as they helped with the fundraising events. They agreed and thanked her for taking on this important challenge. Now they could move forward.

Posters, brochures, and information on the mission trip were ordered; and permission slips that parents would need to sign were printed. The last Sunday in January, Mike would present the youth's mission trip to the church body, as requested by the mission board, so they could be in prayer for the youth and support them with donations as they felt led. Information would be available for the parents to take with them also. They also scheduled their first fundraiser, which would be a bake sale on the Sunday before Valentine's Day. There was much to be done before July.

By the middle of January, Missy's dad was getting stronger and started cardiac rehab three times a week. Liz seemed to be enjoying spending more time with her husband while he was home recuperating. They were reading the Bible and praying together, thanking God for each day they had. They also went shopping together, in order to get Ken out of the house and to go for a walk on the days he didn't have rehab. They also put puzzles together, and her mom was trying out new heart-healthy recipes.

Her dad called a family meeting one evening. Their mom cooked one of her delicious new heart-healthy recipes.

"Since my heart surgery, I've been doing a lot of thinking, and your Mom and I have been doing a lot of talking, praying and evaluating of our lives," Missy's dad began. "I first want to say how thankful I am that God was watching over me and for His answered prayer. I'm also very thankful for my family, for all your love, support, and care for me while I was in the hospital and after I came home.

"You girls have really pitched in, and your mom and I are very grateful. We also realize that things are going to be changing and that I can't do everything I used to. So I've hired Phil Larson to do the snow removal for the rest of the winter and possibly the lawn care this summer as well."

"But, Dad, I can do that. I really don't mind," Emily interrupted.

"No, Emily. I've appreciated you doing it these last few weeks, but your classes have started again and with your studies and work, you have enough on your plate. I'm just glad we haven't had any major snowstorms lately, but we know they'll be coming and it will be too much for you to handle alone," her dad stated. "Your mom will be going back to teaching in February, and after talking to my boss at the bank, I'll be going back to work part time too. I'll start out with four hours a day and increase it as I'm able. Hopefully, by the end of the month, I'll be back to full time."

Then he made a short pause before continuing. "But I also want to apologize for my stubbornness when I was in the hospital and not being cooperative with the nurses when they asked me to get up after my surgery. I was a poor example to you all, and for that, I'm very sorry."

"But you were in a lot of pain, Dad. That was understandable," Missy assured him.

"But not excusable," her dad insisted. "The nurses were just doing their job and what they knew was best for me. And they were right. I soon realized that it was good for me to get up, do the coughing, walking, and breathing exercises they insisted on, in order to prevent pneumonia from settling in, and so I would recover more quickly. I apologized to the nurses before I left, and to your mom and Tony, but now I want to apologize to you girls as well. I acted inappropriately and I'm sorry. Can you forgive me?"

"Of course, Dad," Missy and Emily said at the same time.

"Thank you! But I've been thinking too about how I've been pushing you, Missy, to go back to school and get your BA degree in accounting in order to make something of yourself. I've now realized that you really like what you're doing at the eye clinic. You're helping people with their eyeglasses, making them see better and feel good about themselves. And your work with the youth group, especially with Rose, Missy, you're truly gifted in helping and caring for people. I want you to know that I'm very proud of you. You truly have made something of yourself.

"So no more pushing from me to go for more schooling. You just do what God wants you to do, and I'll support you in it. When

I was praying for you this week, God showed me a verse I want to share with you. It's a familiar verse found in Jeremiah, "For I know the plans I have for you," declares the Lord, "plans to prosper you and not to harm you, plans to give you hope and a future"' (Jer. 29:11). Your future is in God's hands, Missy, so follow His plan, not mine!"

"Thanks, Dad," Missy said with tears in her eyes, getting up to give him a hug. "I love you!"

"I love you too, sweetie," her dad said as his eyes misted over and he put his arms around her.

After Missy went back to her seat, Ken then looked at Emily and said, "Emily, you are a bundle of energy and a true joy to have in our family. You will be wonderful in whatever teaching and coaching field you choose to pursue. Kids love you and you love them, that's obvious. Plus, you have the energy to keep up with them. We are blessed to have you as our daughter, and I know I don't say that enough. You are unique and very special to your mom and I. And I would like to admonish you, as Paul did Timothy, 'Don't let anyone look down on you because you are young, but set an example for the believers in speech, in conduct, in love, in faith and in purity' (1 Tim. 4:12) I love you, Emily, and am so proud of you."

"Thanks, Dad, that means a lot! And I love you and Mom so very much," Emily said as she gave her dad and mom a hug.

"Well, that's enough emotion and hugging for now. I think your mom made dessert, so let's have some of that now," their dad said with a smile.

Missy thought about what her dad had said over the next few days, as well as the verse he'd given her. She had memorized that verse when she was younger but hadn't thought about it for a while.

What is God's plan for my life? Missy asked herself. *How will I recognize it or know if what I'm doing is God's plan for me?*

As she was contemplating these questions her phone rang. It was Linda Reeves.

"Hi, Linda. Do you have some good news for me?"

"Well, yes and no. I didn't get the job at Aspirus Hospital in Ironwood, but I did get the job at the Memorial Medical Center in Ashland. I'll have a forty-five-minute drive to work, but it will be a nice drive, and its Highway 2 most of the way, so the roads will usually be plowed in the wintertime. And it will give me time to wind down after work. Besides, I was very impressed with the way the staff really cared about the patients and worked well together. I think it will be a good experience."

"Oh, I'm so happy for you, Linda! When do you start?"

"I'll start the first full week in February, so I've given my two weeks' notice and would like to move up there the Saturday before. And if you don't mind, I'd like to share the apartment with you."

"Are you kidding?" Missy shrieked. "I would love to have you for a roommate. When you left after Christmas, I was thinking that you're almost like one of the family. You just seem to fit right in. Oh, I'm so excited, I can't wait!"

"I'm sure the time will go fast, especially for me. I have to pack and finish up my job here in Milwaukee. But thankfully, I just have my bedroom things to bring with me. Dad said he should be able to fit it all in his pickup and my car. I'm so glad you have everything else. It will make moving into an apartment so much easier!"

"Yes, well, April left a lot of her furniture here when she moved out, so that made it easier for me as well," Missy said.

"This is so exciting for me! I'll finally be living on my own, will have a great roommate, and be close to Mike too. This is a dream come true!"

"Have you told Mike yet?"

"No, I wanted to talk to you first, to make sure you still wanted me to share your apartment."

"Are you kidding? I was hoping and praying that you would."

"Well, God answered both our prayers then," Linda affirmed. "So how is your Dad doing since I talked to you last?"

"He started cardiac rehab and is doing more walking. He hopes to go back to work part time the first week in February and be back to full time by the end of the month. Mom will be going back to teaching in February too. Things are starting to get back to normal—or at least the new normal. Dad is definitely slowing down and has even hired someone to do the snow removal."

"With all the snow you get up there, it's probably a good idea. I know my dad made a lot of changes after his heart surgery too. I think it makes them realize that they're not as young as they used to be and need to slow down a little."

"Yes, and it has made me realize I shouldn't take them for granted but let them know that I love them and appreciate all they do for me. It can be so easy to take one another for granted and think we'll always have tomorrow to make it right. That's not always the case."

"No, it's not," Linda agreed.

Linda and Missy visited a few more minutes and then concluded their call. After Missy hung up, she went to the now-empty second bedroom and imagined Linda's bedroom furniture in there, seeing her smiling face, enjoying her companionship, and sharing conversations. She was looking forward to Linda coming to live with her. And she also realized that God had answered her prayer for a Christian roommate with whom she could connect and do things.

It seemed God did have a plan for her life, would prosper her, and was giving her hope. She was excited to see what God would do next.

Chapter 19

The next two weeks went by quickly. On Saturday, February 2, Linda arrived at 2:00 p.m. with her parents in their pickup and loaded down with her furniture and boxes. Mike came shortly after, as Linda had called him when they were about ten miles from Ironwood. He brought Luke with him to help unload and carry things up to their apartment.

Mike introduced Luke to his parents and sister.

"Mom, Dad, and Linda, this is my friend Luke. He leads our young adult group on Thursday evenings. He's agreed to help us this afternoon."

"Nice to meet you, Luke," Mike's dad said as he shook his hand. "With two strong young men here to carry the heavy stuff, it makes it that much easier on me."

Luke also shook Lisa and Linda's hands and then said, "Okay, so let's get this truck unloaded."

"All right, I like your style, young man. Let's get to it," Mike's dad agreed.

They unloaded the bed first and set it up where Linda wanted it. Linda was then able to see where they should put her dresser and desk. With all of them working together, they had everything unloaded and carried up in an hour and a half. Then they took a break and sat at the table for some refreshments Missy had prepared. After visiting for a while, Mike and Luke left; and Missy, Linda, and Lisa tackled emptying the boxes and making the bed while Jonathan broke down the boxes and hung Linda's curtains and pictures on the wall.

"All right, job well done!" Lisa said as they looked over Linda's new bedroom after everything was put away. "Everything looks very homey and nice. I think you'll be very comfortable here."

"I think so too," Linda agreed with a smile. She was very pleased with how everything fit and came together. "I have some DVDs to add to your collection, if that's okay with you, Missy."

"Of course. This is your home now too, so please feel free to make yourself at home," Missy insisted.

Missy led them into the living room, and Linda added her DVDs to the shelf.

"I see we have similar taste in movies. But you have some I don't have, so it will be fun to watch them together. The ones that are duplicates—I'll put back in my room."

"If you girls are all set here, your dad and I will get checked into the AmericInn. How about if we meet somewhere for supper, say in an hour?" Lisa suggested.

"Yes, that sounds good. I'm getting hungry but too tired to cook. How does that sound to you, Missy?"

"Sounds good to me too."

"Okay then, what are you girls hungry for?" Lisa asked. "It will be our treat as a housewarming gift for you, Linda, and to thank you, Missy, for being willing to share your apartment with Linda."

"I could go for some pizza. How about you, Missy?"

"Yah, Angelo's has good pizza and it's close to the AmericInn. As long as I get their thin crust, I should be fine. We can meet you at your hotel, Lisa, and you can follow us over there or you can ride with us."

"We'll probably drive ourselves, so yes, we'll meet you at the hotel lobby in an hour."

After Linda's parents left, Missy and Linda reorganized the shelving and drawers in the bathroom so they each had their own spaces, and Missy showed Linda where things were in the kitchen.

"We can work out the grocery budget and meal preparations once we know more of how our schedules will work out. But it sounds like we'll have similar working hours, so that will be nice," Missy said.

"Yes, and I sent the check for my part of this month's rent in the mail last week."

"Good. We'll talk about the electric, cable and internet payments later too. We have time to work out those details before they're due. You already filled out the forms for the building manager, so this is officially your home now too."

"I really want this to work, Missy, so if I do anything that bothers you, or if I can help in any way, please let me know. I want us to talk about things and be able to work them out."

"Me too! We both prayed about this and I'm so glad you're here," Missy said as she gave Linda a hug. "And I'm hungry! Let's go meet your parents and get some pizza!"

"Great idea!" Linda agreed.

Monday morning worked out well. Since Linda had to leave early for her commute to Ashland, there were no conflicts with needing the bathroom at the same time. Missy and Linda ate breakfast together, and Missy wished her well on her first day. Then Missy called and talked with her mom and dad, as they were both going back to work that day also. Afterward, she showered and got ready for work. It was a big day for all of them, so she said a prayer that God would be with each of them in their unique situations and needs.

And God answered her prayer. Her dad was glad to be back at work and found that the half day worked out well. He was able to go home for lunch, take a short rest, and then go to cardiac rehab for his exercise program. Her mom was missed by her students, and she realized how much she missed them as well. One of her classes had even given her a card with their names on it, saying how glad they were she was back. And Linda couldn't stop talking about all the things she'd learned on her first day while they ate supper. Since Linda had the longer drive, Missy had supper ready when she got home.

"Oh, Missy, I think I'm really going to like working at Memorial Medical Center," Linda began. "The people I work with are really friendly and helpful. I still have to get used to how they do things and their computer system, but the basic things are the same. And I was able to assist with some of the patients this afternoon, along with my trainer, Melanie. She is so calm with the patients and explains things so well that they're very willing to do what she instructs them to do. She's been working there for ten years now and says she really loves it and that it's very rewarding to help people become more independent. I know that's why I chose to be an occupational therapist.

"And you know, I don't even mind the longer drive. It was so beautiful! The trees were covered with white snow after the four inches we got last night. The hospital is easy to find and not that far off the highway so I won't have any problems," Linda said as she stopped for a breath. "Oh, here I am going on and on and I didn't even thank you for making supper or ask how your day went."

"That's okay," Missy said with a laugh. "I'm just glad you had a good first day. And I don't mind fixing supper. Since I get home before you, it works out well. That way, we can eat when you get home and have the evening free to do other things. Though you'll be on your own on Wednesdays since I have youth group, and Thursday evenings will have to be something quick and easy since we have young adult group that evening. Oh, I didn't even ask, do you want to go to our young adults' group?"

"Oh yes! I think it will be a good way to get to know the young adults quicker that way," Linda said. "So how was your day?"

"Not quite as exciting as yours but busy as usual. All the doctors are in the clinic on Mondays, so it keeps us on our toes. We're hoping to have time later this week to put up some Valentine's decorations. It's hard to believe Valentine's Day is less than two weeks away."

"Do you have any plans for Valentine's Day?" Linda asked.

"It's on a Thursday this year, so the young adults are having a party for anyone who's able to attend. I've heard some couples are going out to dinner, but for the rest of us, we'll have fun playing games and eating cupcakes, popcorn, and other snacks," Missy informed.

"Sounds fun. But I'm surprised my brother didn't ask you out. He's crazy about you, you know."

"We're just friends and work together with the youth group."

"I've seen the way he looks at you. That's not the way a guy looks at a friend, Missy."

That's what Emma, Julie and Tony said to me too, Missy thought.

"Tell me, Missy. Has Mike ever brought you flowers?"

"Well, yes. When he took me to supper one night to talk about working with the youth group on a regular basis, he brought me flowers. But that was just to be nice and thank me for helping chaperone two youth events."

"What about when he went to the hospital to be with you while your dad was having surgery?" Linda asked.

"He was just doing his job. After all, we work together with the youth and my family attends the church."

"And when I came for the interviews at Christmastime, and you two were all cozy on the couch and spent the evening together?"

"We didn't do anything wrong! He just brought supper over since I was tired and stressed out from being at the hospital that week, and with everything that happened with Dad. Then we watched a movie together and just talked," Missy insisted.

"Missy, I'm not judging you. I'm just trying to open your eyes to the fact that Mike really cares about you. I know he's kind of shy and might need a little push, but I think he's falling in love with you. He talks about you all the time, and whenever you're in the same room, he has eyes only for you."

"Oh, no, that can't be! He's the youth pastor of our church. I could never be involved with a pastor. I'm not good enough!" Missy insisted.

"What do you mean you're not good enough?"

"People expect so much more from a pastor's wife. I would never be able to meet everyone's expectations. And I don't like being in front of people or leading a group. I'm more of a behind-the-scenes, one-on-one type of person. Like what I do at the clinic, or working with Rose, and making snacks for the youth group."

"Missy, what makes you think a pastor's wife has to be perfect and do all those other things? Pastors and their wives are human too. They make mistakes, and each one has their own talents and abilities. Not all pastors' wives are leaders and like being in charge." Linda informed her. "You have great abilities! God doesn't expect you to be like other people—just use the gifts He's given you. You're very caring, kind, and enjoy helping people. That's a wonderful gift.

"You love working with the teens. Mike works with teens. You two make a great team! And you make people feel welcomed, like me and my family. Not everyone can do that. And you're a great organizer. The way you pulled Christmas together amidst all the stress with your dad coming home and then adding in Tony's and my family for Christmas dinner—that was amazing! Missy, you need to see yourself for who you are, how God has gifted you, and be grateful. Stop putting yourself down. You are an amazing woman, and Mike would be very blessed to have you as his wife. And I would love having you as a sister-in-law."

"Whoa, I think you're putting the cart before the horse here," Missy cautioned. "Mike and I aren't even dating."

"You should be. You do like him, don't you?"

"Well, yes. He's very kind and thoughtful. He loves the Lord and really cares about the teens and others in the church as well. He was wonderful with my family at the hospital and even since. My family thinks he's wonderful!"

"The important thing is, what do you think?" Linda insisted.

"I think he's pretty special too." Missy paused as she recalled some of the things she appreciated about Mike. "When I went on the hike to Porcupine Mountain with the youth group, Rose and I had an allergic reaction to the mold as we walked along the swampy area toward the end of the hike, and Mike stayed with us until we got back to the van. He even called me later to make sure I was all right."

"Yah, he's pretty thoughtful that way. What else?"

"Well, he makes me laugh. And he's fun to be with and easy to talk to. The night you came to the apartment before your interviews, I don't think he planned on staying until you got here, but we were having such a good time, I don't think either one of us wanted it to end. So I asked him to pick out a movie, and he chose *A Christmas Prince*. He acted like a prince afterward and treated me like a princess. It was kind of nice. Afterward, we talked about past Christmas memories that were special to us. I felt very relaxed and comfortable talking to him. Usually I'm nervous and don't know what to say or make a fool of myself," Missy admitted.

"Well, it's important to feel comfortable with someone when you begin a relationship," Linda observed.

"Linda, we're not in a relationship!" Missy insisted.

"Then I'll have to give him a little push. You would go out with him if he asked you, wouldn't you?"

"Linda, please don't butt in. If he wanted to ask me out, he would. No pushing necessary."

"Yah, but Mike can be kind of shy when it comes to women he likes. It takes him a while to get up the nerve to ask someone out." Linda paused for a second. "I might be kind of biased, but do you think he's cute?"

"Linda!" Missy said with a laugh.

"Well, do you?"

"Yes, I think he's cute, even handsome when he gets all dressed up," admitted Missy with a smile.

"Okay then. It's time you two stop pussyfooting around and start dating!" Linda concluded. "What are you waiting for?"

Chapter 20

The youth's first fundraiser for their mission trip was on the Sunday before Valentine's Day and was a great success. They had many donations of baked goods; and the youth leaders and some of the teens met at the church on Saturday morning to make cupcakes, heart cookies, and fudge. Even Missy's mom came to help.

Missy let Sue and her mom organize the baking process. Mike, Ron, and Missy set up the tables; priced the products; and laid everything out for the sale. Missy had also made up a schedule so there was an adult and four teens manning the tables before Sunday school, after Sunday school, and again after the church service. After counting up their sales, they took in $1,250. There were donations that had come in for the mission trip previously, so that gave them a total of $2,000 so far. They were well on their way to their $6,000 goal for twenty people to go on the mission, plus transportation expenses.

"I'd say we make a pretty good team," Mike said after the tables were taken down and he, Missy, and Linda were left to lock up the church.

"I agree. Of course, we had a lot of help," Missy pointed out.

"Yes, but your organizational skills made things go smoothly. What could have been chaos turned out to be a great success."

"Well thank you, kind sir. I appreciate the compliment."

"How about I show my appreciation by taking you and Linda out for lunch? It's the least I can do."

Missy and Linda looked at each other, smiled, and said together, "We accept."

The day before Valentine's Day was the youth group's Valentine's party. Missy and Sue decided to keep it simple, so they ordered pizzas, made punch, and baked cupcakes for dessert. Linda helped Missy frost and decorate her cupcakes Tuesday evening. Missy met Sue at the church after work on Wednesday to decorate the youth room with hearts. They put kisses in a clear jar, and Mike and Ron counted them for a guessing game. The teen who guessed the amount closest to the number of kisses in the jar would take the jar home that evening. Once the decorating was done, Mike went to get the pizzas as they decided to eat as soon as the teens arrived. As expected, the pizzas and cupcakes disappeared quickly.

Then they played the games Sue had planned. The first game was, "What kind of candy am I?" The one who guessed correctly got the candy. Then they played another game in which Sue divided the group into three teams. Each team needed to find something in the room that started with each letter of "Valentine's Day." Once the team found all their items, they needed to write an original Valentine's Day poem using each item they found. Then one person from each group read their poem aloud to everyone. They were very original, didn't necessarily make sense or rhyme, but were hilarious. Everyone seemed to have a good time.

Ron then gave a short devotional on what love really is from 1 Corinthians 13. It definitely gave them all something to think about. After the teens left, the leaders pitched in to clean up the room but decided to leave any leftover cupcakes and decorations for the young adults' party the next evening.

Missy looked forward to the party on Thursday evening, as it would give Linda a chance to meet and get to know some of the young adults in their church. Everyone was asked to bring a snack to share with the group, but beverages would be provided. Since Missy had been busy with the party the evening before, Missy and Linda decided to bring something they didn't have to spend a lot of time preparing. They decided to bring Mission chips with salsa and apple slices with caramel dip. Both were items Missy could eat, without worrying about her allergies.

When they arrived, they were each given a heart cut in half with jagged or zigzagged lines. They were to find the other half of his or her heart among the rest of the party guests. It was a great party mixer and got everyone mingling and talking with one another. Linda mixed in well and soon was introducing herself to others as she looked for her matching heart. Once everyone found their matching hearts, Luke welcomed everyone and opened their time in prayer and asked the blessing on the food. There was a great variety, and everyone filled their plates.

After a short time of visiting, Luke announced the next game, which was Valentine's charades. They were to pair up in twos; and when the first pair volunteered to start, they picked a heart-shaped piece of paper from a box and acted out the movie, book, or love song that was on the heart. Whoever guessed the correct answer would then take their turn with their partner and pick another heart.

Some were easier than others to guess, but all were a lot of laughs as they really got into acting out their clues. Luke had asked Linda to be his partner, and Mike asked Missy to be his. Missy didn't know if they'd planned that ahead of time or not, but Linda seemed to be having a good time, as was Missy. The heart that Missy and Mike picked was a movie called, *My Secret Valentine*. They had fun acting it out, but someone guessed it fairly quickly. Everyone went back for more food between charades and the time went by quickly.

Luke ended the evening with a challenging thought. He started out by opening a large box of Valentine's chocolates. As he passed it around, he asked everyone to take a piece without knowing what was in the middle. He watched as they bit into the chocolate. Some were pleased with what they chose; others turned up their nose with disappointment.

"There's a famous quote by Forrest Gump that says, 'Life is like a box of chocolates…you never know what you're gonna get.' With this box of chocolates, you didn't know until you bit into it if it would be chocolate cream or coconut, strawberry or maple flavor, caramel or nuts. Some days you get up in the morning, and nothing goes right. Other days start out okay but then turn sour. There are no guarantees in life that you will succeed or fail—that you will be happy or not have difficulties, that you will not get sick, that people won't disappoint you. God knows that our lives will have circumstances that are uncertain. That's why He says in Psalms 34:8, 'Taste and see that the Lord is good; blessed is the one who takes refuge in him.'

"God is always there to comfort us, and He reminds us many times in His Word that He is our constant companion, our steadfast friend, and consistently our loving God and Savior. We can have confidence and hope in God's unbreakable, spiritual lifeline and know that His love will be there for us, no matter what. I *like* chocolate, but I *love* that I can depend on God. That He will be there for me, in good times and bad. That I can taste and know that He is good and that I can take refuge in Him. I hope that you have tasted and trusted in God as well. If not, do so today."

Missy thought it was an interesting analogy and challenge. She wanted to remember it for future reference. The young adults visited for a while and helped themselves to more snacks before leaving.

Julie came up to her and asked, "So are you and Mike going together now? I noticed that you two paired up for the charades tonight."

"We're just friends, and his sister, Linda, is my new roommate," Missy informed.

"I still say he wants to be more than friends. Emma and Jeremy are going together now. They went out for dinner tonight, so that's why they aren't here. She seems pretty happy. Maybe she found her Prince Charming after all. They really are cute together, and he truly adores her. I think they're a good match."

"That's great! I'm happy for Emma. Jeremy's a great Christian guy and will be good for her."

Julie said good night and left, then Missy looked around to see if Linda was ready to go since they came together, but noticed she was talking to Luke.

Mike approached her and asked, "I was wondering if you'd like to go skiing with me on Saturday afternoon and out for dinner after. Luke and Linda are going too. We could make it a double date if you'd like."

"You're asking me out on a date?" Missy asked.

"Well, yes. I know we work together with the youth and are friends, but I guess I'd like to see if it could be more than that. I really like spending time with you and thought you did too."

"Yes, I do. I just didn't think you'd want to ask me out."

"Well, I do. What do you say? Do you want to go skiing and have dinner with me on Saturday?"

"Yes, I'd like that," Missy said, still surprised that Mike had asked her on a date.

"Good! Luke and I will pick you and Linda up at one-thirty, we'll go to Powderhorn Mountain to ski and then for dinner after."

"Sounds fun. I'll look forward to it," Missy replied.

"Me too," Mike said as he took her hand and smiled. "Me too!"

Then he dropped her hand and got ready to leave.

Linda came over then and asked, "You ready to go home, Missy?"

"Yes, I'm ready."

When they got into the car, Missy turned to Linda and asked, "Did you tell Mike to ask me out and double date with you and Luke on Saturday?"

"He did?" Linda said excitedly. "And no, I didn't. Luke asked if I would mind if another couple went with us on Saturday, but I didn't know it would be you and Mike. I guess Luke wanted to make sure Mike asked you first. But I'm proud of my big brother. He finally asked you out, and I didn't even have to interfere."

"Yah right. Like you didn't give him some hints and pushes along the way?"

"Hey, I've been hinting and pushing since Thanksgiving. It's not my fault it took Mike this long to ask you out. But it will be fun, don't you think? And Luke is so nice, good looking, and smart too. I'd like to get to know him better, and what better way than on a double date with you and Mike."

"Okay, you win! We're double dating on Saturday. And yes, I think it will be fun. Going skiing will be a good, informal way to begin dating, and dinner after will give us time to talk. Are you happy now?"

"Yes," Linda said with a big grin. "I'm happy now. I think I win all the way around."

Saturday turned out to be a wonderful day, as the sun was shining and sparkling on the fresh snow that came down the night before. All four of them had a great time skiing and then decided to go to Mike's Café for dinner afterward. They took a booth in the corner, and after they placed their order with Emily, who was their waitress for the evening, they visited as if they'd been together for a long time. They had a lot in common and enjoyed each other's company. The time went by quickly, and they hadn't realized that two hours had gone by.

"I suppose we better get you ladies home," Luke said as he glanced at his watch. "It's been a great day and I hate to see it end, but I promised Greg that I'd teach his Life group tomorrow morning, and I need to go over the lesson again one more time. Are you ready to go, Linda?"

"Yes I am. But this was great fun. I had a really good time," Linda acknowledged.

"Yeah, and I even learned a few things about Mike I didn't know before," Luke laughed.

"Uh, remind me never to double date with you and my sister again, Luke. She tends to share too much information," Mike said with a smile that said he loved his sister very much, even though she said things he wished she hadn't.

"Oh, but you're so fun to tease," Linda returned. "How else can I get back at you for all the pranks you pulled on me when we were growing up?"

"I think it's time to go," Mike said as he stood and helped Missy with her coat. "We'll get you ladies home before Linda shares any more stories. And, Missy, don't believe everything Linda tells you about me. I wasn't really as bad as she makes me out to be."

"I'm sure you weren't," Missy said, still smiling. "But I can see now why you relate so well to the teens. You're just a kid at heart yourself, and that's not such a bad thing. But you have matured nicely and I'm proud to know you, Mr. Reeves."

"Well, thank you, Miss Andrews. Likewise!" Mike said with a smile, taking her hand as they walked out of the café.

Chapter 21

When Missy saw Rose on Sunday morning, she was all excited. "Missy, I have the best news! Gloria told me they're going to have a Spring Craft and Art Show at the Memorial Building at the end of March. She wants me to put together a display of my pictures for the show and said she'd help me frame them and get them ready. Isn't that simply awesome?"

"Oh, Rose, that's wonderful!" Missy said as she gave Rose a hug. "But then I already knew your pictures were awesome. Now more people will be able to see that too. I'm so proud of you!"

"Thanks! But if it wasn't for you and Pastor Mike, I would still be hiding behind my camera and no one would be seeing my pictures. And I wouldn't have found Jesus or the youth group and my new friends. But you're my best friend ever. I owe you so much!" Rose said with a look of admiration and respect.

"You don't owe me anything," Missy said, placing her hand on her shoulder. "Besides, I got you as a friend out of the deal too, didn't I? Some great pictures for my walls too. What did your parents say when you told them?"

"My mom thought it was pretty cool, but my dad didn't say too much. He's been pretty busy with work," Rose said sadly.

Missy felt bad for Rose. She was such a talented and sweet girl, but her parents didn't seem to take the time to notice.

"Once they see your display, they'll be very impressed."

"I hope so," Rose said doubtfully. "Well, church is starting, and Katie's saving me a place. Thanks for all your encouragement, Missy."

With that, Rose left, and Missy said a silent prayer for Rose and her parents before she went into the sanctuary. She would continue to pray that Rose's parents would come to know the Lord. But she was so thankful to see how God was working in Rose's life. She had come out of her shell, was a much happier girl, and had made many new friends among the youth group. Then the verse her father had given her came to mind again:

> "For I know the plans I have for you," declares the LORD, "plans to prosper you and not to harm you, plans to give you hope and a future. Then you will call on me and come and pray to me, and I will listen to you." (Jer. 29:11–12)

Was this message for her or for Rose? Or both? Whoever it was for, it was a great message of hope.

Mike asked Missy to go out again. In fact, they had gone on two dates, but not with Linda and Luke, who also continued to date. It seemed Linda could talk of nothing else but Luke lately.

"Did I tell you that Luke just got a raise? He's such a good electrician and is busy all the time. He's thinking of buying a house and getting out of his apartment," Linda said as they made lunch together on Saturday.

"That's great! I'm happy for him. So where are you two going tonight? Any special plans?"

"I think we're just going to hang out at his place, order a pizza, and watch a movie. He's had a busy week and just wants a quiet evening."

"That sounds good. Mike planned a gym night at the church tonight for the youth, just to play some basketball or volleyball and hang out together. I'm not very athletic, but I'm going to go and serve some bars and drinks that I'll make this afternoon," Missy informed her.

"I don't have any plans this afternoon, I'll help you. And maybe I can take a plate with me to Luke's place?"

"Sure, why not? And I appreciate the help."

Missy enjoyed doing things with Linda. They cleaned the apartment and usually did grocery shopping together, shared meals when they were both home, and spent time talking or watching a movie in the evenings. It was nice to have someone to do things with and with whom she could relate and talk. Rooming with Linda was working out well. Missy wasn't as lonely or feeling sorry for herself as she once was. Of course, maybe Mike had something to do with that as well. Missy enjoyed spending time with him but was leery of getting too close. After all, he was a pastor at their church.

By the time Missy went to the church, it had started to snow. It was not unusual to get a bad snowstorm in March, so Mike said he would keep an eye on the weather and that if it got too bad, he would send the youth home early. They started playing at seven, but by eight-thirty, the visibility was getting bad, so Mike decided to call it quits and send the youth home.

Mike followed Missy home to make sure she got there safely as well. Linda arrived shortly after. It looked like it was turning out to be a bad blizzard after all, and the wind was really picking up.

By morning, they had twelve inches of new snow with drifts much higher around the buildings. Church on Sunday morning was cancelled, as the plows were still trying to clear the main roads, and many of the side roads were drifted shut. People were also trying to clear their driveways and sidewalks, but it was a difficult task. So Missy and Linda planned on a quiet, restful day.

They read some scripture after breakfast and talked about how it spoke to their hearts, what they learned from it, and how they would apply it to their lives. Then they planned to watch movies and drink hot chocolate during the afternoon. But Missy got a phone call about 1:00 p.m. from Beth, her former roommate.

"Hi, Missy, this is Beth. I was wondering if I could talk to you. Kurt and I were going home after being at a friend's house last night and our car slid into the ditch during the storm. Kurt had to have surgery on his leg and is still in the hospital. I'm okay, mostly just bruises and soreness. Could you come to the hospital? I really need to talk to you."

"Oh my goodness, Beth. Of course I'll come. What room is Kurt in?"

"Room 215. They just gave him some pain medicine, so he's resting now."

"Our parking lot just got plowed a little while ago, but I might have to shovel in front of the garage in order to get my car out. I should be there in about twenty minutes to half an hour."

"Just drive safe, Missy. I wouldn't want anything to happen to you."

"Okay, I'll see you soon," Missy said as she hung up the phone. "Oh my, Linda. That was Beth, my former roommate. She and her husband were in an accident during the storm last night, and Kurt was hurt. She wants me to come to the hospital and talk with her about something. She sounded really concerned. I hope Kurt is going to be all right."

"Do you want me to go with you?" Linda asked.

"No, if Beth wants to talk, it will be better if I go alone. But I would appreciate your prayers."

They prayed together before Missy left, and Linda promised to pray while she was gone and would ask Mike to pray also.

"Thank you. I appreciate it."

Missy was pleased she didn't have a lot of snow to shovel in front of the garage and the roads were mostly plowed in town. When Missy got to the hospital and found Kurt's room, Beth was there to meet her with a warm hug.

"Thanks for coming, Missy. I probably should have waited, but I kept remembering what you said to me once, that I shouldn't keep putting off a relationship with Christ. Oh, Missy, I was so scared. It took a while for someone to find us in that storm and get us out. I thought we were going to freeze to death, and Kurt was hurt, and I couldn't help him," Beth said as tears were streaming down her face. "I knew right away his leg was broken by the way it was twisted under the dash. And his face was bleeding from hitting the steering wheel. I thought we were going to die for sure. When you talked to me about needing a relationship with Jesus, I kept saying I was too busy to think about it, and I thought I had plenty of time. After all, I'm only twenty-three and thought I had my whole life ahead of me. But, Missy, there are no guarantees, are there? We could have died in that storm last night."

"Beth, none of us ever knows when our time to die will come, so yes, we should not put off accepting Jesus Christ as our Savior. Let's sit down over here. You're positively shaking!"

After they sat down, Missy gave Beth some Kleenex to wipe her face and nose. Then she took Beth's hand and calmly shared with her how much God loves her and Kurt, how much God wants to have a relationship with them, and that because we're all sinners, God provided a way for us to find forgiveness of our sins through His Son, Jesus. Missy told Beth that His death on the cross paid the penalty for our sins, and when we repent and trust Christ as our Savior, He forgives us of our sins. And because Jesus had victory over death and rose again, we can have hope of eternal life with Him in heaven as well.

"John 3:16 says it best," Missy concluded. "'For God so loved the world that he gave his one and only Son, that whoever believes in him shall not perish but have eternal life.' So all we have to do is believe."

"You mean it's that simple? I don't have to do something to earn God's forgiveness and love?"

"It's that simple. There's nothing we can do to earn God's love. He gives it freely, even though we often don't deserve it. We just need to acknowledge that we are sinners and in need of a Savior."

"I know I'm a sinner and so in need of a Savior. Will you help me, Missy?"

"Of course, Beth," Missy said with a smile on her face. "Let's pray together. You can repeat the words after me if you mean them with all your heart."

"Okay, I'm ready."

Beth repeated a prayer, one phrase at a time, after Missy.

"Dear Jesus, I know that I'm a sinner and that You died on the cross for my sins. You paid the penalty meant for me. Please forgive me of all the wrong I've done and make my heart clean. I want to be part of God's family and have a relationship with You. Thank You for loving me, even when I didn't deserve it. I believe in You and thank You for forgiving me and making me Your Child. Amen."

As Missy and Beth looked up, Beth had a huge smile on her face and said, "Thank you, Missy, for coming and explaining all this to me. My heart feels so clean. I know God has forgiven me and that I'm part of His family now. This is so awesome! I wish I'd listened to you and done this sooner."

"The important thing is that you did it now while God was speaking to your heart, Beth. Now we are not only friends but sisters in God's family."

And with that, Missy gave Beth a hug.

"I'm so happy for you! Do you still have the Bible I gave you? It's important to grow in your relationship with God by reading His Word every day, learning more about God and how He wants you to live."

"Yes, I still have it, but I may need help in understanding it."

"I'd be happy to help you. You let me know when would be a good time and we can study it together."

"Thanks, I'd like that," said Beth.

Then Judy, Beth's mom, came in with a bag.

"Okay, Beth, I brought you some clean clothes. Once you clean up and change, you'll feel better." She stopped quickly. "Oh, hi, Missy! I didn't know you were here."

"Yes, Beth called and told me about the accident. I'm glad she didn't get hurt too bad and that Kurt will be okay. It was pretty scary to go through an accident like that."

"Yes, it was! We're all so grateful that it wasn't worse. Beth will be bruised and sore for a while from the seatbelt, but I'm glad she had it on or it could have been much worse. Did Kurt's parents arrive yet?" Judy asked as she handed Beth the bag of clothes.

"No, they should arrive later this afternoon. With the storm, their flight was delayed. But Kurt's resting more comfortably now with the pain medicine," Beth informed. "I'm going to go in the bathroom to clean up and change clothes. Thanks again for coming, Missy. I really appreciate it."

"You're very welcome. It was my pleasure!" Missy said with a smile. "So how have you been, Judy? I haven't seen you since the wedding."

"Oh, I've been fine. Busy as usual. How about you? Beth says you've been working a lot with the youth at your church. How do you like that?"

"I'm enjoying it very much. Teens these days have a lot to contend with, even more than when Beth and I were teens. They have a lot more pressure from their peers and parents. But they're great kids, and I enjoy working with them. I mainly just help with snacks, chaperoning, trying to encourage them, and I'm working one-on-one with one girl in particular."

"Well, when it comes to teens, food and a listening ear are very important," Judy concluded.

Chapter 22

As Missy drove home, she thought about what Judy had said.

"Food and a listening ear are very important to teens"—which was very true, Missy mused. *So is what I'm doing really making an impact on the teens? I always think it's insignificant and that my part in helping with the youth is unimportant. I'm not teaching any profound Bible lessons, only interacting, providing food, and giving an encouraging word now and then. But is it making a difference in their lives? It seems to be in Rose's life. What about the others? Only God knows.* Missy decided she would remain faithful, do what she could, and leave the rest to God.

When she arrived at the apartment, Mike was there. He and Linda were both anxious to hear how her meeting with Beth had gone.

"It went well," Missy began. "Beth has some bruises and soreness from the seatbelt, but they will heal. Kurt broke his leg and had to have surgery, but the medication is helping him rest. I'm not sure when he'll be released. But the best news is that Beth accepted Christ as her Savior."

"Wow, that is great news!" Mike said. "How did that come about?"

"Yes, please tell us," Linda said as she motioned for them to sit on the couch.

"Well, I had talked to Beth when she lived here about the importance of accepting Christ, but she always kept putting it off, saying she had plenty of time to do that. But when the accident happened, she realized that one never knows what the day will bring and that life has no guarantees. So she asked me to explain how she could be forgiven and accept Christ as her Savior. I did, and then we prayed together. Now she's a believer and a part of the family of God."

"That is awesome!" Mike said as he took Missy's hand. "Missy, you are so good at taking these opportunities and helping people come to know Christ, first with Rose and now with Beth. This is truly your gift. You befriend people, earn their trust so they can come to you with their concerns, and you win them to Christ. That's why you are such an asset to our youth leadership team. You are so personable, caring, and win them over with your love."

"You really think so?"

"Definitely!"

"Ditto!" Linda agreed. "You won me over, remember?"

"But that was different. You were already a Christian, so we had that in common."

"But you still befriended me, even though you were going through a difficult time with your dad. You cared for me and put your needs aside. That's who you are, and that's what makes you special. It also makes you a great leader and friend," Linda acknowledged.

"You are very special, Missy! To me, Linda, the youth, your family, those you come in contact with at work, and everyone else who knows you. Don't you realize that?" Mike asked.

"I guess I haven't really thought about it that way. I know I'm special and loved by my family, but with others, I just do what comes naturally because I enjoy helping people. I like seeing people smile and making their life better."

"And that's what makes you special, Missy," Mike said as he put his arm around her. "You think of others before yourself. And I want to make sure you realize how special you are to me."

And with that, Mike leaned down and kissed her gently but sweetly.

Missy couldn't say a word when Mike lifted his head but could feel her face turn red and her heart beat faster.

"Well, I think I better get going. I'll continue to pray for Beth and her husband, and I'm so thankful that Beth made a decision for Christ. I'll call you later, okay?"

Missy just nodded her head and watched as Mike left the apartment.

"It's about time Mike realized how special you are and let you know it!" Linda said. "I may get a sister after all."

"Oh, Linda, stop. He was just reacting to the moment."

"Are you kidding me? He was reacting to the special person that you are. It's okay to be humble, but it's not okay to put yourself down and not realize that God is using you in a wonderful way and be grateful for it. So repeat after me, God loves me and made me special."

"Linda, this is crazy."

"Say it!"

"God loves me and made me special."

"Now say, Linda loves me and thinks I'm special."

"Linda loves me and thinks I'm special."

"Mike loves me and thinks I'm special."

"Linda!"

"Say it and believe it!"

"Mike loves me and thinks I'm special," Missy said the words more slowly and with a smile.

"See, it's nice to be loved, isn't it?"

"Yes, it is," Missy agreed, still grinning.

"Missy, God is using you in a wonderful way. You don't have to be a great teacher, singer, or compare yourself to anyone else. Just continue to be the loving, caring person that God made you to be. That's what makes you special and why we love you so much!"

Linda gave Missy a hug.

"Thanks, Linda. I needed that."

It took a while for Missy to get to sleep that night. She thought about the last few days, starting with the snowstorm, her time with Beth, and then what Mike and Linda said about her being special. She had always struggled with feeling inadequate and comparing herself with others. She always felt she had failed her dad by not following in his footsteps and getting her BA and master's degree in accounting. But she liked her job as an optician, where she could help people and not just punch numbers all day. She also liked working with the youth. She wasn't teaching them anything profound; but she enjoyed getting to know them, encouraging them, and helping them see their potential. Even when providing snacks, she was able to use her joy of baking and watch the teens devour the food she made.

But she also realized that she liked where her relationship with Mike was going. His kiss was special. The way he looked at her, praised her, and enjoyed spending time with her was special. Then there was her friendship with Linda. They were becoming such good friends; doing things together and having the same values had really brought them close in the short time they'd shared their apartment.

She also thought of the verses which confirmed that she was "fearfully and wonderfully made" and that God had a plan for her, "plans to prosper you and not to harm you, plans to give you a hope and a future" (Jer. 29:11).

And what was the last part of the next verse? Oh yes, "You will seek me and find me when you seek me with all your heart." That's what I need to do now, Missy decided. *Seek God with all my heart.*

And with that she prayed:

Lord, You did make me special, and You have a plan for my life. I want to follow Your plan, for it will not harm me but will give me a hope and a future. Whether that future includes Mike or not, I don't know. But I trust that You will guide me in the days ahead and make it clear to me. Thank You for loving me and giving me a love for others. I'm grateful for the opportunities You have given me with the teens, and to show Rose and Beth the way to You.

Help me to encourage them in their walk with You. And thank You also for bringing Linda into my life. She has truly filled a void I had and her friendship is very special. You are a good, good God, and I am so grateful I have You to turn to. You are my Great Comforter, Counselor, Friend, and Savior. Without You, I could do nothing. Help me remain humble but usable for Your glory, moldable and shaped into the person You want me to be, and obedient and willing to follow Your plan for my life. In Your Precious Name. Amen.

After Missy prayed, she fell into a peaceful sleep, knowing that God was in control and that she could leave her life in His capable hands.

Beth's husband, Kurt, got out of the hospital a few days later, and Beth took time off work to care for him until he was able to get around on his own. She said she would contact Missy when she could start a Bible study with her. In the meantime, she was reading her Bible, starting with the Gospel of John, as Missy suggested. Missy prayed that God would give Beth understanding and that she would grow in her faith in the Lord.

In the meantime, the snow was melting, and the Spring Craft and Art Show was scheduled for the last Saturday in March. Rose was excited about it and was getting ten of her pictures framed and ready for display. Katie also had some drawings she'd done and was going to display them with Rose's pictures as well. Rose had even gotten several others from the church to reserve a booth and display their crafts. They had quilts, knitted and crocheted items, and even some wood carvings and plaques. Missy was looking forward to the craft show, and Rose said her parents would attend as well.

When the day of the Spring Craft and Art Show arrived, it was well attended. It seemed people had spring fever and were anxious to get out and about. And even the weather had cooperated; for it was a beautiful, sunny spring day with temperatures in the fifties. There were still large piles of snow where the plows had pushed it from the streets and parking lots, but otherwise, there was grass peeking out on the lawns and the streets were dry for the most part, except in the low areas where the melted snow had caused puddles of water.

Many people had admired Rose's framed pictures, including Rose's parents, and she sold all but one of her pictures. Her friend, Katie, sold many of her drawings and she also drew pencil caricatures of people who attended the event for a small fee, which drew many people to their booth. The adults from their church had a great response at their tables as well, and only a few items remained.

As Missy walked around the building, all the exhibitors seemed pleased with the turnout and the sales that were made. It was a great success.

Chapter 23

Missy and Linda started an eight-week Bible study with Beth the first week in April on Monday evenings. Beth had agreed to allow Linda to attend as well and was looking forward to getting to know her. Kurt had gone back to work and was getting around much better on his crutches. He still had some pain, but Tylenol helped.

They decided to do a study on the Book of Colossians called, "Raised Together," by Gloria Furman. Missy had gone through the study in a Life group about a year previously and found it to be very foundational but powerful. She felt it would help Beth begin her walk with the Lord and understand who Christ is and how she could have a vital relationship with Him. The eight lessons included study books and a video to go with it so it would be easy to follow along and help them develop a relationship with Beth during the study.

Missy's relationship with Mike was growing as well. They had gone bowling with Linda and Luke, as well as Emma and Jeremy one Saturday evening and had a blast. She hadn't laughed so hard in a long time. The guys were pretty competitive, but the girls were just there to have fun. Linda and Luke ended up with the highest scores, but they all had a great time and promised to do it again.

On Easter Sunday, the youth prepared the Easter breakfast at church for another fundraiser on a donation basis, as they knew some families couldn't afford a set fee. They decided to serve scrambled eggs, sausage, and pancakes, with juice and coffee for beverages. The teens enjoyed working together, and though there was a lot of fun and laughter, the food was ready when the people arrived, and everyone said it was very good.

They served over 150 people and received $1,200. Minus expenses, they made about $850 dollars. Plus, more gifts had been given toward the mission trip, so now their total was $3,400. They were more than halfway to their goal. God was good.

The Easter service was also very special. The music that celebrated their Risen Savior included a mini orchestra, along with the worship team and special numbers. The message reflected the joy that we can have knowing that our Lord was victorious over death, that Jesus had finished the work God had given Him, and now forgiveness of sin was possible so we can have a relationship with God the Father. All we have to do is believe and accept the gift that Jesus provided. It's our choice. It was a simple but powerful message, and Missy prayed that many hearts were touched and would accept the forgiveness that God offered.

Rose's parents even came to the Easter service, and when the service was over, Rose introduced them to Pastor Mike and Missy.

"Mom, Dad, I want you to meet two of my youth leaders, Pastor Mike and Missy."

Mike shook their hands and said, "Mr. and Mrs. Simms, it's very nice to meet you. We sure enjoy having Rose in our youth group. She has been a true blessing and has made a lot of new friends as well."

"It's nice to see you again, Mr. and Mrs. Simms," Missy added. "We're so glad you came this morning."

"Yes, well Rose has been talking nonstop about this church, the youth group, and now a mission trip. Are you sure it will be safe to take these teens to a place you know nothing about to work with who knows what kind of people?" asked Mr. Simms with a callous tone.

"There will be four adult leaders going along with the teens, as well as trained staff from the mission group that will be working alongside the teens. They will be well chaperoned and never left alone to ensure their safety," assured Mike.

"Well, Rose really wants to go, but Mrs. Simms and I still need to talk more before we sign the permission slip. How soon do you need to have everything signed and turned in?"

"By the end of the month, as we need to have the number of those attending by the first of May. If you have any further questions, don't hesitate to call me. Here's my card with my cell number," Mike said as he handed Mr. Simms his card.

"All right, we'll let you know by then. Rose, are you ready to go?"

Rose looked saddened by her dad's rudeness and abrupt desire to leave but nodded and left with her parents, her smile gone and head down. Missy and Mike watched as they walked out the church doors.

"I'm praying that Rose will be allowed to go on the mission trip," Mike said later when they were alone in the kitchen, making sure everything was clean and put away. "Rose has come a long way spiritually and socially, but we need to continue praying for her parents' salvation as well. It must be difficult for her to live in a home without any encouragement or support."

"Yes, they seem obligated to take care of her physical needs but not her emotional needs," Missy said with deep concern. "They work a lot so aren't home much, and she seems to spend a lot of time alone in her room. It's sad to see. I've been praying for her parents' salvation ever since I met them last fall. Only God can change their hearts. Let's pray for them right now."

Missy and Mike prayed together, asking for God to soften Mr. and Mrs. Simms's hearts to His love and need of salvation, as well as to love their daughter as she needed to be loved.

"I suppose we better get to your parents' home for dinner before they wonder what happened to us," Mike said as he helped Missy with her coat. "By the way, you look very beautiful in that dress. Is it new? I'm sorry I didn't say anything earlier, but it's been pretty crazy all morning with breakfast and then the service."

"Why thank you, kind sir. I was wondering if you were going to notice. And yes, it's new. I got a little spring fever and decided I needed something new to go with the newness of spring," Missy said as she checked the floral scarf she'd tied around the scoop neckline of her solid lagoon-colored and layered knit dress.

"Well, I noticed," Mike said as he kissed her on the cheek. "Let's get going. I was so busy flipping pancakes earlier that I didn't get a chance to eat much. I'm starved!"

Linda and Luke had also been invited for Easter dinner and were already there when Mike and Missy got to the Andrews' home. Liz had the table set and dinner was ready. She'd put a roast in the Crock-Pot before church, so she just had to cook the potatoes and vegetables and make a Watergate salad when she got home. They had waited for Mike and Missy to get there before dishing up the food, so Emily helped her mom put the food on the table. They all sat down, and Missy's dad asked the blessing.

The food and the fellowship were enjoyed by all. They talked about the service that morning and the aspects that were especially meaningful to each of them. Ken was anxious to hear how much they had raised for the mission trip so far and what other fundraisers were planned.

After Missy shared their new totals, she said, "We have our silent auction coming up the second Saturday in May, which we've already been collecting items for. The teens thought we would get more people out if there was food involved, so they suggested we have a simple meal of sloppy joes, chips, carrot sticks, and cookies also, for a charge of five dollars per person—two dollars more if they want an extra sloppy joe. It will start at five-thirty, and the bidding will end at seven, when we'll announce who got the highest bid for each item so they can pay and take their item home the same evening. The youth have designed the posters, printed them, and put them up around the church and community.

"Then in June we'll have a rummage sale and car wash. Hopefully, that will give us the remaining funds that we need. We have twenty signed up so far, including the four leaders, so that's pretty good. Even those who can't go are helping with the fundraisers, and we've had donations come in from church members, so everyone has been really supportive."

"That's good!" her dad replied. "Your mom and I are thinking of some items we can donate for your silent auction and have been going through things for you to put in your rummage sale as well. But we also want to give you a check as our donation toward you going on this mission trip. We believe in you and want you to know that we support you and think you're doing a wonderful job working with the youth. It's a joy to see you excel, use your abilities, and really make a difference in the teens' lives. We're really proud of you, Missy," her dad said as he handed her a check for $266.

Missy accepted it with tears in her eyes.

"Thank you! Your support means so much to me."

"And we definitely couldn't do all this without her," Mike added. "Missy's accounting and organizational skills have been a real asset. She's a great addition to our leadership team, and I think she's pretty special."

With that, Mike took Missy's hand in his and gave her a smile that made her blush.

"Okay, who wants dessert?" Emily asked as she gave her sister a wink and a smile. "I'll warn you ahead of time, I made it, but it's pretty simple and one of my favorites. It's a yellow cake—gluten-free, of course—with holes poked in it and red Jell-O poured over and chilled. Then I made whipped cream to put on top."

They all wanted dessert, so Emily dished it up, and everyone thought it looked very colorful and tasted great. It was a nice light ending to their meal.

Chapter 24

The Bible study with Beth was going well. They were on their fourth lesson, and Beth had many questions. But they found it to be a growing experience for all of them. It was exciting to see Beth's face as she realized how much Christ loved her; had made it possible for her to have a relationship with a Holy God; and the wonderful connection she now had with other believers. Beth was learning things she'd never heard before, and it made Missy and Linda see them in a different light. It also made them appreciate the privilege of being raised in a home where they'd heard the Gospel message and acknowledged it at a young age.

The silent auction was a lot more work than Missy had realized, so she was grateful for the help she was getting from others. Sue and Ron said they would work on the food and had been able to get small bags of chips donated, the grocery store gave them a discount on the buns, someone donated bottles of water, and McDonald's donated a box of orange drinks. Sue and some of the teens' moms would make the meat for the sloppy joes, and other ladies from the church said they would make the cookies. So the food was taken care of.

Mike worked with the advertising for the radio, put pictures of some of the items for the silent auction on Facebook, and wrote an article about the youth's mission trip and their fundraising endeavors that the *Daily Globe* agreed to print. They even sent a photographer on Wednesday evening during youth group to take a picture of those going on the mission trip to go along with the article. They would also be at the silent auction to take pictures and do a follow-up article as they felt it was a good human-interest story. This made the youth and leaders very excited and hoped it would get more of the community involved in the silent auction.

Missy's responsibility was then to keep a list of all the silent auction items as they were donated and make a sign-up sheet to be taped in front of each item so people could place their bids. She also put together an insert for the bulletin the Sunday before the auction to make people aware of the items available. One hundred items were donated, and they had a great variety, something for everyone.

They had candles and jewelry, baked goods and jams, and baby items and books/games for children. There were T-shirts and quilts, tools and housewares, and pictures and crafts, to name a few. Even some of the teens were offering their services for projects to be done such as painting, garden work, babysitting, and other odd jobs. Rose donated three of her framed photos and was anxious to see what people would bid on them. Her parents had finally agreed to let her go on the mission trip and even said they would attend the auction.

The afternoon of the silent auction was very busy. Mike, Ron, and the boys set up rectangle tables to display the auction items around the outside perimeter of the gym, while round tables and chairs for eating were put in the middle. Then they set up the food tables in the foyer so people could get their food as they came in. Sue and some of the teen moms were busy in the kitchen getting the buns, chips, and cookies trayed up; sliced pickles and carrot sticks into bowls; and putting the sloppy joe meat into Nemko warmers. Missy, her mom, Linda, and the girls worked on displaying the auction items on the rectangle tables in the gym, with a taped piece of paper in front of each, which had a description of the item and spaces for people to put their names and bids. It was a time of great excitement, anxiety, and hard work; but for their cause, it was well worth it.

The doors were opened at 5:30 p.m., and they were pleased by the number of people who came. Sue and some of the teens served the food, while the moms watched and brought more of whatever was running low. Missy had two teens at the end of the table to collect the money for the food. They had decided to have the drinks on a separate table in the gym area so people didn't have so much to carry at once. So then more teens were available to help carry drinks for those with young children or older adults. They had a steady stream of people going through the line, and things seemed to be going very smoothly.

It was fun to watch people look at the items displayed, place their bids, and then return again to the items they really wanted in order to rebid when someone outbid them. It would be interesting to see who would be the top bidder. Thankfully, everyone was being civil.

Five minutes before 7:00 p.m., Mike announced that it was their last chance to make a final bid on the items they were interested in. There was a mad dash by some to make their final bids, and then at 7:00 p.m., a loud bell sounded, and Mike announced, "Okay, the bidding has ceased! Everyone please take your seats and I will announce the winners."

He waited silently until everyone had taken their seats and then continued, "On behalf of the youth and leaders, I want to thank all who donated items for our auction and all of you for coming tonight. We received one hundred items for our auction this evening, so you had a great variety of wonderful items to bid on."

Mike paused as people clapped and cheered.

"We really appreciate your support and generosity in supporting our mission trip to Kenosha, Wisconsin, on July 14–19. This is a wonderful opportunity for sixteen of our youth to partner with other youth groups in learning the value of serving others, working together as a team, seeing the joy in people's faces that they minister to, as well as grow in their faith. This wouldn't be possible without your help. So thank you!"

Again, everyone in the gym clapped.

"Okay, I think we're ready to begin, so get your wallets or checkbooks ready, and I'll start at this far end and work my way around the room," Mike said as he walked to the first table on the north end of the gym. "Some of the teens will be helping me by holding up each item for all to see. Then when I call the winning bidder's name, please come up and receive your item and the bidding sheet, and then take your sheet to Missy at the table in front of the platform so she can take your payment. By the end of the evening, we should be able to give you a total of the results of the auction and the meal we enjoyed this evening. And now, the first item we have is this beautiful baby blanket with an animal print, and the winning bid goes to Mary Ellen Larson for twenty-five dollars."

There were many cheers and smiles as people collected their purchases and gratefully made their payment. Rose had been taking pictures throughout the evening, and the *Daily Globe* sent a reporter and photographer around 7:00 p.m. to take pictures of the auction results as well. Missy kept a running total and by the end of the evening was able to announce the total that was collected.

"You have all been most generous, and for that we thank you very much," she said as she stood. "From the auction this evening, we've raised $1,425, the meal this evening adds another $430, so that brings our total this evening to $1,855."

With that announcement, there was loud clapping and cheering that lasted several minutes.

When it subsided, Missy continued, with tears in her eyes, "So our total fundraising money so far comes to $5,521 of our $6,000 goal. Thank you all so very much!"

And with that, Missy sat down, no longer able to speak, as the tears ran down her face. Mike came to her side and placed his hand around her shoulder.

"Your generosity is overwhelming," Mike began. "Thank you all for coming this evening, for supporting this endeavor and our youth. Let's close our time in prayer, and then you are dismissed."

After Mike prayed, people collected their things, while some visited with others in attendance and admired their purchases. Those working in the kitchen started cleaning up, while the teens started taking down the empty display tables. After the people left, the tables and chairs were taken down, garbage bins emptied, and, finally, the room vacuumed. Teamwork made the cleanup go quickly, and they were then able to set up the chairs for church the next morning. What an exhausting but rewarding day.

"Well, that went very well. Thanks for all your hard work in getting this organized. I'd say it went off without a hitch," Mike said as he put his arm around Missy's shoulder as they walked out to the parking lot.

"Except for my tears. I was so embarrassed! I wish I could control my emotions better."

"I don't," Mike said as he stopped Missy, turned her to face him, and put his hands on her shoulders. "It makes you who you are—caring, thoughtful, and compassionate. I wouldn't want you any other way."

They stood there, just looking into each other's eyes, and Missy sensed that Mike was going to kiss her. She looked away to break the spell and continued on to her car.

"Well, it was a great team effort. Everyone really pitched in and made it happen—you, Sue and Ron, the teens and their moms, and even Linda and my mom pitched in. I guess it really does take all our abilities, time, and efforts to do these events. And that's the way it should be. One person can't do it all, but we're all part of His body, the church, and God wants to use each one of us for His purpose in ways that He's gifted us."

"Yes, He does. And you are a very special part of that body and have a wonderful purpose," Mike said as they arrived at Missy's car.

Then he took both her hands in his, looked into her beautiful, brown eyes, and said, "In fact, I hope to one day convince you of that purpose and show you just how much joy you have brought into my life. I'm falling in love with you, Missy, and can't imagine my life without you. One day I hope you'll realize how much I love you. But for now, I am tired and I need to go home and get some sleep. And I'm sure you do too."

Missy just stared into Mike's blue eyes and couldn't say a word, so she just nodded her head.

"Well, good night then," Mike said as he kissed her on the forehead and opened the car door for her before he left. "Sweet dreams."

Sweet dreams? How can I go to sleep after all that has gone on today? Missy thought as she drove to her apartment. *And what about Mike's declaration of falling in love with me? How do I feel about him? Yes, I enjoy being with him—he's handsome, easy to talk to, fun to work with. But love? This is getting complicated!*

Missy took a shower when she got home, thankful that Linda was already done with her shower and had gone to bed so she wouldn't have to be confronted with any of her questions. But Missy tossed and turned in her bed, with no hope of getting the sleep she so desperately needed.

"Lord, it's me again," Missy started praying aloud. "You know I have always wanted to one day fall in love with a wonderful Christian man, marry, and have a family. But not a pastor! You know how people are and what they expect of a pastor's wife. And even in Your Word, You mention that pastors and church leaders are held to high standards, including their wives. I don't know if I could ever measure up to those standards. I would much rather be in the background and not make a fool of myself. Like today, up in front of the church and crying—even if they were happy tears. I hope I didn't embarrass You too badly.

"But then Mike said I cried because I'm a caring, thoughtful, and compassionate person. I guess that's a good thing. So, Lord, what is Your plan for me? Mike is definitely a wonderful Christian man. And I really do like him and enjoy being with him. I like it when he holds me—it makes me feel protected and cared for. When he puts his arm around my shoulders, it makes me feel accepted and that I belong. His soft kisses make me feel cherished. What does all this mean?"

Then the words from Jeremiah came to mind again.

"For I know the plans I have for you," declares the Lord, "plans to prosper you and not to harm you, plans to give you hope and a future." Okay, Lord, I'll take this one step at a time and trust in You to lead me where You want this relationship to go." And with that she soon relaxed and fell asleep.

At church the next morning, three of the teens' moms, who had helped with the silent auction the evening before, came up to Missy with an idea.

"You know, Missy," one of the moms began, "you've worked very hard with all the fundraisers for the mission trip, and the next one is a rummage sale. A big rummage sale is a lot of work, so as we were cleaning up the kitchen last night, we were talking that maybe it would be easier if we had five or six smaller garage sales at different homes. They could be at one of our homes or anyone in the church who would like to host one, rather than having a big one at the church. It would spread out the workload, and we could have them in different areas of our communities. Then people could bring donations to whichever home is closest to them and have them priced beforehand to make it easier on the hosting families."

"We could even draw up a map of all the rummage sales that are supporting the youth's mission trip and hand them out," suggested another mom. "It might draw even more people. If they know it's for the youth, they might even give extra money. What do you think?"

"I think that's a good idea. What did Sue and Ron think about it?"

"They're both for it," said the third mom. "But we wanted to check with you and Mike also to see what you thought about it."

"Okay, I'll talk to Mike. If it's a go, we'll just have to see who's willing to have a garage sale at their home, get the map drawn up, announce it next week, and get it in the paper. It's planned for the first Saturday in June, so that still gives us almost three weeks to get things ready and the word out. I know some people have already been going through their things to put in a garage sale. I know my parents have, and they may be willing to have a sale at their home."

It was time for the Life groups to start, so they each went to their respective groups, and Missy would talk with Mike later. But she didn't get a chance to talk to him until after church was over.

"Mike, some of the teens' moms have come up with an idea that I need to talk to you about. Do you have anything planned for dinner today or can you join me at my parents' home? I'm sure they won't mind if you come."

"No, I don't mind at all. I always like eating at your parents' home."

"Well, Emily and I are doing the cooking today, to give Mom a day off since it's Mother's Day. I have to stop at my apartment to pick up the salad and dessert, so I'll meet you at my parents' house.

Linda is going with Luke and his parent's, as Luke is taking them out for dinner."

And with that, Missy went to find her parents.

Mike watched as Missy walked away.

Missy's acting a bit cold and distant, Mike noticed. *Is it because I said I was falling in love with her? Is it going to be a little strained at her parents' home? I'm not sure what to expect, but I will have to wait and find out.*

Chapter 25

Missy and Emily had planned their mom's favorite meal for dinner—meatloaf, baked potatoes, green beans, a lettuce salad, and chocolate cream pie for dessert. Emily had decided to only go to the church service so she could put the meatloaf and potatoes in the oven, then set the table with their best tablecloth, dishes, and a lovely bouquet of flowers in the center before going to church. Missy and Emily had picked up the bouquet of white daisies and red roses, which were their mom's favorite, from the florist on Saturday morning. All Emily had to do when she got home then was to put the beans on to cook, which wouldn't take long. Missy had made the salad and pie and stopped after church to pick them up at her apartment before going to the house. By the time she got there, everything was ready, and Mike had arrived also.

Everyone enjoyed the food. Liz thought it was nice not to have to cook, and she loved the flowers.

"And to have Mike here makes it special as well. I'm glad Missy invited you," their mom said, but noticed that Missy had gone out of her way to avoid looking at him.

She was polite and passed things to him, as they were seated side by side, but she mostly interacted with the others at the table.

"Actually, I invited him for a reason," Missy explained. "I didn't get a chance to talk to him at church and needed to discuss a situation with him in regard to our next fundraiser. And since it affects you too, Mom and Dad, I thought this would be a good opportunity to talk to all of you at once."

She then went on to tell them what some of the teens' moms had proposed to her about the garage sales.

When she finished, she looked at her parents and said, "Since you had mentioned that you wanted to be involved in the rummage sale at the church and had things you wanted to donate, I thought it might be good if you would host one of the garage sales. That way, you don't have to haul anything but can sell it right from your garage. And others from the church who live close by can bring their items here to sell as well. I would be here to help, of course.

"But first, Mike, what do you think of the idea of separate garage sales rather than one big rummage sale at the church?" Missy asked, looking at him, but in a very businesslike expression.

"I think it's a great idea and I am glad the moms thought of it. It makes good sense and sounds like it will be much easier to manage."

"And I don't mind having a garage sale here, what do you think, Liz?" Ken asked.

"It's fine with me. We'll just have to get busy and clean out the garage more, get things organized, and price the things we have to sell. But we still have about three weeks, so that should be fine."

"Good. That's settled then," Missy concluded. "I'll contact Sue and let her and Ron know that we'll go ahead with the multiple garage sales and see who else is interested in hosting them. Once we have that established, we can get a map made of the different locations, print some signs, and get them put up. Then I'll talk to the church secretary and have it put in the bulletin and on Facebook. Mike, can you put it in the paper again?"

"Sure, not a problem."

"Okay Mom, you and Dad can relax, and Emily and I will get these dishes cleaned up."

"I'll help," Mike volunteered.

Mike offered to wash the dishes while Missy dried and put them away. Emily put away the leftovers and wiped off the table. There was little conversation while Mike and Missy did the dishes.

When they were done, Mike turned to Missy and whispered, "Missy, can we go outside and talk?"

"Okay."

As Mike and Missy went out the back door, Emily went into the living room and quietly said to her parents, "I think there's trouble in paradise. I sure hope they work out whatever is bothering them. That silent treatment was creepy!"

Then Emily went to her room and turned on her music.

Ken and Liz looked at each other. Ken took Liz's hand in his, and they both bowed their heads and prayed.

Mike and Missy sat on the bench under a large maple tree in the backyard, and Mike began by turning to face Missy and asked, "Missy, did I upset you when I said I was falling in love with you?"

"No, you didn't upset me. In fact, Linda has told me several times that you were falling in love with me. And to be honest, I think I'm falling in love with you too. I just don't know what to do about it."

"You don't know what to do about it?" Mike asked as he took one of Missy's hands in his. "I can think of several things I would like to do. First off, stop avoiding each other and talk like we used to. Then I'd like to hold you in my arms and kiss your beautiful, soft lips. And I'd like to see your lovely smile again. But you've put a wall up and won't even let me touch you. Why?"

"Because I'm scared," Missy said as she looked at his pleading face. "You're so good at what you do. You're self-assured, confident, and work well with the teens and adults too. Working with the youth is still new to me, and I don't want to embarrass or fail you."

"Missy, you could never embarrass me, and I have never seen you fail yet. But we will all make mistakes and have disappointments and failures because we're human. But that doesn't mean we turn our backs on each other. That's when we need each other the most—to encourage and support one another. And that's why I need you." Mike took both of Missy's hands in his. "Missy, you make me feel complete, confident, and want to be the best I can be. You make me smile, feel alive, and I'm so proud to know you and have you in my life. I want our relationship to grow and maybe see if God wants it to become permanent someday."

"And that's what scares me," Missy confessed, releasing his hands and standing to put some distance between them. "I don't know if I would be a good pastor's wife."

"Why would you say that?" Mike stood also, not allowing too much distance to come between them.

"Because God and people expect so much more of pastors and their wives. They have to be so perfect and good, always smiling and saying the right things. They have to know more about the Bible than anyone else and have the perfect family. Who can live up to that?"

"No one!" Mike insisted as he moved closer to her, taking her hand in his as he led her toward Liz's flower garden where tulips and daffodils were blooming. "And that's something I struggled with too. Do you remember Harold and Millie? The couple that have the cabin on Lake Gogebic?"

"Yes."

"Well, I told you that they were influential in helping me decide to become a youth pastor. You see, Harold mentored me when I was a teenager and encouraged me to go to Bible school. When I felt God calling me to go into full-time ministry, I fought it. I didn't think I was good enough either. But then Harold reminded me that God doesn't expect perfection—just faithfulness and obedience.

"He pointed out that God always used people who were far from perfect. Moses killed a man, but God used him to lead the Israelites out of Egypt and toward the Promised Land. David was just a shepherd boy, but God made him the greatest king of Israel. He later committed adultery and murder, but he repented, and it was later said that he was a man after God's own heart. Peter denied Christ but became the leader of the first church. Paul was a persecutor of the Christians, until God got a hold of his life, and he became a missionary to the Gentiles.

"You see, God doesn't expect perfection. He just wants those who are willing to be used by Him to trust in Him and be willing to take on the challenge of serving Him, imperfections and all. Then we can say, as Paul did, 'Not that I have already obtained all this, or have already arrived at my goal, but I press on to take hold of that for which Christ Jesus took hold of me. Brothers and sisters, I do not consider myself yet to have taken hold of it. But one thing I do: Forgetting what is behind and straining toward what is ahead, I press on toward the goal to win the prize for which God has called me heavenward in Christ Jesus' (Phil. 3:12–14)."

Then Mike turned Missy so she would have to look at him as he said, "So I ask you, as Harold asked me, are you willing to let God use you, imperfections and all, and follow His plan for your life?"

"Yes, that's what I want," Missy replied sincerely. "And I do enjoy working with the youth. But I always question myself and wonder if I have the capabilities of being a good leader. Like today, why didn't I think of having multiple garage sales rather than one big one? It makes sense, and I think it will be much easier to manage."

"But that's why we have a team who works together to come up with different ideas. We also need to depend on others for help. That's what the body of Christ is all about. We're not on a solo mission, striving on our own, but a unified group, working for the cause of Christ, each one using their abilities and talents for a common goal—to share the Gospel with those who haven't heard, help them grow in their relationship with God, and then disciple others. You don't have to do it alone or know all the answers. That's why we have God and each other."

Mike leaned down, picked one of Liz's red tulips, and placed the stem in Missy's long, curly hair.

He caressed her cheek with his hand and said, "And that's why I need you, Missy. I need someone by my side who loves the Lord, the teens, and me. Someone who will be there in good times and bad, who believes in me, trusts me to care for her, and to love and cherish her. Someone I can share my dreams with, will encourage and support me, and bring out the best in me. I believe that person is you. And I want to do the same for you. I believe in you and want to encourage you to be the best you can be. You have already shown me that you have a real heart for teens and others who don't know the Lord. Look at all you've done for Rose and Beth and with organizing the events for the fundraisers—we couldn't have come this far without you. And I can't be all I can be without you. I love you and want you by my side, Missy."

"Oh, Mike, I love you too. I want our relationship to grow," Missy said as she moved into Mike's waiting arms. "When you hold me in your arms, I feel so complete, loved, and cared for. Your kiss makes me feel cherished, accepted, and valued. I enjoy working beside you, listening to your dreams, encouraging, and supporting you."

Missy looked up into Mike's eyes and said, "God is working on my heart and keeps reminding me that He has a plan for me, one that won't harm me but will give me hope and a future. I hope that future will be with you. But can you give me some time?"

"Of course! As long as there is hope that we can continue moving forward in our relationship, I will keep praying that your future will be with me. Because I like having you by my side, holding you in my arms and kissing you," Mike said, and with that, he kissed her sweetly and with passion.

"Well, Mr. Reeves, you keep kissing me like that, and it won't take much convincing," Missy said with a wide smile.

"But I want to do it right and court you properly. I promise I will be respectful of you, cherish you, and honor you during our time together. Do you mind if we go inside and I ask your parents' permission to court you, with the intent to one day ask you to marry me?"

"It seems a bit old-fashioned but sweet. And I think it would really please my parents and make it more official. So I guess that means we're a couple. I kind of like the sound of that. And it's not as scary as I thought it would be."

"Just promise me—no more silent treatment. If either of us has something bothering us, we'll talk about it and work it out together."

"Definitely! Working things out together is so much better!"

And with that, Missy kissed him.

"I couldn't agree more!" Mike said as he kissed her back. "But I think we better go inside and talk to your parents before they come out looking for us."

"Yes, I'm sure they're wondering what's going on. Emily has probably been peeking out the window already," Missy said with a smile, holding Mike's hand as they went inside.

Mike and Missy found Missy's parents in the living room, and they stood before them as Mike said, "Mr. and Mrs. Andrews, I would like to ask your permission to court your daughter, with the intent of one day asking permission to marry her. I love her and we want to spend time getting to know each other better. I promise to treat her with respect, honor, and will cherish her with all my being."

Missy's parents smiled at each other, stood, and Ken replied, "Mike, it would be my honor to give you permission to court our daughter. And if she would someday agree to be your wife, we would gladly welcome you into our family."

And with that, Ken shook Mike's hand, Liz hugged him, and Missy had tears in her eyes.

"We've been sitting here praying for you two, never imagining it would end like this. But God is good and answers our prayers better than we could ask or think," Liz said as she stepped away from Mike and Missy.

Emily came running around the corner, saying, "Can I join in the celebration too? I love a happy ending. But no more silent treatments—hugging and kissing is much better!"

"I knew you were peeking," Missy said as she smiled and hugged her sister.

"This calls for a special treat. How about we all go out for some ice cream? My treat," Ken announced.

"Yah!" they all agreed.

When Missy went back to her apartment, Mike went with her to share the news with Linda. As expected, Linda was ecstatic with excitement.

"I knew it would happen! What took you so long, big brother?" Linda said as she slugged Mike on the arm, then gave him a hug.

She then hugged Missy, squealed, and said, "I always knew we would be sisters one day. Just don't wait too long, okay?"

"Okay!" Missy said, smiling at Linda and holding her hand. "But remember, we're just courting. This isn't an engagement. We want to get to know each other better and make sure this is what God wants for both of us."

"Hey, you're a match made in heaven—anyone can see that."

Chapter 26

That evening, Missy called Sue and told her that she and Mike agreed with the idea of changing the one big rummage sale to multiple garage sales in different areas of the community.

"My parents are willing to have a sale in their garage. Do you know of others who are willing to have a garage sale at their home as well?"

"I'll contact the moms who were interested," Sue replied. "We can still have the sales on Friday from nine to five and from nine to noon on the first Saturday in June. Ron said he will draw up a map of the various garage sale locations and print posters for the teens to put up on Wednesday evening," Sue replied.

That would leave Missy only with getting the information to the church secretary for the bulletin and their Facebook page and Mike to write up an advertisement for the paper. Things were well on their way. Missy was grateful for everyone's support and help.

Missy helped her parents on her free evenings to get the garage cleaned up, set up tables, and price items. Other people from church dropped off items they wanted to donate for the sale, and Mike came on Saturdays to help as well. They were collecting quite a few items, with a great variety, which should appeal to many garage-sale shoppers. The other garage sale hosts were reporting the same, so they were looking forward to good results. Now they just had to pray for good weather on the days of the sale.

On the Saturday of Memorial weekend, Aaron and April were hosting a cookout at their home, beginning at noon. They invited the couples and their children from their Thursday evening home group and encouraged them to invite friends as well. April had approached Missy and asked if she and Mike would come, as well as Linda and Luke, and asked them to invite Kurt and Beth too. Since Missy and Linda were finishing up their study with Beth, it would be a good opportunity for them to meet other couples in an informal setting. Hopefully, they would then feel more comfortable and want to attend the couples' group on Thursday evenings.

They had a good turnout, even though some couples weren't able to attend due to other family plans. Aaron and April provided the meat for the grill, and each couple were asked to bring a dish to pass. There were sixteen adults and five children, which included Bonnie and Brad's nine-month old son, Sammy. Kurt and Beth decided to come, which pleased Missy and Linda. They enjoyed introducing them to their friends and hosts, Aaron and April Matthews.

Everyone was very friendly, intermingled, and had a great time. There was a large amount of great food that was enjoyed by all, and some of the women exchanged recipes. After the meal, there were lawn games of darts, a beanbag challenge, and croquet. Couples and families began leaving at 4:30 p.m., some with sleeping babies but all with smiling faces after having a great time. Even Kurt and Beth said they enjoyed themselves and would talk about attending the Thursday evening couples' group.

On Memorial Day, Mike asked Missy to go with him to the Black River Scenic Byway and hike from Great Conglomerate Falls to Potawatomi, Gorge, Sandstone, and Rainbow Falls. The total hike was about five miles, and they'd end up at Black River Harbor. Linda and Luke would meet them at the harbor for a picnic, which Missy and Linda would prepare. Missy enjoyed hiking, and it was a good time to go into the woods before it got too hot or buggy. However, Missy still packed some bug spray, bottles of water, and her camera in her backpack.

It turned out to be a beautiful day, with partly cloudy skies, a nice breeze, and temps in the upper sixties. Mike parked his pickup at the Conglomerate Falls parking lot, and Linda would bring it to the harbor later when they came for the picnic. They started with the three-quarter-mile trail through the woods, with a downward trek to the river.

The green leaves were filling out on the trees, and spring flowers were blooming among the undergrowth. Missy took pictures along the way, and when they got to the river, the water was moving fast from all the melted snow and recent rainfalls. It rushed over a huge mound of conglomerate rocks that formed two separate waterfalls, which made it difficult to capture in a single shot. But from the boardwalks and a well-placed viewing platform, Missy was able to get some really nice pictures.

"Wow, this is really beautiful. I'm so glad you chose to bring me here today. It's so nice to get away from all the stress of work and the fundraisers and just get out and enjoy God's creation. This is my first hike of the season, and I'm glad I can do it with you," Missy acknowledged as she gave Mike a kiss.

"I am too," Mike said as he held Missy in his arms. "A beautiful day, a beautiful woman, and a beautiful waterfall—or should I say two?"

"Yes, there actually are two," Missy said as she let out a deep sigh. "I think I could stay here for hours just taking in all the beauty."

"I think I could too," Mike said as he looked down at Missy.

Missy looked up into Mike's eyes and said, "Are we talking about the same thing here?"

"You *are* one of God's creations, so I was admiring you. You are very beautiful, Missy."

"I guess I've never thought of myself as beautiful—more ordinary," Missy admitted.

"Missy, there is nothing ordinary about you. Your skin is soft to touch," Mike said as he caressed her cheek. "And your brown eyes sparkle with passion for whatever you're doing, whether it's admiring the waterfalls, working with the youth, counting money after our fundraising projects, enjoying your family, or with me. It's like your eyes are a window to your heart. Your hair smells like strawberries, shiny and soft, and your ponytail sways as you walk down the trail, so carefree and relaxed. You fit so nicely in my arms, and your lips are so kissable."

Mike bent down and kissed her sweetly.

"Oh, you charmer you. Flattery will get you another kiss," Missy said as she kissed him again.

"As much as I'm enjoying this, we should probably head down the trail to the next waterfall. How about a drink of water before we go?" Mike suggested.

He reached into the backpack he was carrying and took out two water bottles. They each took a good drink, put the bottles back in the backpack, and then Mike took Missy's hand as they headed down the trail along the river. They enjoyed the view but also had to watch where they walked, as there were places that were wet and slippery and tree roots in the trail.

Soon they came to Potawatomi Falls, where again the water was rushing over the rocks and cascading down over twenty feet, leaving a mist in the air and foam as it hit the bottom. It was awesome to see the power of the water and the hills on each side of the river covered in trees and displaying God's glory and majesty. They admired it in silent reverence for a while and then continued on to Gorge Falls where the river squeezed through a narrow gorge lined with cedar. Water spurted over a twenty-foot drop like a ball over a pinball machine, hitting first one side of the rocks and then the other.

Half a mile beyond Gorge Falls was Sandstone Falls. They went down the winding steps to see the water rushing over the sandstone, which gave it a unique appearance. Again, they were awed by the beauty all around them.

After a drink of water, they went on to the last of the waterfalls—Rainbow Falls. It had the longest drop of about forty feet, and they could hear the roar of the water and feel the mist of the waterfall before they saw the water hit the frothy pool at the bottom. Missy had seen it from across the river but not from this side, which again was reached by long, winding steps to an observation platform. But from both sides of the river, it was breathtaking!

"I never tire of seeing these waterfalls," Mike commented.

"Me neither," Missy replied. "We are so blessed to be living in this area and enjoy all this beauty!"

"Amen to that! But how about another drink of water before we head to the picnic area? We'll have to climb these stairs, follow the ridge a short way, and then down to the harbor. I hope you and Linda made a big lunch because after this hike, I'm really hungry."

"I don't think you'll be disappointed," Missy assured him.

And he wasn't.

The following Friday and Saturday were the garage sales at five various homes across the community. The weather was cooperative, though it did start raining on Saturday afternoon after the sales ended. They were well attended, and Missy was surprised when she, Mike, Sue, and Ron added up the funds that were turned in on Sunday after church.

"Mike, this is better than I could ever have imagined! With the five garage sales, we've raised $1,555. Added to our previous total of $5,521, we've raised $7,076—we've surpassed our fundraiser goal and may not even have to do the car wash at all. This is amazing!" Missy said with tears flowing from her eyes.

Mike went to put his arm around Missy and agreed, "God has blessed us amazingly, and all we can say is, thank You, Lord!"

"This mission trip is truly God's plan for our youth this summer, and everyone has put their heart and soul into making it possible. Praise be to God!" Ron added.

"I'm speechless!" Sue said as she shook her head and her eyes overflowed with tears also. "This could only be a God thing! So what do we do with the extra funding?"

"I would like to propose that we pray about it and bring it to the youth on Wednesday evening. They have all worked very hard with the fundraising, and I don't think it should be just our decision," Mike suggested.

The rest of the leaders agreed and promised to pray about the decision that would be made. Mike shared the results with the pastoral staff at their meeting on Tuesday and asked them to pray also that God would lead them in making the right decision.

When Wednesday evening came and the leaders shared the good news of the fundraising success, everyone cheered, clapped their hands, and were filled with joy.

Mike shared a challenge to them and said, "When God blesses us, He expects us to share it with others. We had a goal of raising $6,000 for our mission trip. We've raised $7,076. Do you have any ideas as to what we should do with the extra $1,076?"

After several suggestions, it was agreed to share the extra money with another mission project that was dear to many hearts in their church, which was to purchase cows for a struggling tribe in Kenya whose livelihood had been taken from them. They also suggested that they continue with the car wash, since it was already scheduled in two and a half weeks at the corner of the Holiday Station in Ironwood and that those funds also be donated to the mission in Kenya for food items that were needed. The leaders couldn't have been prouder of their youth. They truly had developed a heart of service and love for others, and they were excited to see how God would use them on their mission trip in July.

To celebrate after all the fundraisers were completed, Mike took Missy to Duluth for a nice dinner and to see the play *Singin' in the Rain* at the Duluth Playhouse. They had a wonderful time; and Missy felt carefree, relaxed, and cherished. Missy loved going to classic plays and musicals, and they sang some of the songs from *Singin' in the Rain* together on the way home.

"Oh, this was such a special evening," Missy said smiling, as they neared Ironwood. "Thanks, Mike! It was so nice to be waited on, have a nice dinner, and then relax in that beautiful old theater to enjoy a fun and delightful musical."

"Well, you deserved it and more. I love seeing you smile and having a good time. How about if we continue this and go kayaking tomorrow after church? We can pick up some lunch at Subway and head over to Little Girls Point. Maybe Linda and Luke can join us."

"Sounds good. I'm sure Linda will be asleep, but I'll ask her in the morning if they have any plans."

After Mike walked her to her apartment, held her in his arms, and kissed her good night, she felt like she was walking on a cloud as she prepared for bed. It was nice to have someone care for her, think she was special, and go out of their way to give her a good time.

Linda and Luke went kayaking with them the next afternoon, and they all had a great time. It turned out to be another beautiful, sunny day. Missy was glad she brought sunscreen along, as the sun shimmering off Lake Superior was very warm, and they would have had some serious sunburn without it.

On the evening of the third of July, Missy and Mike sat with some friends from their young adult group at Sunday Lake for the fireworks display. As always, they had an amazing display and the grand finale was loud and magnificent! On the fourth, they joined Missy's family for a picnic and afternoon at Bond Falls, which is a scenic and popular waterfall in southern Ontonagon County. The falls were created as the middle branch of the Ontonagon river tumbled over a thick belt of fractured rocks, dividing it into numerous small cascades. The total drop of the falls was approximately fifty feet. It was amazing to see, as Missy had never been there before. It was a very enjoyable and relaxing afternoon.

On the way home, they stopped at Harold and Millie's cabin on Lake Ontonagon to say hi and introduce them to Missy's family. Some of Harold and Millie's family were there also, but Harold and Millie insisted they stay and join them for a bonfire, roasting hotdogs, making smores, and then finish the evening by watching the sunset.

"You know, we think of you as family, Mike," Millie said as she gave him a hug. "And, Missy, you're special to us too, and it's so nice to meet your parents and sister, Emily. We're glad you stopped by."

Millie gave Missy a hug too, as well as Liz, Ken, and Emily. With such a warm invitation, they decided to stay and had an enjoyable evening,

When it was time to leave for home, Millie whispered to Mike as she hugged him goodbye, "I think you've made a wonderful choice, son. I liked Missy from the moment I met her."

"Me too," Mike said as he smiled and gave Millie a wink.

Chapter 27

The day to leave for the mission trip at Kenosha, Wisconsin, had finally arrived. There was a real sense of eagerness and anticipation of what lay ahead for the team of four adults and sixteen teens on their Week of Hope experience. Years ago, Kenosha was an active center of manufacturing; but like many other cities in that part of the country, the community had been hurt by factory closures and industry changes.

At the beginning of 2013, the last wall came down as American Motors, a manufacturing plant that once brought hope and income to many families in the city, closed and left many without jobs and hope. They would concentrate their time by entering into the lives of seniors, helping those with disabilities, distributing food for needy families, and working at summer day camps for kids ages five to fifteen. It was sure to be an unforgettable week and a new and adventurous experience for all of them.

By 8:00 a.m. on Saturday, they were loaded into two vans, eight in Ron and Sue's and twelve in the church's fifteen-passenger van, plus luggage. They would be staying at a local church; so they brought sleeping bags, pillows, and air mattresses and would be assigned gender-separate rooms when they arrived. The facility did have air-conditioning and showers, but the showers weren't private, so the church suggested they bring swimsuits, if desired.

The drive from Hurley, Wisconsin, to Kenosha would take seven hours, plus an hour stop for lunch. But they all made the best of it, and there was light conversation and singing most of the way down.

When they arrived, they met other youth groups and leaders they'd be working with throughout the week and staff from the church where they would be staying. The church provided supper and then movies and games for a relaxing evening. Missy, however, hadn't felt good most of the afternoon, so she didn't eat much at suppertime. Mike was concerned and asked her after supper if she was okay, but she'd just said, "My stomach is upset, and I'm pretty tired. I'm just going to lay down and get some rest."

Missy didn't go to the fun events that evening but laid out her sleeping bag in the room designated for the girls and women leaders, and then she tried to get some rest. She was afraid she might be coming down with the flu and hoped none of the others would get it, so she tried to keep her distance. Hopefully, it would just be a twenty-four-hour bug.

But the next morning, she didn't feel any better; in fact, she felt worse—even nauseated. Everyone else went to the worship service, but Missy took some Pepto-Bismol and laid down again. But not for long, as she soon rushed to the bathroom and vomited.

Mike wanted to check on her after the service, but since he wasn't allowed to go into the girl's sleeping area, he asked Sue to check on her. Sue knelt down next to Missy's sleeping bag to check on her. She thought she looked very pale, and her stomach pain was definitely worse.

"I'm so sorry, Sue. I've looked forward to this mission trip since Mike first mentioned it back in January, and now I've got the flu. What bad timing! I hope I'll be able to help out with our service projects tomorrow."

"Don't you worry about it," Sue insisted. "You just rest and get better. Is there anything I can get you? Some 7Up, soda crackers, or more water?"

"Maybe fill up my water bottle and see if you can find a bucket, just in case I can't get to the bathroom in time."

"Of course, I'll see what I can find. There might be something in the kitchen. I'll be right back."

Sue got up and went to inform Mike that she was worse, not better. Then she went to find a bucket for Missy.

Mike prayed that God would touch Missy and help her feel better. It was so hard not to be able to see her or do anything to help.

As the day progressed, Missy's pain continued to get worse, and her moaning began to worry Sue. When she felt Missy's forehead, she felt warm to the touch and probably had a fever. She went to find Ron and suggested they take Missy to the ER. Ron went to get Mike who immediately said he would take her and that Ron and Sue should stay with the teens.

At the ER, Missy underwent a doctor's exam, lab work, and a CT scan. When the doctor came back with the results, he said he wanted to admit Missy, as she had appendicitis, needed to be put on antibiotics, and have surgery the next morning.

Missy was shocked. She thought it was just the flu, though she had never felt that much pain with the flu before. She also never had surgery and was far away from home.

"I'll call your mom and tell her what's happening. I'm sure she'll want to come down. I'll stay with you until she gets here. I won't leave you alone, Missy," Mike promised.

By then, it was nine in the evening. So, as Missy waited to be transferred to a hospital room, Mike called Liz and filled her in on Missy's condition. After talking to Ken, Liz said they would leave early in the morning and get there as soon as possible, as they were both tired and didn't feel comfortable driving late at night.

"I'll stay with Missy until you get here. You get some rest and drive safely," Mike assured her.

He then called Ron and told him that Missy needed surgery in the morning for appendicitis and that he would be staying at the hospital. Mike asked him to explain to the team coordinators that they would be two leaders short for Monday but that he would be there on Tuesday and the rest of the week. However, Missy would not be joining them. He asked for their prayers, for Missy and her parents' safety as they traveled the next morning.

Mike could tell Missy was scared. After the nurses got her settled into her hospital room, Mike came into the room and held Missy's hand. He explained to the nurses that he was the youth pastor and that they were in Kenosha for their Week of Hope mission trip. He told them also that he and Missy were courting and that her parents were a distance away but would be arriving the following afternoon. Missy's charge nurse explained to Missy what was going to happen.

"The doctor ordered an antibiotic and some pain medicine for you. As soon as it gets here, we'll bring it in to you. The antibiotic will go into your IV so it will hit the infection faster. The pain medicine will make you groggy, so we don't want you getting up by yourself. If you need the bathroom, just push the red button on your call button and we'll come in to help you. You won't be able to have anything to eat or drink after midnight. In the morning, the surgeon and anesthesiologist will be in to see you and talk to you about the procedure. I don't have the time of your procedure yet, but it will probably be sometime in the morning. Do you have any questions?"

Missy shook her head no, for she didn't even know what questions to ask.

After the nurse left, she asked Mike, "Have you ever had surgery?"

"Yes, I had my tonsils out when I was little. I don't remember much, though, except that my throat was really sore and I got to eat a lot of popsicles."

"I'm sorry, Mike. I was looking forward to this week, and now I'm in the hospital, will be having surgery, and you'll be short a leader. What will happen now?"

"I'll stay here with you until after the surgery and your parents get here. Ron and Sue will go tomorrow with the teens, and I'm sure they'll be okay without us. You just concentrate on resting and recovering from your surgery."

"You don't have to stay here with me. Besides, they're expecting you to be with the teens tomorrow when they go on their service projects," Missy countered.

"I told you I wouldn't leave you, and I keep my promises," Mike insisted.

"But that's not necessary. Besides, the nurse said the pain medicine will make me sleepy, so I'll probably sleep most of the night."

"I'll feel better if I stay. I can probably catch a few winks here and there. This chair reclines, and one of the nurses said she'd bring in a pillow and blanket for me later. I'll be fine."

"Are you being stubborn?"

"No more than you," Mike said with a smile.

During the night, neither of them got much sleep. Missy moaned often, and it seemed like when she finally drifted off to sleep, a nurse would come in to check her vitals and her stomach to see if the swelling was getting worse. At 6:00 a.m., a technician from the lab came in to take more blood, and shortly after that, they got a call from Missy's parents saying they were on their way and should be there by 2:00 p.m.

At 7:00 a.m., the surgeon came in and introduced himself, examined her, and then explained the procedure to them.

"Since your appendix hasn't burst, we'll be able to do a laparoscopic procedure to remove your appendix. I will make a few small abdominal incisions and then insert special surgical tools and a video camera into your abdomen to remove your appendix. This type of surgery allows you to recover faster and heal with less pain and scarring. After the procedure, you'll be in recovery for about an hour and then brought back to this room. We'll keep you overnight to make sure there are no complications, but you should be able to go home tomorrow. Have you had any other surgeries before?"

"No I haven't."

"Well, we'll take good care of you, and someone will contact you soon for the time of your procedure. The anesthesiologist will also be in to talk with you. I need to go over any risks you need to be aware of, as with any surgery, and then I need you to sign this form, giving us permission to do the operation."

After he explained the risks, Missy signed the permission form and handed it back to him.

"Okay, I'll see you soon, and we'll take out that infected appendix," the surgeon said as he left the room.

When the anesthesiologist came in, he informed her that she was scheduled for 10:00 a.m., so they would be coming for her about 9:30 a.m. He asked her a lot of questions and then explained his part in the surgery.

"Since you've never had an anesthetic before, I'll be watching you very carefully, but I don't expect we'll have any issues."

After he left, Mike took Missy's hand and they prayed together.

When he said "Amen," Missy looked at him and said, with tears in her eyes, "Thank you for being here, Mike. I know I wouldn't have wanted to do this without you."

"I wouldn't want to be anywhere else," he said as he kissed her forehead and wiped her tears.

The surgery went well and the doctor told Mike that they removed the appendix, there was no sign that the infection had spread, and they found no abscess. The doctor said she would be in recovery for an hour, so he should go get some lunch. Mike did so but didn't stay away long as he wanted to be there as soon as he was able to see her.

But Missy had gotten sick from the anesthetic, so she was in the recovery room longer than normal, and they took her directly to her room when she was able to be moved. They'd given her something to settle her stomach, but she still felt nauseated. Mike sat by her side and gave her some ice chips when she asked for them, a cool cloth on her forehead, or whatever else she needed. It was hard to see her so miserable and in pain from the surgery. But soon her parents arrived and were by her side immediately.

Missy was glad to see them but motioned for Mike to again sit by her side and hold her hand.

When her stomach finally settled down and Missy fell asleep, her dad said, "As long as she's resting now, I'm going to check into our hotel and put our luggage in the room. We reserved it for two nights."

Ken then turned to Mike and said, "We weren't sure how soon Missy would feel up to traveling back home. Liz you can stay here, but I should be back in an hour or so."

He then kissed his wife and daughter and left for the hotel.

"Thank you so much, Mike, for being here when we couldn't be. It must have been so scary for her! She's never had surgery before," Liz said to Mike when they were alone.

"It was my privilege! I would never let her go through something like this alone," Mike said.

"I knew you wouldn't. That's what gave me such peace about not leaving last night. Though I knew it would be too much on us to make that long drive at night."

"There was really nothing you could have done last night anyway, and I was already here. She needs you more now, and I'll have to go back and work with the teens and their mission projects for the rest of the week."

"Yes, I know. She's going to be so disappointed not to be able to participate in the projects this week, and after all the work she did to make sure it happened too."

"I know. I don't understand why God allowed this to happen now. But then we're not to question. We just need to trust that God knows what He's doing. But it's not always easy."

"No, it's not," Liz agreed. Liz and Mike both sat back in their chairs and dozed off while Missy slept on.

Chapter 28

When Ken returned to Missy's hospital room, Liz and Mike woke with a start. "Oh, I'm sorry, I didn't mean to wake you," Ken whispered. "But I ran into Sue and Rose in the lobby and wanted to check and see if Missy was up for visitors."

"Sure," they heard Missy say with a raspy voice. "Just give me a minute."

Turning towards her mom, Missy asked, "Mom, do you have a comb or brush with you?"

"Sure, let me get it and run it through your hair."

After Liz brushed Missy's hair and made sure she was comfortable and decent, she went out into the hall and invited them in.

"Hi, Missy," Sue said as she came in. "I know you're not feeling too good yet, but we just wanted to let you know that we've been praying for you, miss you, and hope you'll be feeling better soon." She showed Missy a bouquet of flowers in a vase. "These are from all of us. We thought they would give you something pretty to look at besides four walls."

"Oh, thank you. They're beautiful! Can you put them on the windowsill, Mom?"

"Sure. Would you like to sit down?" Missy's mom asked as she invited the well-wishers in.

"No, we can't stay long," Sue informed. "They'll be serving supper soon, and then we have chapel shortly after. They have it each evening and really make it a fun time for the teens. Last night they had some worship songs, a skit, interaction, and a thought-provoking devotion at the end. But Rose wanted to come too and make sure you're okay."

"I'm not feeling the best yet, but it can only get better now that the surgery is over. Thanks for coming, both of you. It means a lot, and it's so good to see you."

"We were so worried about you, Missy," Rose said. "But we prayed for you and knew that God and Pastor Mike were with you, so you weren't going through this alone. I just wanted to come and say thanks for the opportunity to be here this week. I went to a nursing home today and visited with some of the residents there and even helped with bingo this afternoon. A lot of those people don't get much company and were so glad we were there to visit with them. Before you became my friend, I was alone like that a lot too. It feels really good to help someone else not feel so alone."

Missy got tears in her eyes and was so glad Sue and Rose had come.

"Just to hear you say that, Rose, makes all this pain worth it. Thank you so much for coming and telling me that. I look forward to hearing about the rest of your week and from the others too. Hopefully, I'll feel well enough to come to youth group next week and you can tell me about some of your other experiences."

"That would be great! We'll keep praying that you'll feel better soon, Missy," Rose assured her.

Then Sue and Rose left, and Liz placed Missy's order for supper, since she was awake and felt like eating a little something.

Ken asked Liz to go for a walk with him and left Mike and Missy alone for a while.

"I'm so glad Rose was able to come this week," Missy began. "I think it's really going to make a difference in her life and the rest of the teens."

"I'm sure it will. It will open their eyes to things they haven't seen or done before. Through the fundraising efforts, they got a taste of what it's like to serve others, but this week will take it to a whole new level."

"And I won't be able to be there and see it happen. I'm so sorry for not being able to help, for making you miss today and leaving you short for the rest of the week. I feel like I really failed you," Missy said with tears in her eyes.

"No, you haven't. It's not your fault you had to have surgery today. And remember, I chose to be here with you! I want to be here! I love you, Missy, and would never let you go through this alone. You mean too much to me. And you haven't failed me. Don't even think that. I'm sure everything went fine today and they probably had another volunteer to take our places. Emergencies happen, and you just have to make the best of them and work through them."

"I know, but why me? Why now?"

"I don't know, Missy. But it's going to be okay because I love you no matter what. I'll always be there for you when you need me," Mike said and squeezed her hand.

"Thank you, Mike. And I love you too. I guess I didn't realize how much I've come to depend on you. I've always been able to count on you—when I needed help with Rose and her pictures, when dad had his surgery, with the fundraisers, and now with my surgery. You've always been there for me."

"It goes two ways, you know. I've counted on you too, and you've always been there, faithful and true. We make a good team, you and I," Mike said with a smile and kissed her.

"Yes, we do, don't we?" Missy smiled and kissed him again.

Mike wanted to tell her that he wanted to make it permanent someday but didn't think this was the right time or place to do so. And he was right. Ken and Liz came back from their walk and sat down, with something definitely on their minds.

"Mike, I was just talking to Liz, and we were wondering if you think it would be possible for me to take Missy's place on Tuesday and Wednesday morning. I know she feels bad that you're short of adults to work with the teens, but Liz can handle Missy's discharge tomorrow and take her to the hotel to rest if I leave her the car. Mike, you could pick me up, and since we weren't planning on leaving until Wednesday after checkout time anyway, I might as well make myself useful until she's ready to go home. What do you think?" Ken asked as he looked from Mike to Missy.

"Well, I would have to check it out with the coordinators of the Week of Hope, but it might work out. The teens have Wednesday afternoon off anyway, to do some sightseeing in the area. Can I get back to you on that, Ken?" Mike asked.

"Sure, not a problem."

They brought Missy's supper in, so Mike decided to go and have supper with the teens and others at the church. Hopefully, he could get an answer for Ken and be back later that evening.

Ken had to fill out some paperwork but was approved to take Missy's place. He was excited to work wherever he was needed. On Tuesday, he helped with the food distribution, setting up food items on tables, with the help of the teens and other adults assigned to that project in the morning and early afternoon. From three to five, the doors were opened, and they distributed the food to families in need. Ken was amazed at the amount of food that had been donated and the many families that came to receive it.

Those who served were encouraged to not judge anyone who came but give each item with a loving smile, and it was received gratefully. There were also those from the church who were available to counsel any family members who needed further help, whether spiritually, emotionally, or financially. Theirs was a ministry designed to help all needs. Ken was impressed and grateful to be a part of the ministry.

The next morning, he was assigned to help with the finishing of a ramp for an elderly couple. The husband had recently had a stroke and was wheelchair bound, so it was difficult for him to get in and out of their home. Another leader was in charge of the construction project, which they'd started on Monday and hoped to finish that morning. Ken was asked to do the cutting of the boards with the skill saw. Today they would build the handrails and pour the concrete to stabilize the posts.

Ken enjoyed working alongside the youth. He could tell that many didn't have a lot of experience in building, but they were eager to learn, and by encouraging them and patiently helping when they had questions, the work moved forward. By 11:30 a.m., they finished putting the concrete in the last posthole, and the wife came out and thanked them.

"I can't tell you how grateful we are for your willingness to do this for us. We could never have afforded to pay for a ramp like this to be built. You have done a wonderful job, and I've never seen young people work so hard! Thank you!" she said with tears in her eyes. "Now, I've made you some brownies and lemonade and put them on the picnic table in the backyard as a small thank-you. So go on, before the flies get them."

She waved them off, smiling.

They all enjoyed the refreshments, as it hit the spot on such a warm, summer day. While they finished off the brownies, one of the teen boys came up to Ken and said, "I enjoyed working with you today, Mr. Andrews. You were very patient with me and didn't yell when I made mistakes."

"I enjoyed working with you too, Rob," Ken replied as he put his hand on Rob's shoulder. "And we all make mistakes, but the important thing is that you learned from it and the next board you nailed in perfectly. You didn't even hit your thumb. You did just fine."

That made Rob's face beam and when he turned away, he walked with his head held high.

They got back to the church in time to eat lunch, and it didn't take them long to empty their plates. They had put in a good morning of work, had finished the handicap ramp, and made it possible for a couple to have better access in and out of their home. They were all pleased with what had been accomplished. But now the teens could have some well-deserved time off, and Ken could take his wife and daughter home.

Missy and Liz had eaten their lunch also and were ready to go. Ken thought Missy looked better and hoped the drive home wouldn't be too uncomfortable for her.

Liz had brought extra pillows and blankets so Missy could lay down on the back seat and be more comfortable and cushion some of the bumps in the road. She also insisted that Missy stay at their home till the weekend so she could keep an eye on her in case she needed anything.

But by the weekend, Missy felt better, and Linda would be at the apartment if Missy needed anything, so Missy was able to go home.

"I appreciated all Mom's help, but I'm so glad to be back here," Missy said to Linda as they sat together on the couch. "The pain has lessened, and it's good to be able to get up and around some. I was getting pretty tired of lying in bed and taking those pain pills. They upset my stomach and made me so groggy. I feel better now that I'm just taking Tylenol."

"I'm sure they helped you heal though, since you were forced to rest and stay down. But I'm glad you're feeling better and home now too, though I was shocked to hear about your appendicitis attack. That was sure unexpected!"

"Yes, it was. But your brother was a real Godsend. He wouldn't leave my side 'til my parents got there."

"Ah yes, your knight in shining armor. Or should I say jeans and a T-shirt?" Linda said with a smile.

"Please, don't make me laugh," Missy said holding her stomach. "It still hurts too much."

"Sorry. So what can I get you for lunch?"

"Since you're asking, a BLT sandwich sounds really good, with some applesauce on the side."

"Lucky for you I got groceries this morning before you got here and picked up some bacon. So sit back and relax, and enjoy being waited on, my dear," Linda said as she got up to make lunch. "Can I get you anything else? Something to drink maybe?"

"Just some water, please." Missy appreciated everyone's help but would be so glad when she could move around better and do for herself again.

Chapter 29

Missy didn't go to church on Sunday morning, but Mike came over in the afternoon to watch a movie with her. That gave Linda a chance to spend time with Luke, as it was a beautiful summer day and they had planned on going kayaking.

"You know, we often take our health for granted," Missy acknowledged as they sat on the couch. "We assume that we'll be able to get up every morning and do whatever we want, but you never know what may happen. I know dad was saying on the way home that the man they built the ramp for was pretty active and able to do things around the house, and then he had that stroke and it changed their lives. Now he's in a wheelchair, and without that ramp, he couldn't even get out of the house. And look how quickly I went from being active to being flat on my back and in need of surgery."

"Yes, we need to be thankful for each day God gives us strength and health. I think all our eyes were opened this last week. I've asked the teens who were involved with our Week of Hope to share some of their experiences from this past week and what they learned and took away from it at youth group on Wednesday. Pastor Dale would like them to share next Sunday during the Morning worship service as well. It will be good for those who went to verbalize their experiences and also for those who didn't go to hear about it."

"I'd sure like to hear about it. I wouldn't miss it!"

"Good. I'll pick you up on Wednesday," Mike said as he put his arm around her shoulder and started the movie.

Missy was excited to hear from the teens on Wednesday evening. Some shared about helping with the kids' summer camp and, while talking with them, doing crafts, teaching them to play basketball or archery, sharing a Bible story, and even preparing a snack; it really helped them bond with the children. Some would cling to them, hungry for love and attention. Others caused trouble or would start fights as they had never been disciplined or learned about consequences for their bad behavior. But by the end of the week, they saw behaviors change, and all received hugs and thanks for being there and caring for them.

Those who visited with the elderly at the nursing home, worked at the food distribution, built ramps, or did yard work and gardening for the elderly, as well as those with disabilities, said how good it felt to do something for others and see how much it was appreciated. Also, working together as a team to accomplish a good deed had built a stronger relationship between the youth, and they realized that they had a good time doing it too. Some learned new skills during the building projects, while others found new interests. The work projects at the community center also helped them take pride in the work they accomplished when finished.

They'd each had a chance to work with several different projects throughout the week but found that interacting with the people—and one another—was the most rewarding. Building relationships and helping people feel accepted, loved, and valued is what being Christlike is all about; And that's what Christ did while He was here on earth. When He taught, when He healed people, when He was with His disciples or friends, it was all about others and being selfless.

As the teens and leaders shared, many had tears in their eyes; and even those who weren't able to go on the mission trip were moved. Missy sat back and after listening to their comments, testimonies, and experiences decided that instead of feeling sorry that she wasn't able to be a part of it, she was going to be grateful that she had the opportunity to make this week possible for the teens to experience. It was obvious that it had changed their lives and attitudes and they would be more considerate and caring of others in the days ahead. They would notice people in need and be more willing to help instead of overlooking them or just passing them by.

Even her dad said that he had thoroughly enjoyed the day and a half he spent working on the projects with the teens and other leaders. It made him feel good to help others, working alongside the men and teens to accomplish something good, and he had truly enjoyed the fellowship. He thanked her for allowing him to work in her stead, and he said he would like to go on another mission trip in the future. Missy was sure the teens would too.

It was a week to remember and, hopefully, to do again—except for the surgery part.

Missy and Mike's relationship also changed over the next few weeks. Missy realized how much she enjoyed having Mike by her side and how much she depended on him. She realized how they complemented each other and how much she loved him more each day, and that he loved her. He had proven it to her when she was in the hospital and he wouldn't leave her side. Even when she was at her worst—in pain, hair a mess, in a hospital gown, and sometimes irritable—Mike stood by her. He didn't expect her to be perfect but accepted her for who she was. Mike was her strength and courage, and he gave her hope that everything would be okay.

When they prayed together, they knew that God was with them and that they could get through any difficulty together. It gave them both a real peace. Even the possibility of being a pastor's wife didn't scare her anymore, for Mike had told her many times, "I don't expect you to be perfect or do what other pastors' wives do. The important thing is that you put God first in your life, love Him with all your heart, and then just be willing to use the gifts God has given you. That's all anyone can expect. And all I want is your support, encouragement, and love, and I will give you the same."

Even her dad reminded her often of the verses in Jeremiah: "'For I know the plans I have for you,' declares the Lord, 'plans to prosper you and not to harm you, plans to give you hope and a future. Then you will call on me and come and pray to me, and I will listen to you. You will seek me and find me when you seek me with all your heart.

"Missy, God has a wonderful plan for you. So follow His plan, just as you're doing. You are using the gifts He gave you by caring and encouraging others and by using your organizational skills for His glory. Rose and Beth came to know the Lord because of your caring and compassion, and the youth are growing in the Lord through your example and encouragement. I couldn't be prouder of you."

Missy couldn't be prouder of Rose, for she had been sharing Christ and her experiences from the mission trip with her parents, and now her mom was coming to church with her. Her dad wasn't coming, but Rose was praying, as was the youth group leaders and Missy's parents, that Rose's parents would soon come to know the Lord.

Missy also found out that Aaron and April had kept in contact with Beth and Kurt since the Memorial weekend dinner at their home, and Beth and Kurt were now attending their young married couples' group. They were enjoying interacting with the other couples and making new friends. God was truly at work.

Missy was learning an important lesson—God uses many Christians to accomplish His purposes and draw people to Himself. He gives each one different gifts and abilities to work with people and accomplish different tasks. Some He gives the ability to teach, some to sing, some the gift of hospitality, encouragement, or even leadership. It seemed Missy's gifts and purpose right now was to continue working with the teens by encouraging them and helping organize events. So that's what she would do—until God showed her differently.

Missy didn't have to wait long before God showed her another plan He had for her.

On their next hike to Porcupine Mountain in October, as the teens and leaders reached the observation platform on Summit Peak, Mike knelt down on one knee and said, "Missy, a year ago you came on this hike to help chaperone the youth group. And ever since, you've captured my heart, and I've come to love and cherish you with all my heart. You are beautiful on the inside and outside, you complete me and make me the happiest man on this beautiful earth that God created. I want to work and stand by your side in good times and bad, in sickness and in health, and I promise to encourage you and support you in anything God directs you to do. Will you do me the honor of becoming my wife?" Mike asked as he pulled a small box with an engagement ring out of his shirt pocket.

Missy stood there with tears in her eyes, adoration in her heart, and quickly answered, "Oh yes, I would love to be your wife!"

And with that, Mike stood, put the ring on Missy's finger, took her in his arms and kissed her with the passion he felt in his heart while the youth, Sue, and Ron cheered on. When they descended Summit Peak, Mike held Missy's hand and frequently looked at her with adoring eyes and a smile that reached from ear to ear.

"You have made me the happiest man alive!" Mike said.

"Then that makes me the happiest woman, for I get to marry you and then have you by my side for the rest of my life!"

"Can we make that soon?" Mike asked hopefully.

"We'll talk about that later," Missy whispered back.

When they reached the picnic area, Missy saw that her parents were there to greet them, as well as Linda and Luke.

"We came to congratulate you and give you both our blessing," her mom said excitedly as they gave Missy and Mike each a hug.

"We couldn't be more pleased to give you our blessing to marry our daughter, Mike. You've become like a son to us, and I know that you'll love and care for Missy as much as we do," Ken said as he put his hand on Mike's shoulder.

"And Luke and I came to take your place on the hike to Lost Lake so you two can have some time alone and celebrate," Linda said as she hugged Missy and Mike too.

"Well, that's awful nice of you, and thank you," Missy whispered to Linda as she hugged her.

"I know you'd do the same for me," Linda whispered back with a smile. "Now let me see your ring."

As Missy showed her the ring, Linda looked at Mike and said, "You did good, big brother."

"Well thank you, I'm glad it meets your approval," Mike said with a smile.

Then others swarmed around Missy to look at her ring and offer their congratulations. Their picnic lunch was a great time of celebration and enjoyed by all.

Missy's parents said they wanted to take Missy and Mike out to a restaurant for dinner that evening so they could celebrate with Emily, then call Tony and Shari afterward to give them the good news. They had a good evening together, and Emily was full of questions.

"So have you set a date yet? I'm your only sister, so I will be your maid of honor, right?" Emily began her bombardment. "What color will my dress be? Will it be short or long? Should I wear my hair up or down? Who else will be standing up with you?"

"I don't know. We'll have to wait and see," was all Missy could say. But she was just as excited as Emily and looked forward to planning her wedding with her mom, Emily, and Linda. Like Mike, she didn't want to wait too long.

They called Tony after they got to her parents' house, and Tony and Shari were very excited for them, though not too surprised.

"I knew it was just a matter of time," Shari teased. "You two are so good together!"

When they went back to Missy's apartment, they called Mike's parents, as Linda wanted to be there when they told them.

They also were happy for them and told Missy, "We are very proud to have you as our new daughter. We know Linda already thinks of you as a sister, so welcome to our family."

Missy couldn't have felt more accepted and loved.

Chapter 30

Missy and Mike decided to have a Spring wedding on May 2 at 5:00 p.m., but it was turning out to be a double wedding, as Linda and Luke were engaged on Christmas Eve. Since both couples were making Ironwood, Michigan, their home and wanted to get married at the Community Bible Church, they decided they might as well share the costs and have their relatives come just once, as most of the Reeves family were a distance away.

So Missy and Linda, along with Emily and their moms, had a grand time planning, shopping, sending out invitations, ordering flowers, and doing all the other wedding planning essentials. Rose had agreed to photograph their wedding, as she had been taking more pictures of people and was really very good. Even her boss, Gloria, was giving her tips on what to look for in a good wedding picture. Rose had two weddings to attend before May, so said she would be practicing at those as well.

With all that help, along with Mike and Luke's efforts, you would think the wedding day would go without a hitch. But nerves and emotions were high on their wedding day, and with so many women getting ready at the church, chaos was rampant. They had one room where two friends did their hair, while others did their makeup in the bathroom at the long mirror and counter. Missy and her bridesmaids, Emily, Julie, and Emma, had one room to get dressed in; and Linda, with her three bridesmaids, had another.

"I can't find my other shoe. Has anyone seen my shoe?"

"Help, my zipper is stuck!"

"Oh, look at my hair, the curl didn't stay like I wanted it to."

"Has anyone seen my makeup case?"

And so it continued. Thankfully, the grooms and groomsmen decided to dress at Missy's parents' home so they would be away from all the female emotions. Besides, Missy and Linda didn't want their grooms to see them before they walked down the aisle. Missy's brother, Tony, decided to rent a room at a hotel for his family, since there was already so much going on at the house. Josh was to be the ringbearer, so Shari would make sure he was dressed and at the church on time. But Missy was sure each location had their own chaos going on.

In the end, everyone was ready and at the church before the time came for the bridal procession to commence. The moms and grandparents were seated, the white runner was rolled down the aisle, candles were lit, and then it was finally time for Mike's groomsmen to walk Missy's bridesmaids down the aisle. Missy and Linda had chosen the same knee-length, chiffon V-necked bridesmaid dresses with a pleated bodice, but in different solid colors. Because Missy liked autumn and that was when she and Mike were engaged, she chose Autumn colors of papaya, coral, and gold. Their shoes were a gold, chunky, leatherette heeled sandal pump, with a closed toe and buckle at the ankle. Mike and his groomsmen wore brown suits with ties that matched the bride's and bridesmaid's dresses.

Then Luke's groomsmen walked Linda's bridesmaids down the aisle. Linda liked the color purple, so her bridesmaid's dresses were Tahiti, wisteria, and mauve, with the same shoe as Missy's bridesmaids but in silver. Luke and his groomsmen wore gray suits, with ties that also matched the bride's and bridesmaid's dresses. They climbed stairs to the platform lit with strands of clear lights along the edges of the stairs and platform, with Missy's bridal party on the right and Linda's on the left.

Then Linda's flower girl, dressed in lavender, dropped an array of purple petals as she and Josh, in his little brown suit and holding a papaya-colored pillow proudly, walked down the aisle and to the platform. There was a very full and colorful array of expectant and smiling people on the platform, as well as seated in the sanctuary, who awaited the two brides' entrances.

Missy entered the sanctuary first, holding the arm of her dad. She wore an ivory-colored, princess ball gown made of satin, with a

V-necked sweep train and beaded sequins. The bodice and cap straps had a flowered lace design. She wore her hair in an upsweep style, topped with a tiara, and carried a bouquet of autumn-colored Gerber daisies and ivory roses. She truly looked like a princess. Mike beamed when he saw her, and Missy had eyes only for him as her dad walked her down the aisle.

Then it was Linda and her dad's turn. She wore a white, princess ball gown with a V-neckline, court train, and tulle lace covering the satin gown. It had a beaded silver belt at the waist, and she wore similar beading, shaped like a crown, in her short hair. She carried a bouquet of white and multicolored purple roses. Luke was very pleased with the beauty of his bride and anxiously awaited as she walked down the aisle toward him.

The pastor welcomed the guests and gave an inspiring challenge to the couples getting married to love, honor, and respect one another, as Christ loved each one of us. He reminded them that it was a tall order and can't be done on our own initiative, but only with God's help.

Both couples then repeated their vows to each other, and the song, "To Have and to Hold," was sung by two of their mutual friends. It was all very touching, and Missy and Linda were glad they had asked Mike and Luke to each have handkerchiefs in their pockets, ready and waiting for their tears that were sure to fall. Mike and Luke gladly accommodated them and wiped their tears during the song and dabbed their own as well before putting their handkerchiefs back in their pockets.

Then it was time for the couples to exchange rings, followed by each of the bride's dads coming up to pray a blessing over their daughters and son-in-laws. It was another touching moment with more tears, but it was all very special. Their dads had asked the couples' permission to have this part in their wedding, and it turned out to be one of the favorite parts of their ceremony.

Each couple then went to the table set up on their side of the platform to perform a sand ceremony, which is an alternative to the traditional unity candle. It consisted of the couples taking turns pouring different colored sand into a unity heart vase in the middle of their tables. As they did this ceremony, their friends sang another meaningful song called, "Two Becoming One."

Missy and Mike's table was covered with a gold cloth. It had one vase for Missy with ivory-colored sand and one vase with papaya-colored sand for Mike. As they each poured their sand into the heart-shaped vase in the middle, it became a visible symbol of the joining of their two hearts.

Then it was Linda and Luke's turn. Their table was covered with a silver cloth. It had one vase for Linda with white sand and one for Luke with purple sand. It was amazing to see the beauty that was created when two hearts became one. The heart-shaped vases, with their initials and wedding date, were then able to be kept as a poignant reminder of their special day.

When they returned to their places, the pastor proclaimed both couples as husband and wife and told Mike and Luke they could kiss their brides. Which they did—and didn't have to be told twice.

There was much cheering and clapping from their family and friends, and when it subsided, the pastor was happy to have them turn toward the audience and present them as Mr. and Mrs. Mike Reeves; and Mr. and Mrs. Luke Williams. As the bridal parities walked down the aisle, the song, "From this Moment On" was played. It was a joyous time, a memorable time, and a time to begin new lives together and, with God's help, for many years to come.

When the honeymooners returned, Linda and Luke had decided to keep Linda's apartment while they looked for a house to buy, one that would fulfill both of their hopes and dreams. Missy and Mike rented one side of a brick duplex, which had a deck and big fenced-in backyard with a garden. Missy said the fence would keep the deer out of her garden, but Mike said it could also be good for having a dog.

Missy just smiled and said, "As long as the dog doesn't dig in my garden!"

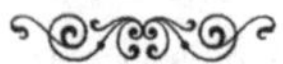

Things hadn't turn out exactly as Missy had thought they would. But she had discovered that God's plan was so much better than hers, that being a "pastor's wife"—or, should we say, "Mike's wife"—wasn't so bad after all. God helped her discover what was really important, that she didn't have to meet everyone's expectations, but only needed to keep her focus on Christ and then trust and follow His plan for her life.

> "For I know the plans I have for you," declares the Lord,
> "plans to prosper you and not to harm you, plans to give
> you hope and a future. Then you will call on me and
> come and pray to me, and I will listen to you.
> You will seek me and find me when you
> seek me with all your heart."
>
> —Jeremiah 29:11–13

To My Readers

I hope you enjoyed my series, *Seasons of Love.* If you haven't been to the Upper Peninsula of Michigan, maybe you can plan to visit sometime. You won't be disappointed! We lived there for fourteen years and enjoyed all the beauty that it offers. The people are pretty amazing too! And if you identified with some of the characters in my stories, I hope you were challenged, encouraged, and found healing as they did.

It was a joy, as well as challenging, to write these stories, as they dealt with issues with which I've struggled, my family has struggled, as well as those we've counseled.

Whiter than Snow is based on my dad's and husband's past, as well as my husband's and my courtship, and offers hope for those who have pain from their past. We've known those who haven't been able to release their pain and lived very unhappy lives; and those who've released their pain and found true joy and peace. I hope you're one of the latter. If not, it's available to you through Jesus Christ!

I have been saddened by the effect of divorce in our world today, even in my own family. The pain and fear that rejection brings is difficult to overcome. But as in *Summer Dreams*, God can bring healing and break that cycle through His love, grace, and forgiveness. We've seen it, and hope you will experience it!

As a young pastor's wife, I struggled with meeting the expectations of others, as Missy did in *Autumn Discoveries.* But I know it's not limited to just pastors' wives, for many people struggle with it. Maybe you do as well. I'm thankful for my husband who told me one day that he didn't want me to think of myself as a pastor's wife but only as *his* wife, to love, support, and encourage. That made a big difference for me, and I've enjoyed being *his* wife ever since. But even more amazing is that I am God's child, and He loves me just as I am, mistakes and all. He loves you too—mistakes and all!

Thank you for reading my series! I hope you will encourage others to read it as well. I'm planning on writing another series, so keep your eyes open for it. I would love to hear from you. Send me a quick hello at joandeppa2@gmail.com.

Discussion Questions

Whiter Than Snow

1. Have you ever been to the UP of Michigan? If so, what were some of your favorite places or activities?
2. Bonnie told Brad, "I can't have a serious relationship with someone who's not a Christian" because of the verses in 2 Cor. 6:14–16. Do you agree or disagree? Why or why not?
3. Have you (or someone you know) ever had pain from your (their) past that left you (them) feeling like you (they) were not loved or accepted? Were you (they) ever able to release it? If so, how? If not, would you like to release it to God and find true peace, joy, and love like Brad did?

Summer Dreams

1. April had dreams that she wanted to accomplish. Do you have dreams that you would like to accomplish? What are they? What do you need to do to make them happen?
2. April had a long history of divorce in her family, which caused her to fear getting married. Many families have been hurt by divorce. Has it affected you or someone you know? In what ways? Do you think it is possible to break the cycle of fear and divorce? Why or why not? April found good counsel from her mom, Jenny, Aaron, and the Bible. Find good counsel from sources you can trust and read the verses that April found helpful as well.
3. One of April's dreams was to renovate an older home and make it into the home of her dreams. Have you ever tackled

a big project like that? What were your challenges? What kept you going until you accomplished it? Would you recommend that others tackle a difficult dream and see it to the finish? Why or why not?

Autumn Discoveries

1. Throughout this series, close friendships have been an important theme. Missy wanted it for herself as well. How important are they to you? Do you have someone in your life that you would consider a close friend? What do you consider important characteristics of a close friend?
2. Missy struggled with her self-esteem and felt she didn't measure up to others expectations of her. Have you ever felt that way? What did you do about it? How do you think God sees you? Does He accept you for who you are? Please explain your answer.
3. Missy finally understood God's purpose and plan for her life. What do you think God's purpose and plan is for your life? How will you go about accomplishing it? Do you think it will change as you mature and grow in your faith in Christ?

Printed in the USA
CPSIA information can be obtained
at www.ICGtesting.com
LVHW040301240923
759035LV00004B/190